Daily
CRICKET
YEAR
BOOK
85

Michael Melford
Bill Frindall

Consultant editor Michael Melford
Statistics Bill Frindall
Special articles E.W. Swanton
Other contributors
George Abbott, Rajan Bala (India), Mike Beddow, Tony Cozier (West Indies), Rachael Flint, John Fogg, David Green, Neil Hallam, Derek Hodgson, Doug Ibbotson, David Leggat (New Zealand), Michael Owen-Smith (South Africa), Qamar Ahmed (Pakistan), D.J. Rutnagur, Alan Shiell (Australia), Sa'adi Thawfeeq (Sri Lanka), A.S.R. Winlaw.

Editor: Norman Barrett
Designer Martin Bronkhorst
Illustrator Dennis Curran

Acknowledgements Thanks are due to David Armstrong and Mike Gear for supplying the statistics for the Minor Counties and Second XI championships, respectively, and to the TCCB for making the first-class fixtures available. The English Schools' Cricket Association material was kindly supplied by Cyril J. Cooper.

Most of the photographs appearing in this book are reproduced by permission of Adrian Murrell/All-Sport. Other pictures were provided by Bill Smith and Associated Sports Photography.

The editors particularly wish to thank Radford Barrett, Daily Telegraph Sports Editor, for his generous help.

Published by Telegraph Publications
135 Fleet Street, London EC4P 4BL

First Published 1984
© Daily Telegraph 1984
Scorecharts © Bill Frindall 1984

British Library Cataloguing in Publication Data
Daily Telegraph cricket year book. ____ '85.
1. Cricket – Periodicals
796.35'8'05   GV911

ISBN 0-86367-038-5
ISBN 0-86367-037-7 Pbk

Conditions of Sale:
This book is sold subject to the conditions that it shall not, by way of trade or otherwise, be lent, re-sold, hired out or otherwise circulated without the publisher's prior consent in any form of binding or cover other than that in which it is published.

Printed in Great Britain
by Redwood Burn Limited, Trowbridge, Wiltshire
Typeset by Shanta Thawani, London

Contents

5 Foreword, by Walter Hadlee

9 Looking Back
10 A Menace to Cricket, by Michael Melford
14 Master of the World, by Derek Hodgson
16 Daily Telegraph 'Twin Hundreds', by E.W. Swanton
17 Daily Telegraph Cricketers of the Year, by E.W. Swanton

19 England's Winter Tour 1983-84
20 England Humbled
22 England in New Zealand
28 England in Pakistan
34 Tour Statistical Summary

35 Overseas Cricket 1983-84
36 India v Pakistan
42 India v West Indies
53 Australia v Pakistan
62 Benson & Hedges World Series Cup
65 West Indies v Australia
75 Sri Lanka v New Zealand
82 Cricket in Australia
86 Cricket in South Africa
90 Cricket in the West Indies
92 Cricket in New Zealand
94 Cricket in India
97 Cricket in Pakistan
99 Cricket in Sri Lanka

101 Tours to England 1984
102 West Indies in England
136 Sri Lanka in England

141 English Season 1984
142 Britannic Assurance Championship
146 Review of the Counties
  146 Derbyshire, 148 Essex,
  150 Glamorgan, 152 Gloucestershire,
  154 Hampshire, 156 Kent,
  158 Lancashire, 160 Leicestershire,
  162 Middlesex,
  164 Northamptonshire,
  166 Nottinghamshire, 168 Somerset,
  170 Surrey, 172 Sussex,
  174 Warwickshire,
  176 Worcestershire, 178 Yorkshire
180 University Cricket
183 First-Class Averages
191 Benson & Hedges Cup
194 NatWest Bank Trophy
197 John Player Special League
199 Second XI County Championship and Under-25 Competition
201 Minor Counties Championship
203 Village and Club Cricket
204 Schools Cricket
205 Women's Cricket

207 Extras
208 Test Career Averages
215 Guide to Newcomers
220 Obituary 1983-84

223 Looking Forward
214 England on Tour 1984-85
225 The 1985 Season
226 Fixtures 1985

Foreword

When I was asked to write the foreword to this edition of the *Daily Telegraph Cricket Year Book*, I regarded it as an opportunity to acknowledge the support given to cricket over the years by the *Daily Telegraph*. It was suggested that I should review the New Zealand cricket scene and look briefly at world cricket today.

My early interest in cricket was stimulated by the visit of the first New Zealand team to tour the United Kingdom in 1927. Since 1937, it has been my privilege to be closely associated with the six teams that have toured the UK.

There was a time when we thought of ourselves as club cricketers. This is no longer so, although club cricket remains the base from which representative teams are selected. In and before my era, C.S. Dempster, W.E. Merritt, K.C. James, and C.C. Dacre were some who took the bold step of committing themselves to county cricket in England. Others played in the Lancashire League. Those with county contracts were lost to New Zealand cricket. They remained in England in an age when there were no fast aeroplanes to enable them to return home.

T.L. Pritchard, one of our finest bowlers, was another whose commitments to Warwickshire denied his country his services at a time when he and Jack Cowie would have comprised an opening attack worthy of any country. In those days, nobody could play cricket for New Zealand without making a financial sacrifice.

Today it is different. I venture to guess that the rewards are now such that players are desperately keen to be selected, not only for the honour, but for a share of the income from Test match and tour fees, plus sponsorships. The part-time professional of recent years appears to have little difficulty in playing a full quota of matches both at home and overseas, yet being able to retain employment when not required for cricket commitments. This would not have been possible in my generation. Employment, of necessity, had to be an absolute priority in years when cricket was financially unrewarding; yet to play for one's country, for no pay, was honour indeed.

For 20 years, from 1929 to 1949, New Zealand's Tests were restricted to three days. Moreover, in that period, there was little opportunity for regular tours. There were but three to the UK, and MCC teams came to New Zealand, usually after touring Australia, for two or three matches. Cash assets were unknown.

Players' preparation was restricted to club cricket and three Plunket Shield matches in December-January, so they were never fully prepared to meet overseas teams in March. It says much for the quality of players of that era that MCC teams managed only 3 wins in 13 encounters, with the rest drawn.

Mercifully, the three-day restriction ended after the 1949 New Zealand team's performance in England. Their batting strength was such that, in the absence of rain, there was no likelihood of obtaining a result in three days. The four Tests were drawn, and the only loss was to Oxford University on a rain-affected pitch. That team, incidentally, averaged 63 runs per hour over a 32-match tour.

The successes of the national teams over the past decade have created an ever-increasing interest in the game. Public support has never been greater – womenfolk have been captivated by the televising of one-day international matches – there are thousands of additional schoolboys wanting to play, and it is no problem to pre-sell 40,000 tickets for a one-day match in Auckland. Spectator interest in Test matches has increased, I think, partly because one-day cricket on television has attracted many new converts to the game. There is generally an awareness that the New Zealand Test team provides worthy opposition, but it remains a fact that gate takings from one-day internationals are vital to cover the ever-increasing costs of hosting visiting teams.

The upsurge of interest in the one-day game is understandable. The pepped-up tempo, and certainty of a result, appeals to a public who traditionally gather in greatest numbers to follow rugby football. Nowadays cricket can attract almost as many to a one-day international. This type of cricket has something in common with rugby sevens. There is more action, faster running between the wickets, sharper fielding, and more frequent tactical adjustments. Special skills are required, but too often do we witness an array of strokes that are a nightmare to the coaches of young batsmen, many of whom do not understand that the basics have to be mastered before the improvised should be attempted. One-day strokes can have a disastrous influence upon the undiscerning schoolboy cricketer and, because of that, ultimately at more senior levels of the game.

Today I am inclined to the view that there is a proliferation of international cricket. It is desirable from a New Zealand point of view that we host an overseas team every year, and that involves return visits. Fair enough. But when, in the period of 26 months from February 1983 to April 1985, our Test team is required to play 21 Tests and something like 35 one-day internationals, visiting five countries to do so, I believe our players are being overcommitted, especially when the full-time professionals have in addition to fulfil their engagements with their English counties. In the almost unseemly rush to meet the various demands of Test-playing countries, we have had a number of back-to-back tours which, whilst keeping the players in gainful employment, provide neither them nor the public with reasonable variety. In a one-sided double series, an element of boredom will soon be apparent.

On the world scene, I hope for a change in bowling tactics. There is nothing more boring than to have to watch a four- or five-pronged pace attack labour through a six-hour day for about 75 overs. Fast, short-pitched bowling has been overdone in several countries. I saw an example of this in the first Test between England and New Zealand at Wellington this past February. When a batsman is exposed to four or five such deliveries in a single over, how can one describe it as other than intimidatory? The Laws are clear and umpires must administer them. Failure to do so is an abdication from duty, and the result can only be serious injuries to batsmen.

It is good to see Sri Lanka playing official Tests. They have established that their pitches, grounds, and facilities meet the necessary standards, and further competition will improve many talented cricketers. They may suffer, as New Zealand has, from insufficient depth, but I am sure their successes will come.

The South African situation seems, as I write, to be no nearer solution. Two separate administrations vie for recognition by the International Cricket Conference. The New Zealand view has been that South Africa should be represented at the Conference table. I am not aware that there has been any change of policy, and I would hope not, for that view has been based on the desirability for dialogue, and the need for all cricketing countries to have access to discussions on the Laws, playing conditions, and problems that are experienced by others. That does not guarantee any commitment by any country to play South Africa, but it does seem churlish to deny them the opportunity to meet fellow administrators of a game they all strive to serve.

Should the Conference recognize the principle that association at administrative level can only help solve mutual problems, it should not be too difficult to decide which of the applicants merits recognition as being the body most representative of cricket in South Africa.

It seems a pity that in the interests of the game in their country, the Cricket Board and the Cricket Union cannot find some common ground and work together. It is clear enough that each body in its own way wishes to make a contribution to an integrated and better society. What better way to achieve this than by understanding and co-operation in the true spirit of cricket?

Walter Hadlee

Looking back

A Menace to Cricket
by Michael Melford

If anything was clarified by the 1984 season, it was the disservice being done to cricket by excessive use of the bouncer. It is distasteful to watch, it is poor entertainment, it is against the spirit of what should be a game, and it is a danger to life and limb. In Test matches alone, two batsmen, Lloyd and Terry, were put out of action for the season.

It is also a contravention of Law 42. The more one reads Section 8 of Law 42, painstakingly worked out over the years and clearly worded, the harder it is to think how it can be improved. It fails only because of the spirit in which the game is often played now and because it has to rely so heavily on the umpire's judgment. Umpires have to make a hard decision at a moment's notice and, quite naturally, as in the throwing controversy, they hesitate to take the tougher and more controversial line.

Nothing emphasized how much the game has been degraded as a spectacle more than the eulogies poured on the Sri Lankan batsmen. They played charmingly with a refreshingly old-fashioned orthodoxy, but they were greatly helped by the fact that England bowled the head-high bouncer only as an occasional variation. Lest this be taken as a fulsome tribute to England's sporting spirit, it has to be added that they had no bowlers fast enough to be a consistent menace on a mild pitch, and those who did bowl short merely provided long-hops which were greeted with enthusiastic hooking.

The problem has been accentuated by the wearing of helmets, which, for all their obvious protective value, have encouraged batsmen to take more risks and bowlers to consider even lower order batsmen as fair game.

'The bowling of fast short-pitched balls is unfair if, in the opinion of the umpire at the bowler's end, it constitutes an attempt to intimidate the striker.' So reads the first paragraph of Law 42 (8). The two key words are 'opinion' and 'intimidate'.

In the following example there should be no room for doubt: The batting side has no chance of winning, does not need runs and must be bowled out if the fielding side is to win. The late-order batsmen show by evasion and stoic acceptance of blows on the helmet and upper body that they are not to be enticed into making strokes unless it is to defend their wicket. What then is the purpose of persisting in bouncing the ball at them? It can only be intimidation.

Yet, when this occurs, the umpires are seldom seen to do much more than mutter at the bowler. They do not go through the phases of action laid down, which culminate with the order to the fielding captain to take the bowler off for the rest of the innings.

It is understandable that the more severe the punishment, the more reluctant the umpire will be to enforce it, especially if it is based purely on his 'opinion'. He has, of course, to take into account the batsman's height and perhaps misjudgment in ducking into a ball. If fact were substituted for opinion, his job might be eased. The most popular suggestion of how this might be implemented is to draw a line about half-way between the wickets short of which the bowler must not pitch. It does provide a clear guideline for the umpire – the square-leg umpire in this case – but that alone is not the answer.

Some advocates of the line would have it drawn so far up that a batsman's life would be one long half-volley – but never a hook. Nobody wants to outlaw the friendly medium-paced long-hop and the hook. They provide much entertainment. Yet there are fast pitches on which a line drawn at half-way would have no effect, because the danger area is much nearer the batsman.

Moreover, the mere calling of a no-ball and the conceding of one run would not stop a bowler really bent on intimidating. The penalty would need to be more severe, but not so severe that umpires would hesitate to enforce it.

I believe that the time has come for some sort of action. The problem seems to be threefold. To find a way of clarifying the umpire's job (perhaps by 'the line'); to find the correct penalty; and, probably hardest of all, to persuade all countries, especially those with fast bowlers, to agree to the action.

Otherwise a lovely game will become an unlovely display of ducking and bruising requiring far more courage than skill.

Triumph by twilight There is something splendidly dotty about a competition such as the NatWest Trophy that is keenly contested and watched for more than two months and has, as in 1981 and 1984, a desperately exciting climax – only for that climax to be more or less invisible to the 20,000 odd gathered to watch it. Television makes it clearer, but many of those watching in the dusk of September 1, 1984, had to interpret the last few balls from the reactions of fielders, not all of whom were entirely confident themselves.

Not all finals will go to the last possible ball, and the light does vary from evening to evening. But there have been more overcast evenings than that of last September 1, and anyhow conditions could be worse next year, when the final falls on September 7. Sunset on September 7, for reasons well outside the TCCB's control, is 14 minutes earlier than on September 1.

How then to prevent repetitions? Playing the final a week earlier would upset a first-class programme already strained by six Test matches. Reducing the number of overs is undesirable, because the 60-overs allotment is one of the NatWest Trophy's big advantages over the other limited-over competitions. An earlier, 10 a.m., start has been tried and has proved unacceptable in view of the mist, dew, and heavy atmosphere of many an autumn morning.

There seem to be two possibilities. One is to have only one interval instead of three – the interval between innings, perhaps with a short break for sustenance on the field in the middle of each innings. The other, of course, is to impress on both captains their responsibility in everybody's interests for sustaining the over-rate of only 16 an hour, which with normal intervals is all that is required for a match beginning at 10.30 to achieve a result by seven o'clock.

A nasty blow to chanting MCC can seldom have earned such bouquets as for their more-seats-and-less-drink operation on the Tavern side for the NatWest final, which allowed the big crowd to enjoy the day unpestered by chanting, drumming, and clanking. Without wishing to appear doubting in any way, I would like to see the arrangement tested by, say, Lancashire and Warwickshire, with the massed ranks of out-of-season Manchester United and Aston Villa supporters arriving after a long coach journey on which they have had plenty of opportunity to stimulate themselves for the day of song ahead. Middlesex and Kent were always likely to be meek stuff by comparison. Middlesex have a cosmopolitan support and nothing like the local following of other counties. Kent have plenty of passionate support, but when it comes to producing massed choirs Canterbury Cathedral lacks the raucous volume of Old Trafford.

ICC future An article in *The Cricketer* by Gerry Gomez, the eminent West Indies all-rounder of the 1950s and since then a wise administrator, called for the ICC to be turned into a stronger international cricket authority, one with teeth. Mr Gomez has been involved with the administration of soccer as well as cricket in Trinidad and thus is in a position to compare the ICC, which was never intended to be much more than a forum for discussion, with FIFA. He cites the 'Packer scenario' and the post-Packer influence, which has brought 'the unsavoury notion that for cricket to be entertaining and draw crowds it must be violent, controversial, and ill-mannered', as things that would not have been allowed to develop under FIFA. He also indicates, as follows, the areas in which the ICC, given a thoroughly authoritative new constitution, would become a body able to benefit cricket throughout the world:

It would help to promote and develop the game universally and at all levels; to establish a Coaching Council; to preserve the independence of the ICC against the intervention of an outside body in its relations with its affiliated member-countries; to establish an Umpires Council designed to improve the standards and consistency of umpiring and the recruiting and teaching of umpires throughout the world.

This is a noble ideal. Its supporters in this country put up one other virtue for it. An all-powerful ICC would not stand for one member-country refusing to play another or objecting to players in another's side. A country that did so refuse would be suspended.

So far so good. But would there not still be governments looking over the shoulders of cricket boards? It is governments, not cricketers, who make the political decisions.

Moreover, the plan seems to hold little to attract English backing for a number of reasons. To turn the ICC into a sort of FIFA would mean an expensive proliferation of staff and accommodation, a new bureaucracy, not only at the ICC headquarters but at the HQ of each member-country, for what would be the point of having an efficient central organization if it was regularly frustrated by not receiving answers to its letters? The financing of the new ICC, it is proposed, would come from member-countries, but, however, sensitively graded, would be hard to collect and perhaps grudgingly given.

One of the main reasons for starting the World Cup was to provide income for associate member-countries who have none from gate receipts. In nearly all of them cricket is for the player, not the watcher. They would have to be persuaded of the ultimate benefit of an annual contribution or would have to be excused it.

As for encouraging coaching, umpiring, and the nurturing of the game wherever it is played, English cricket has always tried to do that anyhow, seeing it as a traditional obligation of the country where the game was born.

The most compelling reason for full member-countries resisting a strengthening of the ICC is that many have always prized their autonomy and have resented outside interference from other members.

Few would deny that the ICC is ill-equipped to cope with many problems afflicting the modern sporting world or that its troubles have often come through the weaknesses of individual boards. But FIFA, I gather, is not always considered perfect. Nor is the United Nations. And I imagine that the ICC will carry on doing the best it can until some alternative sure of unanimous support turns up.

Master of the World
by Derek Hodgson

Clive Lloyd, master of the world, has now dominated cricket for almost 10 years, a tyranny exercised through a regiment of fast bowlers and an unceasing fusillade of bouncers. Had Jardine, or Bradman or even Gavaskar been in charge of West Indies in this era, the International Cricket Conference would have been rent apart.

But for Lloyd the world laughs, cheers, and applauds. There has never been such a popular despot, probably because the public have not realized what the players have long known: there are two Clive Hubert Lloyds.

There is the man other teams fear, one of the most devastating batsmen in history ('Cover and midwicket automatically step back a yard when Hubert takes guard' says David Gower) and one of the most ruthless captains: witness the systematic destruction of Mohinder Armanath's confidence when, very briefly, the Indian appeared to be the one player in the world to be getting on top of the fast attack. Off the field, there is the big (6 feet 4 inches) shambling man of inoffensive moustache and glasses and slow, engaging smile, with such a transparent love of children he is every little girl's favourite uncle. What endears him to players and public is a bubbling sense of humour.

There is a fund of stories, which he tells himself: He was lucky to arrive in England first at the Lancashire League club of Haslingden where, as a 22-year-old, he realized that he was in the land of Constantine, Martindale, Weekes, and Walcott, where every West Indian cricketer was a local legend. After smiting the ball over the neighbouring Woolpack Hotel, his introduction to the home crowd, he was soon able to buy his first small car. What is more, he learned that the Englishman washes his car on Sunday mornings. He was so engaged, bent down over the hub caps, when he heard a voice from across the road: 'Hey, Nigger.' This was the first instance of a racial slur that Clive had encountered. He hoped the man would go away. 'Hey, Nigger. I won't tell you again', the voice repeated. Clive felt his anger rising. He rose slowly to his full height and glared across the roof of the car to where a little man in a flat cap quailed before him: 'Eeh, mister. Ah'm reight sorry. Ah were calling me dog.'

From Haslingden he almost joined Warwickshire, but Lancashire intervened, and it was as a young member of the staff that he heard Barry Wood, a stickler for tea after a meal, complaining to a waiter that there was only demerara sugar on the table. 'Why can't I have white sugar?' he demanded. The young Lloyd, his face set in mock anger, leaned across and drawled: 'You got a colour problem, man?'

On another occasion, he was hitting the Kent bowling so hard that he was knocking tiles off the roofs of surrounding houses. An elderly lady, terrified, rang the police who sent a panda car to investigate. By accident, the sergeant's first call was the press box where the Kent 12th man, who was visiting, responded to his enquiry by saying: 'Glad you're here, officer. It's that big black man out there. I think you should arrest him before he does any more damage.'

He loved Manchester, a swinging city in the late 1960s. For a spell of about five years success came to clubs in every sport; the social scene was thick with internationals. At Old Trafford, on what must have been a far cry from today's pitches, Middlesex knocked out Farokh Engineer (his nose was broken), while Clive was hit on the head by a ball that bounced away to the boundary. 'I hope Matt Busby was watching' said Clive.

There is no reason to suppose that Clive would have been unhappy just playing his cricket with Lancashire and West Indies. He did not actively seek captaincy, although he has admitted that he was disappointed when David Lloyd was preferred to him as the county captain and suspects there was a definite racial bias in the committee at that time. Today, it is such a joke in the dressing-room that when manager Jack Bond introduced John Abrahams, a Cape Coloured from South Africa, as the county captain in succession to Clive, Bond said, straight-faced and to the consternation of a TV crew: 'Step by step we are working our way back towards a white captain.'

Clive Lloyd has been playing Test cricket since 1966 and has led West Indies in 69 Test matches, more than any other captain. More than that, he has given a group of Caribbean islands, bound together only by a language, a unity far stronger than any politician could confer. He has given West Indians everywhere, no matter what their circumstances, one good reason why they can look the world in the eye. He has given them pride and happiness, a good measure of which can be seen on the shining faces of little West Indian children when Clive or Vivian or Gordon go in to bat at the Oval. West Indies have lost but one of their last 39 Tests.

Nor should his accomplishments for his fellow professionals be overlooked. He was severely castigated for leading West Indies into Kerry Packer's World Series, but his common sense told him, and natural justice ordained, that poor men from poor islands could not be held back from the proper rewards for their labours.

He celebrated his 40th birthday at the end of August. Fitness permitting, there is no reason why, as each autumn approaches, Clive should not solemnly announce he is retiring and then return, chuckling, with blessings, to play again the following spring. We shall not see his like again.

Daily Telegraph 'Twin Hundreds'

by E.W. Swanton

Let me start with the happier half first. The first bowler to 100 wickets last summer, and therefore the winner of the award with which my name is associated, is **John Kenneth Lever**, whose fastish left-arm bowling has for so long been both the spearhead and the mainstay of Essex. Lever is 35, and he was in his 15th season as a capped player. Yet, playing in every first-class match, he bowled more overs (874) than anyone in England bar the spinner Geoff Miller. He took his 116 wickets at 22 runs each, and though Richard Hadlee, whose 117 were collected at a cost of only 14, can be accounted unlucky to be beaten on the post, no one can begrudge the winner his success. These two alone, by the way, reached three figures.

Essex, who needed 103 years to win their first county competition, have now collected six successes between 1979 and 1984, an astonishing change of fortune for which a nucleus of able and whole-hearted cricketers are responsible. The names one thinks of automatically are those of Fletcher, Gooch, Lever, McEwan, East, Acfield, Phillip, and Turner, a seasoned band if ever there was one. Fletcher leads what is essentially a team, and he has had no more whole-hearted trier than Lever, who might, incidentally, have won the Trophy last year if he had not had to miss seven matches recovering from a serious operation.

Now for the lament. A year ago I was obliged to describe the farcical circumstances which presented the Walter Lawrence Award for the fastest hundred of the season to Steven O'Shaughnessy, who to his credit was embarrassed to find himself presented by Leicestershire with a hundred that made him the joint holder with P.G.H. Fender of the fastest ever. This time the proprieties were observed during most of the last day of a sterile, disappointing match between Middlesex and Kent which brought the Lord's season to an end. Nevertheless **Michael William Gatting** was faced by irregular bowlers towards the end of his innings, and it was the 17 that he made off the last over, bowled by Chris Tavaré, that brought him to three figures in 79 minutes.

It so happened that earlier on this same day Allan Lamb at Worcester had clipped a couple of minutes off the fastest time which had been to the credit of Gatting for most of the summer. Perhaps that fact makes the destination of the Lawrence Trophy rather less phoney. But the oldest of the individual county trophies deserves better than this, and if the patrons should decide to withdraw their prize, the players will have only themselves to blame.

Daily Telegraph Cricketers of the Year

by E.W. Swanton

It is a sign of the times, I suppose, that of the cricketers selected by our correspondents in the eight countries to which this list is confined only one named previously has earned top place again in 1983/4. Nor is he a Test player, since he is the South African Peter Kirsten. The wholesale proliferation of Test matches has led – among other effects, including the cheapening of each individual match – to a more rapid turn-round of the cast. Even Imran Khan and Richard Hadlee, the only other men to have been nominated twice in the three years of this Year Book's life, have been superseded this time.

In the Year Book's inaugural year, the accent turned out to be on all-rounders. Last year, batsmen led the field. Now we have a mixed assortment of five batsmen, two bowlers, and, to add novelty, a batsman-keeper.

Michael Melford and I weighed up with due care the respective claims of John Lever, Graham Gooch, and **Mike Gatting,** three highly worthy candidates, and in the end plumped narrowly for the Middlesex captain, partly because, as such, he had led his side by such admirably enterprising and unselfish example. If anyone had distinguished himself for England over the period, he could hardly have been overlooked. As it is, let us pay tribute to the man who has led the averages of all currently available for England for four summers running (first with 68.39 in 1984), and who, returning after spasmodic absences to a county side that had gone two months without a win, scored four hundreds in the next five games, leading them to victory in each case.

Alan Shiell had much difficulty in assessing the respective claims of Graham Yallop and **Allan Border.** The former, after being in and out of Test sides for almost a decade, established himself with a vengeance against Pakistan, averaging 92 in the five-match series. However, Border was little behind him, and while Yallop was deprived by injury from taking part in the West Indies tour following, he took on those formidable opponents almost single-handed. I cannot recall since the days of George Headley a man standing so far above his fellows as Border, whose Test average of 74 was followed by the 25 of the next man.

By contrast with Shiell, there was no doubt in the mind of Tony Cozier that **Malcolm Marshall** was the top star in the bright West Indian galaxy. In 14 Tests over the 12-month period, this strong, indefatigable fast bowler actually took 78 wickets, against India, Australia, and England. Whether Marshall is soon burnt out by the excessive demands made on him remains to be seen – but he is only 26, and with such an exemplary action may well learn to conserve his energies rather as did Lillee and his own compatriot, Roberts.

The New Zealand winner, chosen by David Leggat, is – surprisingly – not Hadlee, though he made his usual mark on the five Tests contested by his country – but **I.D.S. Smith,** who, it seems, had a very good series against England behind the stumps and illustrated his improving skill as a batsman by making his first Test hundred.

The strain of continuous Test cricket is telling, not indeed surprisingly, so Rajan Bala records, on **Sunil Gavaskar,** who will seek to counteract it by demoting himself henceforward from No.1 to No.4. With his 100th Test just coming up, the ultra-patient, technically admirable little Sunil has now made more runs (8,394) than even Boycott and Sobers, and has had the ultimate effrontery to exceed by one, in his 99th Test, the 29 hundreds compiled by Sir Donald Bradman in 52. It was reassuring to read how modestly Gavaskar rated the respective achievements.

Sarfraz Nawaz, whom by the standards of Test opening bowlers one may call (coming up to his 36th birthday) the old war-horse, was the choice of Qamar Ahmed for Pakistan. Not only in his own country did he play a prominent part in the successive defeats of both India and England; but, sent to Australia as a reinforcement, 'he put new life into a battered team', a view supported, by the way, by cricket's eternal globe-trotter, Henry Blofield.

It is a pleasure to have the chance of paying a tribute to Sri Lankan batting in the light of their splendid showing against England at Lord's. As it happened, Sa'adi Thawfeeq's choice, **Ranjan Madugalle,** failed in the Test against England, whereas Wettimuny, Silva, Ranatunga, and, above all, the captain, Duleep Mendis, delighted us all. However, Madugalle 'showed guts, determination, and the skill to tackle Hadlee' on Sri Lankan pitches, and to average 60 in the three-Test series. Like all countries new to Test cricket, Sri Lanka will need time to break through. May the memory of Lord's encourage them.

Michael Owen-Smith had no qualms about awarding South Africa's palm to **Peter Kirsten,** who, despite his smallness, stood up manfully to the fast bowling of the 'West Indian XI' which won the four-match series 2-1 and the one-day games 4-2. During the season, Kirsten was replaced as captain by Clive Rice, a questionable decision according to our correspondent. Kirsten survived many bruises to average 50, the South African umpires apparently being no more willing to check intimidatory bowling than those of any other country. The name of Kirsten's nearest rival brings back in memory a young left-hander of peerless grace and power who in his few years of Test cricket in the 1960s showed all the hall-marks of greatness – Graeme Pollock, now aged 40, who averaged 48 against the West Indians.

England's winter tour 1983-84

England Humbled

England's tour of Fiji, New Zealand, and Pakistan was widely voted a disaster when the team returned to England in late March. The main evidence in support of this was that they had lost series to New Zealand and Pakistan, both for the first time. Moreover, the players returned amid lurid reports of drug-taking parties.

In a wider context, the results of the two series could be judged as not unpredictable. Before the England party left home in the week after Christmas, it was not considered of world-beating potential. The fact that Bob Willis, aged 35, was still the fastest and most effective bowler was evidence in itself of a weakness in one vital department. The decline in Ian Botham's bowling seriously upset the penetration of the attack and the balance of the side. It was hoped that some of the younger bowlers would develop during the tour, and this expectation was in fact fulfilled by the performances of Foster and Cowans.

The team anyhow was not fully representative of English cricket. Only a few of the 15 banned by the TCCB in 1982 would have come under consideration for this tour, but two or three would have improved the side in vital quarters, and it takes only two or three players to turn a losing side into a good average one.

One other fact not generally taken into account was that, since the last tour of Pakistan and New Zealand in 1977-78, the standards in those two countries had certainly not declined, perhaps had risen. And in that previous tour of 1977-78 England could only draw each series. Since then, New Zealand had played more international cricket than ever before and had won a Test match in England for the first time. Pakistan, at home, had routed Australia, and even without Imran Khan and other experienced players had a depth of talent that was always going to make them formidable opponents on their own mud pitches.

The itinerary, congested and latterly with no relief from international matches, was widely condemned afterwards and was certainly no help. The defeat in Karachi could certainly be attributed to the unkind arrangement whereby England started a Test match there only about 48 hours after a delayed flight from New Zealand and, of course, in conditions entirely different from those which they had been experiencing. The TCCB, by introducing a stop for two days' cricket in Fiji, had tried to lessen the habitual difficulties of acclimatization experienced by a side plucked from an English midwinter. But that could not solve the main problem, which is the modern proliferation of international cricket sprung on the game for commercial reasons and for which the players themselves bear their share of responsibility.

The old style of tour, with its country matches and its less important contests against states and provinces, may have had its dull and financially unrewarding moments, but it did provide opportunities for the most successful players to relax, and for the less successful and the recently convalescent to seek a return to form in the middle.

The limited-over game has much to answer for, and the fact that

England won the one-day series in New Zealand 2-1 and drew the series in Pakistan 1-1 rightly did not have much emphasis put on it in the post-mortems. It is in the general interest of the game that Test cricket should not lose its attraction, and it is right that success in Test matches should still be considered the main objective.

If England had won the two Tests that they lost, those in Christchurch and Karachi, the tour would certainly have been regarded as successful, and it can be argued that both matches were played in freakish circumstances. The one at Christchurch was played on a thoroughly bad pitch and the one at Karachi under the influence of jet-lag and by an unhappy chance on the one pitch encountered in Pakistan that held out promise of a definite result.

Test matches in New Zealand have been played on bad pitches in the past, but this time at Christchurch, as at Wellington in 1978, it was the New Zealand bowlers who used the conditions the better, and England who bowled in a way that made a mockery of the modern boast of leading players that their way is the 'professional' way. It was much to New Zealand's credit that they were able to make over 300 on such a pitch, but incredible that they should have been allowed to do so.

Anyone who knew New Zealand cricket in its less successful days, when it was regarded as very much the poor relation of New Zealand rugby, would have been delighted to have seen how it has progressed. No longer do New Zealand cricket teams go on the field heavy with inferiority, thinking not of winning but of how to avoid defeat. The real test of the depth of the cricketing talent in the country will come when the present senior players, especially Richard Hadlee, retire.

Pakistan, by contrast, surprised the visitors by fielding in the first Test, for various reasons, a side of relative unknowns. Of those who played in the deciding Test at Headingley in 1982, won rather agonizingly by England, only three, Mohsin, Zaheer, and Abdul Qadir, remained. Certainly some old hands, such as Sarfraz and Wasim Raja, showed themselves to be still good enough, but the less well known players chosen, especially Saleem Malik, looked far from outclassed in Test cricket.

The defeat in Karachi was less culpable than the one in Christchurch, not only because of the difficulty of instant acclimatization but because the England batsmen, with no recent practice against leg-spinners, were confronted with a bowler of Qadir's class and subtlety on a pitch giving him some help. It marked David Gower's return to form, and indeed it led to the tour's ending on a slightly more optimistic note than had seemed possible earlier.

Even this had to be qualified, on the last day of the series, when England stooped to time-wasting tactics – 11 overs an hour – for which there could be no excuse. One hopes that on reflection those involved will realize that even if other sides do it, there is no satisfaction in winning or saving a match in this way.

England in New Zealand

First Test: Wellington, January 20, 21, 22, 23, 24.
Drawn.

Nothing happened in the first three days of the first Test to suggest that England might lose the series. Basin Reserve in Wellington had been soaked four days before the match, but the pitch was never difficult and became even easier as the match progressed. New Zealand batted without distinction, Botham had one of his better days with the ball, England fielded brilliantly, and New Zealand were out early on the second day for 219.

The England batsmen had some early problems against Cairns, who took the first four wickets, but Botham was dropped by Cairns off Chatfield at third slip. If taken, the catch would have made England's score 93 for 5. As it was, Botham, 138, and Randall, 164, shared in a fifth-wicket stand of 232 in three-and-a-half hours. It seemed then likely that Cairns's error might have decided the match.

On the third afternoon, New Zealand batted again 244 behind. They started reasonably well, but wickets were thrown away and their captain Geoff Howarth had the ill luck to be run out, as the non-striker, by the bowler's deflection of a straight drive. At 165 for 4 on the fourth morning, New Zealand still seemed on the road to defeat.

Then it was that Martin Crowe, the great young hope of New Zealand cricket, made a maiden Test century of high quality, and Jeremy Coney, an ever-useful all-rounder but one who had not made a first-class 100 for seven years, scored 174 not out. The match was comfortably saved.

Second Test: Christchurch, February 3, 4, 5.
New Zealand won by an innings and 132 runs.

The second Test, decisive, as it proved, brought the best out of New Zealand and the worst out of England, who because of injuries to fast bowlers were forced to recruit Tony Pigott from his winter coaching and playing job. On a pitch well below Test standard, they bowled themselves to defeat on the first day, Botham being particularly wayward. Richard Hadlee ruthlessly punished errors in length while making 99 in 110 minutes, and New Zealand scored 307, a huge and unbeatable total in the conditions.

Only Gatting fought the conditions for any length of time in England's innings of 82. Hadlee, Cairns, and Chatfield made the most of the conditions as England had singularly failed to do. Following on, England made only a few runs more in their second innings and, though play was not possible until after tea on the second day, the match was over on the third day.

Third Test: Auckland, 10, 11, 12, 14, 15.
Drawn.

Of the world's Test grounds, Eden Park, Auckland, nowadays provides one of the milder and truer batting pitches. It was a near-certainty that New Zealand would preserve their 1-0 lead there and, winning the toss, they made no mistake. Centuries by John Wright, Jeff Crowe, and Ian Smith allowed them to declare just short of 500, and in a dull match there was barely time to fit in an innings apiece in the five days.

ENGLAND'S WINTER TOUR 1983-84/IN NEW ZEALAND

New Zealand v England 1983-84 1st Test
Match Drawn
Played at Basin Reserve, Wellington, January 20, 21, 22, 23, 24
Toss: New Zealand. Umpires: F.R. Goodall and S.J. Woodward
Debuts: Nil

New Zealand

J.G. Wright	c Cook b Botham	17	c Foster b Cook		35
B.A. Edgar	c Taylor b Botham	9	c Taylor b Willis		30
G.P. Howarth*	c Gower b Botham	15	run out		34
M.D. Crowe	b Willis	13	c Botham b Gatting		100
J.J. Crowe	c Taylor b Foster	52	lbw b Botham		3
J.V. Coney	c Gower b Cook	27	not out		174
R.J. Hadlee	c Gatting b Botham	24	c Lamb b Foster		18
M.C. Snedden	c Taylor b Willis	11	c Taylor b Foster		16
I.D.S. Smith†	lbw b Botham	24	b Cook		29
B.L. Cairns	c Gatting b Willis	3	c sub (G. Fowler) b Willis		64
E.J. Chatfield	not out	4	b Cook		0
Extras	(B 4, LB 9, NB 7)	20	(B 4, LB 14, W 2, NB 14)		34
		219			**537**

England

C.J. Tavaré	b Cairns	9
C.L. Smith	c Hadlee b Cairns	27
D.I. Gower	c Hadlee b Cairns	33
A.J. Lamb	c M.D. Crowe b Cairns	13
M.W. Gatting	lbw b Cairns	19
I.T. Botham	c J.J. Crowe b Cairns	138
D.W. Randall	c M.D. Crowe b Hadlee	164
R.W. Taylor†	run out	14
N.G.B. Cook	c Smith b Cairns	7
N.A. Foster	c Howarth b Hadlee	10
R.G.D. Willis*	not out	5
Extras	(LB 8, NB 16)	24
		463

not out		36
not out		30
(NB 3)		3
(0 wickets)		**69**

England	O	M	R	W	O	M	R	W
Willis	19	7	37	3	37	8	102	2
Botham	27.4	8	59	5	36	6	137	1
Foster	24	9	60	1	37	12	91	2
Cook	23	11	43	1	66.3	26	153	3
Gatting					8	4	14	1
Smith					3	1	6	0

New Zealand	O	M	R	W	O	M	R	W
Hadlee	31.5	6	97	2				
Snedden	21	3	101	0	7	2	28	0
Cairns	45	10	143	7				
Chatfield	28	6	68	0	5	0	24	0
M.D. Crowe	3	0	20	0	6	1	11	0
Coney	4	1	10	0				
Edgar					3	1	3	0
J.J. Crowe					1	1	0	0

Fall of Wickets

Wkt	NZ 1st	E 1st	NZ 2nd	E 2nd
1st	34	41	62	
2nd	39	51	79	
3rd	56	84	153	
4th	71	92	165	
5th	114	115	279	
6th	160	347	302	
7th	174	372	334	
8th	200	386	402	
9th	208	426	520	
10th	219	463	537	

*Captain †Wicket-keeper

New Zealand v England 1983-84 2nd Test
New Zealand won by an innings and 132 runs
Played at Lancaster Park, Christchurch, February 3, 4, 5
Toss: New Zealand. Umpires: F.R. Goodall and S.J. Woodward
Debuts: England, A.C.S. Pigott

New Zealand

J.G. Wright	c Taylor b Cowans	25
B.A. Edgar	c Randall b Pigott	1
G.P. Howarth*	b Cowans	9
M.D. Crowe	c Tavaré b Botham	19
J.J. Crowe	lbw b Cowans	47
J.V. Coney	c Botham b Pigott	41
R.J. Hadlee	c Taylor b Willis	99
I.D.S. Smith†	not out	32
B.L. Cairns	c Taylor b Willis	2
S.L. Boock	c Taylor b Willis	5
E.J. Chatfield	lbw b Willis	0
Extras	(B 8, LB 11, W 2, NB 6)	27
		307

England

C. Fowler	b Boock	4	c Howarth b Boock		10
C.J. Tavaré	c J.J. Crowe b Hadlee	3	c Smith b Hadlee		6
D.I. Gower	lbw b Hadlee	2	c Cairns b Hadlee		8
A.J. Lamb	c Smith b Chatfield	11	c Coney b Chatfield		9
D.W. Randall	c Coney b Hadlee	0	(7) c Cairns b Hadlee		25
I.T. Botham	c Chatfield b Cairns	18	c M.D. Crowe b Boock		0
M.W. Gatting	not out	19	(5) c Hadlee b Boock		0
R.W. Taylor†	c J.J. Crowe b Cairns	2	run out		15
A.C.S. Pigott	lbw b Cairns	4	not out		8
R.G.D. Willis*	b Chatfield	6	c Howarth b Hadlee		0
N.G. Cowans	c Coney b Chatfield	4	c Smith b Hadlee		7
Extras	(LB 5, NB 4)	9	(LB 2, NB 3)		5
		82			**93**

England

	O	M	R	W
Willis	22.1	5	51	4
Botham	17	1	88	1
Pigott	17	7	75	2
Cowans	14	2	52	3
Gatting	2	0	14	0

New Zealand

	O	M	R	W	O	M	R	W
Hadlee	17	9	16	3	18	6	28	5
Cairns	19	5	35	3	9	3	21	0
Boock	6	3	12	1	13	3	25	3
Chatfield	8.2	3	10	3	11	1	14	1

Fall of Wickets

Wkt	NZ 1st	E 1st	E 2nd
1st	30	7	15
2nd	42	9	23
3rd	53	10	25
4th	87	10	31
5th	137	41	31
6th	203	41	33
7th	281	47	72
8th	291	58	76
9th	301	72	80
10th	307	82	93

*Captain †Wicket-keeper

New Zealand v England 1983-84 3rd Test
Match Drawn
Played at Eden Park, Auckland, February 10, 11, 12, 14, 15
Toss: New Zealand. Umpires: F.R. Goodall and S.J. Woodward
Debuts: Nil

New Zealand

J.G. Wright	b Willis	130	not out	11
B.A. Edgar	lbw b Willis	0	not out	0
G.P. Howarth*	c Randall b Cowans	35		
M.D. Crowe	c Botham b Willis	16		
J.J. Crowe	b Marks	128		
J.V. Coney	b Cowans	9		
R.J. Hadlee	b Marks	3		
I.D.S. Smith†	not out	113		
B.L. Cairns	c Cowans b Foster	28		
S.L. Boock	lbw b Marks	2		
E.J. Chatfield	not out	6		
Extras	(LB 19, NB 7)	26	(LB 1, NB 4)	5
	(9 wickets declared)	**496**	(0 wickets)	**16**

England

G. Fowler	c Smith b Hadlee	0
C.L. Smith	c Smith b Cairns	91
D.I. Gower	b Boock	26
A.J. Lamb	lbw b Cairns	49
D.W. Randall	c Wright b Chatfield	104
R.W. Taylor†	st Smith b Boock	23
I.T. Botham	run out	70
V.J. Marks	c Smith b Chatfield	6
N.A. Foster	not out	18
R.G.D. Willis*	c Smith b Hadlee	3
N.G. Cowans	c Cairns b Boock	21
Extras	(B 7, LB 13, NB 8)	28
		439

England	O	M	R	W	O	M	R	W
Willis	34	7	109	3	3	1	7	0
Botham	29	10	70	0				
Cowans	36	11	98	2	2	1	4	0
Foster	30	8	78	1				
Marks	40.2	9	115	3				

New Zealand	O	M	R	W
Hadlee	43	12	91	2
Cairns	40	19	52	2
Boock	61.3	28	103	3
Chatfield	46	23	72	2
M.D. Crowe	17	5	62	0
Coney	13	8	13	0
Howarth	7	1	18	0

Fall of Wickets

Wkt	NZ 1st	E 1st	NZ 2nd
1st	3	0	
2nd	74	48	
3rd	111	143	
4th	265	234	
5th	293	284	
6th	302	371	
7th	385	387	
8th	451	391	
9th	461	396	
10th		439	

*Captain †Wicket-keeper

Test Match Averages: New Zealand v England 1983-84

New Zealand

Batting/Fielding	M	I	NO	HS	Runs	Avge	100	50	Ct	St
I.D.S. Smith	3	4	2	113*	198	99.00	1	–	8	1
J.V. Coney	3	4	1	174*	251	83.66	1	–	3	–
J.J. Crowe	3	4	0	128	230	57.50	1	–	3	–
J.G. Wright	3	5	1	130	218	54.50	1	–	1	–
M.D. Crowe	3	4	0	100	148	37.00	1	–	3	–
R.J. Hadlee	3	4	0	99	144	36.00	–	1	3	–
B.L. Cairns	3	4	0	64	97	24.25	–	1	3	–
G.P. Howarth	3	4	0	35	93	23.25	–	–	3	–
B.A. Edgar	3	5	1	30	40	10.00	–	–	–	–
E.J. Chatfield	3	4	2	6*	10	5.00	–	–	1	–
S.L. Boock	2	2	0	5	7	3.50	–	–	–	–

Played in one Test: M.C. Snedden 11, 16.

Bowling	O	M	R	W	Avge	Best	5wI	10wM
R.J. Hadlee	109.5	33	232	12	19.33	5-28	1	–
S.L. Boock	80.3	34	140	7	20.00	3-25	–	–
B.L. Cairns	113	37	251	12	20.91	7-143	1	–
E.J. Chatfield	98.2	33	188	6	31.33	3-10	–	–

Also bowled: J.V. Coney 17-9-23-0; J.J. Crowe 1-1-0-0; M.D. Crowe 26-6-93-0; B.A. Edgar 3-1-3-0; G.P. Howarth 7-1-18-0; M.C. Snedden 28-5-129-0.

England

Batting/Fielding	M	I	NO	HS	Runs	Avge	100	50	Ct	St
C.L. Smith	2	3	1	91	148	74.00	–	1	–	–
D.W. Randall	3	4	0	164	293	73.25	2	–	2	–
I.T. Botham	3	4	0	138	226	56.50	1	1	3	–
N.A. Foster	2	2	1	18*	28	28.00	–	–	1	–
A.J. Lamb	3	4	0	49	82	20.50	–	–	1	–
M.W. Gatting	2	3	1	19*	38	19.00	–	–	2	–
C.J. Tavaré	2	4	1	36*	54	18.00	–	–	1	–
D.I. Gower	3	4	0	33	69	17.25	–	–	2	–
R.W. Taylor	3	4	0	15	54	13.50	–	–	9	–
N.G. Cowans	2	3	0	21	32	10.66	–	–	1	–
G. Fowler	2	3	0	10	14	4.66	–	–	–	–
R.G.D. Willis	3	4	1	6	14	4.66	–	–	–	–

Played in one Test: N.G.B. Cook 7 (1 ct); V.J. Marks 6; A.C.S. Pigott 4, 8*.

Bowling	O	M	R	W	Avge	Best	5wI	10wM
R.G.D. Willis	115.1	28	306	12	25.50	4-51	–	–
N.G. Cowans	52	14	154	5	30.80	3-52	–	–
N.G.B. Cook	89.3	37	196	4	49.00	3-153	–	–
I.T. Botham	109.4	25	354	7	50.57	5-59	1	–
N.A. Foster	91	29	229	4	57.25	2-91	–	–

Also bowled: M.W. Gatting 10-4-28-1; V.J. Marks 40.2-9-115-3; A.C.S. Pigott 17-7-75-2; C.L. Smith 3-1-6-0.

Statistical Highlights of the Tests

1st Test, Wellington. Howarth won his ninth toss in 18 Tests as captain and chose to bat for the first time. Willis took his 308th wicket (Cairns) in 84 Tests to supersede F.S. Trueman (67 Tests) as England's leading wicket-taker. It was his 51st wicket v New Zealand. Botham scored a hundred and took five wickets in an innings of the same Test for the fifth time – no one else has achieved this feat more than twice. Cairns, who took the first six wickets to fall, including his 100th (Lamb) in 33 Tests, recorded the best analysis (7-143) for New Zealand against England in New Zealand. Coney's 174 not out was the highest score of his career, a record against England in New Zealand and for New Zealand in all Tests at The Basin Reserve, and his first century in first-class matches in 131 innings since 1977. With Cairns he shared a ninth-wicket partnership of 118 – a record for New Zealand v England. The total of 537 was New Zealand's highest on any home ground and the record by any country at Wellington. They have not lost a Test on that ground since 1968, a sequence of nine matches without defeat.

2nd Test, Christchurch. Failing to include a specialist spin bowler for only the third time in 596 Tests, England's defeat echoed the result of both previous instances (Melbourne 1932-33 and Brisbane 1954-55). New Zealand, who were able to enforce the follow-on for the first time in 59 matches, gained their 17th victory (third v England) by their largest margin of an innings and 132 runs. It was England's heaviest defeat since 1973, when West Indies won by an innings and 226 runs at Lord's, and their first by an innings for 33 Tests, since 1980-81 (Port-of-Spain). For the first time since 1894-95, England failed to reach 100 in either innings. The last of the previous 14 instances was inflicted upon New Zealand by England in 1958.

3rd Test, Auckland. Howarth became the first New Zealand captain to win three successive tosses in a home series. The fourth-wicket partnership of 154 by Wright and J.J. Crowe broke New Zealand's record against England set by M.L. Page and R.C. Blunt at Lord's in 1931. Smith improved his highest Test score for the fourth time in successive innings and celebrated his maiden Test hundred by hitting the last two balls of the innings for six before catching Fowler off the first ball of England's reply. Smith's five dismissals equalled the New Zealand Test record. After 54 years and at their 21st attempt, New Zealand won their first series against England.

One-Day Internationals

18 February at Christchurch. ENGLAND won by 54 runs. Toss: New Zealand. England 188-9 closed (50 overs) (D.W. Randall 70; R.J. Hadlee 10-2-32-5). New Zealand 134 (42.1 overs). Match award: D.W. Randall (70).

22 February at Wellington. ENGLAND won by 6 wickets. Toss: New Zealand. New Zealand 135 (47.1 overs) (V.J. Marks 10-3-20-5 – England's best analysis in one-day internationals). England 139-4 (45.1 overs) (C.L. Smith 70). Match award: V.J. Marks (5-20 and 1 ct).

25 February at Auckland. NEW ZEALAND won by 7 wickets. Toss: England. England 209-9 closed (50 overs) (A.J. Lamb 97*). New Zealand 210-3 (45.3 overs) (G.P. Howarth 72, M.D. Crowe 105*). Match award: M.D. Crowe (105*).

England in Pakistan

First Test: Karachi, March 2, 3, 4, 6, 7.
Pakistan won by three wickets.
Despite England's unhelpful preliminaries to the first Test – injuries, a long and interrupted flight, and the abrupt change of conditions – they might have escaped defeat, even won, but for one man and his craft. Few of the England side had ever played a leg-spinner of Abdul Qadir's class and guile and his influence on the match, with bat as well as ball, was decisive.

Their new opening pair of Smith and Gatting made a promising start, but the difficulty in reading Qadir plus the steadiness of Sarfraz had them out for 182. This was not enough even on a pitch more favourable to bowlers than most in Pakistan, where England had for the past 22 years only drawn Test matches.

Yet Cook, who had bowled only 16 overs in the middle in the previous five and a half weeks, bowled tidily enough to prompt errors from the early Pakistan batsmen, and if he had taken a return catch from Qadir Pakistan would have been 141 for 7 with no great lead in prospect. The catch escaped, Saleem Malik and Qadir put on 75, and the eventual lead was 95.

Though David Gower, the only England batsman to reach 50 in the first innings, did so again, England left Pakistan needing only 65 to win. When Pakistan were 40 for 6 against Cook and Marks, a miracle was just possible, but the wickets had been lost mainly through carelessness and the later batsmen took Pakistan home by three wickets. The margin may have flattered England, but the defeat was not a dishonourable one in the circumstances.

Second Test: Faisalabad, March 12, 13, 14, 16, 17.
Drawn.
As in New Zealand, when they were one down going to Auckland, England could have little hope of remedying the situation on a pitch of notorious innocuousness in Faisalabad. Moreover, in the five days between the first two Tests, Willis had dropped out through illness and Botham had gone home with a knee injury. Only four specialist bowlers remained, and most of those who took the field were plagued at some time by sore throats and disturbed stomachs.

However, after Pakistan had made the sort of score which seemed inevitable, Zaheer declaring at 449 for 8, Gatting led a spirited England reply which soon settled fears that the size of the Pakistan total plus weariness and the prevailing ailments might bring about a collapse not warranted by the easy batting conditions. Gower, coming in late because of slight indisposition, batted for seven hours, and eventually England led on first innings.

Third Test: Lahore, March 19, 20, 21, 23, 24.
Drawn.

Having been put in and bowled out for 241, England hit back, as in Karachi, but were thwarted by a ninth-wicket stand of 161 between a limping Zaheer and Sarfraz, the acting captain for much of the match. Batting again 102 behind, England made enough runs, through Gower's splendid 173 not out and Marks's second fine innings of the match, to declare with nine wickets down, leaving Pakistan needing 243 in 59 overs. The declaration was a sensible one by a side one down in the series. Only the subsequent time-wasting, when it was realized early in the opening stand of 173 between Mohsin and Shoaib that Pakistan might be heading for victory, marred a commendable English effort in adversity.

ENGLAND'S WINTER TOUR 1983-84/IN PAKISTAN

Pakistan v England 1983-84 1st Test
Pakistan won by 3 wickets
Played at National Stadium, Karachi, March 2, 3, 4, 6
Toss: England. Umpires: Khizer Hayat and Shakoor Rana
Debuts: Pakistan, Anil Dalpat, Ramiz Raja

England

C.L. Smith	c Wasim b Sarfraz	28	lbw b Sarfraz	5
M.W. Gatting	b Tauseef	26	lbw b Sarfraz	4
D.I. Gower	lbw b Qadir	58	c Mohsin b Tauseef	57
A.J. Lamb	c Ramiz b Sarfraz	4	c Anil b Qadir	20
D.W. Randall	b Qadir	8	b Qadir	16
I.T. Botham	c Ramiz b Qadir	22	b Tauseef	10
V.J. Marks	c Ramiz b Sarfraz	5	b Qadir	1
R.W. Taylor†	lbw b Qadir	4	c Mohsin b Tauseef	19
N.G.B. Cook	c Salim b Qadir	9	c Mohsin b Wasim	5
R.G.D. Willis*	c Wasim b Sarfraz	6	c Tauseef b Wasim	2
N.G. Cowans	not out	1	not out	0
Extras	(LB 6, NB 5)	11	(B 6, LB 6, NB 8)	20
		182		**159**

Pakistan

Mohsin Khan	c Botham b Cook	54	b Cook	10
Qasim Omar	lbw b Cook	29	c Botham b Cook	7
Ramiz Raja	c Smith b Cook	1	c Botham b Marks	1
Zaheer Abbas*	c Lamb b Botham	0	b Cook	8
Salim Malik	lbw b Willis	74	run out	11
Wasim Raja	c Cowans b Cook	3	c Cowans b Cook	0
Anil Dalpat†	c Taylor b Willis	12	not out	16
Abdul Qadir	c Lamb b Botham	40	b Cook	7
Sarfraz Nawaz	c Botham b Cook	8	not out	4
Tauseef Ahmed	not out	17		
Azim Hafeez	c Willis b Cook	24		
Extras	(LB 5, NB 10)	15	(B 1, NB 1)	2
		277	(7 wickets)	**66**

Pakistan	O	M	R	W	O	M	R	W
Azim	11	3	21	0	8	3	14	0
Sarfraz	25.5	8	42	4	15	1	27	2
Tauseef	24	11	33	1	21	6	37	3
Wasim	3	2	1	0	3.3	1	2	2
Qadir	31	12	74	5	31	4	59	3

England	O	M	R	W	O	M	R	W
Willis	17	6	33	2	2	0	13	0
Cowans	12	3	34	0	2.3	1	10	0
Botham	30	5	90	2				
Cook	30	12	65	6	14	8	18	5
Marks	13	4	40	0	12	5	23	1

Fall of Wickets

Wkt	E 1st	P 1st	E 2nd	P 2nd
1st	41	67	6	17
2nd	90	79	21	18
3rd	94	80	63	26
4th	108	96	94	38
5th	154	105	121	38
6th	159	138	128	40
7th	164	213	128	59
8th	165	229	157	
9th	180	240	159	
10th	182	277	159	

*Captain †Wicket-keeper

Pakistan v England 1983-84 2nd Test
Match Drawn
Played at Iqbal Stadium, Faisalabad, March 12, 13, 14, 16, 17
Toss: Pakistan. Umpires: Javed Akhtar and Mahboob Shah
Debuts: Nil

Pakistan

Mohsin Khan	c Lamb b Dilley	20	b Dilley		2
Mudassar Nazar	c Gatting b Cook	12	lbw b Foster		4
Qasim Omar	c Gatting b Foster	16	c Taylor b Dilley		17
Salim Malik	c Lamb b Cook	116	c sub (N.G. Cowans) b Marks		76
Zaheer Abbas*	lbw b Gatting	68	not out		32
Wasim Raja	b Marks	112	not out		5
Abdul Qadir	c Foster b Dilley	50			
Anil Dalpat†	lbw b Dilley	8			
Sarfraz Nawaz	not out	16			
Tauseef Ahmed	not out	1			
Azim Hafeez	did not bat				
Extras	(LB 11, W 2, NB 17)	30	(LB 1)		1
	(8 wickets declared)	**449**	(4 wickets)		**137**

England

C.L. Smith	b Sarfraz	66
M.W. Gatting	c Salim b Tauseef	75
D.W. Randall	b Sarfraz	65
A.J. Lamb	c Anil b Azim	19
D.I. Gower*	st Anil b Mudassar	152
G. Fowler	c Omar b Wasim	57
R.W. Taylor†	c Salim b Qadir	0
V.J. Marks	b Sarfraz	83
G.R. Dilley	not out	2
N.G.B. Cook	not out	1
N.A. Foster	did not bat	
Extras	(B 10, LB 4, NB 12)	26
	(8 wickets declared)	**546**

England	O	M	R	W	O	M	R	W
Foster	30	7	109	1	5	1	10	1
Dilley	28	6	101	3	9	0	41	2
Cook	54	14	133	2	16	6	38	0
Marks	27	9	59	1	8	2	26	1
Gatting	3	0	17	1	2	0	18	0
Fowler					1	0	3	0

Pakistan	O	M	R	W
Azim	19	3	71	1
Sarfraz	50	11	129	3
Wasim	26	6	61	1
Qadir	51	14	124	1
Tauseef	30	8	96	1
Mudassar	13	1	39	1

Fall of Wickets

Wkt	P 1st	E 1st	P 2nd
1st	35	127	6
2nd	53	163	6
3rd	70	214	56
4th	200	245	123
5th	323	361	
6th	416	361	
7th	430	528	
8th	433	545	

*Captain †Wicket-keeper

ENGLAND'S WINTER TOUR 1983-84/IN PAKISTAN

Pakistan v England 1983-84 3rd Test
March Drawn
Played at Gaddafi Stadium, Lahore, March 19, 20, 21, 23, 24
Toss: Pakistan. Umpires: Amanullah Khan and Khizer Hayat
Debuts: Pakistan, Mohsin Kamal

England

C.L. Smith	c Salim b Sarfraz	18	(2) not out	15
M.W. Gatting	lbw b Sarfraz	0	(3) run out	53
D.I. Gower*	c Anil b Mohsin Kamal	9	(4) not out	173
A.J. Lamb	c Ramiz b Qadir	29	(5) c and b Qadir	6
D.W. Randall	c Salim b Qadir	14	(6) c Salim b Qadir	0
G. Fowler	c Omar b Qadir	58	(1) c Anil b Mohsin Kamal	19
V.J. Marks	c Mohsin Khan b Qadir	74	c sub (Akram Raza) b Qadir	55
R.W. Taylor†	lbw b Sarfraz	1	(10) b Sarfraz	5
N.A. Foster	lbw b Qadir	6	(8) lbw b Qadir	0
N.G.B. Cook	c Anil b Sarfraz	3		
N.G. Cowans	not out	3	(9) st Anil b Qadir	3
Extras	(B 4, LB 5, W 9, NB 8)	26	(B 6, LB 3, W 1, NB 5)	15
		241	(9 wickets declared)	**344**

Pakistan

Mohsin Khan	lbw b Foster	1	c Smith b Cowans	104
Shoaib Mohammad	lbw b Cowans	7	c Gatting b Cowans	80
Qasim Omar	c Fowler b Foster	73	run out	0
Salim Malik	b Marks	38	c Gatting b Cowans	7
Ramiz Raja	c Smith b Foster	26	(8) not out	6
Wasim Raja	c Gower b Cowans	12	lbw b Cowans	0
Zaheer Abbas*	not out	82	(5) c Gatting b Cowans	5
Abdul Qadir	c Taylor b Foster	3		
Anil Dalpat†	c Gower b Foster	2		
Sarfraz Nawaz	c Gatting b Smith	90	(7) not out	10
Mohsin Kamal	c Gower b Cook	0		
Extras	(LB 9)	9	(LB 5)	5
		343	(6 wickets)	**217**

Pakistan	O	M	R	W	O	M	R	W
Mohsin Kamal	15	0	66	1	17	3	59	1
Sarfraz	22.5	5	49	4	27.4	1	112	1
Qadir	30	7	84	5	42	5	110	5
Wasim	11	4	16	0	21	5	48	0

England	O	M	R	W	O	M	R	W
Cowans	29	5	89	2	14	2	42	5
Foster	32	8	67	5	15	4	44	0
Cook	46	12	117	1	18.3	2	73	0
Marks	20	4	59	1	10	0	53	0
Smith	1	0	2	1	1	1	0	0

Fall of Wickets

Wkt	E 1st	P 1st	E 2nd	P 2nd
1st	5	9	35	173
2nd	20	13	38	175
3rd	47	99	175	187
4th	77	138	189	197
5th	83	151	189	199
6th	203	166	308	199
7th	205	175	309	
8th	222	181	327	
9th	237	342	344	
10th	241	343		

*Captain †Wicket-keeper

Test Match Averages: Pakistan v England 1983-84

Pakistan

Batting/Fielding	M	I	NO	HS	R	Avge	100	50	Ct	St
Sarfraz Nawaz	3	5	3	90	128	64.00	-	1	-	-
Salim Malik	3	6	0	116	322	53.66	1	2	6	-
Zaheer Abbas	3	6	2	82*	195	48.75	-	2	-	-
Mohsin Khan	3	6	0	104	191	31.83	1	1	4	-
Wasim Raja	3	6	1	112	132	26.40	1	-	2	-
Abdul Qadir	3	4	0	50	100	25.00	-	1	1	-
Azim Hafeez	2	1	0	24	24	24.00	-	-	-	-
Qasim Omar	3	6	0	73	142	23.66	-	1	2	-
Tauseef Ahmed	2	2	2	17*	18	-	-	-	1	-
Anil Dalpat	3	4	1	16*	38	12.66	-	-	5	2
Ramiz Raja	2	4	1	26	34	11.33	-	-	4	-

Played in one Test: Mohsin Kamal 0; Mudassar Nazar 12, 4; Shoaib Mohammad 7, 80.

Bowling	O	M	R	W	Avge	Best	5wI	10wM
Abdul Qadir	185	42	451	19	23.73	5-74	3	1
Sarfraz Nawaz	141.2	26	359	14	25.64	4-42	-	-
Tauseef Ahmed	75	25	166	5	33.20	3-37	-	-

Also bowled: Azim Hafeez 38-9-106-1; Mohsin Kamal 32-3-125-2; Mudassar Nazar 13-1-39-1; Wasim Raja 64.3-18-128-3.

England

Batting/Fielding	M	I	NO	HS	R	Avge	100	50	Ct	St
D.I. Gower	3	5	1	173*	449	112.25	2	2	3	-
G. Fowler	2	3	0	58	134	44.66	-	2	1	-
V.J. Marks	3	5	0	83	218	43.60	-	3	-	-
M.W. Gatting	3	5	0	75	158	31.60	-	2	6	-
C.L. Smith	3	5	0	66	132	26.40	-	1	3	-
D.W. Randall	3	5	0	65	103	20.60	-	1	-	-
A.J. Lamb	3	5	0	29	78	15.60	-	-	4	-
N.G. Cowans	2	4	3	3*	7	7.00	-	-	2	-
N.G.B. Cook	3	4	1	9	18	6.00	-	-	-	-
R.W. Taylor	3	5	0	19	29	5.80	-	-	3	-
N.A. Foster	2	2	0	6	6	3.00	-	-	1	-

Played in one Test: I.T. Botham 22, 10 (4 ct); G.R. Dilley 2*; R.G.D. Willis 6, 2 (1 ct).

Bowling	O	M	R	W	Avge	Best	5wI	10wM
N.G. Cowans	57.3	11	175	7	25.00	5-42	1	-
G.R. Dilley	37	6	142	5	28.40	3-101	-	-
N.G.B. Cook	178.3	54	444	14	31.71	6-65	2	1
N.A. Foster	82	20	230	7	32.85	5-67	1	-

Also bowled: I.T. Botham 30-5-90-2; G. Fowler 1-0-3-0; M.W. Gatting 5-0-35-1; V.J. Marks 90-24-260-4; C.L. Smith 2-1-2-1; R.G.D. Willis 19-6-46-2.

Statistical Highlights of the Tests

1st Test, Karachi. Botham made the last of his 65 consecutive Test appearances to equal A.P.E. Knott's England record. England's totals of 182 and 159 were their lowest in Pakistan. Pakistan beat England in Pakistan for the first time in 13 attempts and so ended a sequence of 11 drawn matches. They have never lost a Test at Karachi – played 21, won 10, drawn 11. Cook (11-83) became the first England bowler to take more than eight wickets in a Test in Pakistan.

2nd Test, Faisalabad. Salim Malik emulated G.A. Headley (West Indies) and R.G. Pollock (South Africa) by scoring a third Test hundred before his 21st birthday. Gower, who became the 14th batsman to score 4,000 runs for England, recorded the first century by an England captain since A.W. Greig scored 103 at Calcutta in 1976-77. His seventh-wicket partnership of 167 with Marks established a new England record against Pakistan. England's total of 546-8 declared was their highest in a Test in Pakistan (previously 507 at Karachi in 1961-62).

3rd Test, Lahore. This was England's 600th official Test match (won 222, lost 152, drawn 226). Mohsin Kamal became the 100th player to represent Pakistan in Test cricket. During his highest Test innings, Sarfraz Nawaz (90) completed 1,000 runs and became the third Pakistani after Intikhab Alam and Imran Khan to complete the career double of 1,000 runs and 100 wickets. Mohsin Khan and Shoaib Mohammad added 173 for the first wicket to set a new record against England (previously 122 by Shoaib's father, Hanif, and Alim-ud-Din at Dacca in 1961-62). Abdul Qadir (10-194) was the first bowler to take more than seven wickets against England in Pakistan. His total of 19 wickets set a Pakistan series record at home against England. Gower (449 runs) and Cook (14 wickets) set England series records in Pakistan. After 12 attempts during a period of 30 years, Pakistan won their first series against England. England lost two Test series during the same season for the first time.

One-Day Internationals

9 March at Gaddafi Stadium, Lahore. PAKISTAN won by 6 wickets. Toss: Pakistan. England 184-8 closed (40 overs) (A.J. Lamb 57). Pakistan 187-4 (38.4 overs) (Zaheer Abbas 59*). Match award: Zaheer Abbas (59*).

26 March at National Stadium, Karachi. ENGLAND won by 6 wickets. Toss: England. Pakistan 163-8 closed (40 overs) (Saadat Ali 78*). England 164-4 (38.4 overs). Match award: M.W. Gatting (38*, 8-1-32-3, and 1ct).

Tour Statistical Summary

England Tour of Fiji, New Zealand, and Pakistan 1983-84

First-Class Matches: Played 10; Won 1, Lost 2, Drawn 7
All Matches: Played 18; Won 7, Lost 4, Drawn 7

First-Class Averages

Batting/Fielding	M	I	NO	HS	R	Avge	100	50	Ct	St
D.I. Gower	9	14	1	173*	746	57.38	2	4	7	–
D.W. Randall	8	13	2	164	624	56.72	3	2	5	–
V.J. Marks	6	9	2	83	293	41.85	–	4	–	–
C.L. Smith	8	14	2	138*	502	41.83	1	3	6	–
I.T. Botham	7	10	0	138	409	40.90	1	2	8	–
G. Fowler	7	12	0	104	397	33.08	1	3	2	–
M.W. Gatting	8	13	2	75	357	32.45	–	4	8	–
G.R. Dilley	4	4	2	28	47	23.50	–	–	1	–
C.J. Tavaré	6	12	2	89	204	20.40	–	1	6	–
A.J. Lamb	9	15	0	51	307	20.46	–	1	5	–
R.W. Taylor	10	13	1	86	216	18.00	–	1	20	–
N.A. Foster	6	6	1	21	63	12.60	–	–	3	–
N.G. Cowans	7	7	3	21	39	9.75	–	–	5	–
N.G.B. Cook	7	8	2	9	44	7.33	–	–	3	–
R.G.D. Willis	7	8	3	6	28	5.60	–	–	5	–

Also batted: A.C.S. Pigott (one match) 4,8*.

Bowling	O	M	R	W	Avge	Best	5wI	10wM
R.G.D. Willis	188.5	51	495	19	26.05	4-51	–	–
G.R. Dilley	99	27	291	11	26.45	3-28	–	–
N.G. Cowans	170.3	45	503	18	27.94	5-42	1	–
N.A. Foster	224	61	614	20	30.70	6-30	2	–
V.J. Marks	195.3	54	538	17	31.64	5-52	2	–
N.G.B. Cook	348	116	849	24	35.37	6-65	2	1
I.T. Botham	193.5	46	589	16	36.81	5-59	1	–

Also bowled: G. Fowler 1-0-3-0; M.W. Gatting 25-9-82-3; A.C.S. Pigott 17-7-75-2; C.L. Smith 5-2-8-1.

Overseas cricket
1983-84

India v Pakistan

It was not only because they missed the advantage of playing at home that Pakistan failed to re-establish such superiority as they held over India in the previous winter's series. The absence of Imran Khan and Sarfraz Nawaz made so much difference that the rubber was drawn, with none of the Tests producing a result.

Pakistan were also without Abdul Qadir, but his absence seemed a handicap less weighty, as the leg-spinner had never previously bewildered India's batsmen as he had England's and Australia's. Man for man, Pakistan were a stronger batting side, particularly as Amarnath, such a heavy scorer against them a year earlier, was miserably out of form. In fact, all of India's front-line batsmen, save Gavaskar, seemed the worse for having played no cricket since the World Cup, as far back as in June.

Yet, Pakistan's bowling did not have the cutting edge to exploit the fragility of the Indian batting. If India's attack looked more respectable, it was only because it contained Kapil Dev who, as always, bowled superbly. Pakistan's most likely bowler was a newcomer, Azeem Hafeez. Left-arm fast-medium, Hafeez was not undermined by slow pitches. He was always a threat because of his angle of delivery from over the wicket and across the batsman towards the slips. However, he suffered from lack of experience and even more from the way Zaheer Abbas handled him.

The strengths and weaknesses of the rivals made little difference in the final analysis. Rain interfered significantly with every Test match and the decisive factor really was the weather. However, despite loss of time, the third Test, played on a dubious pitch at Nagpur, could have been won by Pakistan if Zaheer had only reached for victory. It was put within his range by India's forthright efforts to force the issue.

Zaheer's negative approach gave credence to a statement made by Sarfraz Nawaz half way through the series. The controversial Sarfraz said that he was left out of the touring side because he refused to subscribe to the predetermined policy of playing to draw every match. It indeed appeared as if the Pakistanis were using this tour as a warm-up for their Australian campaign which followed immediately.

The confidence India had gained from winning the World Cup was reflected in the manner in which they demolished Pakistan in the one-day internationals. The Test series did not rouse the fanatical interest which is normally a feature of battles between the two neighbouring countries and, by Indian standards, crowds were small. But there was no keeping them away from the limited-over games.

India v Pakistan 1983-84 1st Test
Match Drawn
Played at Karnataka SCA Stadium, Bangalore, September 14, 15, 17, 18, 19
Toss: India. Umpires: M.V. Gothoskar and Swaroop Kishen
Debuts: Pakistan, Azim Hafeez

India

S.M. Gavaskar	lbw b Tahir	42	not out	103
A.D. Gaekwad	b Mudassar	11	not out	66
M. Amarnath	b Mudassar	4		
Yashpal Sharma	c Wasim Bari b Mudassar	16		
S.M. Patil	c Miandad b Tahir	6		
Kapil Dev*	c Mohsin b Azim	0		
R.M.H. Binny	not out	83		
Madan Lal	c Wasim Bari b Azim	74		
S.M.H. Kirmani†	c Wasim Bari b Tahir	14		
S. Venkataraghavan	c Salim b Tahir	5		
D.R. Doshi	lbw b Tahir	0		
Extras	(B1, LB 8, W 6, NB 5)	20	(LB 4, W 1, NB 2)	7
		275	(0 wickets)	**176**

Pakistan

Mohsin Khan	c Kirmani b Madan Lal	17
Mudassar Nazar	c Kirmani b Kapil Dev	25
Salim Malik	c Amarnath b Kapil Dev	5
Javed Miandad	c sub (K. Srikkanth) b Madan Lal	99
Zaheer Abbas*	c Kapil Dev b Madan Lal	22
Wasim Raja	b Doshi	39
Wasim Bari†	b Kapil Dev	64
Tahir Naqqash	b Kapil Dev	1
Iqbal Qasim	c Gaekwad b Venkat	9
Azim Hafeez	b Kapil Dev	0
Mohammad Nazir	not out	0
Extras	(B 1, LB 4, NB 2)	7
		288

Pakistan‡	O	M	R	W	O	M	R	W
Tahir	34.5	11	76	5	17	2	54	0
Azim	39	11	102	2	8	2	20	0
Nazir	10	2	26	0	21	4	47	0
Mudassar	23	6	44	3	2.1	0	19	0
Qasim	13	7	18	0	12	2	29	0
Zaheer					1	0	3	0

India‡	O	M	R	W
Kapil Dev	29	6	68	5
Madan Lal	24	5	72	3
Binny	18	2	42	0
Venkat	21.1	4	49	1
Doshi	20	5	52	1

Fall of Wickets

Wkt	I 1st	P 1st	I 2nd
1st	38	32	
2nd	42	37	
3rd	72	58	
4th	80	99	
5th	81	187	
6th	85	243	
7th	240	244	
8th	269	288	
9th	275	288	
10th	275	288	

*Captain †Wicket-keeper ‡Wides and no-balls included in bowling analyses

India v Pakistan 1983-84 2nd Test
Match Drawn
Played at Burlton Park, Jullunder, September 24, 25, 26 (no play), 28, 29
Toss: India. Umpires: D.N. Dotiwalla and B. Ganguli
Debuts: Pakistan, Qasim Omar, Shoaib Mohammad

Pakistan

Mohsin Khan	lbw b Kapil Dev	0	not out	7
Shoaib Mohammad	c Kirmani b Kapil Dev	6	not out	6
Qasim Omar	c Kirmani b Binny	15		
Zaheer Abbas*	b Shastri	49		
Javed Miandad	c Shastri b Kapil Dev	66		
Mudassar Nazar	c sub (K. Srikkanth) b Shastri	24		
Wasim Raja	c Kirmani b Shastri	125		
Wasim Bari†	c Kirmani b Kapil Dev	0		
Tahir Naqqash	b Binny	37		
Mohammad Nazir	run out	2		
Azim Hafeez	not out	2		
Extras	(B 3, LB 6, W 1, NB 1)	11	(NB 3)	3
		337	(0 wickets)	16

India

S.M. Gavaskar	b Azim	5
A.D. Gaekwad	c and b Wasim Raja	201
M. Amarnath	c Wasim Bari b Azim	7
Yashpal Sharma	lbw b Tahir	7
S.M. Patil	c Wasim Bari b Tahir	26
R.J. Shastri	c Wasim Bari b Azim	26
R.M.H. Binny	b Zaheer	54
Kapil Dev*	lbw b Wasim Raja	4
Madan Lal	c Wasim Bari b Wasim Raja	11
S.M.H. Kirmani†	not out	8
S. Venkataraghavan	b Wasim Raja	6
Extras	(B 2, LB 4, W 9, NB 4)	19
		374

India‡	O	M	R	W	O	M	R	W
Kapil Dev	32	8	80	4	2	0	9	0
Madan Lal	20	4	61	0	1	0	1	0
Binny	16	1	69	2				
Shastri	37.2	12	63	3	3	2	1	0
Venkat	28	5	55	0				
Patil					2	1	2	0
Gavaskar					1	0	3	0

Pakistan‡	O	M	R	W
Tahir	27	3	74	2
Azim	23	3	65	3
Mudassar	28	6	80	0
Nazir	52	16	76	0
Wasim Raja	28.5	5	50	4
Mohsin	5	2	9	0
Zaheer	6	1	14	1

Fall of Wickets

Wkt	P 1st	I 1st	P 2nd
1st	0	5	
2nd	7	20	
3rd	55	73	
4th	101	131	
5th	154	209	
6th	169	330	
7th	169	345	
8th	264	353	
9th	309	368	
10th	337	374	

*Captain †Wicket-keeper ‡Wides and no-balls included in bowling analyses

India v Pakistan 1983-84 3rd Test
Match Drawn
Played at Vidarbha CA Ground, Nagpur, October 5, 6, 8, 9, 10
Toss: India. Umpires: S.R. Bose and M.G. Subramaniam
Debuts: India, R. Bhat

India

S.M. Gavaskar	c Mudassar b Azim	50	c Mudassar b Nazir	64
A.D. Gaekwad	c Wasim Bari b Tahir	6	c Wasim Raja b Nazir	29
D.B. Vengsarkar	c Wasim Bari b Salim	21	c Mohsin b Nazir	40
Yashpal Sharma	lbw b Nazir	13	c Wasim Bari b Azim	15
S.M. Patil	c Wasim Raja b Azim	6	lbw b Wasim Raja	26
Kapil Dev*	c Wasim Bari b Mudassar	32	(8) st Wasim Bari b Wasim Raja	10
R.J. Shastri	c Mudassar b Azim	52	(6) c Mudassar b Nazir	0
Kirti Azad	c Mohsin b Azim	11	(7) c Zaheer b Nazir	0
Madan Lal	c Salim b Nazir	5	not out	32
S.M.H. Kirmani†	run out	30	not out	31
R. Bhat	not out	0		
Extras	(B 9, LB 6, W 1, NB 3)	19	(B 7, LB 7, NB 1)	15
		245	(8 wickets declared)	**262**

Pakistan

Mohsin Khan	c Kirmani b Shastri	44		
Shoaib Mohammad	c Yashpal b Kapil Dev	9		
Salim Malik	lbw b Kapil Dev	0	not out	0
Javed Miandad	lbw b Bhat	60		
Zaheer Abbas*	c Kirmani b Kapil Dev	85		
Mudassar Nazar	st Kirmani b Bhat	78		
Wasim Raja	c Yashpal b Shastri	16		
Wasim Bari†	c Patil b Shastri	1		
Tahir Naqqash	c Gaekwad b Shastri	6	(1) not out	18
Mohammad Nazir	not out	13		
Azim Hafeez	c Patil b Shastri	4	(2) b Kirmani	18
Extras	(B 1, LB 1, NB 4)	6	(B 4, LB 1, NB 1)	6
		322	(1 wicket)	**42**

Pakistan‡	O	M	R	W	O	M	R	W
Azim	27	10	58	4	19	1	67	1
Tahir	19.3	3	72	1	23	7	55	0
Mudassar	14	2	43	1				
Salim	3	0	7	1				
Nazir	22	5	50	2	50	19	72	5
Zaheer					1	1	0	0
Wasim Raja					10	1	46	2
Mohsin					3	1	7	0
Miandad					1	0	1	0

India‡	O	M	R	W	O	M	R	W
Kapil Dev	27	8	68	3	1	1	0	0
Madan Lal	13	2	44	0				
Bhat	39	16	65	2				
Kirti Azad	25	7	68	0				
Shastri	30.4	7	75	5				
Vengsarkar					2	0	15	0
Yashpal					1	0	10	0
Kirmani					2	0	9	1
Gaekwad					1	0	3	0
Gavaskar					1	1	0	0

Fall of Wickets

Wkt	I 1st	P 1st	I 2nd	P 2nd
1st	27	20	78	42
2nd	66	26	125	
3rd	96	83	148	
4th	103	153	172	
5th	103	254	172	
6th	171	287	188	
7th	190	289	188	
8th	205	305	207	
9th	242	309		
10th	245	322		

*Captain †Wicket-keeper ‡Wides and no-balls included in bowling analyses

Test Match Averages: India v Pakistan 1983-84

India

Batting/Fielding	M	I	NO	HS	R	Avge	100	50	Ct	St
R.M.H. Binny	2	2	1	83*	137	137.00	-	2	-	-
A.D. Gaekwad	3	5	1	201	313	78.25	1	1	2	-
S.M. Gavaskar	3	5	1	103*	264	66.00	1	2	-	-
S.M.H. Kirmani	3	4	2	31*	83	41.50	-	-	8	1
Madan Lal	3	4	1	74	122	40.66	-	1	-	-
R.J. Shastri	2	3	0	52	78	26.00	-	1	1	-
S.M. Patil	3	4	0	26	64	16.00	-	-	2	-
Yashpal Sharma	3	4	0	16	51	12.75	-	-	2	-
Kapil Dev	3	4	0	32	46	11.50	-	-	1	-
M. Amarnath	2	2	0	7	11	5.50	-	-	1	-
S. Venkataraghavan	2	2	0	6	11	5.50	-	-	-	-

Played in one Test: R. Bhat 0*; D.R. Doshi 0; Kirti Azad 11, 0; D.B. Vengsarkar 21, 40.

Bowling	O	M	R	W	Avge	Best	5wI	10wM
R.J. Shastri	71	21	139	8	17.37	5-75	1	-
Kapil Dev	91	23	225	12	18.75	5-68	1	-

Also bowled: R. Bhat 39-16-65-2; R.M.H. Binny 34-3-111-2; D.R. Doshi 20-2-52-1; A.D. Gaekwad 1-0-3-0; S.M. Gavaskar 2-1-3-0; S.M.H. Kirmani 2-0-9-1; Kirti Azad 25-7-68-0; Madan Lal 58-11-178-3; S.M. Patil 2-1-2-0; D.B. Vengsarkar 2-0-15-0; S. Venkataraghavan 49.1-9-104-1; Yashpal Sharma 1-0-10-0.

Pakistan

Batting/Fielding	M	I	NO	HS	R	Avge	100	50	Ct	St
Javed Miandad	3	3	0	99	225	75.00	-	3	1	-
Wasim Raja	3	3	0	125	180	60.00	1	-	3	-
Zaheer Abbas	3	3	0	85	156	52.00	-	1	1	-
Mudassar Nazar	3	3	0	78	127	42.33	-	1	4	-
Mohsin Khan	3	4	1	44	68	22.66	-	-	3	-
Wasim Bari	3	3	0	64	65	21.66	-	1	11	1
Tahir Naqqash	3	4	1	37	62	20.66	-	-	-	-
Mohammad Nazir	3	3	2	13*	15	15.00	-	-	-	-
Shoaib Mohammad	2	3	1	9	21	10.50	-	-	-	-
Azim Hafeez	3	4	1	18	24	8.00	-	-	-	-
Salim Malik	2	3	1	5	5	2.50	-	-	2	-

Played in one Test: Iqbal Qasim 9; Qasim Omar 15.

Bowling	O	M	R	W	Avge	Best	5wI	10wM
Wasim Raja	38.5	6	96	6	16.00	4-50	-	-
Azim Hafeez	116	27	312	10	31.20	4-58	-	-
Mohammad Nazir	155	46	271	7	38.71	5-72	1	-
Tahir Naqqash	121.2	26	331	8	41.37	5-76	1	-

Also bowled: Iqbal Qasim 25-9-47-0; Javed Miandad 1-0-1-0; Mohsin Khan 8-3-16-0; Mudassar Nazar 67.1-14-186-4; Salim Malik 3-0-7-1; Zaheer Abbas 8-2-17-0.

Statistical Highlights of the Tests

1st Test, Bangalore. Javed Miandad became the second batsman after Zaheer Abbas to score 4,000 runs for Pakistan in Test cricket. He was the fourth Pakistani after Maqsood Ahmed, Majid Khan, and Mushtaq Mohammad to be dismissed for 99 in a Test. The seventh-wicket partnership of 155 between Binny and Madan Lal established a new Indian record against Pakistan.

2nd Test, Jullundur. Burlton Park became the 55th ground to stage an official Test match and the 13th to do so in India. Gaekwad (201) recorded the first double century for India against Pakistan. The previous highest innings for India in this series was C.G. Borde's 177 not out at Madras in 1960-61. Gaekwad's sixth-wicket partnership of 121 with Binny set a new Indian record for this series. By adding 95 for the eighth wicket, Wasim Raja and Tahir Naqqash set a new Pakistan record against India.

3rd Test, Nagpur. The Vidarbha Cricket Association Ground staged its second Test match, the first being against New Zealand in October 1969. Pakistan's total of 322 set a new record for a Test at Nagpur. Kapil Dev took his 75th wicket in 18 Tests against Pakistan; the only other bowler to take 50 or more in this series is Imran Khan, with 73 in 14 matches.

One-Day Internationals

10 September at Hyderabad. INDIA won by 4 wickets. Toss: India. Pakistan 151-8 closed (46 overs) (Javed Miandad 66*). India 152-6 (43 overs) (M. Amarnath 60*). Match award: M. Amarnath (60*, 10-0-27-0, and 1 ct).

21 September at Delhi. INDIA won by 1 wicket. Toss: Pakistan. Pakistan 197-3 closed (50 overs) (Mohsin Khan 50, Mudassar Nazar 65). India 201-9 (49.3 overs) (Kirti Azad 71*). Match award: Kirti Azad (71*, 10-1-28-3, and 1 ct). Attendance: 60,000. This was the first floodlit one-day international to be staged in India. The match was reduced from 60 to 50 overs per side when a lighting failure caused 24 minutes to be lost.

2 October at Jaipur. INDIA won by 4 wickets. Toss: India. Pakistan 166-9 closed (46 overs). India 169-6 (40.4 overs) (S.M. Patil 51). Match award: S.M. Patil (51 and 1 ct).

Note: Penalty runs for wides and no-balls were debited against the bowler's analysis in all matches on this tour.

India v West Indies

It will be recalled that Clive Lloyd, following the loss of the World Cup, relinquished the captaincy of the West Indies, announced his unavailability for the tour of India, and expressed doubts about playing international cricket ever again. Less than two weeks later, Lloyd was back at Lord's, captaining Lancashire in a cup tie. Before play started, he and Allan Rae, President of the West Indies Board, were observed to hold a long, earnest conversation. Mr Rae, a solicitor, used his powers of persuasion to get Lloyd to think again, and it was probably during those moments when he and Lloyd were closeted together that the destiny of the 1983 series between India and the West Indies was forged.

Apparently, Mr Rae told Lloyd that the team to India would contain a fair sprinkling of inexperienced youngsters whose development needed the supervision and guidance of an old hand. Lloyd's role on the tour exceeded the grooming of the newcomers. For the second consecutive series, he proved the ballast of the West Indies batting and the team's main run-getter. His glory lay not just in the runs he accumulated, but in playing big innings when they were most needed.

West Indies won the series 3-0, each victory clinched in four days. Yet, in every one of these Tests, there was a stage when they were in grievous trouble. As often as not, it was Lloyd who dispelled the crisis. He made a century at a crucial time in the drawn second Test in which West Indies were replying to a massive Indian total. His second century of the series, a marathon 161 not out which spanned 496 minutes, had its roots in a dismal collapse and a score of 42 for 4. On this, his third tour of India, Lloyd was not the volatile batsman of his youth. He was weighed down by responsibility and limited by slow pitches. In these circumstances, he batted in the image of the dedicated Lancashire professional rather than the Caribbean cavalier.

The full might of the West Indian batting was not manifest in this series. Haynes, Gomes, and Logie fell on lean times. And while Viv Richards's form could not be described as poor, he certainly did not do justice to his genius. Apart from Lloyd, the most consistent run-scorer was Jeff Dujon. No matter what the state of the match, he got his runs with style and a degree of fluency none of the other batsmen achieved. Although he seemed to lack the concentration to play a really big innings – twice he was dismissed within short range of a century – it seemed he would have had more to offer had he batted higher in the order.

Greenidge, with a dour 194, was one of the architects of West Indies' win in the first Test. His touch never really deserted him, but he could never re-summon the discipline that went into the making of that first huge score.

With the batting at the top uneven, West Indies were for ever reliant on their bowlers to make runs, and they did not let them down. Marshall, twice, and Holding and Roberts all took turns to play major innings, and Davis and Daniel were also concerned in useful stands. The consistency with which the West Indian tail wagged was, perhaps, a reflection of the lack of depth of the Indian bowling.

On the other hand, the West Indies attack was many times quite uncontainable. It firepower was no less awesome for the absence of Garner, who stayed home to give his various injuries a long rest, and the restricted appearances of Roberts because of fitness problems early in the tour. Marshall, who touched supreme heights, and Holding combined speed and control to great advantage. There were times when each sealed the fate of a Test match in a single spell. The quality of the Indian batting notwithstanding, it took bowling of high class to give Marshall and Holding tallies of 33 and 30 wickets, respectively.

Of the younger brigade, Roger Harper, 20, made runs as well as took wickets with his off-breaks in the zonal matches, besides gaining a reputation as an outstanding fielder both in the slips and in the deep.

Baptiste, a rapid learner, was an improved cricketer at the end of the tour. Logie, unfortunately, did not establish himself as a Test batsman, seeming to want in temperament. Richardson, who played only one Test, looked dubious against spin.

India's supporters could take consolation only in Gavaskar's climb up three major statistical peaks. During the series, Gavaskar beat Boycott to the highest aggregate of Test runs. In scoring 236 not out in the final Test, Gavaskar replaced Don Bradman as the scorer of the most Test centuries, and also achieved the highest Test score by an Indian.

When it came to bowling, India's resources were even leaner than in their batting. But the gallant Kapil Dev distinguished himself by taking 29 wickets, and that without having the support that the West Indian fast bowlers gave each other. However, two young pace bowlers, Chetan Sharma, only 17, and Raju Kulkarni, performed impressively in the zonal matches and looked as if they will bowl effectively in English conditions when India come on tour in 1986.

West Indies made a clean sweep of the five-match series of one-day internationals and gained total revenge for indignities suffered in the Prudential World Cup competition.

India v West Indies 1983-84 1st Test
West Indies won by an innings and 83 runs
Played at Green Park, Kanpur, October 21, 22, 23, 25
Toss: West Indies. Umpires: B. Ganguli and Swaroop Kishen
Debuts: West Indies, E.A.E. Baptiste

West Indies

C.G. Greenidge	c Kirmani b Amarnath	194
D.L. Haynes	c Madan Lal b Kapil Dev	6
I.V.A. Richards	c Kirmani b Kapil Dev	24
H.A. Gomes	c Gaekwad b Shastri	21
C.H. Lloyd*	c Kirmani b Bhat	23
A.L. Logie	lbw b Bhat	0
P.J.L. Dujon†	b Binny	81
M.D. Marshall	c and b Kapil Dev	92
E.A.E. Baptiste	run out	6
M.A. Holding	lbw b Kapil Dev	0
W.W. Davis	not out	0
Extras	(B 4, LB 2, NB 1)	7
		454

India

S.M. Gavaskar	c Dujon b Marshall	0	c Davis b Marshall	7
A.D. Gaekwad	c Dujon b Marshall	4	c Richards b Marshall	5
M. Amarnath	lbw b Marshall	0	(6) b Davis	0
D.B. Vengsarkar	b Marshall	14	c Davis b Marshall	65
S.M. Patil	c Richards b Davis	19	b Davis	3
R.J. Shastri	c Dujon b Davis	0	(7) not out	46
S.M.H. Kirmani†	b Holding	20	(9) b Holding	14
Kapil Dev*	c Gomes b Baptiste	27	c Dujon b Holding	3
R.M.H. Binny	c Richards b Holding	39	(3) c Dujon b Marshall	7
Madan Lal	not out	63	b Holding	0
R. Bhat	b Holding	0	b Davis	6
Extras	(B 6, LB 6, W 3, NB 6)	21	(B 2, LB 2, W 1, NB 3)	8
		207		**164**

India‡	O	M	R	W				
Kapil Dev	24.2	3	99	4				
Madan Lal	17	5	50	0				
Binny	17	2	74	1				
Bhat	34	6	86	2				
Shastri	38	7	103	1				
Gaekwad	1	0	6	0				
Amarnath	7	1	30	1				

West Indies‡	O	M	R	W	O	M	R	W
Marshall	15	7	19	4	17	7	47	4
Holding	14.4	6	37	3	19	2	59	3
Davis	13	2	57	2	16.3	3	46	3
Baptiste	11	0	58	1	6	1	8	0
Gomes	6	0	24	0				

Fall of Wickets

Wkt	WI 1st	I 1st	I 2nd
1st	9	0	8
2nd	58	0	13
3rd	102	9	38
4th	157	18	43
5th	157	29	43
6th	309	49	105
7th	439	90	109
8th	449	90	135
9th	451	207	143
10th	454	207	164

*Captain †Wicket-keeper ‡Wides and no-balls included in bowling analyses

India v West Indies 1983-84 2nd Test
Match Drawn
Played at Feroz Shah Kotla, Delhi, October 29, 30, November 1, 2, 3
Toss: India. Umpires: D.N. Dotiwalla and M.V. Gothoskar
Debuts: Nil

India

S.M. Gavaskar	b Gomes	121	lbw b Holding	15
A.D. Gaekwad	c Richards b Holding	8	b Daniel	32
D.B. Vengsarkar	c Richards b Holding	159	b Marshall	63
Yashpal Sharma	b Holding	5	lbw b Daniel	0
R.J. Shastri	lbw b Davis	49	lbw b Holding	26
R.M.H. Binny	lbw b Holding	52	b Daniel	32
M. Amarnath	c Dujon b Daniel	1	c Davis b Marshall	0
Kapil Dev*	c Lloyd b Marshall	18	c Gomes b Marshall	0
Kirti Azad	lbw b Daniel	5	run out	9
Madan Lal	c sub (R.A. Harper) b Daniel	3	not out	24
S.M.H. Kirmani†	not out	1	c Logie b Gomes	3
Extras	(B 4, LB 9, W 2, NB 27)	42	(B 5, LB 10, W 2, NB 12)	29
		464		**233**

West Indies

C.G. Greenidge	lbw b Kirti Azad	33
D.L. Haynes	c Yashpal b Kapil Dev	12
W.W. Davis	b Kirti Azad	19
I.V.A. Richards	lbw b Kapil Dev	67
H.A. Gomes	c Kirmani b Shastri	19
C.H. Lloyd*	lbw b Kapil Dev	103
A.L. Logie	c and b Kapil Dev	63
P.J.L. Dujon†	lbw b Kapil Dev	22
M.D. Marshall	b Kapil Dev	17
M.A. Holding	b Shastri	14
W.W. Daniel	not out	1
Extras	(B 5, LB 7, NB 2)	14
		384

	not out	72
	b Shastri	17
(3)	c Gaekwad b Shastri	22
(4)	not out	1
	(LB 4, W 1, NB 3)	8
	(2 wickets)	**120**

West Indies‡

	O	M	R	W	O	M	R	W
Marshall	24	1	105	1	18	4	52	3
Holding	28.1	1	107	4	12	4	36	2
Davis	25	2	87	1	12	0	45	0
Daniel	21	2	86	3	15	3	38	3
Gomes	21	2	58	1	20.1	2	47	1
Richards	3	1	8	0				

India‡

	O	M	R	W	O	M	R	W
Kapil Dev	31	2	77	6	7	2	26	0
Madan Lal	15	2	59	0	7	0	15	0
Binny	15	3	35	0	3	0	16	0
Shastri	37.5	7	106	2	17	3	36	2
Kirti Azad	26	5	84	2	14	4	22	0
Gaekwad	3	1	11	0	1	1	0	0
Gavaskar					1	0	1	0

Fall of Wickets

Wkt	I 1st	WI 1st	I 2nd	WI 2nd
1st	28	44	20	50
2nd	206	45	73	107
3rd	221	112	73	
4th	366	143	133	
5th	382	173	151	
6th	383	304	152	
7th	422	331	153	
8th	452	357	166	
9th	462	370	218	
10th	464	384	233	

*Captain †Wicket-keeper ‡Wides and no-balls included in bowling analyses

India v West Indies 1983-84 3rd Test
West Indies won by 138 runs
Played at Gujarat Stadium, Ahmedabad, November 12, 13, 14, 16
Toss: India. Umpires: S.N. Hanumantha Rao and K.B. Ramaswamy
Debuts: India, Navjot Singh

West Indies

C.G. Greenidge	c Maninder b Binny	7	b Kapil Dev	3
D.L. Haynes	lbw b Binny	9	c Patil b Sandhu	1
I.V.A. Richards	c Kirti Azad b Binny	8	c sub (Gursharan Singh) b Kapil Dev	20
H.A. Gomes	c Gavaskar b Maninder	38	lbw b Kapil Dev	25
C.H. Lloyd*	c sub (Gursharan Singh) b Maninder	68	c Gavaskar b Kapil Dev	33
A.L. Logie	c Kirmani b Maninder	0	lbw b Kapil Dev	0
P.J.L. Dujon†	c Kapil Dev b Shastri	98	c sub (Gursharan Singh) b Kapil Dev	20
M.D. Marshall	b Maninder	10	c sub (Gursharan Singh) b Kapil Dev	29
W.W. Daniel	run out	6	(10) Kapil Dev	0
M.A. Holding	b Kapil Dev	16	(9) lbw b Kapil Dev	58
W.W. Davis	not out	3	not out	1
Extras	(B 8, LB 6, NB 4)	18	(LB 9, NB 2)	11
		281		**201**

India

S.M. Gavaskar	c Lloyd b Holding	90	lbw b Holding	1
A.D. Gaekwad	b Holding	39	b Davis	29
Navjot Singh	run out	15	c Dujon b Holding	4
S.M. Patil	c Dujon b Marshall	22	c Daniel b Marshall	1
R.J. Shastri	c Lloyd b Daniel	13	c Dujon b Holding	1
R.M.H. Binny	c Haynes b Davis	5	(8) c Greenidge b Holding	1
Kapil Dev*	lbw b Daniel	31	b Davis	1
Kirti Azad	b Daniel	0	(6) b Marshall	3
S.M.H. Kirmani†	c Haynes b Daniel	5	not out	24
B.S. Sandhu	not out	7	lbw b Davis	1
Maninder Singh	lbw b Daniel	0	lbw b Daniel	15
Extras	(B 7, LB 4, NB 3)	14	(B 6, LB 12, NB 4)	22
		241		**103**

India‡	O	M	R	W	O	M	R	W
Kapil Dev	27	9	52	1	30.3	6	83	9
Sandhu	14	6	33	0	10	1	45	1
Binny	6	0	18	3				
Maninder Singh	34	6	85	4	14	1	48	0
Kirti Azad	7	0	34	0	4	2	7	0
Shastri	16.3	2	45	1	2	0	9	0

West Indies‡	O	M	R	W	O	M	R	W
Marshall	26	9	66	1	13	3	23	2
Holding	26	5	80	2	17	5	30	4
Daniel	11.5	0	39	5	6.1	2	11	1
Davis	11	3	23	1	11	1	21	3
Gomes	6	0	22	0				

Fall of Wickets

Wkt	WI 1st	I 1st	WI 2nd	I 2nd
1st	16	127	4	1
2nd	22	148	8	7
3rd	27	174	43	8
4th	134	186	74	24
5th	134	197	74	27
6th	158	213	107	38
7th	168	214	114	39
8th	190	222	188	61
9th	230	241	188	63
10th	281	241	201	103

*Captain †Wicket-keeper ‡Wides and no-balls included in bowling analyses

OVERSEAS CRICKET 1983-84/INDIA v WEST INDIES 47

India v West Indies 1983-84 4th Test
Match Drawn
Played at Wankhede Stadium, Bombay, November 24, 26, 27, 28, 29
Toss: India. Umpires: M.V. Gothoskar and Swaroop Kishen
Debuts: West Indies, R.B. Richardson

India

S.M. Gavaskar	lbw b Marshall	12		c Davis b Marshall	3
A.D. Gaekwad	b Holding	48		c Richards b Holding	3
D.B. Vengsarkar	c Richards b Davis	100			
A. Malhotra	c Dujon b Holding	32	(3)	not out	72
R.J. Shastri	b Holding	77	(4)	run out	38
R.M.H. Binny	lbw b Marshall	65	(5)	lbw b Davis	18
Kapil Dev*	b Holding	8	(6)	c Dujon b Daniel	1
Madan Lal	lbw b Marshall	0	(7)	not out	26
S.M.H. Kirmani†	not out	43			
N.S. Yadav	b Daniel	12			
Maninder Singh	c Lloyd b Holding	9			
Extras	(B 16, LB 14, W 1, NB 26)	57		(B 1, LB 6, NB 5)	12
		463		(5 wickets declared)	**173**

West Indies

C.G. Greenidge	b Yadav	13		b Kapil Dev	4
D.L. Haynes	handled the ball	55		b Maninder	24
R.B. Richardson	lbw b Yadav	0		b Shastri	26
I.V.A. Richards	st Kirmani b Shastri	120		c Kirmani b Shastri	4
H.A. Gomes	b Kapil Dev	26		not out	37
P.J.L. Dujon†	c Kirmani b Yadav	84			
C.H. Lloyd*	run out	67	(6)	not out	9
M.D. Marshall	c Gavaskar b Yadav	4			
M.A. Holding	c and b Yadav	2			
W.W. Daniel	c Gavaskar b Shastri	0			
W.W. Davis	not out	4			
Extras	(B 4, LB 8, NB 6)	18			
		393		(4 wickets)	**104**

West Indies‡	O	M	R	W	O	M	R	W
Marshall	32	6	88	3	13	3	47	1
Holding	40.5	10	102	5	11	1	39	1
Davis	36	3	127	1	8	0	35	1
Daniel	30	3	113	1	14	3	45	1
Gomes	4	1	3	0				

India‡	O	M	R	W	O	M	R	W
Kapil Dev	23	10	41	1	5	1	13	1
Shastri	35	8	98	2	13	4	32	2
Maninder Singh	27	7	71	0	15	7	25	1
Madan Lal	13	6	29	0	3	1	8	0
Binny	4	1	11	0				
Yadav	44.1	8	131	5	12	5	22	0
Gaekwad					1	0	4	0
Gavaskar					1	1	0	0
Malhotra					1	1	0	0

Fall of Wickets

Wkt	I 1st	WI 1st	I 2nd	WI 2nd
1st	12	47	4	4
2nd	145	47	6	40
3rd	190	128	91	48
4th	234	205	118	68
5th	361	238	121	
6th	372	357		
7th	373	377		
8th	385	383		
9th	433	384		
10th	463	393		

*Captain †Wicket-keeper ‡Wides and no-balls included in bowling analyses

India v West Indies 1983-84 5th Test
West Indies won by an innings and 46 runs
Played at Eden Gardens, Calcutta, December 10, 11, 12, 14
Toss: India. Umpires: M.V. Gothoskar and Swaroop Kishen
Debuts: West Indies, R.A. Harper

India

S.M. Gavaskar	c Dujon b Marshall	0	c Dujon b Holding	20
A.D. Gaekwad	b Marshall	2	b Holding	4
D.B. Vengsarkar	b Holding	23	lbw b Marshall	1
M. Amarnath	c and b Marshall	0	b Holding	0
A. Malhotra	c Gomes b Davis	20	(6) c Dujon b Marshall	30
R.J. Shastri	b Holding	12	(7) b Marshall	2
R.M.H. Binny	lbw b Roberts	44	(8) c Harper b Marshall	6
Kapil Dev*	b Holding	69	(9) c Dujon b Marshall	0
S.M.H. Kirmani†	b Roberts	49	(10) b Roberts	13
N.S. Yadav	c Greenidge b Roberts	10	(5) b Marshall	4
Maninder Singh	not out	0	not out	0
Extras	(LB 6, NB 6)	12	(B 1, LB 5, NB 4)	10
		241		**90**

West Indies

C.G. Greenidge	c Yadav b Binny	25
D.L. Haynes	lbw b Kapil Dev	5
I.V.A. Richards	c Kirmani b Kapil Dev	9
H.A. Gomes	b Yadav	18
P.J.L. Dujon†	c Gaekwad b Kapil Dev	0
C.H. Lloyd*	not out	161
M.D. Marshall	lbw b Maninder	54
M.A. Holding	c Shastri b Maninder	17
R.A. Harper	lbw b Kapil Dev	0
A.M.E. Roberts	c Amarnath b Yadav	68
W.W. Davis	lbw b Yadav	0
Extras	(B 8, LB 7, W 1, NB 4)	20
		377

West Indies‡	O	M	R	W	O	M	R	W
Marshall	22	7	65	3	15	4	37	6
Roberts	23.4	9	56	3	4	1	11	1
Davis	14	1	39	1	2	0	7	0
Holding	20	4	59	3	9	3	29	3
Harper	8	2	16	0				

India‡	O	M	R	W
Kapil Dev	35	5	91	4
Binny	13	2	62	1
Amarnath	7	1	19	0
Yadav	27	1	80	3
Shastri	18	2	56	0
Maninder Singh	28	7	54	2

Fall of Wickets

Wkt	I 1st	WI 1st	I 2nd
1st	0	32	14
2nd	9	41	29
3rd	13	42	29
4th	41	42	33
5th	63	88	36
6th	63	175	50
7th	145	213	77
8th	212	213	77
9th	240	374	80
10th	241	377	90

*Captain †Wicket-keeper ‡Wides and no-balls included in bowling analyses

India v West Indies 1983-84 6th Test
Match Drawn
Played at Chidambaram Stadium, Chepauk, Madras, December 24 (no play), 26, 27, 28, 29
Toss: West Indies. Umpires: M.G. Subramaniam and Swaroop Kishen
Debuts: Nil

West Indies

C.G. Greenidge	c Gavaskar b Shastri	34	not out	26
D.L. Haynes	b Maninder	23	c Vensarkar b Shastri	24
I.V.A. Richards	c Kirmani b Maninder	32		
H.A. Gomes	b Yadav	28	(3) not out	10
P.J.L. Dujon†	c Kapil Dev b Binny	62		
C.H. Lloyd*	lbw b Kapil Dev	32		
W.W. Davis	c Navjot Singh b Binny	12		
M.D. Marshall	lbw b Kapil Dev	38		
M.A. Holding	lbw b Kapil Dev	34		
A.M.E. Roberts	not out	0		
R.A. Harper	c and b Maninder	0		
Extras	(LB 12, NB 6)	18	(LB 2, NB 2)	4
		313	(1 wicket)	**64**

India

A.D. Gaekwad	c Harper b Marshall	0
Navjot Singh	c Richards b Roberts	20
D.B. Vengsarkar	c Harper b Marshall	0
S.M. Gavaskar	not out	236
A. Malhotra	c sub (R.B. Richardson) b Harper	9
N.S. Yadav	c Dujon b Marshall	3
R.J. Shastri	lbw b Davis	72
R.M.H. Binny	c sub (E.A.E. Baptiste) b Marshall	1
Kapil Dev*	c sub (E.A.E. Baptiste) b Marshall	26
S.M.H. Kirmani†	not out	63
Maninder Singh	did not bat	
Extras	(B 1, LB 5, W 9, NB 6)	21
	(8 wickets declared)	**451**

India‡	O	M	R	W	O	M	R	W
Kapil Dev	15	3	44	3	6	2	11	0
Binny	12	1	48	2	2	0	14	0
Shastri	28	6	72	1	6	3	10	1
Yadav	28	4	96	1				
Maninder Singh	29.3	9	41	3	6	2	10	0
Navjot Singh					1	0	9	0
Kirmani					1	0	4	0
Vengsarkar					1	0	4	0

West Indies‡	O	M	R	W
Marshall	26	8	72	5
Roberts	28	4	81	1
Davis	30	4	75	1
Holding	26	2	85	0
Harper	42	7	108	1
Gomes	8	0	24	0

Fall of Wickets

Wkt	WI 1st	I 1st	WI 2nd
1st	47	0	38
2nd	91	0	
3rd	100	54	
4th	136	67	
5th	200	92	
6th	226	262	
7th	232	269	
8th	303	308	
9th	312		
10th	313		

*Captain †Wicket-keeper ‡Wides and no-balls included in bowling analyses

Test Match Averages: India v West Indies 1983-84
India
Batting/Fielding	M	I	NO	HS	R	Avge	100	50	Ct	St
D.B. Vengsarkar	5	8	0	159	425	53.12	2	2	1	-
S.M. Gavaskar	6	11	1	236*	505	50.50	2	1	5	-
A. Malhotra	3	5	1	72*	163	40.75	-	1	-	-
S.M.H. Kirmani	6	10	4	63*	235	39.16	-	1	9	1
Madan Lal	3	6	3	63*	116	38.66	-	1	1	-
R.J. Shastri	6	11	1	77	336	33.60	-	2	1	-
R.M.H. Binny	6	11	0	65	270	24.54	-	2	-	-
Kapil Dev	6	11	0	69	184	16.72	-	1	4	-
A.D. Gaekwad	6	11	0	48	174	15.81	-	-	3	-
Navjot Singh	2	3	0	20	39	13.00	-	-	1	-
S.M. Patil	2	4	0	22	45	11.25	-	-	1	-
Maninder Singh	4	5	2	15	24	8.00	-	-	2	-
N.S. Yadav	3	4	0	12	29	7.25	-	-	2	-
Kirti Azad	2	4	0	9	17	4.25	-	-	1	-
M. Amarnath	3	6	0	1	1	0.16	-	-	1	-

Played in one Test: R. Bhat 0, 6; B.S. Sandhu 7*, 1; Yashpal Sharma 5, 0 (1 ct).

Bowling	O	M	R	W	Avge	Best	5wI	10wM
Kapil Dev	203.5	43	537	29	18.51	9-83	2	1
Maninder Singh	153.3	39	334	10	33.40	4-85	-	-
N.S. Yadav	111.1	18	329	9	36.55	5-131	1	-
R.M.H. Binny	72	9	278	7	39.71	3-18	-	-
R.J. Shastri	211.2	42	567	12	47.25	2-32	-	-

Also bowled: M. Amarnath 14-2-49-1; R. Bhat 34-6-86-2; A.D. Gaekwad 6-2-21-0; S.M. Gavaskar 2-1-1-0; S.M.H. Kirmani 1-0-4-0; Kirti Azad 51-11-147-2; Madan Lal 55-14-161-0; A. Malhotra 1-1-0-0; Navjot Singh 1-0-9-0; B.S. Sandhu 24-7-78-1; D.B. Vengsarkar 1-0-4-0.

West Indies
Batting/Fielding	M	I	NO	HS	R	Avge	100	50	Ct	St
C.H. Lloyd	6	8	2	161*	496	82.66	2	2	4	-
P.J.L. Dujon	6	7	0	98	367	52.42	-	4	16	-
C.G. Greenidge	6	10	2	194	411	51.37	1	1	2	-
M.D. Marshall	6	7	0	92	244	34.85	-	2	1	-
I.V.A. Richards	6	9	0	120	306	34.00	1	1	8	-
H.A. Gomes	6	10	3	38	223	31.85	-	-	3	-
M.A. Holding	6	7	0	58	141	20.14	-	1	-	-
D.L. Haynes	6	10	0	55	176	17.60	-	1	2	-
A.L. Logie	3	4	0	63	63	15.75	-	1	1	-
W.W. Davis	6	7	4	19	39	13.00	-	-	4	-
W.W. Daniel	3	4	1	6	7	2.33	-	-	1	-

Also batted: E.A.E. Baptiste (1 Test) 6; R.A. Harper (2 Tests) 0, 0 (3 ct); R.B. Richardson (1 Test) 0, 26; A.M.E. Roberts (2 Tests) 68, 0*.

Bowling	O	M	R	W	Avge	Best	5wI	10wM
M.D. Marshall	221	59	621	33	18.81	6-37	2	-
M.A. Holding	223.4	43	663	30	22.10	5-102	1	-
W.W. Daniel	98	13	332	14	23.71	5-39	1	-
A.M.E. Roberts	55.4	14	148	5	29.60	3-56	-	-
W.W. Davis	178.3	19	562	14	40.14	3-21	-	-

Also bowled: E.A.E. Baptiste 17-1-66-1; H.A. Gomes 65.1-5-178-2; R.A. Harper 50-9-124-1; I.V.A. Richards 3-1-8-0.

Statistical Highlights of the Tests

1st Test, Kanpur. Greenidge, who scored 194 in 522 minutes, recorded his highest score in Tests and also became the 12th West Indies batsman to complete 3,000 runs at that level. His seventh-wicket partnership of 130 with Marshall set a new West Indies record against India.

2nd Test, Delhi. Gavaskar's hundred was scored off only 94 balls and was the fastest of his 29 three-figure innings in Test cricket. It brought him level with D.G. Bradman's world-record tally of Test match centuries in 166 innings compared with the Australian's 80. Gavaskar's first 50 came off 37 balls. He became the third batsman after G. St A. Sobers (8,032) and G. Boycott (8,114) to score 8,000 runs in Test cricket.

3rd Test, Ahmedabad. The Gujarat Stadium became the 56th Test match venue and the 14th in India (more than any other country). When Gavaskar glanced a ball from Holding for his 83rd run, he overtook G. Boycott's aggregate of 8,114 runs to establish a new world Test record. He also became the first batsman to score 1,000 runs in a calendar year of Test cricket for the fourth time. Kapil Dev was the tenth bowler to take nine or more wickets in a Test innings, the third to do so and finish on the losing side, and the first to achieve the feat as captain.

4th Test, Bombay. Haynes was the fourth batsman to be given out for handling the ball in a Test match, the others being W.R. Endean (South Africa), A.M.J. Hilditch (Australia), and Mohsin Khan (Pakistan); when a ball from Kapil Dev took the inside edge of his bat and rolled slowly towards his wicket, Haynes brushed it away with his hand. Madan Lal reached 1,000 runs in Test cricket.

5th Test, Calcutta. Gavaskar became the first batsman in Test history to be dismissed by the very first ball of a match on more than one occasion. G.G. Arnold had inflicted the first such dismissal upon him at Birmingham in 1974. Roberts was the third bowler to take 200 Test wickets for West Indies and later shared in a national record ninth-wicket partnership against India of 161 with Lloyd. Shastri scored his 1,000th run in Tests. India's total of 90 was the lowest by either country in this series. The match aggregate of 708 runs was the lowest in a completed Test between the two countries in India.

6th Test, Madras. Gavaskar scored his 30th hundred in Test cricket to surpass D.G. Bradman's world record. His innings of 236 not out was the highest for India in Tests, beating the 231 by V. Mankad against New Zealand at Madras in 1955-56. He was the first batsman to score three double centuries against West Indies. His stands of 170 for the sixth wicket with Shastri and 143 unbroken for the ninth with Kirmani were records for India in this series. Marshall's total of 33 wickets in the series equalled the West Indies record previously shared by A.L. Valentine (v England 1950) and C.E.H. Croft (v Pakistan 1976-77). India extended their sequence of matches since they beat England at Bombay in December 1981 to 29 without a victory (20 draws, 9 losses). Only New Zealand, who failed to win any of their first 44 Tests, have had a more disastrous run.

West Indies Tour of India 1983-84
Results: Played 12; Won 4, Lost 0, Drawn 8

Batting/Fielding	M	I	NO	HS	R	Avge	100	50	Ct	St
C.H. Lloyd	9	12	3	161*	671	74.55	2	4	6	-
C.G. Greenidge	10	17	4	194	715	55.00	2	2	4	-
P.J.L. Dujon	10	13	2	98	582	52.90	-	6	23	3
E.A.E. Baptiste	5	7	3	64*	181	45.25	-	1	3	-
M.D. Marshall	7	8	0	92	305	38.12	-	3	1	-
I.V.A. Richards	10	14	0	120	527	37.64	2	2	10	-
R.B. Richardson	7	12	0	77	380	31.66	-	2	5	-
D.L. Haynes	11	19	1	67*	560	31.11	-	4	5	-
H.A. Gomes	12	21	6	65*	441	29.40	-	1	4	-
A.M.E. Roberts	7	7	2	68	131	26.20	-	1	-	-
M.R. Pydanna	4	6	0	59	126	21.00	-	1	5	-
R.A. Harper	8	10	0	70	204	20.40	-	1	8	-
A.L. Logie	8	12	1	63	214	19.45	-	2	2	-
M.A. Holding	8	9	0	58	171	19.00	-	1	2	-
W.W. Daniel	6	7	3	28*	69	17.25	-	-	1	-
W.W. Davis	10	12	6	19	61	10.16	-	-	4	-

Bowling	O	M	R	W	Avge	Best	5wI	10wM
M.D. Marshall	234	64	641	34	18.85	6-37	2	-
E.A.E. Baptiste	91.5	14	245	12	20.41	5-55	1	-
M.A. Holding	256.4	53	726	34	21.35	5-102	1	-
R.A. Harper	240	54	571	25	22.84	5-62	2	-
W.W. Daniel	145	20	474	17	27.88	5-39	1	-
H.A. Gomes	133.1	23	368	12	30.66	4-30	-	-
A.M.E. Roberts	147.4	43	355	11	32.27	3-56	-	-
W.W. Davis	251.3	35	791	21	37.66	3-21	-	-

Also bowled: D.L. Haynes 0.4-0-6-1; I.V.A. Richards 21.3-5-88.3.

Note: Penalty runs for wides and no-balls were debited against the bowler's analysis in all first-class matches on this tour.

One-Day Internationals

13 October at Srinagar. WEST INDIES won by a faster scoring rate. Toss: West Indies. India 176 (41.2 overs). West Indies 108-0 (22.4 overs) (D.L. Haynes 55*). Bad light and strong winds caused the match to be abandoned. India had scored 80 after 22 overs. Match award: D.L. Haynes (55* and 1 ct).

9 November at Baroda. WEST INDIES won by 4 wickets. Toss: India. India 214-6 closed (49 overs) (R.J. Shastri 65). West Indies 217-6 (47.5 overs) (C.G. Greenidge 63). Match award: C.G. Greenidge (63).

1 December at Indore. WEST INDIES won by 8 wickets. Toss: India. India 240-7 closed (47 overs) (M. Amarnath 55). West Indies 241-2 (45.2 overs) (C.G. Greenidge 96, D.L. Haynes 54). Match award: C.G. Greenidge (96).

7 December at Jamshedpur. WEST INDIES won by 104 runs. Toss: India. West Indies 333-8 closed (45 overs) (C.G. Greenidge 115, I.V.A. Richards 149 off 99 balls). India 229-5 closed (45 overs) (S.M. Gavaskar 83, A. Malhotra 65). Match award: I.V.A. Richards (149 and 1-0-8-0). West Indies recorded their highest total in one-day internationals. The partnership of 221 for the second wicket between Greenidge and Richards is the highest for any wicket by all countries in these matches.

17 December at Gauhati. WEST INDIES won by 6 wickets. Toss: West Indies. India 178-7 closed (44 overs). West Indies 182-4 (41.4 overs). Match award: G.A. Parkar (42 and 1 ct).

Australia v Pakistan

This will be remembered as the last Test series for three of Australia's greatest players – Greg Chappell, Dennis Lillee, and Rod Marsh. As such, it marked the end of an era in Australian cricket. Chappell, Lillee, and Marsh started their Test careers against Ray Illingworth's England team in Australia in 1970-71, were largely responsible for Australia's climb to world cricket supremacy in the mid-1970s, and retired with a host of individual records that will be beaten only by men of exceptional skill and steel.

Chappell and Lillee announced their retirements on the second and third days of the fifth and last Test in Sydney. Marsh announced his a month later, a few days before the World Series Cup finals against the West Indies. Each gave mental tiredness and family commitments as the reasons for his decision. Fittingly, the trio bowed out in grand style, helping Australia defeat Pakistan by 10 wickets for a 2-0 series victory. The deeds of Chappell, especially, overshadowed the fifth Test. The result seemed almost immaterial as records tumbled, the Sydney Cricket Ground was awash with nostalgia and emotion, and most Australians paused to salute their legendary cricket heroes.

Australia won this series, in a season billed by the marketing people as 'Thunder Down Under', because of their vastly superior fast-bowling resources. Speed merchants Geoff Lawson (24), Lillee (20), Carl Rackemann (16 in two Tests), and Rodney Hogg (9 in four) shared 69 wickets. The Pakistani batsmen floundered on the bouncy pitches of Perth, where Australia won by an innings and 9 runs with more than a day to spare, and Brisbane, where Australia probably would have won by an innings but for rain. The Pakistanis justified their batting reputations only on the more docile pitches in Adelaide and Melbourne, where the Tests were drawn, before Australia won comfortably in Sydney.

Pakistan missed their captain Imran Khan, one of the finest fast bowlers in the world, in the first three Tests while he was recovering from a stress fracture of the left shin. He played solely as a batsman in the last two Tests. The Pakistanis were forced to rely too heavily on Abdul Qadir as their potential match-winner, and his bustling style of leg-breaks, topspinners, and 'wrong 'uns' gained him only 12 wickets at 61 runs apiece compared with his series-winning haul of 22 in 1982.

Imran said at the end of the series that Qadir had been 'demoralized' after the third Test, had not adjusted to Australian wickets, and had been 'put off' by the many left-handed batsmen in the Australian team. It also was significant that Chappell said after his memorable 182 in the fifth Test: 'We decided long ago that the best way to play him was to try to be aggressive and not let him dictate to us.'

Pakistan looked to have found two players for the future in courageous and stylish little batsman Qasim Omar, *the* personality of the touring party, and tall, willing left-arm opening bowler Azeem Hafeez. Looking ahead, Australia were heartened particularly by the successful comeback of Yallop, the promise of Phillips, and the sustained hostility of Lawson.

Australia v Pakistan 1983-84 1st Test

Australia won by an innings and 9 runs
Played at WACA Ground, Perth, November 11, 12, 13, 14
Toss: Pakistan. Umpires: M.W. Johnson and P.J. McConnell
Debuts: Australia, W.B. Phillips

Australia

K.C. Wessels	c Wasim Bari b Azim	12
W.B. Phillips	c Tahir b Nazir	159
G.N. Yallop	b Azim	141
K.J. Hughes*	b Qadir	16
A.R. Border	c Wasim Raja b Azim	32
G.S. Chappell	c Azim b Qadir	17
R.W. Marsh†	c Wasim Bari b Azim	24
G.F. Lawson	c Nazir b Qadir	9
D.K. Lillee	c Wasim Raja b Azim	0
R.M. Hogg	not out	7
C.G. Rackemann	did not bat	
Extras	(LB 9, W 3, NB 7)	19
	(9 wickets declared)	**436**

Pakistan

Mohsin Khan	c Marsh b Hogg	8	c Border b Rackemann	24
Mudassar Nazar	c Phillips b Lillee	1	c Chappell b Rackemann	27
Qasim Omar	c Yallop b Rackemann	48	c Marsh b Rackemann	65
Javed Miandad	c Phillips b Hogg	0	lbw b Rackemann	46
Zaheer Abbas*	c Phillips b Hogg	0	c Marsh b Rackemann	30
Wasim Raja	c Chappell b Rackemann	14	c Marshall b Lawson	4
Wasim Bari†	c Chappell b Rackemann	0	c Marsh b Lawson	7
Tahir Naqqash	not out	29	c Marsh b Rackemann	26
Abdul Qadir	b Rackemann	5	run out	18
Mohammad Nazir	c Chappell b Rackemann	16	c Border b Hogg	18
Azim Hafeez	c Border b Lawson	1	not out	0
Extras	(LB 3, NB 4)	7	(B 4, LB 7, W 2, NB 20)	33
		129		**298**

Pakistan‡

	O	M	R	W
Tahir	22	6	76	0
Azim	27.3	5	100	5
Mudassar	15	1	39	0
Nazir	29	5	91	1
Qadir	32	4	121	3

Australia‡

	O	M	R	W	O	M	R	W
Lillee	13	3	26	1	29	6	56	0
Hogg	12	4	20	3	21.1	2	72	1
Rackemann	8	0	32	5	26	6	86	6
Lawson	7.2	0	48	1	13	1	53	2
Chappell					9	1	20	0

Fall of Wickets

Wkt	A 1st	P 1st	P 2nd
1st	34	7	62
2nd	293	13	63
3rd	321	15	188
4th	369	15	197
5th	386	65	206
6th	404	68	218
7th	424	90	257
8th	424	105	267
9th	436	124	281
10th		129	298

*Captain †Wicket-keeper ‡Wides and no-balls included in bowling analyses

Australia v Pakistan 1983-84 2nd Test
Match Drawn
Played at Woolloongabba, Brisbane, November 25, 26, 27, 28, 29 (no play)
Toss: Pakistan. Umpires: R.A. French and M.W. Johnson
Debuts: Nil

Pakistan

Mohsin Khan	c Chappell b Lawson	2	b Lawson	37
Mudassar Nazar	c Marsh b Lawson	24	c Wessels b Rackemann	18
Qasim Omar	c Hughes b Lawson	17	not out	11
Javed Miandad	c Marsh b Hogg	6	c Phillips b Rackemann	5
Zaheer Abbas*	c Border b Lawson	56	not out	3
Wasim Raja	c Hughes b Rackemann	27		
Wasim Bari†	c Border b Rackemann	2		
Abdul Qadir	b Rackemann	0		
Rashid Khan	not out	13		
Mohammad Nazir	c Marsh b Hogg	1		
Azim Hafeez	b Lawson	2		
Extras	(LB 3, W 1, NB 2)	6	(LB 6, NB 2)	8
		156	(3 wickets)	**82**

Australia

K.C. Wessels	c Omar b Azim	35
W.B. Phillips	b Rashid	46
G.N. Yallop	c Wasim Bari b Rashid	33
K.J. Hughes*	c Nazir b Azim	53
A.R. Border	c Wasim Bari b Rashid	118
G.S. Chappell	not out	150
R.W. Marsh†	b Azim	1
G.F. Lawson	b Qadir	49
D.K. Lillee	did not bat	
R.M. Hogg	,, ,,	
C.G. Rackemann	,, ,,	
Extras	(B 2, LB 6, W 1, NB 15)	24
	(7 wickets declared)	**509**

Australia‡	O	M	R	W	O	M	R	W
Lawson	17.1	1	49	5	10	3	24	1
Hogg	15	2	43	2	3	0	11	0
Rackemann	10	3	28	3	8	1	31	2
Lillee	8	1	33	0	2	0	10	0

Pakistan‡	O	M	R	W
Azim	37	7	152	3
Rashid	43	10	129	3
Mudassar	16	2	47	0
Qadir	32	5	112	1
Nazir	24	6	50	0
Wasim Raja	3	0	11	0

Fall of Wickets

Wkt	P 1st	A 1st	P 2nd
1st	10	56	57
2nd	39	120	59
3rd	46	124	74
4th	62	232	
5th	124	403	
6th	128	406	
7th	128	509	
8th	146		
9th	147		
10th	156		

*Captain †Wicket-keeper ‡Wides and no-balls included in bowling analyses

Australia v Pakistan 1983-84 3rd Test
Match Drawn
Played at Adelaide Oval, December 9, 10, 11, 12, 13
Toss: Australia. Umpires: A.R. Crafter and R.A. French
Debuts: Nil

Australia

K.C. Wessels	c Zaheer b Qadir	179	c Wasim Bari b Sarfraz		2
W.B. Phillips	c Wasim Bari b Azim	12	c Mudassar b Qadir		54
G.N. Yallop	c Omar b Sarfraz	68	c Miandad b Qadir		14
K.J. Hughes*	c Wasim Bari b Azim	30	c Mudassar b Azim		106
A.R. Border	not out	117	lbw b Azim		66
G.S. Chappell	c Wasim Bari b Sarfraz	6	run out		4
R.W. Marsh†	c Mohsin b Sarfraz	2	retired hurt	•	33
T.G. Hogan	run out	2	c Omar b Salim		8
G.F. Lawson	c Wasim Bari b Azim	4	not out		7
D.K. Lillee	c Sarfraz b Azim	25	not out		4
R.M. Hogg	c Miandad b Azim	5			
Extras	(LB 7, W 4, NB 4)	15	(B 3, LB 4, W 1, NB 4)		12
		465	(7 wickets)		**310**

Pakistan

Mohsin Khan	c Phillips b Lawson	149
Mudassar Nazar	c Marsh b Lillee	44
Qasim Omar	c Marsh b Lillee	113
Javed Miandad	lbw b Lawson	131
Zaheer Abbas*	c Yallop b Hogg	46
Salim Malik	c Lawson b Hogan	77
Sarfraz Nawaz	c Yallop b Lillee	32
Abdul Qadir	b Lillee	10
Wasim Bari†	c Marsh b Lillee	0
Mohammad Nazir	not out	5
Azim Hafeez	c Wessels b Lillee	5
Extras	(B 1, LB 4, NB 7)	12
		624

Pakistan‡	O	M	R	W	O	M	R	W
Azim	38.2	8	167	5	19	4	50	2
Sarfraz	42	7	105	3	30	8	69	1
Qadir	20	1	96	1	47	9	132	2
Mudassar	10	2	45	0				
Nazir	9	0	37	0	27	14	39	0
Mohsin	3	0	8	0	1	1	0	0
Miandad					3	0	10	0
Salim					1	0	3	1
Omar					1	1	0	0

Australia‡	O	M	R	W
Lawson	37	7	127	2
Hogg	34	3	123	1
Lillee	50.2	8	171	6
Hogan	37	8	107	1
Chappell	32	6	82	0
Border	1	0	9	0

Fall of Wickets

Wkt	A 1st	P 1st	A§ 2nd
1st	21	73	3
2nd	163	306	44
3rd	219	314	121
4th	353	371	216
5th	376	557	228
6th	378	590	293
7th	383	604	305
8th	394	612	
9th	451	613	
10th	465	624	

*Captain †Wicket-keeper ‡Wides and no-balls included in bowling analyses
§In Australia's second innings, R.W. Marsh retired hurt at 288-5

Australia v Pakistan 1983-84 4th Test
Match Drawn
Played at Melbourne Cricket Ground, December 26, 27, 28, 29, 30
Toss: Pakistan. Umpires: A.R. Crafter and P.J. McConnell
Debuts: Australia, J.N. Maguire, G.R.J. Matthews

Pakistan

Mohsin Khan	lbw b Lillee	152	c Hughes b Lillee		3
Mudassar Nazar	c Marsh b Lawson	7	lbw b Matthews		35
Qasim Omar	b Maguire	23	b Lawson		9
Javed Miandad	c Marsh b Maguire	27	lbw b Lillee		11
Zaheer Abbas	run out	44	(6) b Matthews		50
Salim Malik	c Maguire b Lawson	35	(8) b Lillee		14
Imran Khan*	c Marsh b Lillee	83	not out		72
Sarfraz Nawaz	c Hughes b Maguire	22	(9) not out		11
Abdul Qadir	c Lawson b Matthews	45	(5) b Lawson		12
Wasim Bari†	not out	6			
Azim Hafeez	c Maguire b Matthews	7			
Extras	(LB 11, NB 8)	19	(B 10, LB 9, W 2)		21
		470	(7 wickets)		**238**

Australia

K.C. Wessels	c Wasim Bari b Azim	11
W.B. Phillips	lbw b Azim	35
G.N. Yallop	c Wasim Bari b Sarfraz	268
K.J. Hughes*	lbw b Azim	94
A.R. Border	lbw b Qadir	32
G.S. Chappell	c Salim b Qadir	5
R.W. Marsh†	c Mudassar b Qadir	0
G.R.J. Matthews	lbw b Sarfraz	75
G.F. Lawson	c Mudassar b Qadir	0
J.N. Maguire	c Wasim Bari b Qadir	4
D.K. Lillee	not out	2
Extras	(B 15, LB 9, W 2, NB 3)	29
		555

Australia‡	O	M	R	W	O	M	R	W
Lawson	38	8	125	2	21	8	47	2
Lillee	38	11	113	2	29	7	71	3
Maguire	29	7	111	3	12	3	26	0
Matthews	28.4	7	95	2	21	8	48	2
Chappell	7	3	15	0	8	3	13	0
Border					5	3	9	0
Marsh					2	0	3	0
Wessels					2	1	2	0

Pakistan‡	O	M	R	W
Sarfraz	51	12	106	2
Azim	35	8	115	3
Qadir	54.3	12	166	5
Mudassar	20	0	76	0
Miandad	5	0	16	0
Zaheer	22	5	42	0
Salim	2	1	10	0

Fall of Wickets

Wkt	P 1st	A 1st	P 2nd
1st	13	21	3
2nd	64	70	18
3rd	112	273	37
4th	244	342	73
5th	294	354	81
6th	321	354	160
7th	349	539	213
8th	457	540	
9th	459	553	
10th	470	555	

*Captain †Wicket-keeper ‡Wides and no-balls included in bowling analyses

Australia v Pakistan 1983-84 5th Test
Australia won by 10 wickets
Played at Sydney Cricket Ground, January 2, 3, 4, 5, 6
Toss: Australia. Umpires: R.A. French and M.W. Johnson
Debuts: Nil

Pakistan

Mohsin Khan	c Border b Lillee	14	c Chappell b Lawson	1
Mudassar Nazar	c Chappell b Lawson	84	b Lawson	21
Qasim Omar	c Border b Lillee	15	c Marsh b Lawson	26
Abdul Qadir	c Hughes b Lawson	4	(9) c Marsh b Lillee	5
Javed Miandad	c Lillee b Matthews	16	(4) c Marsh b Lawson	60
Zaheer Abbas	c Yallop b Lawson	61	(5) c Marsh b Hogg	33
Imran Khan*	c Yallop b Lawson	5	(6) c Marsh b Hogg	10
Salim Malik	c Lillee b Lawson	54	(7) c Chappell b Lillee	7
Sarfraz Nawaz	lbw b Lillee	5	(8) c Phillips b Lillee	20
Wasim Bari†	not out	7	c Phillips b Lillee	20
Azim Hafeez	c Marsh b Lillee	4	not out	2
Extras	(B 2, LB 7)	9	(LB 4, NB 1)	5
		278		**210**

Australia

K.C. Wessels	c Wasim Bari b Azim	3	not out	14
W.B. Phillips	c Salim b Sarfraz	37	not out	19
G.N. Yallop	c Wasim Bari b Mudassar	30		
G.S. Chappell	lbw b Mudassar	182		
K.J. Hughes*	lbw b Sarfraz	76		
A.R. Border	c Wasim Bari b Mudassar	64		
G.R.J. Matthews	not out	22		
R.W. Marsh†	not out	15		
G.F. Lawson	did not bat			
R.M. Hogg	,, ,,			
D.K. Lillee	,, ,,			
Extras	(LB 15, W 1, NB 9)	25	(NB 2)	2
	(6 wickets declared)	**454**	(0 wickets)	**35**

Australia‡

	O	M	R	W	O	M	R	W
Lillee	31.2	10	65	4	29.5	5	88	4
Hogg	18	1	61	0	14	2	53	2
Chappell	8	0	25	0				
Lawson	25	5	59	5	20	7	48	4
Matthews	18	4	59	1	7	4	17	0

Pakistan‡

	O	M	R	W	O	M	R	W
Sarfraz	53	13	132	2	3	1	7	0
Azim	36	7	121	1	2.4	0	28	0
Mudassar	31	9	81	3				
Qadir	34	9	105	0				

Fall of Wickets

Wkt	P 1st	A 1st	P 2nd	A 2nd
1st	18	11	5	
2nd	57	66	47	
3rd	67	83	56	
4th	131	254	104	
5th	150	407	132	
6th	158	436	163	
7th	254		163	
8th	267		173	
9th	267		191	
10th	278		210	

*Captain †Wicket-keeper ‡Wides and no-balls included in bowling analyses

Test Match Averages: Australia v Pakistan 1983-84

Australia

Batting/Fielding	M	I	NO	HS	R	Avge	100	50	Ct	St
G.N. Yallop	5	6	0	268	554	92.33	2	1	5	–
A.R. Border	5	6	1	118	429	85.80	2	2	7	–
G.S. Chappell	5	6	1	182	364	72.80	2	–	8	–
K.J. Hughes	5	6	0	106	375	62.50	1	3	5	–
W.B. Phillips	5	7	1	159	362	60.33	1	1	7	–
K.C. Wessels	5	7	1	179	256	42.66	1	–	2	–
R.W. Marsh	5	6	2	33*	75	18.75	–	–	21	–
G.F. Lawson	5	5	1	49	69	17.25	–	–	2	–
D.K. Lillee	5	4	2	25	31	15.50	–	–	2	–

Also batted: T.G. Hogan (1 Test) 2, 8; R.M. Hogg (4 Tests) 7*, 5; J.N. Maguire (1 Test) 4 (2 ct); G.R.J. Matthews (2 Tests) 75, 22*. C.G. Rackemann (2 Tests) did not bat.

Bowling	O	M	R	W	Avge	Best	5wI	10wM
C.G. Rackemann	52	10	177	16	11.06	6-96	2	1
G.F. Lawson	188.3	40	580	24	24.16	5-49	2	–
D.K. Lillee	230.3	51	633	20	31.65	6-171	1	–
R.M. Hogg	117.1	14	383	9	42.55	3-20	–	–
G.R.J. Matthews	74.4	23	219	5	43.80	2-48	–	–

Also bowled: A.R. Border 6-3-18-0; G.S. Chappell 64-13-155-0; T.G. Hogan 37-8-107-1; J.N. Maguire 41-10-137-3; R.W. Marsh 2-0-3-0; K.C. Wessels 2-1-2-0.

Pakistan

Batting/Fielding	M	I	NO	HS	R	Avge	100	50	Ct	St
Imran Khan	2	4	1	83	170	56.66	–	2	–	–
Mohsin Khan	5	9	0	152	390	43.33	2	–	1	–
Qasim Omar	5	9	1	113	327	40.87	1	1	3	–
Zaheer Abbas	5	9	1	61	323	40.37	–	3	1	–
Salim Malik	3	5	0	77	187	37.40	–	2	2	–
Javed Miandad	5	9	0	131	302	33.55	1	1	2	–
Mudassar Nazar	5	9	0	84	261	29.00	–	1	4	–
Sarfraz Nawaz	3	5	1	32	90	22.50	–	–	1	–
Wasim Raja	2	3	0	27	45	15.00	–	–	2	–
Mohammad Nazir	3	4	1	18	40	13.33	–	–	2	–
Abdul Qadir	5	8	0	45	99	12.37	–	–	–	–
Wasim Bari	5	7	2	20	42	8.40	–	–	15	–
Azim Hafeez	5	7	2	7	21	4.20	–	–	1	–

Played in one Test: Rashid Khan 13*; Tahir Naqqash 29*, 26 (1 ct).

Bowling	O	M	R	W	Avge	Best	5wI	10wM
Azim Hafeez	195.3	39	733	19	38.57	5-100	2	–
Sarfraz Nawaz	179	41	419	8	52.37	3-105	–	–
Abdul Qadir	219.3	40	732	12	61.00	5-166	1	–

Also bowled: Javed Miandad 8-0-26-0; Mohammad Nazir 89-25-217-1; Mohsin Khan 4-1-8-0; Mudassar Nazar 92-14-288-3; Qasim Omar 1-1-0-0; Rashid Khan 43-10-129-3; Salim Malik 3-1-13-1; Tahir Naqqash 22-6-76-0; Wasim Raja 3-0-11-0; Zaheer Abbas 22-5-42-0.

Statistical Highlights of the Tests

1st Test, Perth. Phillips became the ninth batsman to score a century in his first innings for Australia. His second-wicket partnership of 259 with Yallop was the highest for any wicket by either country in this series. Rackemann's match analysis of 11-118 was a record for Australia against Pakistan and also set a record for Test cricket at the WACA Ground.

2nd Test, Brisbane. Hogg became the 20th bowler to take 100 Test wickets for Australia. The partnership of 171 between Border and Chappell equalled the fifth-wicket record in this series.

3rd Test, Adelaide. Pakistan's total of 624 was the highest by either country in this series, their second-highest in all Tests, the fifth-highest by any country against Australia, and the highest in all Test cricket since 1979 when England scored 633-5 declared against India at Edgbaston. It was also the highest total made against Australia since England amassed their world record 903-7 declared at The Oval in 1938. Pakistan set new partnership records against Australia for the second wicket (233 by Mohsin Khan and Qasim Omar) and the fifth wicket (186 by Javed Miandad and Salim Malik). Six individual hundreds were scored during the match, just one short of the record for any Test.

4th Test, Melbourne. Yallop's innings of 268 was the highest of his first-class career, the record for either country in this series, and the third-highest by any batsman against Pakistan. Lasting 716 minutes, it was the sixth-longest recorded innings in all first-class cricket, the third-longest for Australia in Tests, and the longest by any batsman scoring under 300. His innings enabled him to eclipse D.G. Bradman's record Australian first-class aggregate for a calendar year of 1,763 runs in 1929 (Yallop finished with 1,834 runs in 1983). It also took him beyond 1,000 runs in the Australian first-class season before the end of December, a feat previously achieved only by W.H. Ponsford, H. Sutcliffe, R.B. Simpson (twice), G. Boycott, and D.W. Hookes. Yallop shared record Australian partnerships against Pakistan of 203 for the third wicket with Hughes and 185 with Matthews for the seventh. Imran Khan became the fifth player and first Pakistani to complete the double of 2,000 runs and 200 wickets in Tests.

5th Test, Sydney. Chappell became the sixth player to score 7,000 runs in Test cricket and exceeded D.G. Bradman's Australian record aggregate of 6,996. He also emulated the feats of fellow-Australians R.A. Duff and W.H. Ponsford by scoring centuries in both his first and his final Test. Later, he broke M.C. Cowdrey's world record of 120 catches by a non-wicket-keeper in Test matches. Lillee became the first bowler to take 350 wickets in Test cricket and Marsh the first wicket-keeper to make 350 dismissals. Their 95 shared dismissals (ct Marsh b Lillee) also constitutes a world record. The three Australian world-record holders (Lillee 355 wickets, Marsh 355 dismissals, and Chappell 122 catches) all announced their retirements either during or immediately after this match. Wasim Bari, who was also playing in his last Test, became the third wicket-keeper after Marsh and A.P.E. Knott to take 200 catches in Test cricket.

Pakistan Tour of Australia 1983-84

Results: Played 11; Won 3, Lost 3, Drawn 5

Batting/Fielding	M	I	NO	HS	R	Avge	100	50	Ct	St
Javed Miandad	10	18	3	141*	952	63.46	3	6	3	–
Mudassar Nazar	10	19	1	139	1071	59.50	5	3	9	–
Salim Malik	4	7	0	80	306	43.71	–	3	2	–
Qasim Omar	11	20	2	131	767	42.61	2	3	4	–
Imran Khan	3	6	1	83	202	40.40	–	2	–	–
Zaheer Abbas	8	14	2	61	448	37.33	–	4	3	–
Mohsin Khan	10	19	0	152	699	36.78	2	2	5	–
Rashid Khan	6	8	3	45*	122	24.40	–	–	1	–
Wasim Raja	7	11	0	83	268	24.36	–	2	4	–
Mansoor Akhtar	3	6	3	25*	68	22.66	–	–	2	–
Tahir Naqqash	5	6	2	29*	86	21.50	–	–	3	–
Mohammad Nazir	8	8	5	20*	63	21.00	–	–	3	–
Sarfraz Nawaz	4	6	1	32	104	20.80	–	–	2	–
Wasim Bari	8	11	3	73*	154	19.25	–	1	23	–
Ashraf Ali	3	5	1	39	71	17.75	–	–	8	1
Abdul Qadir	10	15	2	45	223	17.15	–	–	–	–
Azim Hafeez	9	8	3	7	22	4.40	–	–	3	–

Atiqur Rehman (2 matches) did not bat.

Bowling	O	M	R	W	Avge	Best	5wI	10wM
Tahir Naqqash	163.3	31	555	15	37.00	4-80	–	–
Mohammad Nazir	252.5	59	627	16	39.18	4-73	–	–
Azim Hafeez	316.2	62	1217	27	45.07	5-100	1	–
Abdul Qadir	441.5	78	1413	28	50.46	7-122	2	–
Sarfraz Nawaz	223	55	516	10	51.60	3-105	–	–
Rashid Khan	224	51	633	12	52.75	3-129	–	–
Mudassar Nazar	164	26	534	8	66.75	3-76	–	–

Also bowled: Atiqur Rehman 30-2-177-2; Javed Miandad 21-5-80-0; Mohsin Khan 8-2-24-0; Qasim Omar 5-1-22-1; Salim Malik 7-1-39-1; Wasim Raja 62-15-160-0; Zaheer Abbas 27-5-63-0.

Note: Penalty runs for wides and no-balls were debited against the bowler's analysis in all first-class matches on this tour.

Benson & Hedges World Series Cup

Having avenged their shock World Cup loss to India by winning the Test and one-day series in India, the West Indies then reaffirmed their status as the champions of the limited-overs game by trouncing Australia and Pakistan in the Benson and Hedges World Series Cup in Australia. They did it in awesome fashion, winning 8 of their 10 preliminary matches and defeating Australia 2-0 in the best-of-three finals, the second of which produced a remarkable tie – a mini-repetition of the tied Test between Australia and the West Indies in Brisbane in 1960.

The West Indies believed they had won the Cup when Australia scored 222 for 9 in reply to their 222 for 5. But the playing conditions included a provision that in the event of a tie no account would be taken of the wickets that had fallen. The playing conditions also stated that for an incompleted series, the team with the greater number of wins in the preliminary series (the West Indies) would be the winner. However, with one match decided, one tied and nothing to stop the third from being played, the finals were deemed not to be incomplete.

A Melbourne Sunday crowd of only 19,210 saw the third final after 42,430 had seen the tied match (and 28,190 had attended the first final under lights in Sydney the previous Wednesday).

On the morning of the deciding final, the Australian Cricket Board increased the prize money by $A30,000, lifting the winning team's cheque by $A20,000 to $A52,000 and the losing side's cheque by $A10,000 to $A26,000. But after the thrills and drama of the tie the previous day (when Australia scored 10 runs off the last over – from Joel Garner), the third final was anticlimactic, with the West Indies, captained by Michael Holding, often appearing to have an indifferent attitude and to be merely going through the motions of bowling and fielding – and exchanging words with the Australian batsmen.

Clive Lloyd (hamstring and finger injuries) and Viv Richards (groin injury) did not play in the third final, nor did Lloyd attend the presentation ceremony on the ground, which smacked of a form of protest over the staging of the match. The West Indians' wrath was appeased by their receiving prize money of $A85,000, including $A31,000 from the preliminary round and $A2,000 from Garner's Player of the Finals award. The Australians shared $A53,000, including $A27,500 from their 10 preliminary games (of which they won five). The hapless Pakistanis won only one match (against the West Indies), yet still pocketed $A17,500.

Richards, whose 106 against Australia in Melbourne in the ninth match was the batting jewel of the series, won a Nissan sports car, valued at more than $A20,000 for being adjudged the International Cricketer of the Year – and the Australians complained about the voting system, which they claimed was weighted too heavily in favour of the side that did not compete in the Test series before the Cup competition.

While, as usual, there were some cries about there being too much of the 'pyjama game', the aggregate attendance for the 18 WSC fixtures, including the three finals, was 541,432 – an average of 30,079 per game – with gate-takings of about $A2¾m, nearly double the receipts for the five Tests between Australia and Pakistan.

Qualifying Rounds

8 January at Melbourne. WEST INDIES beat AUSTRALIA by 27 runs. West Indies 221-7 closed (50 overs) (I.V.A. Richards 53, C.H. Lloyd 65). Australia 194 (46 overs) (A.R. Border 84*). Match award: I.V.A. Richards (53 and 6-1-24-1). Attendance: 72,610.

10 January at Sydney. AUSTRALIA beat PAKISTAN by 34 runs. Australia 264-8 closed (50 overs) (K.C. Wessels 92, A.R. Border 54, R.W. Marsh 66; Sarfraz Nawaz 10-2-27-4). Pakistan 230-9 closed (50 overs) (Javed Miandad 67). Match award: K.C. Wessels (92). Attendance: 30,315.

12 January at Melbourne. PAKISTAN beat WEST INDIES by 97 runs. Pakistan 208-8 closed (50 overs) (Qasim Omar 69). West Indies 111 (41.4 overs) (Azim Hafeez 10-1-22-4). West Indies were dismissed for their lowest total in one-day internationals. Match award: Qasim Omar (69). Attendance: 13,295.

14 January at Brisbane. WEST INDIES beat PAKISTAN by 5 wickets. Pakistan 174-9 closed (50 overs) (Mudassar Nazar 68). West Indies 175-5 (40.2 overs) (D.L. Haynes 53). Match award: Mudassar Nazar (68 and 10-0-46-2). Attendance: 13,894.

15 January at Brisbane. AUSTRALIA v PAKISTAN – no result (match abandoned – rain). Pakistan 184-6 closed (42 overs). Australia 15-0 (3.5 overs). No match award. Attendance: 21,689.

17 January at Sydney. WEST INDIES beat AUSTRALIA by 28 runs. West Indies 223-7 closed (49 overs) (D.L. Haynes 108*). Australia 195-9 closed (49 overs). Match award: D.L. Haynes (108*). Attendance: 42,303.

19 January at Sydney. WEST INDIES beat PAKISTAN by 5 wickets. Pakistan 184-8 closed (50 overs) (Qasim Omar 67*; M.A. Holding 10-2-26-4). West Indies 185-5 (48.3 overs) (R.B. Richardson 53). Match award: R.B. Richardson (53). Attendance: 15,194.

21 January at Melbourne. AUSTRALIA beat PAKISTAN by 43 runs. Australia 209-8 closed (50 overs) (K.C. Wessels 86; Abdul Qadir 10-1-53-5). Pakistan 166 (45 overs) (Javed Miandad 56; R.M. Hogg 10-2-33-4). Match award: K.C. Wessels (86, 7-0-28-0, and 1 ct). Attendance: 24,273.

22 January at Melbourne. WEST INDIES beat AUSTRALIA by 26 runs. West Indies 252-6 closed (50 overs) (D.L. Haynes 64, I.V.A. Richards 106). Australia 226 (49.5 overs) (K.C. Wessels 60, K.J. Hughes 71). Match award: I.V.A. Richards (106 and 10-0-51-2). Attendance: 86,133 – a world record for one-day matches.

25 January at Sydney. AUSTRALIA beat PAKISTAN by 87 runs. Australia 244-8 closed (50 overs) (S.B. Smith 106). Pakistan 157 (47.2 overs) (R.M. Hogg 10-0-37-4). Match award: S.B. Smith (106). Attendance: 26,106.

28 January at Adelaide. WEST INDIES beat PAKISTAN by 1 wicket. Pakistan 177-8 closed (50 overs). West Indies 180-9 (49.1 overs) (M.D. Marshall 56*). Match award: M.D. Marshall (56* and 9-1-28-3). Attendance: 13,101.

29 January at Adelaide. WEST INDIES beat AUSTRALIA by 6 wickets. Australia 165-7 closed (50 overs) (S.B. Smith 55). West Indies 169-4 (45.1 overs). Match award: A.L. Logie (49*). Attendance: 31,424.

30 January at Adelaide. AUSTRALIA beat PAKISTAN by 70 runs. Australia 210-8 closed (50 overs) (K.C. Wessels 61; Ijaz Faqih 10-1-43-4). Pakistan 140 (45.2 overs) (C.G. Rackemann 8.2-2-16-5). Match award: K.C. Wessels (61 and 9-0-32-2). Attendance: 22,758.

4 February at Perth. WEST INDIES beat PAKISTAN by 7 wickets. Pakistan 182-7 closed (50 overs) (Mudassar Nazar 54). West Indies 183-3 (45.1 overs) (D.L. Haynes 78*). Match award: I.V.A. Richards (40, 5-0-24-0, and 1 ct). Attendance: 14,000.

15 March at Perth. AUSTRALIA beat WEST INDIES by 14 runs. Australia 211-8 closed (50 overs) (K.C. Wessels 50, K.J. Hughes 67). West Indies 197 (43.3 overs) (D.L. Haynes 52, M.A. Holding 64). Match award: M.A. Holding 64 and 10-1-31-2). Attendance: 27,027.

Qualifying Table	P	W	L	NR	Points
WEST INDIES	10	8	2	-	16
AUSTRALIA	10	5	4	1	11
Pakistan	10	1	8	1	3

Final Round Results

8 February at Sydney. WEST INDIES beat AUSTRALIA by 9 wickets. Australia 160 (44.4 overs) (S.B. Smith 50). West Indies 161-1 (43.1 overs) (R.B. Richardson 80*). Attendance: 28,190.

11 February at Melbourne. AUSTRALIA tied with WEST INDIES. West Indies 222-5 closed (50 overs) (I.V.A. Richards 59). Australia 222-9 closed (50 overs) (K.C. Wessels 77, K.J. Hughes 53). Attendance: 42,430.

12 February at Melbourne. WEST INDIES beat AUSTRALIA by 6 wickets. Australia 212-8 closed (50 overs) (K.J. Hughes 65; J. Garner 10-1-31-5). West Indies 213-4 (45.3 overs) (A.L. Logie 88, P.J.L. Dujon 82*). Attendance: 19,210.

WEST INDIES won the WSC Finals by two matches to nil, the third final being tied. Player of the Preliminary Series: K.C. Wessels (Australia). Player of the Finals: J. Garner (West Indies).

Leading Averages

Batting	Team	M	I	NO	HS	R	Avge	100	50
A.L. Logie	WI	9	9	5	88	220	55.00	-	1
K.C. Wessels	A	13	13	1	92	495	41.25	-	6
D.L. Haynes	WI	13	13	2	108*	450	40.90	1	4
S.B. Smith	A	8	7	0	106	285	40.71	1	2
R.B. Richardson	WI	8	8	1	80*	248	35.42	-	2
P.J.L. Dujon	WI	13	10	4	82*	212	35.33	-	1
R.W. Marsh	A	11	10	2	66	282	35.25	-	1
I.V.A. Richards	WI	12	11	0	106	348	31.63	1	2
C.H. Lloyd	WI	10	9	1	65	245	30.62	-	1
Javed Miandad	P	10	10	0	67	295	29.50	-	2
Qasim Omar	P	10	10	1	69	241	26.77	-	2
K.J. Hughes	A	13	12	0	71	309	25.75	-	4
Mudassar Nazar	P	10	10	0	68	210	21.00	-	2
A.R. Border	A	13	12	1	84*	226	20.54	-	2

Bowling	Team	O	M	R	W	Avge	Best	r/o
J. Garner	WI	56	11	150	14	10.71	5-31	2.7
M.A. Holding	WI	113.3	9	411	23	17.86	4-26	3.6
Abdul Qadir	P	76	11	272	15	18.13	5-53	3.6
M.D. Marshall	WI	95	14	297	14	21.21	3-28	3.1
R.M. Hogg	A	119	10	481	22	21.86	4-33	4.0
G.F. Lawson	A	105	23	298	13	22.92	3-30	2.8
W.W. Daniel	WI	93	8	369	16	23.06	3-27	4.0
C.G. Rackemann	A	120.2	20	454	19	23.89	5-16	3.8
E.A.E. Baptiste	WI	110	7	401	13	30.84	2-10	3.6
Mudassar Nazar	P	85.4	5	328	10	32.80	2-33	3.8

r/o = runs per over.

West Indies v Australia

Australia's 1984 tour of the West Indies was one of the least successful in the history of their ventures abroad, their only significant achievement being a win in the second of four one-day internationals. Of the territories, Leeward Islands, well below full strength, was the only one the Australians could beat. They lost the Test series 3-0 and, but for wet weather during the first two Tests, would have been whitewashed.

The retirement *en masse* of Greg Chappell, Dennis Lillee, and Rod Marsh left a void that the Australians did not have the reserves to fill. Chappell's departure was felt even more keenly because of the absence in the tour party of another experienced batsman in Graham Yallop, who had a magnificent season at home, but who had also sustained a long-term injury. There was hardly a week during the tour when a new fitness problem did not crop up to undermine the side's morale which, in any case, was never high.

Australia got the opportunity to rectify their selectors' initial error in leaving out Graeme Wood. It arose when Keppler Wessels's knee broke down during the second Test, requiring him to go back for immediate surgery. Wood joined the team in Barbados before they had fallen behind in either the Test or one-day series and immediately justified his presence. Batting with discipline which none of the batsmen originally selected could muster, save Allan Border, Wood scored 76 and 3 against Barbados and then 68 and 20 in the third Test. But he fractured his finger during the last of his four innings, which was another pugnacious effort, and within a fortnight of his arrival had to pack his bags for home.

If Australia salvaged even a small measure of honour from this disastrous tour, it was thanks to Allan Border, who aggregated 825 runs at 75 per innings and totalled 521 runs in the Tests at just under 75. Only in the third Test did Border fail to score at least 50 in either innings. He had a part-share in saving the first Test and prevented a major rout in the second with two innings of heroic proportions – 98 not out and 100 not out – which kept the West Indies bowlers at bay for a total of 10¾ hours, during which he faced 535 balls.

In the second innings, Border and Terry Alderman, the last man, came together with Australia only 25 runs in front. They foiled the West Indies with a re-enactment of the celebrated Mackay-Kline stand at Adelaide, 24 years earlier. They stood their ground for 105 minutes.

Kim Hughes, the captain, had a particularly disappointing tour, although it must be said in fairness to him that his failure could have been due to the fact that in the earlier matches he batted too quickly in the interests of entertainment when he should have sought a long innings to establish his form. His inability to make an adequate contribution of runs affected Hughes's authority as captain of a young and inexperienced side which needed to be led with firmness. David Hookes, too, did not fulfil the hopes placed in the most experienced Test batsman in the party.

Of the younger batsmen, Greg Ritchie looked a player of immense personality and ability in the early days of the tour, but did not make the runs that seemed to lie within his scope. Steve Smith scored heavily against the territories, but was vulnerable in the Tests. Left-handed Wayne Phillips, picked as an opener but used lower down the order, played two sizeable Test innings, including a century, but made little impact on other occasions.

Where the Australian bowling was concerned, there was a heavy dependence on their two front-line bowlers, Geoff Lawson and Rodney Hogg, who were not at their freshest after a long home season and were prone to minor injuries. It was not until the final Test, when the rubber was lost, that they both simultaneously bowled at their best.

If the West Indies could not assert their superiority until the third Test, it was as much because of the weather as the fact that their bowling was not at full strength in the first two. Neither Marshall nor Holding was fit for the first two Tests and the latter missed the second as well. Once they joined forces with Garner, West Indies were absolutely irresistible. Garner, who had opted out of the Indian tour and come into the series absolutely fresh, bowled with unprecedented fire and took 31 wickets.

Not one of West Indies' main batsmen, except Gomes, who was utterly off-form, failed to play at least one major innings. And Haynes, who had a poor tour of India, scaled great heights, scoring 468 runs, including two hundreds. These came on top of three unbeaten centuries in the one-day internationals, which gave him an average of 340 in the four limited-over games!

Keep the Facts at your Fingertips with the Daily Telegraph
Pocket Sports Facts

Designed to appeal to the dedicated fan and the armchair sports follower.

If you want to know who won what and when, read about the greats past and present or merely check the rules of each sport, then don't miss out on this great new series. Titles published to date:

Athletics   **Cricket**   **Flat Racing**   **Golf**

Available from leading bookshops price £3.95 each or by post from Dept. PSF, Daily Telegraph, 135 Fleet Street, London EC4 (please add 55p for postage and packing).

West Indies v Australia 1983-84 1st Test
Match Drawn
Played at Bourda, Georgetown, March 2, 3, 4, 6, 7
Toss: Australia. Umpires: D.M. Archer and D.J. Narine
Debuts: Australia, S.B. Smith

Australia

S.B. Smith	c Dujon b Garner	3	c Dujon b Garner	12
K.C. Wessels	c Lloyd b Garner	4	c Lloyd b Daniel	20
G.M. Ritchie	c Davis b Harper	78	lbw b Garner	3
K.J. Hughes*	b Garner	18	c Haynes b Daniel	0
A.R. Border	b Garner	5	run out	54
D.W. Hookes	c Dujon b Harper	32	b Garner	10
W.B. Phillips†	c Greenidge b Harper	16	b Daniel	76
G.F. Lawson	c Richards b Harper	11	not out	35
T.G. Hogan	not out	42	lbw b Davis	18
T.M. Alderman	lbw b Garner	1	(11) not out	3
R.M. Hogg	lbw b Garner	52	(10) b Davis	6
Extras	(B 2, LB 3, W 1, NB 11)	17	(B 10, LB 15, NB 11)	36
		279	(9 wickets declared)	**273**

West Indies

C.G. Greenidge	c Wessels b Lawson	16	not out	120
D.L. Haynes	lbw b Hogg	60	not out	103
R.B. Richardson	lbw b Lawson	19		
I.V.A. Richards	c Phillips b Hogg	8		
H.A. Gomes	c Border b Hogan	10		
C.H. Lloyd*	c Phillips b Alderman	36		
P.J.L. Dujon†	b Hogan	21		
R.A. Harper	b Hogan	10		
J. Garner	not out	16		
W.W. Davis	c Ritchie b Hogan	11		
W.W. Daniel	lbw b Lawson	4		
Extras	(LB 7, NB 12)	19	(B 10, LB 13, NB 4)	27
		230	(0 wickets)	**250**

West Indies‡	O	M	R	W	O	M	R	W
Garner	27.2	10	75	6	24	5	67	3
Daniel	12	3	60	0	27	4	86	3
Davis	19	3	45	0	14	3	35	2
Harper	24	7	56	4	15	4	27	0
Gomes	15	1	35	0	11	2	25	0
Richards	5	2	3	0	6	2	8	0

Australia‡	O	M	R	W	O	M	R	W
Lawson	20.4	4	59	3	18	0	54	0
Alderman	21	3	64	1	11	0	43	0
Hogg	12	0	44	2	13	0	56	0
Hogan	25	9	56	4	19	2	74	0

Fall of Wickets

Wkt	A 1st	WI 1st	A 2nd	WI 2nd
1st	6	29	37	
2nd	23	72	41	
3rd	55	93	42	
4th	63	110	50	
5th	139	154	60	
6th	166	181	185	
7th	180	191	209	
8th	181	203	248	
9th	182	225	263	
10th	279	230		

*Captain †Wicket-keeper ‡Wides and no-balls included in bowling analyses

West Indies v Australia 1983-84 2nd Test
Match Drawn
Played at Queen's Park Oval, Port-of-Spain, March 16, 17, 18, 20, 21
Toss: West Indies. Umpires: D.M. Archer and C.E. Cumberbatch
Debuts: Australia, D.M. Jones; West Indies, M.A. Small

Australia

K.C. Wessels	c Gomes b Garner	4	lbw b Garner	4
W.B. Phillips†	c Dujon b Garner	4	run out	0
G.M. Ritchie	b Garner	1	b Small	26
K.J. Hughes*	c Dujon b Garner	24	lbw b Marshall	33
A.R. Border	not out	98	(6) not out	100
D.W. Hookes	b Garner	23	(7) c Richardson b Gomes	21
D.M. Jones	c and b Richards	48	(8) b Richards	5
G.F. Lawson	c and b Daniel	14	(9) b Marshall	20
T.G. Hogan	c Greenidge b Daniel	0	(5) c Logie b Daniel	38
R.M. Hogg	c Marshall b Daniel	11	c Garner b Richards	9
T.M. Alderman	c Richardson b Garner	1	not out	21
Extras	(B 6, LB 4, NB 17)	27	(B 6, LB 1, W 1, NB 14)	22
		255	(9 wickets)	**299**

West Indies

C.G. Greenidge	c Phillips b Hogg	24
D.L. Haynes	run out	53
R.B. Richardson	c Wessels b Alderman	23
I.V.A. Richards*	c Phillips b Alderman	76
H.A. Gomes	b Lawson	3
A.L. Logie	lbw b Hogan	97
P.J.L. Dujon†	b Hogan	130
M.D. Marshall	lbw b Lawson	10
J. Garner	not out	24
W.W. Daniel	not out	6
M.A. Small	did not bat	
Extras	(B 7, LB 12, W 2, NB 1)	22
	(8 wickets declared)	**468**

West Indies‡	O	M	R	W	O	M	R	W
Garner	28.1	9	60	6	15	4	35	1
Marshall	19	4	73	0	22	3	73	2
Daniel	15	3	40	3	9	3	11	1
Small	10	3	24	0	14	2	51	1
Gomes	10	0	33	0	27	5	53	1
Richards	10	4	15	1	25	5	65	2
Logie					0.1	0	4	0

Australia‡	O	M	R	W
Lawson	32	3	132	2
Hogg	31	2	103	1
Alderman	35	9	91	2
Hogan	28	3	123	2

Fall of Wickets

Wkt	A 1st	WI 1st	A 2nd
1st	4	35	1
2nd	7	93	35
3rd	16	124	41
4th	50	129	114
5th	85	229	115
6th	185	387	153
7th	233	430	162
8th	233	462	196
9th	253		238
10th	255		

*Captain †Wicket-keeper ‡Wides and no-balls included in bowling analyses.

West Indies v Australia 1983-84 3rd Test
West Indies won by 10 wickets
Played at Kensington Oval, Bridgetown, March 30, 31, April 1, 3, 4
Toss: West Indies. Umpires: D.M. Archer and L. Barker
Debuts: Nil

Australia

S.B. Smith	c Dujon b Marshall	10	b Marshall		7
G.M. Wood	c Dujon b Holding	68	lbw b Garner		20
G.M. Ritchie	c and b Harper	57	c Haynes b Marshall		0
K.J. Hughes*	c Dujon b Holding	20	c Lloyd b Holding		25
A.R. Border	c Richardson b Marshall	38	(6) c Dujon b Holding		8
D.W. Hookes	c Dujon b Garner	30	(7) b Holding		9
T.G. Hogan	b Garner	40	(5) c Richardson b Holding		2
W.B. Phillips†	c Dujon b Garner	120	b Marshall		1
G.F. Lawson	b Baptiste	10	c Harper b Marshall		2
R.M. Hogg	c Garner b Harper	3	not out		5
T.M. Alderman	not out	2	b Marshall		0
Extras	(B 14, LB 8, NB 9)	31	(B 1, LB 6, NB 11)		18
		429			**97**

West Indies

C.G. Greenidge	run out	64
D.L. Haynes	b Hogg	145
R.B. Richardson	not out	131
I.V.A. Richards	b Lawson	6
E.A.E. Baptiste	b Lawson	11
P.J.L. Dujon†	b Alderman	2
C.H. Lloyd*	b Hogg	76
M.D. Marshall	b Hogg	10
R.A. Harper	b Hogg	19
J. Garner	c Phillips b Hogg	9
M.A. Holding	c Smith b Hogg	0
Extras	(LB 25, NB 11)	36
		509

	not out	10
	not out	11
(0 wickets)		**21**

West Indies‡

	O	M	R	W	O	M	R	W
Garner	33.5	6	110	3	8	4	9	1
Marshall	26	2	83	2	15.5	1	42	5
Holding	30	5	94	2	15	4	24	4
Baptiste	17	5	34	1	3	0	14	0
Harper	43	9	86	2	2	1	1	0

Australia‡

	O	M	R	W	O	M	R	W
Lawson	33.2	4	150	2	2	1	3	0
Alderman	42.4	6	152	1	1.4	0	18	0
Hogg	32.4	4	77	6				
Hogan	34	8	97	0				
Border	3	1	8	0				

Fall of Wickets

Wkt	A 1st	WI 1st	A 2nd	WI 2nd
1st	11	132	13	
2nd	114	277	13	
3rd	158	289	62	
4th	171	313	65	
5th	223	316	68	
6th	263	447	80	
7th	307	465	85	
8th	350	493	85	
9th	363	509	92	
10th	429	509	97	

*Captain †Wicket-keeper ‡Wides and no-balls included in bowling analyses.

West Indies v Australia 1983-84 4th Test
West Indies won by an innings and 36 runs
Played at Recreation Ground, St. John's, April 7, 8, 9, 11
Toss: Australia. Umpires: D.M. Archer and A. Weekes
Debuts: Nil

Australia

W.B. Phillips	c Dujon b Garner	5	b Garner		22
G.M. Ritchie	c Holding b Marshall	6	c Dujon b Garner		23
A.R. Border	c Dujon b Baptiste	98	c Greenidge b Baptiste		19
K.J. Hughes*	c Marshall b Harper	24	c Richards b Marshall		29
D.M. Jones	b Harper	1	c Dujon b Garner		11
D.W. Hookes	c Richardson b Baptiste	51	c Greenidge b Holding		29
R.D. Woolley†	c Dujon b Baptiste	13	lbw b Marshall		8
T.G. Hogan	c Harper b Holding	14	c Baptiste b Garner		6
G.F. Lawson	b Holding	4	not out		17
J.N. Maguire	not out	15	b Marshall		0
C.G. Rackemann	b Holding	12	b Garner		0
Extras	(B 5, LB 4, NB 10)	19	(B 19, LB 7, NB 10)		36
		262			**200**

West Indies

C.G. Greenidge	c Ritchie b Lawson	0
D.L. Haynes	b Lawson	21
R.B. Richardson	c Woolley b Rackemann	154
I.V.A. Richards	c Woolley b Rackemann	178
P.J.L. Dujon†	c Hughes b Rackemann	28
C.H. Lloyd*	c Jones b Rackemann	38
M.D. Marshall	c Hookes b Maguire	6
E.A.E. Baptiste	b Maguire	6
R.A. Harper	c Ritchie b Maguire	27
J. Garner	c Hogan b Rackemann	10
M.A. Holding	not out	3
Extras	(B 12, LB 14, NB 1)	27
		498

West Indies‡	O	M	R	W	O	M	R	W
Marshall	18	2	70	1	17	5	51	3
Garner	18	5	34	1	20.5	2	63	5
Holding	19.5	3	42	3	14	2	22	1
Harper	19	4	58	2	6	0	24	0
Baptiste	17	2	42	3	8	2	14	1
Richards	5	0	7	0				

Australia‡	O	M	R	W
Lawson	29	4	125	2
Rackemann	42.4	8	160	5
Maguire	44	9	122	3
Hogan	30	9	65	0

Fall of Wickets

Wkt	A 1st	WI 1st	A 2nd
1st	14	0	50
2nd	14	43	57
3rd	67	351	97
4th	78	390	116
5th	201	405	150
6th	208	426	167
7th	217	442	176
8th	224	468	185
9th	246	491	185
10th	262	498	200

*Captain †Wicket-keeper ‡Wides and no-balls included in bowling analyses.

West Indies v Australia 1983-84 5th Test
West Indies won by 10 wickets
Played at Sabina Park, Kingston, April 28, 29, 30, May 2
Toss: West Indies. Umpires: D.M. Archer and L. Barker
Debuts: Nil

Australia

W.B. Phillips†	c Dujon b Garner	12	b Garner		2
S.B. Smith	c Greenidge b Marshall	9	absent hurt		–
A.R. Border	c Dujon b Marshall	41	not out		60
G.M. Ritchie	c Dujon b Marshall	5	b Holding		8
K.J. Hughes*	c Harper b Holding	19	c Greenidge b Marshall		23
D.W. Hookes	b Harper	36	c Dujon b Marshall		7
G.R.J. Matthews	st Dujon b Harper	7	(2) b Holding		7
T.G. Hogan	c and b Garner	25	(7) b Marshall		10
G.F. Lawson	c Harper b Garner	15	(8) b Marshall		4
R.M. Hogg	not out	1	(9) b Marshall		14
J.N. Maguire	b Baptiste	9	(10) b Garner		0
Extras	(B 8, LB 3, W 1, NB 8)	20	(B 17, LB 4, NB 4)		25
		199			**160**

West Indies

C.G. Greenidge	c Ritchie b Hogan	127
D.L. Haynes	b Hogan	60
R.B. Richardson	c Phillips b Lawson	0
I.V.A. Richards	run out	2
C.H. Lloyd*	c Phillips b Lawson	20
P.J.L. Dujon†	c Phillips b Maguire	23
M.D. Marshall	c Hookes b Maguire	19
E.A.E. Baptiste	c Lawson b Maguire	27
R.A. Harper	c Phillips b Maguire	0
J. Garner	c Phillips b Lawson	7
M.A. Holding	not out	0
Extras	(B 1, LB 11, NB 8)	20
		305

not out 32
not out 15

(B 2, LB 3, NB 3) 8
(0 wickets) **55**

West Indies‡

	O	M	R	W	O	M	R	W
Marshall	18	4	37	3	23	3	51	5
Garner	17	4	42	3	16.4	6	28	2
Holding	12	2	43	1	11	4	20	2
Baptiste	11	3	40	1	6	3	11	0
Harper	20	8	26	2	9	2	25	0
Richards					2	0	4	0

Australia‡

	O	M	R	W	O	M	R	W
Lawson	30	8	91	3	5	0	24	0
Hogg	16	2	67	0	5.2	0	18	0
Hogan	30	8	68	2				
Maguire	16.4	2	57	4	1	0	8	0
Matthews	2	0	10	0				

Fall of Wickets

Wkt	A 1st	WI 1st	A 2nd	WI 2nd
1st	22	162	7	
2nd	23	169	15	
3rd	34	174	27	
4th	73	213	89	
5th	113	228	109	
6th	124	260	125	
7th	142	274	131	
8th	181	274	159	
9th	190	297	160	
10th	199	305		

*Captain †Wicket-keeper ‡Wides and no-balls included in bowling analyses.

Test Match Averages: West Indies v Australia 1983-84

West Indies

Batting/Fielding	M	I	NO	HS	R	Avge	100	50	Ct	St
D.L. Haynes	5	8	3	145	468	93.60	2	3	2	-
R.B. Richardson	5	5	1	154	327	81.75	2	-	5	-
C.G. Greenidge	5	8	3	127	393	78.60	2	1	6	-
I.V.A. Richards	5	5	0	178	270	54.00	1	1	3	-
C.H. Lloyd	4	4	0	76	170	42.50	-	1	3	-
P.J.L. Dujon	5	5	0	130	204	40.80	1	-	20	1
J. Garner	5	5	2	24*	66	22.00	-	-	3	-
E.A.E. Baptiste	3	3	0	27	44	14.66	-	-	1	-
R.A. Harper	4	4	0	27	56	14.00	-	-	5	-
M.D. Marshall	4	4	0	19	45	11.25	-	-	2	-
W.W. Daniel	2	2	1	6*	10	10.00	-	-	1	-
H.A. Gomes	2	2	0	10	13	6.50	-	-	1	-
M.A. Holding	3	3	2	3*	3	3.00	-	-	1	-

Played in one Test: W.W. Davis 11 (1 ct); A.L. Logie 97 (1 ct); M.A. Small (did not bat).

Bowling	O	M	R	W	Avge	Best	5wI	10wM
J. Garner	208.5	55	523	31	16.87	6-60	3	-
M.A. Holding	101.5	20	245	13	18.84	4-24	-	-
M.D. Marshall	158.5	24	480	21	22.85	5-42	2	-
E.A.E. Baptiste	62	15	155	6	25.83	3-42	-	-
W.W. Daniel	63	13	197	7	28.14	3-40	-	-
R.A. Harper	138	35	303	10	30.30	4-56	-	-

Also bowled: W.W. Davis 33-6-80-2; H.A. Gomes 63-8-146-1; A.L. Logie 0.1-0-4-0; I.V.A. Richards 53-13-102-3; M.A. Small 24-5-75-1.

Australia

Batting/Fielding	M	I	NO	HS	R	Avge	100	50	Ct	St
A.R. Border	5	10	3	100*	521	74.42	1	4	1	-
W.B. Phillips	5	10	0	120	258	25.80	1	1	10	-
D.W. Hookes	5	10	0	51	248	24.80	-	1	2	-
T.G. Hogan	5	10	1	42*	195	21.66	-	-	1	-
K.J. Hughes	5	10	0	33	215	21.50	-	-	1	-
G.M. Ritchie	5	10	0	78	207	20.70	-	2	4	-
R.M. Hogg	4	8	2	52	101	16.83	-	1	-	-
G.F. Lawson	5	10	2	35*	132	16.50	-	-	1	-
D.M. Jones	2	4	0	48	65	16.25	-	-	1	-
T.M. Alderman	3	6	3	21*	28	9.33	-	-	-	-
S.B. Smith	3	5	0	12	41	8.20	-	-	-	-
K.C. Wessels	2	4	0	20	32	8.00	-	-	2	-
J.N. Maguire	2	4	1	15*	24	8.00	-	-	-	-

Played in one Test: G.R.J. Matthews 7, 7; C.G. Rackemann 12, 0; G.M. Wood 68, 20; R.D. Woolley 13, 8 (2 ct).

Bowling	O	M	R	W	Avge	Best	5wI	10wM
J.N. Maguire	61.4	11	187	7	26.71	4-57	-	-
C.G. Rackemann	42.4	8	160	5	32.00	5-160	1	-
R.M. Hogg	110	8	365	9	40.55	6-77	1	-
G.F. Lawson	170	24	638	12	53.16	3-59	-	-
T.G. Hogan	166	39	483	8	60.37	4-56	-	-

Also bowled: T.M. Alderman 111.2-18-368-4; A.R. Border 3-1-8-0; G.R.J. Matthews 2-0-10-0.

Statistical Highlights of the Tests

1st Test, Georgetown. For the first time since December 1980 (against Pakistan at Faisalabad), West Indies included only three fast bowlers in their team. Hogan and Hogg, who scored his first fifty in Test cricket, shared a record tenth-wicket partnership of 97 – the highest by either country in this series. Lawson was fined $200 by the tour management committee for showing dissent over umpire Narine's decision concerning his lbw appeal on the second day. Border (4,000 runs) and Haynes (2,000) reached Test career batting milestones. The unbroken first-wicket partnership of 250 between Greenidge and Haynes was a record for West Indies against Australia.

2nd Test, Port-of-Spain. Australia were saved from defeat by two courageous innings by Border. The left-hander scored 198 runs without being out in either innings, survived 555 balls, and batted for 10 hours 42 minutes. Alderman partnered him for the last 105 minutes of the match, negotiating 83 deliveries and helping to add 61 runs in an unbroken tenth-wicket partnership.

3rd Test, Bridgetown. Hogg and Alderman helped Phillips to add 99 runs for the last two Australian wickets, contributing 3 and 2 respectively. Australia's second-innings total of 97 was the lowest by any country in a Test at Bridgetown.

4th Test, St John's, Antigua. Richards and Richardson, playing on their home ground, shared a record third-wicket partnership of 308 – the highest for that wicket by either side in this series. Richards recorded the highest score in a Test at St John's (178). Marshall took his 100th Test wicket when he dismissed Woolley.

5th Test, Kingston. Lloyd became the first West Indian to appear in 100 Test matches. Only M.C. Cowdrey and G. Boycott, who made 114 and 108 appearances respectively for England, played in more. Hogg bowled six bouncers in one over to Haynes in the first innings. West Indies achieved their largest margin of victory (3-0) in any series against Australia, and became the first side not to lose a single second-innings wicket during a five-match rubber. Garner set a new West Indies record against Australia by taking 31 wickets in the series.

Australia Tour of West Indies 1983-84

Results: Played 10; Won 1, Lost 3, Drawn 6 (Abandoned 1)

Batting/Fielding	M	I	NO	HS	R	Avge	100	50	Ct	St
A.R. Border	8	15	4	113	825	75.00	2	6	3	-
K.C. Wessels	4	7	1	126*	333	55.50	1	2	3	-
R.D. Woolley	6	9	4	56*	236	47.20	-	2	11	1
G.M. Wood	2	4	0	76	167	41.75	-	2	-	-
S.B. Smith	7	12	0	127	479	39.91	3	1	5	-
D.W. Hookes	9	18	2	103*	623	38.93	1	4	4	-
D.M. Jones	5	10	0	95	336	33.60	-	3	2	-
W.B. Phillips	9	18	3	120	475	31.66	1	3	16	-
G.R.J. Matthews	5	8	2	54	188	31.33	-	1	4	-
K.J. Hughes	9	18	1	73	486	28.58	-	3	9	-
G.M. Ritchie	10	18	0	99	494	27.44	-	4	6	-
T.G. Hogan	8	14	2	42*	248	20.66	-	-	1	-
G.F. Lawson	6	10	2	35*	132	16.50	-	-	1	-
R.M. Hogg	6	9	2	52	101	14.42	-	1	2	-
T.M. Alderman	6	8	5	21*	41	13.66	-	-	4	-
J.N. Maguire	6	8	2	19	59	9.83	-	-	3	-
C.G. Rackemann	4	4	1	12	25	8.33	-	-	2	-

Bowling	O	M	R	W	Avge	Best	5wI	10wM
J.N. Maguire	210	38	645	26	24.80	4-57	-	-
C.G. Rackemann	149	19	546	19	28.73	6-105	2	-
R.M. Hogg	164	15	569	15	37.93	6-77	2	-
T.G. Hogan	281.1	58	869	22	39.50	5-95	1	-
T.M. Alderman	203.2	37	654	15	43.60	3-47	-	-
G.R.J. Matthews	150	27	472	9	52.44	3-83	-	-
G.F. Lawson	199	29	768	14	54.85	3-59	-	-

Also bowled: A.R. Border 10.1-2-35-1; D.W. Hookes 42-0-215-4; D.M. Jones 19.3-1-74-2; G.M. Ritchie 2-0-10-1; S.B. Smith 1-0-5-0; K.C. Wessels 4-0-14-0.

One-Day Internationals

29 February at Albion, Berbice, Guyana. WEST INDIES won by 8 wickets. Toss: Australia. Australia 231-5 closed (50 overs) (S.B. Smith 60). West Indies 233-2 (48 overs) (D.L. Haynes 133*, R.B. Richardson 61). Match award: D.L. Haynes (133*).

14 March at Queen's Park Oval, Port-of-Spain, Trinidad. AUSTRALIA won by 4 wickets. Toss: Australia. West Indies 190-6 closed (37 overs) (C.G. Greenidge 63, I.V.A. Richards 67). Australia 194-6 (36.4 overs) (K.C. Wessels 67). Match award: K.C. Wessels (67 and 4-0-25-1).

19 April at Castries, St Lucia. WEST INDIES won by 7 wickets. Toss: West Indies. Australia 206-9 closed (45 overs) (A.R. Border 90, K.J. Hughes 78; M.D. Marshall 10-2-34-4). West Indies 208-3 (41.4 overs) (D.L. Haynes 102*). Match award: D.L. Haynes (102*).

26 April at Sabina Park, Kingston, Jamaica. WEST INDIES won by 9 wickets. Toss: Australia. Australia 209-7 closed (50 overs) (S.B. Smith 50, G.M. Ritchie 84). West Indies 211-1 (47.4 overs) (D.L. Haynes 104*, R.B. Richardson 51*). Match award: D.L. Haynes (104* and 1 ct).

Sri Lanka v New Zealand

New Zealand's 35-day maiden tour of Sri Lanka ended on a triumphant note for captain Geoff Howarth. He won the short series of three Tests by 2-0 (1 drawn) and the three-match one-day Internationals by 2-1.

New Zealand's successes in the Tests were largely due to one man – Richard Hadlee. His ability to seam the ball even on dead-pan tracks was more than the Sri Lanka batsmen could take. Hadlee's immaculate line and length off his shortened run-up and the effective use of the short-pitched ball also restricted the free-scoring Sri Lanka batsmen. They presented their wickets to him 23 times in the series at a cost of only 10 runs apiece – a New Zealand record for a Test series.

The second innings of the first and third Tests clearly showed how inexperienced Sri Lanka still were in the five-day game. At Asgiriya, Kandy, venue of the first Test, when Howarth set Sri Lanka 263 to win in 190 minutes, the batsmen were still attacking the bowling even after Hadlee had reduced them to 18 for 6. Victory was offered to a surprised Howarth on a platter. Sri Lanka were shot out for 97 in under two hours and the innings lasted only 27 overs.

In the final Test at the CCC grounds, Colombo, Sri Lanka's second innings lasted nearly four hours and 57 overs, but the batsmen failed to come to terms with Hadlee even on a pitch which was still good for batting on the final day. Sri Lanka were bundled out for 142 and lost by an innings. In these two Tests, Hadlee took 18 wickets – 8 at Asgiriya and 10 at CCC.

The only Test where Sri Lanka were in a dominant position was the second, played at the SSC grounds, Colombo. Here they were spearheaded by a magnificent century from Roy Dias, who unfortunately had a run of bad luck with injuries and was fully fit only for this Test. New Zealand, set a reasonable target of 266 for victory in 350 minutes, were not interested, and the match ended in a stalemate.

With injury to Ashantha de Mel, Vinodhan John spearheaded Sri Lanka's attack, taking 16 wickets at 23.31. The batting successes were left-hander John Reid, with a marathon 180 in the final Test, Jeremy Coney, and Howarth for New Zealand, and Ranjan Madugalle and Arjuna Ranatunga for Sri Lanka.

Sri Lanka v New Zealand 1983-84 1st Test
New Zealand won by 165 runs
Played at Asgiriya Stadium, Kandy, March 9 (no play), 10, 11, 13, 14
Toss: New Zealand. Umpires: H.C. Felsinger and P.W. Vidamagamage
Debuts: Sri Lanka, A.M.J.G. Amerasinghe, S.M.S. Kaluperuma

New Zealand

Batsman	Dismissal	Runs	Dismissal (2nd)	Runs
G.P. Howarth*	c de Alwis b John	62	lbw b John	60
J.G. Wright	lbw b John	45	c de Alwis b John	4
J.F. Reid	c Kaluperuma b Amerasinghe	26	c Ranatunga b De Silva	30
M.D. Crowe	c Ratnayake b De Silva	26	(5) st de Alwis b De Silva	8
J.J. Crowe	c sub (U. Karnain) b John	20	(8) c Amerasinghe b Kaluperuma	9
J.V. Coney	lbw b Ratnayake	25	(10) not out	3
R.J. Hadlee	c Ratnayake b John	29	(6) c sub (U. Karnain) b Kaluperuma	27
I.D.S. Smith†	b Ranatunga	30	(9) not out	31
B.L. Cairns	c de Alwis b Ranatunga	0	(7) c Wettimuny b De Silva	2
J.G. Bracewell	c De Silva b John	2	(4) c Amerasinghe b John	21
S.L. Boock	not out	4		
Extras	(B 1, LB 1, W 5)	7	(B 2, LB 1, W 3)	6
		276	(8 wickets declared)	**201**

Sri Lanka

Batsman	Dismissal	Runs	Dismissal (2nd)	Runs
S. Wettimuny	c Coney b Hadlee	0	c Smith b Hadlee	5
E.R.N.S. Fernando	c Hadlee b Boock	29	lbw b Hadlee	2
S.M.S. Kaluperuma	c Howarth b Bracewell	18	c J.J. Crowe b Boock	5
R.J. Ratnayake	c Smith b Hadlee	6	(9) lbw b Boock	12
L.R.D. Mendis*	c Bracewell b Hadlee	5	(4) b Hadlee	0
R.S. Madugalle	c M.D. Crowe b Hadlee	33	(5) c Bracewell b Hadlee	2
A. Ranatunga	c Bracewell b Cairns	20	(6) c and b Bracewell	51
D.S. De Silva	b Bracewell	11	(7) c Coney b Boock	0
R.G. de Alwis†	lbw b Boock	26	(8) c Howarth b Boock	19
V.B. John	not out	27	c Wright b Boock	0
A.M.J.G. Amerasinghe	run out	34	not out	0
Extras	(LB 2, NB 4)	6	(NB 1)	1
		215		**97**

Sri Lanka Bowling

	O	M	R	W	O	M	R	W
John	29.1	7	86	5	17.5	1	73	3
Ratnayake	15	4	45	1				
Ranatunga	9	3	17	2	4	0	14	0
De Silva	29	6	69	1	21	2	59	3
Amerasinghe	12	3	45	1	8	2	32	0
Kaluperuma	6	3	7	0	4	0	17	2

New Zealand Bowling

	O	M	R	W	O	M	R	W
Hadlee	20.5	7	35	4	7	4	8	4
Cairns	18	3	71	1	4	1	6	0
M.D. Crowe	3	1	4	0				
Boock	23	7	63	2	9	3	28	5
Bracewell	15	4	36	2	7	1	54	1

Fall of Wickets

Wkt	NZ 1st	SL 1st	NZ 2nd	SL 2nd
1st	97	0	14	3
2nd	124	38	75	12
3rd	165	55	126	12
4th	189	55	126	14
5th	210	61	133	18
6th	236	89	137	18
7th	266	120	167	55
8th	266	132	167	97
9th	272	155		97
10th	276	215		97

*Captain †Wicket-keeper

Sri Lanka v New Zealand 1983-84 2nd Test
Match Drawn
Played at Singhalese Sports Club Ground, Colombo, March 16, 17, 18, 20, 21
Toss: New Zealand. Umpires: D. Buultjens and H.C. Felsinger
Debuts: Nil
Sri Lanka

S. Wettimuny	c Coney b Chatfield	26	c Hadlee b Chatfield		65
E.R.N.S. Fernando	b M.D. Crowe	8	c J.J. Crowe b Hadlee		0
S.M.S. Kaluperuma	b Boock	23	c Wright b Hadlee		2
R.L. Dias	run out	16	b Cairns		108
L.R.D. Mendis*	b Hadlee	1	(6) b Chatfield		36
R.S. Madugalle	not out	44	(7) c J.J. Crowe b Chatfield		36
A. Ranatunga	c Smith b Cairns	6	(8) run out		7
J.R. Ratnayeke	lbw b Hadlee	22	(5) c and b Hadlee		12
D.S. De Silva	c Coney b Cairns	0	not out		13
R.G. de Alwis†	c Smith b Cairns	2	b Chatfield		2
V.B. John	c Smith b Cairns	0	not out		3
Extras	(B 5, LB 7, W 8, NB 6)	26	(LB 4, NB 1)		5
		174	(9 wickets declared)		**289**

New Zealand

G.P. Howarth*	b John	24	c Kaluperuma b John		10
J.G. Wright	c Dias b John	20	c De Silva b Ranatunga		48
J.F. Reid	c de Alwis b John	7	lbw b John		0
J.J. Crowe	b Ratnayeke	50	c de Alwis b Ranatunga		16
J.V. Coney	c John b De Silva	30	(6) not out		20
R.J. Hadlee	b Ratnayeke	19			
S.L. Boock	c Madugalle b Ratnayeke	4			
M.D. Crowe	c Kaluperuma b Ratnayeke	0	(5) not out		19
I.D.S. Smith†	c Kaluperuma b Ratnayeke	7			
B.L. Cairns	lbw b De Silva	14			
E.J. Chatfield	not out	9			
Extras	(B 4, LB 6, W 1, NB 3)	14	(B 4, LB 4, NB 2)		10
		198	(4 wickets)		**123**

New Zealand	O	M	R	W	O	M	R	W
Hadlee	22	12	27	2	30	13	58	3
Cairns	24.5	6	47	4	22	3	79	1
Chatfield	20	7	35	1	29	9	78	4
M.D. Crowe	13	5	21	1				
Boock	7	2	18	1	42	16	65	0
Coney					4	3	4	0

Sri Lanka	O	M	R	W	O	M	R	W
John	24	1	89	3	21	11	26	2
Ratnayeke	21	8	42	5	21	11	17	0
Kaluperuma	1	0	3	0	6	3	10	0
Ranatunga	4	1	11	0	18	7	29	2
De Silva	14.3	6	39	2	19	10	31	0
Madugalle					1	1	0	0

Fall of Wickets

Wkt	SL 1st	NZ 1st	SL‡ 2nd	NZ 2nd
1st	25	38	3	10
2nd	66	53	13	10
3rd	68	66	176	48
4th	69	127	209	89
5th	99	151	234	
6th	111	166	244	
7th	152	166	245	
8th	153	171	278	
9th	165	178	282	
10th	174	198		

*Captain †Wicket-keeper ‡In Sri Lanka's second innings, S. Wettimuny retired hurt at 172-2, when 65, and resumed at 244-6

Sri Lanka v New Zealand 1983-84 3rd Test

New Zealand won by an innings and 61 runs
Played at Colombo Cricket Club Ground, March 23, 25, 26, 28, 29
Toss: Sri Lanka. Umpires: K.T. Francis and P.W. Vidamagamage
Debuts: Nil

Sri Lanka

S. Wettimuny	b Hadlee	4		c Coney b Hadlee	2
S.M.S. Kaluperuma	b Hadlee	16		c Coney b Hadlee	18
J.R. Ratnayeke	lbw b Hadlee	0	(7)	b Boock	2
R.L. Dias	c Smith b Chatfield	10		absent hurt	–
L.R.D. Mendis*	c J.J. Crowe b Chatfield	19	(6)	b Boock	10
R.S. Madugalle	not out	89	(3)	c Wright b Bracewell	38
A. Ranatunga	c sub (B.A. Edgar) b Chatfield	37	(4)	c Wright b Boock	50
D.S. De Silva	c Smith b Hadlee	17	(5)	c Smith b Hadlee	1
R.G. de Alwis†	c Boock b Hadlee	28	(8)	c Bracewell b Hadlee	10
A.M.J.G. Amerasinghe	c Wright b Chatfield	15	(9)	b Hadlee	5
V.B. John	c and b Chatfield	12	(10)	not out	0
Extras	(LB 4, NB 5)	9		(LB 1, NB 5)	6
		256			**142**

New Zealand

G.P. Howarth*	lbw b Ratnayeke	7
J.G. Wright	c de Alwis b Ratnayeke	18
J.F. Reid	c and b Amerasinghe	180
M.D. Crowe	c de Alwis b Ratnayeke	45
S.L. Boock	b John	35
J.J. Crowe	lbw b John	18
J.V. Coney	c de Alwis b Amerasinghe	92
R.J. Hadlee	c Kaluperuma b De Silva	0
I.D.S. Smith†	b John	42
J.G. Bracewell	c Kaluperuma b De Silva	0
E.J. Chatfield	not out	1
Extras	(B 4, LB 10, W 2, NB 5)	21
		459

New Zealand	O	M	R	W	O	M	R	W
Hadlee	22	4	73	5	16	7	29	5
Chatfield	22	5	63	5	9	2	27	0
M.D. Crowe	6	2	22	0	5	2	13	0
Boock	20	9	51	0	16	2	32	3
Bracewell	9	2	31	0	11	4	35	1
Coney	3	0	7	0				

Sri Lanka	O	M	R	W
John	37	8	99	3
Ratnayeke	40	9	128	3
Ranatunga	16	5	18	0
De Silva	42	4	95	2
Amerasinghe	30	4	73	2
Kaluperuma	10	2	25	0

Fall of Wickets

Wkt	SL‡ 1st	NS 1st	SL 2nd
1st	4	13	16
2nd	4	32	63
3rd	22	132	63
4th	32	214	79
5th	63	253	101
6th	182	386	105
7th	222	391	136
8th	227	429	138
9th	249	436	142
10th	256	459	

*Captain †Wicket-keeper ‡In Sri Lanka's first innings, R.S. Madugalle retired hurt at 172-5, when 87, and resumed at 249-9

Test Match Averages: Sri Lanka v New Zealand 1983-84

Sri Lanka

Batting/Fielding	M	I	NO	HS	R	Avge	100	50	Ct	St
R.S. Madugalle	3	6	2	89*	242	60.50	-	1	1	-
R.L. Dias	2	3	0	108	134	44.66	1	-	1	-
A. Ranatunga	3	6	0	51	171	28.50	-	2	1	-
A.M.J.G. Amerasinghe	2	4	1	34	54	18.00	-	-	3	-
S. Wettimuny	3	6	0	65	102	17.00	-	1	1	-
R.G. de Alwis	3	6	0	28	87	14.50	-	-	8	1
V.B. John	3	6	3	27*	42	14.00	-	-	1	-
S.M.S. Kaluperuma	3	6	0	23	82	13.66	-	-	6	-
L.R.D. Mendis	3	6	0	36	71	11.83	-	-	-	-
E.R.N.S. Fernando	2	4	0	29	39	9.75	-	-	-	-
J.R. Ratnayeke	2	4	0	22	36	9.00	-	-	-	-
D.S. De Silva	3	6	1	17	42	8.40	-	-	2	-

Played in one Test: R.J. Ratnayeke 6, 12 (2 ct).

Bowling	O	M	R	W	Avge	Best	5wI	10wM
V.B. John	129	28	373	16	23.31	5-86	1	-
J.R. Ratnayeke	82	28	187	8	23.37	5-42	1	-
D.S. De Silva	125.3	28	293	8	36.62	3-59	-	-

Also bowled: A.M.J.G. Amerasinghe 50-9-150-3; S.M.S. Kaluperuma 27-8-62-2; R.S. Madugalle 1-1-0-0; A. Ranatunga 51-16-89-4; R.J. Ratnayeke 15-4-45-1.

New Zealand

Batting/Fielding	M	I	NO	HS	R	Avge	100	50	Ct	St
J.V. Coney	3	5	2	92	170	56.66	-	1	6	-
J.F. Reid	3	5	0	180	243	48.60	1	-	-	-
I.D.S. Smith	3	4	1	42	110	36.66	-	-	8	-
G.P. Howarth	3	5	0	62	163	32.60	-	2	2	-
J.G. Wright	3	5	0	48	135	27.00	-	-	5	-
M.D. Crowe	3	5	1	45	98	24.50	-	-	1	-
J.J. Crowe	3	5	0	50	113	22.60	-	1	4	-
S.L. Boock	3	3	1	35	43	21.50	-	-	1	-
R.J. Hadlee	3	4	0	29	75	18.75	-	-	3	-
J.G. Bracewell	2	3	0	21	23	7.66	-	-	5	-
B.L. Cairns	2	3	0	14	16	5.33	-	-	-	-

Also batted: E.J. Chatfield (2 Tests) 9*, 1* (1 ct).

Bowling	O	M	R	W	Avge	Best	5wI	10wM
R.J. Hadlee	117.5	47	230	23	10.00	5-29	2	1
E.J. Chatfield	80	23	203	10	20.30	5-63	1	-
S.L. Boock	117	39	257	11	23.36	5-28	1	-
B.L. Cairns	68.5	13	203	6	33.83	4-47	-	-

Also bowled: J.G. Bracewell 42-11-156-4; J.V. Coney 7-3-11-0; M.D. Crowe 27-10-60-1.

Statistical Highlights of the Tests

1st Test, Kandy. This was New Zealand's first official Test in Sri Lanka; the two countries had played a two-match rubber in New Zealand a year earlier. Howarth opened the batting in both innings of a Test match for the first time for seven years. Hadlee was warned by umpire Vidamagamage for intimidation after bowling successive bouncers at John. The latter's partnership of 60 with Amerasinghe was a tenth-wicket record for Sri Lanka against all countries. Needing 263 runs to win in 130 minutes plus 20 overs, Sri Lanka were bowled out in under two hours for their lowest total in a home Test.

2nd Test, Colombo. The Singhalese Sports Club Ground became Test cricket's 57th venue. 'Ravi' Ratnayeke (5-42) recorded Sri Lanka's best analysis in their ten Tests. For only the second time Sri Lanka dismissed their opposition for under 200 (England scored 175 in the second innings of the inaugural Test in February 1982). Dias scored Sri Lanka's first century in a home Test. His partnership of 163 with Wettimuny was a third-wicket record for Sri Lanka against all countries. M.D. Crowe batted 221 minutes for 19 runs in drawing the match; he had remained on 1 for 65 minutes. Only 117 runs were scored in 330 minutes on the last day.

3rd Test, Colombo. Colombo became the first city to boast three current Test match venues by staging this match at the Colombo Cricket Club Ground (the inaugural Test against England was played at the Saravanamuttu Stadium). Recalled for his first Test series for three years, Reid scored New Zealand's first hundred against Sri Lanka and went on to record the highest innings against Sri Lanka in their 11 Tests. He batted for 580 minutes. Boock, who equalled his highest score in first-class cricket, reached double figures for the first time in 24 Test innings. Hadlee's match analysis of 10-102 was a record for Tests in Sri Lanka. New Zealand won a series overseas for the first time since they defeated Pakistan in November 1969.

One-Day Internationals

3 March at Colombo. NEW ZEALAND won by 104 runs. Toss: Sri Lanka. New Zealand 234-6 closed (42 overs) (J.F. Reid 80). Sri Lanka 130 (37.3 overs). Match award: J.F. Reid (80).

31 March at Moratuwa. SRI LANKA won by 41 runs. Toss: New Zealand. Sri Lanka 157-8 closed (40 overs) (A. Ranatunga 50*). New Zealand 116 (34 overs) (U.S.H. Karnain 8-1-26-5). Match award: U.S.H. Karnain (28 and 5-26 on his debut in international cricket).

1 April at Colombo. NEW ZEALAND won by 86 runs. Toss: Sri Lanka. New Zealand 201-8 closed (44 overs) (M.D. Crowe 68). Sri Lanka 115 (38.1 overs). Match award: B.L. Cairns (40* – including 26 off V.B. John's final over of the innings – and 7-2-14-2).

THE MAGAZINE THE PLAYERS READ TOO

A probe into the past, present and future
The best in words and pictures

MONTHLY THROUGHOUT THE YEAR

**Take out a subscription from:
WISDEN CRICKET MONTHLY
313 KILBURN LANE, LONDON W9 3EQ**

Cricket in Australia

Admiration abounded for Western Australia's winning of the Sheffield Shield for the ninth time and the eighth in 17 seasons. But there was much sympathy for Queensland, whose impossible dream of taking the trophy for the first time since they entered the competition in 1926-27 was again a case of so near, yet so far.

For the second successive season, the destiny of the Shield was decided by a five-day final. Western Australia had lost to New South Wales by 54 runs at Perth's WACA Ground in 1982-83. But this time they triumphed over Queensland by four wickets, the match finishing soon after tea on the fifth day when the home team had passed their second innings target of 223 runs.

Western Australia had finished on top of the Shield table, just two points clear of Queensland, after the preliminary round. Tasmania, in only their second full season in the competition, climbed from fourth to third position, defending champions New South Wales plunged to fourth, South Australia slipped from third to fifth, and Victoria were bottom for the third consecutive season.

Western Australia were denied the double when South Australia scored a surprise eight-run win in the McDonald's Cup final. It was South Australia's first success in the limited-overs competition.

The Western Australia Shield victory was a source of immense satisfaction for the state's two greatest players, Dennis Lillee and Rod Marsh, who were making their farewell first-class appearances in the final. Equally, the result was especially disappointing for Greg Chappell, whom Queensland had lured from South Australia in 1973-74 for the express purpose of winning them the Shield.

Chappell relinquished the captaincy to his former Test team-mate Jeff Thomson for the last three matches so that he could concentrate solely on his batting. He scored his 74th and last first-class century in Queensland's last preliminary match – 129 against Tasmania in Hobart – and topscored with 85 in the first innings of the final. He bowed out of first-class cricket as the Shield competition's third-highest run-getter, behind John Inverarity and Sir Donald Bradman. Their figures are: Inverarity – 9,036 (avg 39.28) for Western Australia and South Australia, Bradman – 8,926 (avg 110.19) for New South Wales and South Australia, Chappell – 8,762 (avg 57.26) for South Australia and Queensland. Chappell also became only the fourth batsman to score more than 5,000 Shield runs for Queensland, after Sam Trimble (8,647 at 39), Peter Burge (7,084 at 56), and Ken Mackay (6,341 at 45). Chappell made 5,037 at 69.

The Shield final also marked the last first-class appearance of Western Australian Bruce Laird, a brave, stubborn little batsman who scored 1,331 runs (avg 35.02) in 21 Tests for Australia between 1979 and 1982 and who amassed 3,760 (avg 36.01) first-class runs for his State from 1972-73. Laird's 63 and 54 not out helped pave the way for Western Australia's win in the final.

The other retirement of note was that of New South Wales' former

Test opening batsman Rick McCosker, who accumulated 8,983 runs, with 27 centuries, at an average of 44.03 in 127 first-class games for New South Wales and Australia. In 25 Tests, from 1974-75 to 1979-80, he made 1,622 runs (avg 39.56), with four hundreds – and an unforgettable display of courage when he batted with a broken jaw in the Centenary Test in Melbourne in 1977.

In the absence of Kim Hughes, captaining Australia in the West Indies, Lillee led Western Australia in the final – immediately after having served a two-match suspension for calling for drinks against the umpires' wishes during the match against Queensland in Brisbane. Lillee, who was also fined $A1,000, failed in a Western Australian Supreme Court action to have declared invalid the suspension, imposed by the Australian Cricket Board. The fine was imposed because Lillee was found to have breached the players' code of behaviour within 14 months of having been given a $A1,000 suspended fine for using abusive language to spectators at Adelaide Oval the previous season.

Only 14 outright results from 31 matches helped underline the dominance of batsmen over bowlers in the 1983-84 Shield season, and contributed to the ACB's decision to increase playing times by two hours (half an hour a day) to 26 hours for each four-day match. Players would have preferred five-day matches of 30 hours, as in Tests, but this was considered impractical because of the huge losses already incurred by the Shield competition.

Indicative of the continuing decline in Shield attendances, caused partly by some matches being up against live national television coverage of Tests and one-day internationals, was the aggregate crowd of 1,940 (771, 618, 501, and 50) at the Victoria-New South Wales match at the Melbourne Cricket Ground in late January. As a distant, some may say irrelevant, comparison, the corresponding match in 1929 drew 22,348 to the third day's play alone.

Two prolific-scoring batsmen, Tasmania's Brian Davison, formerly of Rhodesia (Zimbabwe) and Leicestershire, and New South Wales' John Dyson, tied for the Benson and Hedges Shield Player of the Year award ($A1,000 each and a gold tray and goblets). With umpires casting votes on a 3-2-1 basis in each match, Davison and Dyson polled 15 votes – one more than South Australian (and former New South Wales and Australian) batsman Andrew Hilditch, and three more than Queensland new-ball bowler John Maguire and batsman Greg Ritchie and Western Australian left-handed opening batsman Graeme Wood. Dyson hit the highest score of the season – 241 against South Australia in Adelaide – in topping 1,000. It will not be a surprise if he regains his Test place against West Indies in Australia in 1984-85 and tours England again in 1985.

Western Australia v Queensland 1983-84 Sheffield Shield Final
Western Australia won by 4 wickets
Played at WACA Ground, Perth, March 9, 10, 11, 12, 13
Toss: Western Australia. Umpires: M.W. Johnson and P.J. McConnell

Queensland

B.A. Courtice	b MacLeay	77	c R.W. Marsh b MacLeay		22
R.B. Kerr	c R.W. Marsh b MacLeay	56	lbw b Lillee		4
C.B. Smart	c R.W. Marsh b Graf	57	c and b Graf		62
G.S. Chappell	c Laird b Lillee	85	c Laird b MacLeay		1
G.S. Trimble	c R.W. Marsh b Graf	0	c Graf b MacLeay		6
T.V. Hohns	c Clements b Milosz	39	c Shipperd b MacLeay		17
R.B. Phillips†	not out	61	lbw b Graf		10
C.J. McDermott	c R.W. Marsh b Graf	16	not out		21
G.K. Whyte	not out	18	c Graf b Milosz		1
H. Frei	did not bat		run out		0
J.R. Thomson*	" "		b Graf		0
Extras	(B 2, LB 7, W 4, NB 9)	22	(LB 4, W 1, NB 5)		10
	(7 wickets declared)	**431**			**154**

Western Australia

G.M. Wood	c Kerr b Thomson	53	c Smart b Thomson		13
S.C. Clements	c Kerr b Frei	6	b Thomson		28
G. Shipperd	c Phillips b Frei	21	c Kerr b Whyte		41
G.R. Marsh	b Thomson	107	c Phillips b McDermott		0
B.M. Laird	c Phillips b Hohns	63	not out		54
M.R.J. Veletta	c Trimble b Thomson	12	c and b Whyte		0
R.W. Marsh†	b Frei	7	c and b Whyte		45
S.F. Graf	c Chappell b Hohns	14	not out		17
K.H. MacLeay	b Thomson	21			
D.K. Lillee*	c Phillips b Thomson	18			
S.J. Milosz	not out	0			
Extras	(B 5, LB 6, W 4, NB 26)	41	(B 5, LB 10, W 2, NB 9)		26
		363	(6 wickets)		**224**

W Australia	O	M	R	W	O	M	R	W
Lillee	48	8	116	1	12	2	34	1
MacLeay	52	13	115	2	21	3	58	4
Graf	42	5	111	3	18.2	6	34	3
Milosz	26	4	78	1	9	3	24	1
Laird	1	0	2	0				

Queensland	O	M	R	W	O	M	R	W
McDermott	20	5	67	0	10	3	20	1
Frei	37	10	104	3	12	2	28	0
Thomson	25.2	6	85	5	19	0	96	2
Whyte	14	4	26	0	13	6	28	3
Hohns	23	12	35	2	5.5	2	22	0
Courtice	11	1	35	0				
Chappell					11	4	15	0

Fall of Wickets

Wkt	Q 1st	WA 1st	Q 2nd	WA 2nd
1st	103	12	4	34
2nd	163	81	40	52
3rd	291	105	42	53
4th	292	244	62	134
5th	293	289	104	138
6th	352	291	130	199
7th	391	309	139	
8th		321	150	
9th		363	152	
10th		363	154	

*Captain †Wicket-Keeper

Sheffield Shield 1983-84
Final Table

	P	W	L	D	1st Inngs points	Total points
Western Australia	10	4	0	6	28	76
Queensland	10	4	2	4	26	74
Tasmania	10	2	3	5	20	44
New South Wales	10	1	4	5	24	36
South Australia	10	1	2	7	14	26
Victoria	10	1	2	7	8	20

Leading First-Class Averages

Batting	State	M	I	NO	HS	R	Avge	100	50
G.N. Yallop	V	8	11	1	268	1132	113.20	5	2
P.C. Clifford	NSW	5	8	3	152*	443	88.60	1	3
G.M. Ritchie	Q	7	12	1	196	905	82.27	3	6
A.R. Border	Q	10	14	2	118	929	77.41	3	7
M.D. Taylor	V	11	18	4	172*	1010	72.14	4	3
B.F. Davison	T	11	20	4	171	1036	64.75	4	4
J. Dyson	NSW	11	19	3	241	1015	63.43	3	3
K.J. Hughes	WA	10	14	0	130	867	61.92	3	4
A.M.J. Hilditch	SA	10	17	1	230	937	58.56	3	3
W.B. Phillips	SA	10	15	1	234	763	54.50	2	2
D.M. Jones	V	8	15	1	128	762	54.42	2	6
P.R. Sleep	SA	10	14	5	144	486	54.00	2	2

Qualification: 8 innings.

Bowling	State	O	M	R	W	Avge	Best	5WI
C.G. Rackemann	Q	188.4	46	523	28	18.67	6-86	2
G.F. Lawson	NSW	325	77	927	40	23.17	6-43	3
H. Frei	Q	212.2	61	554	23	24.08	6-52	2
T.M. Alderman	WA	293.3	74	758	30	25.26	5-79	1
R.M. Hogg	SA	281.1	50	814	32	25.43	5-53	1
D.K. Lillee	WA	610.5	142	1513	59	25.64	6-62	3
J.R. Thomson	Q	373.5	64	1361	48	28.35	5-85	1
K.H. MacLeay	WA	396.1	99	1005	35	28.71	4-50	–
J.N. Maguire	Q	275	60	870	30	29.00	6-62	2
R.G. Holland	NSW	310.3	115	718	24	29.91	7-56	1
L.S. Pascoe	NSW	192.3	43	599	20	29.95	5-53	2
D.R. Gilbert	NSW	276	75	762	25	30.48	5-56	1

Qualification: 20 wickets

McDonald's Cup
Semi-Finals

21 December at Sydney. WESTERN AUSTRALIA beat NEW SOUTH WALES by 46 runs. W. Australia 230-5 closed (49 overs) (M.R.J. Veletta 83, G. Shipperd 67); NSW 184 (45.2 overs) (D.M. Wellham 64). Man of the Match: M.R.J. Veletta (83).

21 December at Launceston. SOUTH AUSTRALIA beat TASMANIA by 5 wickets. Tasmania 163 (50 overs) (P. Brinsley 4-45); S. Australia 167-5 (49.4 overs) (M.D. Haysman 54). Man of the Match: R.M. Hogg (10-2-10-1).

Final

4 March at Adelaide. SOUTH AUSTRALIA beat WESTERN AUSTRALIA by 8 runs. S. Australia 256-6 closed (49 overs) (D.F. O'Connor 96*); W. Australia 248-9 closed (49 overs) (R.W. Marsh 54; I.R. Carmichael 4-50). Man of the Match: D.F. O'Connor (96* and 1 ct).

Cricket in South Africa

Transvaal's domination of South African domestic cricket finally came to an end in the Benson & Hedges night series, but it took the intervention of the weather, rather than the efforts of the other provinces, to do it. The South African Cricket Union took the mystifying decision that, in the event of teams finishing level on points in the round-robin section, final places would be decided by runs aggregate regardless of the number of games played or overs faced. Transvaal, Natal, and Eastern Province all finished bottom on six points. But, because their game against Eastern Province had been completely washed out and their match against Northern Transvaal badly rain-affected, the champions found themselves knocked out because they had the worst runs aggregate.

The road seemed to be open for Western Province, so long in Transvaal's shadow, to emerge and win a major trophy. But it was not to be. Peter Kirsten's men were badly beaten on their home ground by a rejuvenated Natal under the new captaincy of Paddy Clift. In the other semi-final, Eastern Province caused something of a surprise by beating Northern Transvaal at Pretoria, having previously lost their round-robin fixture at the same venue. So two teams who had finished joint bottom in the qualifying competition contested the final! In the event, Eastern Province were no match for Natal, and the final was extremely one-sided.

If Transvaal felt they had been done out of one of their trophies, they made no mistake in defence of two others. Both the first-class Castle Currie Cup and the 55-overs Nissan Shield produced embarrassingly one-sided finals, both against the outclassed Western Province.

Western Province had enjoyed an excellent first half of the season when they stood top of the round-robin Currie Cup section (four matches only) before the start of the West Indies tour. But, when the domestic competitions got into full swing again a couple of months later, their performances were nowhere near the same standard.

In the limited overs final, Transvaal, put into bat, rattled up an imposing 305 for 5, thanks largely to a brilliant century by Alvin Kallicharran. The little left-hander had been woefully out of touch since scoring a century for the West Indies in the first four-day game against the Springboks at Kingsmead at Christmas, but he came bouncing back. He needed only 107 balls for his 104 runs. Western Province, in reply, were bowled out for 216 with 25 balls still available to be bowled.

The four-day Currie Cup final was even more humiliating. Western Province had home ground advantage but came off second best on three of the four days. They got off to a bad start when they won the toss and sent Transvaal into bat on a typical, slow Newlands turner. And the champions responded by knocking up an impressive 406 for 7 off 97 overs in the first six hours. This total became even more substantial in the light of the limit of 100 overs on the first innings. Western Province, in fact, did well to trail by no more than 98 runs.

Stephen Jefferies then gave the home side an outside chance of victory on the third afternoon when he bowled Transvaal out almost single-handed for 179. He sent down 31.2 overs out of a possible 34.2 from the one end, taking 7 for 105. He had two catches dropped and his only rest came when John Emburey bowled the other three overs from his end. Jefferies' effort still left Western Province needing 278 for victory in six hours, and their chickens – for not batting first – duly came home to roost when Alan Kourie (6-57) spun them out for a miserable 136.

In the semi-finals, Transvaal, although leading by a mere 53 runs on the first innings, had cantered home by 234 runs against Northern Transvaal after making a mammoth 488 in their second innings. Western Province had left matters late before beating Eastern Province by 67 runs. The latter led by 41 runs on the first innings, but collapsed against Jefferies' second new-ball onslaught on the final afternoon. The left-hander ran through Eastern Province in eight overs before and after the tea interval, as Eastern collapsed from 195 for 4 to 245 all out.

Graham Gooch also had a lot to do with this Western Province victory. His second innings score of 171 – the highest of the South African season – came at the rate of five to the over and gave his side extra time in which to force victory.

High scoring by individual batsmen was, in fact, a feature of the South African season. Apart from his 171 in this match, Gooch also passed 150 when he and Lawrence Seeff put on 293 for the first wicket against Eastern Province at Newlands, while Jimmy Cook and Henry Fotheringham shared an opening stand of 226 for Transvaal in their semi-final against Northern Transvaal, Cook's contribution being 166.

Although all these batsmen are fine players, this state of affairs was also a reflection on the poor standard of bowling in the Currie Cup competition. Jefferies and the West Indian Sylvester Clarke stood out head and shoulders above all others. The retirement of Vintcent van der Bijl left a huge gap in South Africa's bowling resources, Garth le Roux broke down with recurring injuries for the second successive season – he took five wickets in an innings only once and he is no longer the feared fast bowler of old – and even Alan Kourie did not match his form of the previous season. Others, such as Kenny Watson and Rupert Hanley, lack the pace of international opening bowlers, while Clive Rice can only be considered a medium-pacer in the twilight of his bowling career.

Comment on the South African season cannot pass without reference to Mike Procter, who retired during the course of the summer. He played only seven tests, in two series against Australia, but nevertheless established himself as one of the world's great all-rounders of the 1970s – a player who could stand comparison with the likes of Imran Khan, Ian Botham, Kapil Dev, and Richard Hadlee. Had he had the international opportunities granted to that quartet, there is no knowing how many runs he would have scored or wickets he would have taken. In a Springbok contest he was probably a superior all-rounder and a greater match-winner than any other – and there were some pretty good ones, such as Aubrey Faulkner, Trevor Goddard, and Eddie Barlow.

Western Province v Transvaal 1983-84 Currie Cup Final
Transvaal won by 141 runs
Played at Newlands, Cape Town, February 24, 25, 26, 27

Transvaal

S.J. Cook	c Gooch b Kuiper	93	c Ryall b Jefferies	19
H.R. Fotheringham	lbw b Jefferies	14	c Ryal b Jefferies	21
A.I. Kallicharran	c Ryall b Kuiper	73	c Emburey b Jefferies	0
R.G. Pollock	b Emburey	94	b Jefferies	7
C.E.B. Rice*	c Kirsten b Hobson	41	run out	28
K.A. McKenzie	c Rayner b Emburey	45	not out	61
A.J. Kourie	not out	20	c and b Emburey	4
R.V. Jennings†	c Kirsten b Jefferies	0	c Seeff b Emburey	7
N.V. Radford	not out	12	c and b Jefferies	0
S.T. Clarke	did not bat		c Rayner b Jefferies	11
R.W. Hanley	,, ,,		lbw b Jefferies	7
Extras	(B 8, LB 17, NB 8)	33	(B 2, LB 5, NB 7)	14
	(7 wickets declared)	425		179

Western Province

G.A. Gooch	lbw b Hanley	11	c Radford b Kourie	15
L. Seeff	c Jennings b Clarke	41	c Jennings b Clarke	8
P.N. Kirsten*	c Radford b Kourie	57	b Kourie	22
P.H. Rayner	c Kourie b Clarke	36	run out	2
R.F. Pienaar	c sub b Kallicharran	51	not out	38
A.P. Kuiper	c Fotheringham b Kourie	37	lbw b Clarke	16
S.T. Jefferies	b Clarke	26	c Rice b Kourie	2
O. Henry	c Clarke b Hanley	44	lbw b Hanley	7
J.E. Emburey	b Hanley	8	lbw b Kourie	8
R.J. Ryall†	lbw b Hanley	3	b Kourie	4
D.L. Hobson	not out	0	c Fotheringham b Kourie	4
Extras	(B 3, LB 7, NB 3)	13	(B 4, LB 5, NB 1)	10
		327		136

W Province	O	M	R	W	O	M	R	W
Jefferies	23	1	103	2	31.2	3	105	7
Kuiper	20	1	96	2	10	2	20	0
Pienaar	5	0	21	0	10	2	17	0
Emburey	39	5	110	2	17	6	23	2
Hobson	12	1	54	1				
Henry	1	0	8	0				

Transvaal	O	M	R	W	O	M	R	W
Clarke	26	8	59	3	21	8	26	2
Hanley	24	6	85	4	11	1	21	1
Kourie	35	6	111	2	34.1	14	57	6
Radford	9	1	45	0	4	2	8	0
Rice	4	1	10	0	7	2	14	0
Kallicharran	2	0	4	1	1	1	0	0

Fall of Wickets

Wkt	T 1st	WP 1st	T 2nd	WP 2nd
1st	31	22	40	15
2nd	193	97	40	42
3rd	212	142	41	55
4th	280	162	64	55
5th	390	221	102	72
6th	390	253	113	88
7th	393	285	139	108
8th	–	308	144	120
9th	–	327	168	128
10th	–	327	179	136

*Captain †Wicket-keeper

Currie Cup Semi-Finals

10, 11, 12, 13 February at Port Elizabeth. WESTERN PROVINCE beat EASTERN PROVINCE by 67 runs. Western Province 293 (G.A. Gooch 67, P.H. Rayner 54; T.G. Shaw 5-127) and 353-6 dec (G.A. Gooch 171, A.P. Kuiper 64*); Eastern Province 334 (G.S. Cowley 98, T.G. Shaw 66; S.T. Jefferies 4-86) and 245 (P. Willey 88; S.T. Jefferies 6-45).

10, 11, 12, 13 February at Johannesburg. TRANSVAAL beat NORTHERN TRANSVAAL by 234 runs. Transvaal 252 (H.R. Fotheringham 99) and 488 (S.J. Cook 166, H.R. Fotheringham 115, R.G. Pollock 53; A.M. Ferreira 6-115); Northern Transvaal 199 (N.T. Day 70; S.T. Clarke 6-62) and 307.

Leading Currie Cup Averages

Batting	Province	M	I	NO	HS	R	Avge	100	50
S.J. Cook	T	6	11	1	166	741	74.10	2	5
R.G. Pollock	T	6	11	1	154	563	56.30	2	2
A.P. Kuiper	WP	6	10	2	104	435	54.37	1	3
G.A. Gooch	WP	6	11	0	171	573	52.09	2	1
R.A. Smith	N	4	7	1	109	309	51.50	1	2
R.F. Pienaar	WP	6	10	2	151*	404	50.50	1	1
R.M. Bentley	N	4	7	1	110*	286	47.66	1	3
W. Larkins	EP	5	8	0	116	370	46.25	2	1
M.B. Logan	N	4	7	0	84	289	41.28	-	3
P.N. Kirsten	WP	6	11	0	100	428	38.90	1	4
H.R. Fotheringham	T	6	11	0	115	417	37.90	1	3
P. Willey	EP	5	8	0	111	281	35.12	1	1

Qualification: 7 innings.

Bowling	Province	O	M	R	W	Avge	Best	5wI
R.W. Hanley	T	204	67	512	29	17.65	7-31	2
S.T. Clarke	T	170.5	61	322	18	17.88	6-62	1
A.M. Ferreira	NT	193.5	52	535	25	21.40	6-26	3
S.T. Jefferies	WP	138.2	22	469	21	22.33	7-105	2
A.P. Kuiper	WP	130	21	432	17	25.41	6-55	1
D.L. Hobson	WP	111.2	24	468	18	26.00	5-43	2
G. Miller	N	206.5	48	528	18	29.33	4-24	-
P.A. Robinson	NT	130	23	487	16	30.43	6-46	1
P. Willey	EP	206.2	47	534	17	31.41	4-45	-
A.J. Kourie	T	279.1	80	724	23	31.47	6-57	1
J.A. Carse	EP	152.4	26	517	16	32.31	4-43	-

Qualification: 15 wickets.

Nissan Shield Final (formerly the Datsun Shield)

3 March at Johannesburg. TRANSVAAL beat WESTERN PROVINCE by 89 runs. Transvaal 305-5 closed (55 overs) (A.I. Kallicharran 107, S.J. Cook 51, R.G. Pollock 49, C.E.B. Rice 45*); Western Province 216 (R.F. Pienaar 84; S.T. Clarke 3-20).

Notes: Transvaal's total was a record for this one-day final. S.T. Clarke took 23 wickets (avge 6.30) during the season's Nissan Shield matches.

Cricket in West Indies

The 1984 Shell Shield competition was staged without the majority of the leading West Indian players, absent for one reason or another. This obviously affected the standard. Yet it provided a unique opportunity for the true level of domestic cricket at the amateur club level in the various territories to be assessed.

Missing were the players in Australia for the Benson & Hedges World Series Cup, the rebels banned for their tours of South Africa, and a few injured players. As a result, 39 of those who played in the Shield in 1982 were unavailable in 1984, although a few did return from Australia for a single, irrelevant match at the end.

It meant that the teams were comprised for once almost entirely of players chosen from the club systems. Normally the reverse is true. For instance, nine of Barbados's Shield-winning team of 1982 were professionals who played most of their cricket in England or Holland and turned out in little or no club cricket at home. Clive Lloyd and Faoud Bacchus, of the 1983 Shield champions, Guyana, had played no club cricket there for some years. Michael Holding's last club match in Jamaica was in 1977. This time, every single Barbadian had appeared in the previous season's club championship, and the same was true of the other territories.

In the circumstances, Barbados again proved the overall strength of their structure which has produced so many great players over the years. Even though they had more players unavailable than any other team, they won the Shield for the 11th time in its 18th season.

Barbados's triumph was based mainly on the strength of their bowling, their fielding, and the leadership of their new captain, Carlisle Best, at 24 the youngest in the tournament. They beat Trinidad & Tobago and Jamaica and led the Windward Islands and the Leeward Islands on first innings in drawn matches to clinch the Shield even before their record was spoiled by a heavy defeat in the final match against the 1983 champions, Guyana.

The outstanding individuals of the tournament were provided by the other teams. The 26-year-old Antiguan Ralston Otto at last fulfilled his potential for the Leeward Islands with centuries against Jamaica, Barbados, and Trinidad & Tobago for a new Shield record aggregate of 572 in a season. This beat the record of 1966 set by Jamaican Easton McMorris in the Shield's inaugural season. Two other batsmen, the forthright Jamaican Mark Neita, who made centuries against Guyana and Barbados, and the aggressive Guyana opener Andrew Lyght, also passed 400 runs.

Of the bowlers, the tall, 21-year-old Jamaican Courtney Walsh was well ahead of the rest with 30 wickets, seldom failing to make early inroads into opposition batting. It was the veteran Andy Roberts, leading the Leewards' team after being dropped from the West Indies tour of Australia, who topped the overall averages, however.

Milton Small, a 20-year-old newcomer who would hardly have played a match if all of Barbados's plethora of fast bowlers had been available, took his chance so keenly that his 18 wickets in four Shield matches (at 18.44 each) earned him a Test place against Australia and selection on the summer's tour of England.

There were other batting records to add to that of Otto. The Leewards pair Richie Richardson and Livingstone Lawrence broke the first-wicket Shield record by making 290 against Trinidad & Tobago at the start of an innings of 613 for 5 declared. This was the second highest total ever recorded in the competition, surpassing the 586 which the same Leewards had scored against Guyana in the preceding match.

The limited-overs Geddes Grant/Harrison Line Trophy provided a tense final in which Jamaica beat the Leeward Islands by three wickets. Both teams were bolstered by the return of their Test players from Australia. Jamaica won their first major trophy since 1969 because they got more from theirs (Michael Holding 4 for 22 and Man of the Match, Jeffrey Dujon 57 not out) than the Leewards (Vivian Richards run out 15, Richie Richardson 4, Eldine Baptiste 32 and 0 for 43).

Shell Shield

Final Table

	P	W	L	D	Points
BARBADOS	5	2	1	2	48
Guyana	5	1	1	3	41
Jamaica	5	2	2	1	36
Leeward Islands	5	1	0	4	36
Windward Islands	5	1	0	4	32
Trinidad and Tobago	5	0	3	2	17

Shell Shield Winners

10 Barbados
3 Guyana
2 Trinidad and Tobago
1 Combined Islands, Jamaica
Shared titles: 1 Barbados, Trinidad and Tobago.

Leading Shell Shield Averages

Batting

	Team	M	I	NO	HS	R	Avge	100	50
R.M. Otto	LI	5	8	1	136	572	81.71	3	1
C.B. Lambert	G	3	5	1	123	315	78.75	1	2
P. Moosai	T	3	5	1	97	273	68.25	–	3
V.A. Eddy	LI	5	8	3	120	305	61.00	1	–
L.C. Sebastien	WI	5	6	1	107	275	55.00	1	2
M.C. Neita	J	5	9	0	133	482	53.55	2	3
A. Rajah	T	5	10	2	141*	395	49.37	1	3
A.F.D. Jackman	G	5	8	1	100	334	47.71	1	2
A.A. Lyght	G	5	9	0	122	403	44.77	1	2
G.L. Linton	B	5	9	3	83	260	43.33	–	2

Bowling

		O	M	R	W	Avge	Best	5wI
A.M.E. Roberts	LI	142.5	34	374	21	17.80	6-80	1
M.A. Small	B	109.1	15	332	18	18.44	5-57	1
C.A. Walsh	J	154	17	606	30	20.20	6-35	3
S.J. Hinds	WI	179.1	33	455	21	21.66	6-97	1
R.O. Estwick	B	110.3	11	412	19	21.68	6-68	1
T. Kentish	WI	158	33	350	15	23.33	4-73	–
G.L. Linton	B	128.1	20	432	17	25.41	5-75	1
G. Mahabir	T	181.3	37	476	18	26.44	4-57	–
C. Butts	G	302.4	88	652	24	27.16	6-76	2
D.I. Kallicharran	G	185.5	35	499	15	33.26	5-59	1

Cricket in New Zealand

Fierce determination and an admirable team spirit were the chief attributes that carried Canterbury from the bottom to the top of the pack to win the 1983-84 Shell Trophy competition. Canterbury had not won the major domestic title since 1976. That they did so after a dismal previous season was largely due to the role played by their reappointed captain, Cran Bull. His qualities as a leader, with a knack of getting the best out of his troops, were vital.

Certainly there was the advantage of playing four of their eight games on a Lancaster Park oval of dubious quality, which always guaranteed a result. But that should not detract from the four outright wins they achieved. In three of those matches, Canterbury had to bat last, and no player contributed more to the success than Paul McEwan.

The former Test batsman, who was dropped from the representative side a year ago, had a marvellous summer. Batting as always like a man late for his wedding, he amassed 713 runs, including two centuries and seven scores over 50. He was the most entertaining batsman in the country, and the most prolific.

The bowling revolved around Vaughan Brown's tidy off-spin, which brought 27 wickets, although Richard Hadlee, briefly, and Dayle Hadlee were important contributors.

Canterbury's winning margin would have been greater but for a controversial 16 points awarded to Central Districts for their contrived victory over Auckland. Rain restricted play to just three hours in the first two days. Auckland then declared their first innings at 37 for 3. Central's captain, Richard Hayward, the Hampshire professional, forfeited his team's second innings, leaving Auckland 188 to win in a late afternoon thrash. The rules clearly state that no collusion between captains is allowed, but despite overwhelming circumstantial evidence – both teams needed outright points to stay in the title hunt – Central retained their points.

Peter Visser achieved a hat-trick in the match, while Steve Maguiness of Wellington took another against Northern Districts, the 26th in New Zealand first-class cricket.

Of the other teams, Central were the best, combining a lively and varied bowling attack, spearheaded by the New Zealand representatives Derek Stirling and Gary Robertson, with a positive batting approach. Ronnie Hart and Scott Briasco set a series of records with their second-wicket partnership of 317 against Canterbury, including the all-time New Zealand mark of 301, set by C.S. Dempster and C.F.W. Allcott for New Zealand against Warwickshire 57 years ago.

Wellington finished third, but relied heavily on Bruce Edgar for runs and Maguiness for wickets. Auckland did not seem to get over their humiliation by Canterbury in the first round, although John Bracewell had a fine all-round season and only three players took more wickets than Martin Shedden. Otago had their moments, and Richard Webb and Neil Mallender formed a useful opening attack. But Northern Districts, one of the favourites for the trophy, failed dismally. Two first innings wins were a pathetic return for a team boasting five international players.

The Shell Cup one-day competition was won by Auckland, in a low-scoring final against Wellington.

Shell Trophy

Final Table	P	W	L	D	1st inngs points	Penalty points	Total points
CANTERBURY	8	4	1	3	16	-	64
Central Districts	8	3	1	4	20	2	54
Wellington	8	3	2	3	16	-	52
Auckland	8	2	4	2	16	-	40
Otago	8	1	2	5	20	-	32
Northern Districts	8	0	3	5	8	2	6

Leading First-Class Averages

Batting	Team	M	I	NO	HS	R	Avge	100	50
P.E. McEwan	Canterbury	8	12	0	155	713	59.41	2	5
M.D. Crowe	C. Districts	9	14	1	151	649	49.92	3	1
J.J. Crowe	Auckland	9	13	0	151	630	48.46	2	2
I.D.S. Smith	C. Districts	9	13	4	113*	390	43.33	1	1
P.S. Briasco	C. Districts	8	13	2	157	472	42.90	1	2
J.V. Coney	Wellington	8	13	1	174*	513	42.75	1	1
T.J. Franklin	Auckland	8	15	3	106	483	40.25	1	4
R.J. Hadlee	Canterbury	6	9	1	99	305	38.12	-	2
J.G. Bracewell	Auckland	7	10	2	104*	303	37.87	1	2
J.F. Reid	Auckland	6	9	1	106	293	36.62	1	1

Qualification: 8 innings.

Bowling	Team	O	M	R	W	Avge	Best	5wI
R.J. Hadlee	Canterbury	181.2	62	329	25	13.16	5-28	1
V.R. Brown	Canterbury	249.4	91	456	27	16.88	7-50	1
S.J. Maguiness	Wellington	255.1	82	546	26	21.00	5-72	1
B.P. Bracewell	N. Districts	170.2	44	444	21	21.14	4-23	-
G.K. Robertson	C. Districts	251.1	60	728	34	21.41	5-80	1
N.A. Mallender	Otago	177.4	35	517	24	21.54	4-53	-
J.G. Bracewell	Auckland	342.1	123	705	32	22.03	6-32	2
D.R. O'Sullivan	C. Districts	271	79	714	32	22.31	5-99	1
E.J. Chatfield	Wellington	337.4	115	676	29	23.31	5-81	1
R.J. Webb	Otago	231	52	677	29	23.34	6-20	2

Qualification: 20 wickets.

Shell Cup

Final = 17 (no play), 18 March at Wellington. AUCKLAND beat WELLINGTON by 5 wickets. Wellington 129-6 closed (35 overs) (G.B. Troup 3-26). Auckland 130-5 (33.3 overs) (M.J. Greatbatch 47; E.J. Gray 3-22). Match award: M.J. Greatbatch (47).

Cricket in India

It is but inevitable that after a full and hectic season involving nine Test matches and seven one-day internationals there should be a drop in the enthusiasm for more competitive cricket. The domestic fare was interesting, with Bombay carving out their 29th triumph in the 50-year-old Ranji Trophy Championship under the leadership of ace batsman Sunil Gavaskar. Days before, he had been nominated to lead India in the Asia Cup in Sharjah, with Kapil Dev having withdrawn on medical grounds.

Gavaskar, however, was not inclined to extend himself, missing the Duleep Trophy, in which the West Zone skipper, the bespectacled Anshuman Gaekwad, excelled. Gaekwad compiled combative centuries in the semi-final against South and in the final against North. He was the only batsman to weather the fire of young paceman Chetan Sharma, whose bowling won North, without Kapil, the trophy.

On generally docile pitches, batsmen held the upper hand all over the country. The talking point in the league stage of the Ranji Trophy was the elimination of the previous season's champions, Karnataka, because of the new points system. This involved bonus points for fast scoring and taking wickets. Karnataka planned poorly, and paid the penalty when Hyderabad, despite being beaten outright by Tamil Nadu, qualified for the knock-out phase of the Championship. Under the old system, Karnataka would have gone through.

Because the Indian under-25 team had a trip to Zimbabwe involving more limited-over games than anything else, the players in this age group concentrated on the one-day competitions such as the Deodhar Trophy, won by West Zone, and the Wills Trophy, won by the Board President's XI. There was a similar incentive for the senior players in the Asia Cup (April 6-13), and the national selectors concentrated on these tournaments.

Significant during the season was the batting form shown by Surinder Khanna, who accompanied Venkataraghavan's Indian team to England in 1979 and kept wicket in the World Cup. His blazing century against West Zone for North Zone in the Duleep Trophy final was a classic, and he never quite let up taking to pieces all bowling he encountered. His form gained him selection in the Indian squad to Sharjah. Ghulam Parkar, the opener who toured England in 1982, came back into contention with a string of fine scores in the one-day tournaments and also booked his seat to Sharjah.

A valiant double century by Orissa's Asjit Jayaprakasham could not prevent Rajasthan from qualifying further in the Ranji Trophy knock-out. The final between Bombay and Delhi saw Gavaskar make an unbeaten double century, while Vengsarkar, who missed the Duleep Trophy, finished the Ranji Trophy in glory, making three centuries in succession – in the quarter-final against Rajasthan, the semi-final against Haryana, and the final against Delhi.

Bombay v Delhi 1983-84 Ranji Trophy Final
Match drawn; Bombay won Ranji Trophy by leading on first innings
Played at Wankhede Stadium, Bombay, March 30, 31, April 1, 2, 3

Bombay

L.S. Rajput	c Khanna b Maninder	53	b Madan Lal	43
G.A. Parkar	c Khanna b Prabhakar	15	c Kirti Azad b Prabhakar	2
D.B. Vengsarkar	c Lamba b Rajinder	123	(6) c Khanna b Madan Lal	9
S.M. Patil	c Amarnath b Rajinder	31	(8) b Lamba	72
S.M. Gavaskar*	not out	206	c and b Madan Lal	19
R.J. Shastri	c Amarnath b Maninder	48	(7) c Madan Lal b Rajinder	56
C.S. Pandit†	c Khanna b Kirti Azad	71	(4) c Amarnath b Valson	14
R. Baindur	c Maninder b Valson	20	(3) retired hurt	1
S.V. Nayak	lbw b Valson	0	c Madan Lal b Rajinder	5
B.S. Sandhu	c Kirti Azad b Maninder	7	not out	7
R.R. Kulkarni	c Pillai b Maninder	1	lbw b Lamba	3
Penalty runs		24		4
Extras	(B 4, LB 8, W 1, NB 13)	26	(B 1, LB 1, NB 8)	10
		625	(9 wickets declared)	**245**

Delhi

M. Prabhakar	c and b Nayak	27	lbw b Pandit	122
R. Lamba	c Pandit b Kulkarni	0	c Pandit b Sandhu	7
Bhaskar Pillai	lbw b Sandhu	6	c Pandit b Kulkarni	0
M. Amarnath*	c Nayak b Shastri	49	not out	103
Kirti Azad	st Pandit b Nayak	106		
Madan Lal	c Pandit b Nayak	30		
S.C. Khanna†	c Baindur b Sandhu	42	not out	19
Rajinder Singh	c and b Shastri	8	(5) run out	7
R.S. Shukla	not out	36		
Maninder Singh	c Pandit b Kulkarni	3		
S. Valson	c Nayak b Kulkarni	0		
Penalty runs		16		
Extras	(B 1, LB 4, W 1, NB 4)	10	(B 5, NB 3)	8
		333	(4 wickets)	**266**

Delhi	O	M	R	W	O	M	R	W
Valson	27	3	108	2	11	0	40	1
Prabhakar	20	5	56	1	6	0	34	1
Madan Lal	22	2	74	0	15	2	35	3
Maninder	67.1	18	172	4	23	6	58	0
Amarnath	10	2	24	0				
Shukla	17	0	53	0				
Kirti Azad	20	1	63	1	10	2	37	0
Rajinder	17	2	39	2	9	2	26	2
Lamba					4.5	2	9	2

Bombay	O	M	R	W	O	M	R	W
Kulkarni	21.4	2	81	3	5	1	18	1
Sandhu	14	2	55	2	6	3	19	1
Nayak	25	2	98	3	9	1	32	0
Shastri	26	2	61	2	9	5	13	0
Baindur	6	1	17	0				
Parkar					4	0	19	0
Rajput					22	0	92	0
Gavaskar					8	0	42	0
Pandit					10	1	26	1

Fall of Wickets

Wkts	B 1st	D 1st	B 2nd	D 2nd
1st	33	3	6	27
2nd	121	15	31	32
3rd	229	47	77	216
4th	250	149	94	243
5th	356	220	95	
6th	492	233	211	
7th	563	244	230	
8th	570	294	230	
9th	583	315	241	
10th	601	317		

*Captain †Wicket-keeper

Leading Ranji Trophy Averages

Batting	Team	M	I	NO	HS	R	Avge	100	50
Arun Lal	Bengal	4	5	2	135	478	159.33	4	–
Subroto Das	Bihar	3	5	2	151	347	115.66	2	1
S.M. Gavaskar	Bombay	6	8	3	206*	541	108.20	2	2
K. Bramhabhatt	Gujarat	4	8	2	136	619	103.16	3	2
D.B. Vengsarkar	Bombay	5	8	2	149	570	95.00	3	2
Madan Lal	Delhi	6	7	2	157*	473	94.60	2	2
P. Roy	Bengal	4	6	2	206*	358	89.50	1	2
R.J. Shastri	Bombay	5	8	3	161*	433	86.60	1	2
A. Mitra	Bengal	4	4	0	137	302	75.50	1	2
P. Shastri	Rajasthan	5	9	1	131	568	71.00	2	3
A.V. Jayaprakash	Orissa	4	6	1	208*	354	70.80	1	1
S.C. Khanna	Delhi	8	13	3	126	685	68.50	2	4

Qualification: 300 runs.

Bowling	Team	O	M	R	W	Avge	5wI
R. Goel	Haryana	363.3	116	689	48	14.35	6
Madan Lal	Delhi	160	40	400	24	16.66	–
J. Prasad	Hyderabad	137.4	31	403	24	16.79	2
Arshad Ayub	Hyderabad	139.5	24	349	20	17.45	1
S. Venkataraghavan	Tamil Nadu	172.1	45	391	22	17.77	1
R. Bhat	Karnataka	187	29	549	27	20.33	3
R.C. Shukla	Delhi	151.4	24	415	20	20.75	–
Chetan Sharma	Haryana	152.5	15	592	28	21.14	3
R.S. Hans	Uttar Pradesh	204.2	57	445	21	21.19	2
D.R. Doshi	Bengal	200.4	41	626	29	21.58	3
M.V. Narasimha Rao	Hyderabad	126.5	9	451	20	22.55	3
B.S. Sandhu	Bombay	209.4	42	715	30	23.83	1

Qualification: 20 wickets.

Ranji Trophy Winners
29 Bombay
 4 Baroda, Holkar
 3 Delhi, Karnataka (formerly Mysore)
 2 Maharashtra
 1 Bengal, Hyderabad, Madras (now Tamil Nadu), Nawanagar, Western India States

Irani Cup
1, 2, 3, 4 September at Rajkot. KARNATAKA (1982-83 Ranji Trophy champions) beat REST OF INDIA on first innings. Karnataka 350 (M.R. Srinivas Prasad 117, B. Sudhakar Rao 67) and 405-9 dec (R.M.H. Binny 158, B. Sudhakar Rao 62, J. Abhiram 50; R.J. Shastri 4-101); Rest 185 (Yashpal Sharma 76; B. Vijaykrishna 5-63, R. Bhat 5-65) and 186-3 (M. Amarnath 66*, Yashpal Sharma 53*). Toss: Karnataka. Match Award: M.R. Srinivas Prasad (117, 20 and 0-12).

Duleep Trophy
Final: 17, 18, 19, 20 January at Cuttack. NORTH ZONE beat WEST ZONE on first innings. North 401 (S.C. Khanna 146, A. Malhotra 70; A. Patel 4-87) and 283-7 (M. Amarnath 79, Gursharan Singh 69), West 343 (A.D. Gaekwad 143, M.D. Gunjal 59; Chetan Sharma 7-83).

Cricket in Pakistan

In a season lasting no less than six months, a record number of 88 first-class matches were played during 1983-84. The BCCP Patron's Trophy, which had served as a qualifying tournament for the Quaid-e-Azam Trophy Championship since 1979-80, was again upgraded to the first-class level and no commercial or departmental teams were allowed to participate in it except the zonal and association teams. However, players employed by the various organizations could appear for the zone or associations of their birth or residence. The Patron's Trophy, which was contested by 19 teams divided into four groups, was won by Karachi Blues, who defeated Lahore City Whites by three wickets in a thrilling final.

The Punjab province had entered 10 teams – Multan, Bahawalpur, Sargodha, Rawalpindi, Gujranwala, Faisalabad, and four teams from Lahore. Sind province had five – three from Karachi and one each from Hyderabad and Sukkur. Peshawar, Hazara, and Dera Ismail Khan from North West Frontier, and Quetta, the only team from Baluchistan, made up the number.

Pakistan's major domestic tournament, the Quaid-e-Azam Trophy, was won by National Bank, last year's runners-up, who regained the title by outplaying the champions, United Bank. But the surprise of the competition was the HBFC (House Building Finance Corporation), who finished third in the table, above Habib Bank, PIA, and Railways. The tournament, which is played between the commercial organization teams, had three new sides in HBFC, PACO, and State Bank.

Sri Lanka's under-23 team, which visited Pakistan during the season, played three representative four-day games against Pakistan, losing the series 1-0. These matches enjoyed first-class status. Some of the players, such as Anil Dalpat, Shoaib Mohammad, and Rameez Raja, who performed well in the series, later became Test players, gaining their caps against England.

Another major championship in Pakistan cricket, the PACO Pentangular, was not played because of an overcrowded domestic schedule and also because of the non-availability of Pakistan's leading cricketers, who were already committed to take up their professional assignments abroad.

PIA's three-year run of success in the only one-day competition, the Wills Cup, was finally broken when Habib Bank, led by Test star Mohsin Khan, clinched the trophy for the first time.

HBFC and Lahore City's Saadat Ali was the most prolific batsman of the season. His aggregate of 1,649 runs broke a ten-year-old record set up by Zaheer Abbas (1,597). Saadat's 1,217 runs in the Quaid-e-Azam Trophy was another new record. Wicket-keeper Anil Dalpat, with 69 victims, and Ali Zia, with 25 catches, also set new records.

Quaid-e-Azam trophy

Final Table	P	W	L	D	Tied	Points
NATIONAL BANK	9	6	1	2	0	128
United Bank	9	5	3	1	0	103
HBFC	9	4	2	3	0	102
Habib Bank	9	3	0	6	0	98
PIA	9	3	1	5	0	94
Railways	9	3	3	2	1	84
Muslim Commercial Bank	9	2	2	4	1	83
PACO	9	2	4	3	0	75
Allied Bank	9	2	5	2	0	71
State Bank	9	0	9	0	0	38

Leading First-Class Averages

Batting	Team	M	I	NO	HS	R	Avge	100	50
Saadat Ali	LC/HBFC	14	27	1	208	1649	63.42	4	7
Arshad Pervez	Sg/HB	12	20	2	181	1051	58.38	4	5
Rizwan-uz-Zaman	K/PIA	11	18	3	189	864	57.60	2	5
Salim Malik	HB	6	11	0	132	607	55.18	2	3
Shafiq Ahmed	LC/UB	12	22	3	125	1007	53.00	2	6
Azhar Khan	G/HB	10	17	4	155	676	52.00	3	2
Munir-ul-Haq	HBFC	6	12	3	132*	461	51.22	2	2
Sajid Ali	K/NB	14	24	0	146	1180	49.16	3	7
Shaukat Mirza	K/PACO	11	22	4	137*	882	49.00	3	4
Sadiq Mohammad	UB	7	14	1	124	635	48.84	2	3
Shoaib Mohammad	K/PIA	15	26	3	151*	1118	48.60	5	4
Azmat Rana	MCB	7	12	1	172	531	48.27	1	4

Qualification: 8 innings

Bowling	Team	O	M	R	W	Avge	Best	5wI
Ehtesham-ud-Din	UB	175	42	494	33	14.96	8-61	1
Iqbal Qasim	NB	324.1	109	617	35	17.62	5-42	2
Naved Anjum	LC/Rwy	365	80	1022	55	18.58	6-67	3
Afzaal Butt	LC/NB	417.1	75	1362	66	20.63	7-104	7
Sikander Bakht	K/UB	273.1	35	952	46	20.69	6-44	4
Liaquat Ali	HB	304.2	50	897	41	21.87	7-62	2
Tauseef Ahmed	K/UB	526.1	149	1224	54	22.66	5-38	2
Zahid Ahmed	K/PIA	302.2	64	827	36	22.97	6-120	2
Jalal-ud-Din	K/AB	388	56	1339	58	23.08	6-49	5
Iqbal Sikander	K/PIA	399.4	91	1144	49	23.34	6-40	4
Ijaz Faqih	K/MCB	539.5	107	1258	53	23.73	6-42	5
Raess-ur-Rehman	AB	176.4	17	714	30	23.80	6-82	2

Qualification: 30 wickets

Teams: AB – Allied Bank; G – Gujranwala; HB – Habib Bank; HBFC – House Building Finance Corporation; K – Karachi; LC – Lahore City; MCB – Muslim Commercial Bank; NB – National Bank; PACO – Pakistan Automobile Corporation; PIA – Pakistan International Airlines; Rwy – Railways; Sg – Sargodha; UB – United Bank.

Cricket in Sri Lanka

Singhalese SC and Nondescript CC, the two clubs worst hit by Test calls, finished one-two in the 1983-84 Lakspray Trophy championship. SSC, who for half the final round were without their captain Duleep Mendis, Roy Dias, Sidath Wettimuny, Arjuna Ranatunga, Guy de Alwis, and Ashantha de Mel, won all their matches to finish over 18 points clear. NCC, also minus their captain, Ranjan Madugalle, as well as Ravi and Rumesh Ratnayake, lost their opening final-round game against SSC, but won the remaining seven matches and kept up a hot pace behind the champions.

SSC completed their matches one weekend ahead of the others and collected enough points to make the final weekend one of only academic interest. Mendis, the Sri Lanka captain, was in outstanding form, averaging 82.75 in the four matches he played. These included an innings of 172 against Tamil Union, which was the highest in the final round. In his absence, SSC were captained by Ranil Abeynaike, who played a few seasons in England for Minor County Bedfordshire.

SSC's young opener Kapila Jayasooriya, with 522 runs, had the highest final-round aggregate. This was in complete contrast to last season, when 10 batsmen passed the 500-run mark.

Asoka de Silva, NCC's right-arm leg-spinner, headed the bowling averages with 25 wickets at 12.52 apiece. SSC's key bowlers were Priyantha Udayaratne, a 20-year-old off-spinner with 33 wickets, and fast-medium bowler Saliya Ahangama, with 39 wickets – the highest in the final round.

Saracens SC, a club with a lot of experienced cricketers, were expected to be one of the teams to give SSC and NCC a run for the title. But they lost to both clubs, their only defeats in the final round. Against NCC, they suffered the humiliation of being dismissed for the lowest total – 76.

Colombo CC, the oldest cricket club in Sri Lanka, with a history dating back to 1863, and Tamil Union, last year's runners-up, performed in fits and starts and had an equal share of wins and losses. What each lacked was an experienced captain to guide a team brimming with talent.

Police SC, who finished at the bottom last season, improved by three places, while Nomads suffered the reverse and went through the final round without a single win. Air Force SC depended heavily on their captain, Test opener Susil Fernando, while Moors SC, despite the presence of former Cambridge University opener A.M. Mubarak, won only one match.

All the Lakspray Trophy final-round matches were played over three days – thus conforming to first-class standards. The preliminary-round matches, played over two days, saw 17 clubs participate in two groups.

Bloomfield C and AC, last season's Lakspray Trophy champions, surprisingly failed to qualify. They gained some consolation, however, by winning the Raheman Hathy Trophy – a two-day final-round tournament for clubs that failed to find a place in the premier tournament.

Lakspray Trophy Final Round 1983-84

Final Table

	P	W	WF	L	LF	NR	Pts
SINGHALESE SPORTS CLUB	8	3	5	0	0	0	100.940
Nondescript Cricket Club	8	2	5	0	1	0	82.095
Saracens Sports Club	8	2	4	0	2	0	75.565
Colombo Cricket Club	8	3	1	3	1	0	73.385
Tamil Union C&AC	8	3	1	0	4	0	67.935
Police Sports Club	8	0	3	1	4	0	41.675
Air Force Sports Club	8	0	3	3	2	0	40.505
Moors Sports Club	8	1	0	2	5	0	35.480
Nomads Sports Club	8	0	0	5	3	0	20.325

WF = won first innings, LF = lost first innings in drawn match; NR = no result

Leading Lakspray Trophy Averages

Batting (Minimum qualification: 250 runs)

	M	I	NO	HS	R	Avge	100	50
R.S. Madugalle (NCC)	4	5	3	82	294	147.00	0	4
L.R.D. Mendis (SSC)	4	4	0	172	331	82.75	2	1
S.A.R. Silva (NCC)	7	9	2	106*	491	70.14	2	2
S. Wettimuny (SSC)	5	7	0	83	366	52.28	0	3
R.G. Abeynaike (SSC)	8	11	2	105	430	47.77	1	3
K. Jayasooriya (SSC)	8	12	1	97	522	47.45	0	3

Bowling (Minimum qualification: 15 wickets)

	O	M	R	W	Avge	5wI	10wM
E.A.R. de Silva (NCC)	179	52	313	25	12.52	3	1
P. Udayaratne (SSC)	168.1	42	446	33	13.51	1	0
H.S.M. Pieris (Saracens)	140.2	32	375	27	13.88	1	1
S. Jeganathan (NCC)	151.4	50	274	19	14.42	1	0
R.G.C.E. Wijesuriya (CCC)	193.3	68	332	22	15.09	0	0
H. Musafer (CCC)	107.4	25	275	18	15.27	1	0

SST

Tours to England 1984

West Indies in England

West Indies' tour of 1984 had been expected to be successful and to provide them with a comfortable win over England. They had just beaten Australia easily in the Caribbean and nothing had happened to suggest that batsmen such as Vivian Richards and bowlers such as Michael Holding and Malcolm Marshall were in decline. The surprise, if any, was the completeness of their success and the all-round contribution to it.

Any thought that West Indies had been on top for so long that it was time they had the recession that comes to most countries from time to time was scotched. More realistic, perhaps, was the fact that the form of the many West Indian Test cricketers playing for English counties was known to be maintained – and the readiness of the counties to sign on young West Indians who would soon acquire priceless experience of English conditions. A West Indies side nowadays is probably less at home in the Caribbean, where there can be inter-island rivalries, than in England.

One unexpected feature of the huge West Indian success, with its 5-0 Test win and easy passage against the counties, was the relatively small contribution of Richards and the way in which less heralded players did their share. The side was soon being talked about, not without some reason, as probably the strongest West Indian side of all, certainly better balanced than those of recent years.

One of its two great strengths lay, as usual, in its fast bowling. But now there was also a high-class off-spinner (and close catcher) in the young giant Roger Harper, by no means new to English conditions for he toured with the Young West Indies side of 1982. Whereas recent sides had used the rather makeshift slow bowling of Richards as variety, if they needed it, this one had a bowler who would pose problems of his own.

The other strength was the depth of the batting. On several occasions the England bowlers began by taking four or five wickets cheaply, but there was still more batting left than any other country would be able to muster. Larry Gomes, with his early grounding with Middlesex, provided a stability that made the batting even more reliable. Unlike many other countries, West Indies did not bother about the shortage of runs in an opening batsman. They persevered with Desmond Haynes and in the last innings of the series he handsomely repaid the confidence.

On those occasions when a recovery was needed, Clive Lloyd was usually able to lead it, as so often in the past. But if he did fail, others stepped in to dowse English hopes and to strengthen the belief that this West Indian team had a versatility not even achieved by most of its highly successful predecessors.

Dujon is not one of the world's great wicket-keepers – anyhow, not at present. That did not matter in this context, for wickets were being taken with such frequency that a chance missed, if he did miss one, was unlikely to be costly. What did matter was that he was a batsman of quality who boosted an already strong middle order. England might well fear that his

101 at Old Trafford was only the first of many hundreds against them.

Of the late order batsmen, Marshall was not in his Hampshire form but, as he is now the main attacking bowler, consistency with the bat is less likely. But Baptiste, with many runs for Kent behind him, was a dangerous opponent to find still around when more eminent batsmen had gone. Harper showed himself to be a very capable batsman for a number nine, Holding's power and experience enabled him to destroy tiring bowling or hold an end, whichever was required, and no side expects to remove Joel Garner easily if he is required to stay. It was a side almost without a tail.

The reserve strength is simply illustrated in figures. Logie, though not required in Test matches, averaged 73 in other matches. And Winston Davis, when he played at Old Trafford instead of the injured Marshall, not only maintained the hostility of the bowling but made 77 as a nightwatchman.

The only distasteful feature of the tour was the excessive use of the bouncer, especially against lower-order batsmen ill-equipped to defend themselves. The defence will be that the umpires in their interpretation of the law of unfair play allowed it, but it did not make for attractive watching and one heard of spectators being kept away by it. It certainly seemed a pity that bowlers of such pace and talent should need to resort to short bowling when they were good enough to prosper by attacking the stumps.

Of the bowlers, Marshall confirmed his position at the moment as the fastest and most menacing. His skidding trajectory was seemingly hard to focus and in sharp contrast to the steeper bounce of Joel Garner, obtained from an arm nearly a foot higher than Marshall's.

Holding showed in the last Test at the Oval, where once he took 14 wickets in a Test match by bowling a full length on a slow pitch, that off his full run he was still as fast as any. But for most of the tour he was off a shorter run, content to move the ball about and vary his pace with a control that gave the batsmen no rest. Baptiste's contribution with the ball as a stock fast-medium bowler was a great help to the team's overall performance as providing variation from sheer pace with a method well suited to most English conditions.

It was a tour which, despite the forthcoming retirement of Clive Lloyd, gave no hint of any weakening in West Indian supremacy but rather of an indefinite prolongation of it.

First Test: Edgbaston, June 14, 15, 16, 18.
West Indies won by an innings and 180 runs.

Very little went right for England throughout the first Test and, in settled weather, it was always certain that nothing would save them from a heavy defeat. West Indies outplayed them and won soon after lunch on the fourth day.

England's limitations and West Indies' strengths were well known and were quickly demonstrated on the first morning when England were reduced to 49 for 4. It was said subsequently that Gower should have put West Indies in, but the slight moisture in the pitch was scarcely likely to have stopped West Indies from making a big score.

The 49 for 4 was in effect 49 for 5, for Andy Lloyd, twisting away from a shortish ball from Marshall which rose less than he expected, had been hit on the side of the head and had to retire. It was soon learnt that he would take no further part, indeed would be in hospital for a week. Marshall was not at his most accurate, but Garner bowled superbly throughout the match, and Holding, at reduced pace, also gave the batsmen little rest.

If Botham had been caught at third slip before scoring – he was also bowled by a no-ball – England would never have reached 191. But Botham for a time exploited his luck with an ideal partner in Downton, who played the fast bowlers soundly and with great composure. This made all the more undesirable Botham's charge down the pitch at the off-spin of Harper almost before the ball left the bowler's hand. A skier to mid-off ended the seventh wicket stand of 65. Downton was last out for a stoutly made 33.

That evening, Willis brought the ball back twice in the same over to have Greenidge and Haynes lbw. But West Indies' modest start of 53 for 2 was soon left far behind next day when Richards, though unwell, made 117, Gomes batted nearly all day for 143, Clive Lloyd played at his best, and West Indies, having scored at over four runs an over, finished at 421 for 7.

They had lost three wickets for three runs just before the close but that again was no augury of relief for England. On the Saturday morning, Baptiste and Holding flogged the England bowlers at will, another 185 were added, and England went in soon after lunch 415 behind.

They had little for which to hope and, with one exception, little to offer. The exception was Downton who, opening the innings in place of Lloyd, again batted with resolution and good sense. He was still there at the end of Saturday's play when at 112 for 4 – Garner 3 for 22 – England were hopelessly placed. Botham had again been Downton's most effective partner – 62 they added this time – but he was soon out on the Monday morning. When Downton's sturdy resistance ended at last after he had batted for four and three-quarter hours, Pringle played with some enterprise and Willis swung the bat for a few minutes. But nothing happened to make this look anything but one of West Indies' most conclusive victories.

WEST INDIES IN ENGLAND 1984

ENGLAND 1ST INNINGS v. WEST INDIES at EDGBASTON, BIRMINGHAM (1ST TEST) on 14, 15, 16, 18 JUNE 1984. TOSS: ENGLAND

IN	OUT	MINS	No.	BATSMAN	HOW OUT	BOWLER	RUNS	WKT	TOTAL	6s	4s	BALLS	NOTES ON DISMISSAL
11.00	11.07	7	1	G. FOWLER	C' DUJON	GARNER	0	1	1	.	.	9	Vicious lifter - simple catch off glove
11.00	11.33	33	2	T. A. LLOYD	RETIRED HURT		10	(2)	20	.	1	17	Ducked into lifting ball - hit on side of helmet, bowled by Marshall. Hospitalised - vision blurred - cut above right temple.
11.09	11.15	6	3	D. W. RANDALL	BOWLED	GARNER	0	2	5	.	.	3	Played on - middled back foot defensive stroke rebounded
11.17	12.30	73	4	D. I. GOWER *	C' HARPER	HOLDING	10	4	49	.	1	49	3rd slip - cut at wide long hop.
11.35	12.17	42	5	A. J. LAMB	C' LLOYD	BAPTISTE	15	3	45	.	2	32	Edged low to 1st slip. Excellent catch - dived forward.
12.19	3.23	144	6	I. T. BOTHAM	C' GARNER	HARPER	64	7	168	.	10	82	Mishmed lofted drive - skier to mid-off. (HIS HS v. WEST INDIES)
12.32	1.55	43	7	G. MILLER	C' DUJON	GARNER	22	5	89	.	4	43	Low right-handed catch - very well-judged - defensive stroke.
1.57	2.10	13	8	D. R. PRINGLE	C' DUJON	HOLDING	4	6	103	.	.	7	Back defensive stroke - edged lifting off-side ball.
2.11	4.22	110	9	P. R. DOWNTON†	LBW	GARNER	33	9	191	.	3	101	HS in TESTS. Played back - beaten by breakback.
3.25	3.41	16	10	N. G. B. COOK	C' LLOYD	MARSHALL	2	8	173	.	.	15	Edged defensively to 1st slip - held at third attempt.
4.02	(4.22)	20	11	R. G. D. WILLIS	NOT OUT		10			.	1	12	(800 TEST MATCH RUNS when 3)
				EXTRAS	b 8 lb 5	w - nb 8	21						53* not out (world Test record)
				TOTAL	(59.3 OVERS, 261 MINUTES)		191						all out at 4.22 pm on 1st day.

*CAPTAIN †WICKET-KEEPER

13 OVERS 4 BALLS / HOUR
3.21 RUNS / OVER
52 RUNS / 100 BALLS

BOWLER	O	M	R	W	nb	HRS	OVERS	RUNS
MARSHALL	14	4	37	1	4	1	12	39
GARNER	14.3	2	53	4	7	2	14	34
HOLDING	16	4	44	2	.	3	14	66
BAPTISTE	11	3	28	1	2	4	14	34
HARPER	4	1	8	1	-			
	59.3	14	191	9				

	RUNS	MINS	OVERS	LAST 50 (in mins)
	50	94	19.3	94
	100	148	32.1	54
	150	192	43.0	44

LUNCH: 73-4 BOTHAM 12* (41 min.) MILLER 12* (28 min.)
OFF 26 OVERS IN 120 MINUTES

TEA: 172-8 DOWNTON 25* (90 min.)
OFF 54.3 OVERS IN 241 MINUTES

WKT	PARTNERSHIP		RUNS	MINS
1st	Fowler	Lloyd	1	7
2nd	Lloyd	Randall	4	6
3rd	Lloyd Lamb	Gower	15* 25	33 42
4th	Gower	Botham	4	11
5th	Botham	Miller	40	43
6th	Botham	Pringle	14	13
7th	Botham	Downton	65	72
8th	Downton	Cook	5	16
9th	Downton	Willis	18	20
10th			10.1	

© BILL FRINDALL 1984

106 WEST INDIES IN ENGLAND 1984

WEST INDIES 1st INNINGS — IN REPLY TO ENGLAND'S 191 ALL OUT

IN	OUT	MINS	No.	BATSMAN	HOW OUT	BOWLER	RUNS	WKT	TOTAL	6s	4s	BALLS	NOTES ON DISMISSAL
4.36	5.28	52	1	C.G. GREENIDGE	LBW	WILLIS	19	2	35	.	3	47	Played back - sharp breakback.
4.36	5.24	48	2	D.L. HAYNES	LBW	WILLIS	8	1	34	.	1	24	Played back - sharp breakback. (2nd off no ball previous ball)
5.26	5.49	380	3	H.A. GOMES	c Miller	PRINGLE	143	5	418	.	16	279	(6th in TESTS; (1st v ENGLAND. HS in TESTS. Edged to 1st slip
5.30	2.35	204	4	I.V.A. RICHARDS	c Randall	COOK	117	3	241	1	17	154	5000 runs when 13. (1st in TESTS. (1st v ENGLAND. Drove to mid-off
2.37	4.03	64	5	P.J. DUJON †	c Gower	MILLER	23	4	294	.	2	51	Edged off-break via pad to silly-point.
4.05	5.53	108	6	C.H. LLOYD *	c Pringle	BOTHAM	71	6	418	.	8	89	Edged outswinger (from round the wicket) to 1st slip
5.51	5.59	8	7	M.D. MARSHALL	LBW	PRINGLE	2	7	421	.	.	5	Hit across line. Slower ball.
5.55	11.40	44	8	R.A. HARPER	BOWLED	PRINGLE	14	8	455	.	3	31	Missed lofted straight drive.
11.00	(2.18)	161	9	E.A.E. BAPTISTE	NOT OUT		87			.	11	131	HS = TESTS.
11.42	2.13	114	10	M.A. HOLDING	c Willis	PRINGLE	69	9	605	4	8	80	HS in TESTS. Hooked bouncer to long-leg. 50 off 43 balls.
2.15	2.18	3	11	J. GARNER	c Lamb	PRINGLE	0	10	606	.	.	6	Edged low to 3rd slip
				EXTRAS	b 6 lb 17 w 2 nb 28		53			5	69*	897 balls (including 39 no balls)

* CAPTAIN † WICKET-KEEPER

TOTAL (143 OVERS, 601 MINUTES) 606 all out at 2:18 pm 3rd day

(LEAD: 415)

	RUNS	MINS	OVERS	LAST 50 (in mins)
	50	69	13.3	69
	100	131	26.5	62
	150	193	41.5	62
	200	229	52.3	36
	250	271	62.3	42
	300	332	78.1	61
	350	369	88.2	37
	400	410	97.1	41
	450	475	112.0	65
	500	518	121.4	43
	550	543	128.1	25
	600	590	140.3	47

STUMPS: 53-2 (1st day) OFF 17 OVERS IN 84 MINUTES GOMES 4* RICHARDS 14* (34 min / 30 min)

LUNCH: 159-2 OFF 45 OVERS IN 204 MINUTES GOMES 46* (154 min) RICHARDS 60* (150 min)

TEA: 293-3 OFF 76 OVERS IN 323 MINUTES GOMES 102* (273 min) DUJON 23* (63 min)

STUMPS: 421-7 103.3 OVERS IN 440 MIN HARPER 0* (4 min)

LUNCH: 578-8 OFF 133 OVERS IN 563 MINUTES BAPTISTE 72* (123 min) HOLDING 60* (81 min)

BOWLER	O	M	R	W	HRS	OVERS	RUNS
WILLIS	25	3	108	2	2½	1	12	41
BOTHAM	34	7	127	1	-	2	12	52
PRINGLE	31	5	108	5	1½	3	14	48
COOK	38	6	127	1	-	4	17	70
MILLER	15	1	83	1		5	16	69
			55			6	16	61
	143	22	606	10		7	12	67
						8	14	47
						9	14	89
						10	16	62

2nd NEW BALL taken at 4.36pm 2nd day
- WEST INDIES 341-4 after 86 overs

© BILL FRINDALL 1984

14 OVERS 1 BALL/HOUR
4.24 RUNS/OVER
68 RUNS/100 BALLS

WKT	PARTNERSHIP		RUNS	MINS
1st	Greenidge	Haynes	34	48
2nd	Greenidge	Gomes	1	2
3rd	Gomes	Richards	206	204
4th	Gomes	Dujon	53	64
5th	Gomes	Lloyd	124	104
6th	Lloyd	Marshall	0	2
7th	Marshall	Harper	3	4
8th	Harper	Baptiste	34	40
9th*	Baptiste	Holding	150	114
10th	Baptiste	Garner	1	3

* WEST INDIES 9th WKT RECORD v ENGLAND.

WEST INDIES IN ENGLAND 1984

ENGLAND 2ND INNINGS — 415 BEHIND ON FIRST INNINGS

IN	OUT	MINS	No.	BATSMAN	HOW OUT	BOWLER	RUNS	WKT	TOTAL	6s	4s	BALLS	NOTES ON DISMISSAL
2·32	3·18	46	1	G. Fowler	LBW	Garner	7	1	17	·	·	40	Late on stroke – shuffled across stumps.
2·32	12·29	276	2	P.R. Downton †	c' Greenidge	Harper	56	7	181	·	3	187	HS IN TESTS Edged off-break via pad to silly point.
3·20	3·28	8	3	D.W. Randall	c' Lloyd	Garner	1	2	21	·	·	9	Top-edged cut to 1st slip.
3·30	4·07	16	4	D.I. Gower *	c' Dujon	Garner	7	3	37	·	1	17	Top-edged cut to 'keeper.
4·09	4·58	49	5	A.J. Lamb	c' Richards	Marshall	13	4	65	·	1	32	Edged backfoot offside force to 2nd slip. Misjudged bounce.
5·00	11·20	80	6	I.T. Botham	LBW	Garner	38	5	127	1	4	66	Beaten by breakback that kept low.
11·22	11·34	12	7	G. Miller	c' Harper	Marshall	11	6	138	·	1	10	Gloved bouncer via helmet to 3rd slip – simple catch.
11·36	(1·56)	101	8	D.R. Pringle	NOT OUT		46			·	5	88	–
12·31	12·47	16	9	N.G.B. Cook	RUN OUT (GOMES)		9	8	193	·	1	12	Backed up – failed to regain ground. – direct throw from mid-on.
12·49	1·56	28	10	R.G.D. Willis	c' Dujon	Garner	22	9	235	·	3	13	Followed offside ball.
		–	11	T.A. Lloyd	ABSENT HURT		–			·	·	·	Detained in hospital with blurred vision in right eye.
				EXTRAS	b 1 lb 5 w 4 nb 10		20				1⁶	19⁴	474 balls (including 13 no balls)
				TOTAL	(76·5 OVERS, 324 MINUTES)		235	all out at 1·56 pm on 4th day

* CAPTAIN   † WICKET-KEEPER

14 OVERS / HOUR
3·06 RUNS / OVER
50 RUNS / 100 BALLS

BOWLER	O	M	R	W	HRS	OVERS	RUNS
Marshall	23	7	65	2	¾	1	14	27
Garner	23·5	7	55	5	¾	2	14	37
Holding	12	3	29	0	¾	3	13	40
Harper	13	3	48	1	–	4	14	42
Baptiste	5	1	18	0	¾	5	15	49
			20	1				
	76·5	21	235	9				

	RUNS	MINS	OVERS	LAST 50 (in mins)
	50	89	20·3	89
	100	171	39·2	82
	150	238	55·2	67
	200	300	70·3	62

WKT	PARTNERSHIP			RUNS	MINS
1st	Fowler	Downton		17	46
2nd	Downton	Randall		4	8
3rd	Downton	Gower		16	16
4th	Downton	Lamb		28	49
5th	Downton	Botham		62	80
6th	Downton	Miller		11	12
7th	Downton	Pringle		43	53
8th	Pringle	Cook		12	16
9th	Pringle	Willis		42	28
–					235

TEA: 32-2 [16 OVERS / 68 MIN.]   DOWNTON 12" (68 min) / GOWER 8" (10 min)

STUMPS: 112-4 [43 OVERS / 187 MIN.] (3RD DAY) 303 BEHIND   DOWNTON 24" (187 min) / BOTHAM 30" (60 min)

LUNCH: 221-8 [73 OVERS / 309 MIN]   PRINGLE 35" (86 min) / WILLIS 19" (13 min)
194 BEHIND

WEST INDIES WON BY INNINGS & 180 RUNS
(ONLY THE SECOND ENGLAND DEFEAT AT EDGBASTON)

MAN OF THE MATCH: H.A. GOMES
(Adjudicator: F.S. Trueman)

TOTAL TIME LOST: NIL

© Bill Frindall 1984

Second Test: Lord's, June 28, 29, 30, July 2, 3.
West Indies won by nine wickets.

This was a match that England need not have lost, for they led on first innings and, for much of the fourth day, seemed to be building a position that would, at worst, make them safe from defeat.

West Indies put England in on the first day, when, despite stoppages for drizzle and bad light, England's left-handed opening pair of Fowler and, in his first Test, Broad made 101 together. Next day Fowler went on to make 106, but 286 was a disappointing total after the score had once stood at 183 for 2.

Marshall, from the Nursery End, had taken six wickets, and from the same end Botham soon had three West Indian batsmen out for 35. Richards and Lloyd took the score to 119 that evening, but next day Botham, moving the ball both in the air and off the pitch and bowling with much of his old rhythm, worked steadily through the West Indian batting so that England batted again in mid-afternoon with a 41-run lead. When they lost three wickets for 36 to Garner and Small, their slight advantage had disappeared, but Gatting brought a new confidence into the batting until for the second time in the match he was lbw playing no stroke to Marshall.

From 88 for 4, Lamb and Botham took the score briskly on to 114 on the Saturday evening and, despite the loss of nearly all Monday morning's play through light rain, to 216 before Botham was fifth out. For once, the West Indian attack, which in this match was short of the injured Holding, was being made to look ordinary, and Lamb passed 100 going well. This made all the more inexplicable his decision to go off early in the extra hour which had been added on for the earlier stoppage. Marshall had just come on and bowled him one bouncer, but the light was not desperately bad, the initiative was with the batsmen, and the bowlers were tired. England, 328 ahead with three wickets left, might have hoped for 40 more runs, which would enable them to declare sometime the next morning, leaving West Indies needing nearly 400.

They did declare on the last morning after losing two wickets, including Lamb's, to fresh bowlers in the first 20 minutes. This left West Indies needing 342 in nearly six hours at the prevailing over-rate. For a side of their great batting strength operating on a predictably innocuous Lord's last-day pitch against ineffectual bowling, this was an easy task unless something went strangely wrong.

Very little did go wrong for them. Greenidge was in such fluent form that the score was already 57 when Haynes was run out by Lamb. Greenidge, when 29, had been caught off a no-ball from Willis but was 110 before he gave his first genuine chance. This was missed, as was one when Gomes was 5.

But these were rare moments of uncertainty as Greenidge, with active support from Gomes, maintained a pace which meant that there was never a need for risks to be taken. Nor were Richards, Lloyd, and others required. West Indies won with nearly 12 overs to spare, Greenidge having rattled up 214, the third highest Test score ever made at Lord's, in only 66.1 overs.

WEST INDIES IN ENGLAND 1984

ENGLAND 1st INNINGS v. WEST INDIES (2ND TEST) AT LORD'S, LONDON ON 28, 29, 30 JUNE, 2, 3 JULY, 1984.

TOSS: WEST INDIES

IN	OUT	MINS	No.	BATSMAN	HOW OUT	BOWLER	RUNS	WKT	TOTAL	6s	4s	BALLS	NOTES ON DISMISSAL
11.03	12.45	366	1	G. FOWLER	c† HARPER	BAPTISTE	106	5	243	.	13	259	H.S. in TESTS [2nd] Edged drive to 2nd slip
11.03	5.00	156	2	B.C. BROAD	c† DUJON	MARSHALL	55	1	101	.	9	115	Leg-glanced short ball – excellent leg-side catch.
5.02	5.14	12	3	D.I. GOWER *	LBW	MARSHALL	3	2	106	.	.	9	Played back – beaten by pace – breakback.
5.16	11.20	109	4	A.J. LAMB	LBW	MARSHALL	23	3	183	.	3	77	Played back – fast ball kept low.
11.22	11.30	8	5	M.W. GATTING	LBW	MARSHALL	1	4	185	.	.	7	Padded up to ball on off stump.
11.33	12.58	85	6	I.T. BOTHAM	c† RICHARDS	BAPTISTE	30	6	248	.	4	66	Square gully – ball 'popped' – off shoulder of bat.
12.48	(3.10)	97	7	P.R. DOWNTON †	NOT OUT		23			.	3	62	
1.43	1.54	11	8	G. MILLER	RUN OUT (BAPTISTE)		0	7	251	.	.	6	Beaten by astonishing throw from deep fine leg – bowler's end middle stump
1.56	2.15	19	9	D.R. PRINGLE	LBW	GARNER	2	8	255	.	.	13	Padded up to break back that would have hit middle & off
2.17	2.41	24	10	N.A. FOSTER	c† HARPER	MARSHALL	6	9	264	.	.	24	Edged push to 3rd slip.
2.43	3.10	27	11	R.G.D. WILLIS	BOWLED	MARSHALL	2	10	286	.	.	14	Late on stroke.
				EXTRAS	b 4 lb 14	w 2 nb 15	35			0 32† 652 balls (including 17 no balls)			
				TOTAL	(105.5 OVERS; 466 MINUTES)		286		all out at 3.10 pm on second day.				

* CAPTAIN † WICKET-KEEPER

13 OVERS 4 BALLS / HOUR
2.70 RUNS / OVER
44 RUNS / 100 BALLS

	RUNS	MINS	OVERS	LAST 50 (in mins)
	50	69	17.2	69
	100	147	35.0	78
	150	233	54.0	86
	200	316	73.0	83
	250	388	89.3	72

WKT	PARTNERSHIP		RUNS	MINS
1st	Fowler	Broad	101	156
2nd	Fowler	Gower	5	12
3rd	Fowler	Lamb	77	109
4th	Fowler	Gatting	2	8
5th	Fowler	Botham	58	73
6th	Botham	Downton	5	10
7th	Downton	Miller	3	11
8th	Downton	Pringle	4	19
9th	Downton	Foster	9	24
10th	Downton	Willis	22	27
			286	

LUNCH: 46-0 [16 OVERS] FOWLER 11* BROAD 29*
BAD LIGHT, RAIN STOPPED PLAY 11:55 TO 12:50 PM (55 MIN. LOST) (63 MIN.)

TEA: 100-0 [36 OVERS] FOWLER 30* BROAD 54*
BAD LIGHT & RAIN STOPPED PLAY 3:15 TO 3:37 PM (62 MIN. LOST) (151 MIN.)

STUMPS: 167-2 [61 OVERS] FOWLER 76 (NO) LAMB 13 (96)
1ST DAY – NETT TIME LOST 96 MIN (262 MIN.)

LUNCH: 248-6 87 OVERS 379 MINUTES DOWNTON 0* (10 MIN)

MARSHALL TOOK FIVE WICKETS IN A TEST INNINGS FOR THE SIXTH TIME (FIFTH IN LAST EIGHT MATCHES).

BOWLER	O	M	R	W	nb/w	HRS	OVERS	RUNS
GARNER	32	10	67	1	2/-	1	15	44
SMALL	9	0	38	0		2	13	42
MARSHALL	36.5	10	85	6	9/-	3	13	20
BAPTISTE	20	6	36	2	4/-	4	14	46
HARPER	8	0	25	0		5	14	35
			35	1		6	14	52
	105.5	26	286	10		7	13	17

2ND NEW BALL TAKEN AT 2:10 PM 2ND DAY.
ENGLAND 253-7 AFTER 93.1 OVERS.

© BILL FRINDALL 1984

WEST INDIES 1st INNINGS

IN REPLY TO ENGLAND'S 286 ALL OUT

IN	OUT	MINS	No.	BATSMAN	HOW OUT	BOWLER	RUNS	WKT	TOTAL	6s	4s	BALLS	NOTES ON DISMISSAL
3·24	3·29	5	1	C.G. GREENIDGE	C* MILLER	BOTHAM	1	1	1	·	·	7	Edged outswinger low to 2nd slip. Superb falling catch.
3·24	3·42	18	2	D.L. HAYNES	LBW	BOTHAM	12	2	18	·	2	12	Played back - hit on back leg by breakback.
3·31	4·25	35	3	H.A. GOMES	C* GATTING	BOTHAM	10	3	35	·	2	24	Edged via pad to forward short leg - dived forward (right-hand ct.)
4·01	11·33	153	4	I.V.A. RICHARDS	LBW	BOTHAM	72	4	138	·	11	94	Beaten by breakback.
4·27	12·24	178	5	C.H. LLOYD *	LBW	BOTHAM	39	5	173	·	6	129	7th to 7000 RUNS when 25. Missed 7 off 59 balls on 3rd morning.
11·35	11·46	11	6	P.J. DUJON †	C* FOWLER	BOTHAM	8	6	147	·	1	8	Top-edged hook - skier to mid-wicket.
11·48	1·43	75	7	M.D. MARSHALL	C* PRINGLE	WILLIS	29	7	213	1	4	39	Edged lifting ball to 1st slip.
12·26	2·25	79	8	E.A.E. BAPTISTE	C* DOWNTON	WILLIS	44	8	241	·	7	56	Edged low to keeper's right.
1·45	2·01	16	9	R.A. HARPER	C* GATTING	BOTHAM	8	9	231	·	1	12	Drove half-volley low to cover.
2·03	2·32	29	10	J. GARNER	C* DOWNTON	BOTHAM	6	10	245	·	·	19	Edged low to keeper's right.
2·27	(2·32)	5	11	M.A. SMALL	NOT OUT		3			·	·	3	First innings in Tests.
				EXTRAS	b - lb 5	w 1 nb 7	13			1b 33⁴	4s	403 balls (including 9 no balls)	

TOTAL (65.4 OVERS; 310 MINUTES) **245** ALL OUT AT 2:32 pm on third day.

12 OVERS 4 BALLS/HOUR
3·73 RUNS/OVER
61 RUNS/100 BALLS

BOWLER	O	M	R	W	w/w	HRS	OVERS	RUNS	RUNS	MINS	OVERS	LAST 50 (in mins)
WILLIS	19	5	48	2	4	1	12	41	50	75	15·4	75
BOTHAM	27·4	6	103	8	-1	2	13	59	100	119	24·5	44
PRINGLE	11	0	54	0	5	3	14	43	150	194	41·3	75
FOSTER	6	2	13	0	·	4	12	46	200	244	51·5	50
MILLER	2	0	14	0	·	5	13	52				
	65·4	13	245	10								

ENGLAND'S LEAD: 41 RUNS

TEA 18-2

GOMES 5* (11 minutes)
4 OVERS, 18 MINUTES.

STUMPS: 119-3 [30 OVERS] RICHARDS 6* (121')
(2nd DAY) 167 BEHIND [139 MIN] LLOYD 32* (95')

LUNCH: 213-6 [56 OVERS] MARSHALL 25* (74')
73 BEHIND [240 MIN] BAPTISTE 32* (36')

WKT	PARTNERSHIP		RUNS	MINS
1st	Greenidge	Haynes	1	5
2nd	Haynes	Gomes	17	18
3rd	Gomes	Richards	17	24
4th	Richards	Lloyd	103	127
5th	Lloyd	Dujon	9	11
6th	Lloyd	Marshall	26	36
7th	Marshall	Baptiste	40	37
8th	Baptiste	Harper	18	16
9th	Baptiste	Garner	10	22
10th	Garner	Small	4	5
			245	

* CAPTAIN † WICKET-KEEPER

© BILL FRINDALL 1984

WEST INDIES IN ENGLAND 1984

ENGLAND 2ND INNINGS — 41 RUNS AHEAD ON FIRST INNINGS

IN	OUT	MINS	No.	BATSMAN	HOW OUT	BOWLER	RUNS	WKT	TOTAL	6s	4s	BALLS	NOTES ON DISMISSAL
2.44	4.21	76	1	G. FOWLER	LBW	SMALL	11	3	36	.	2	53	Played back to ball that moved back sharply
2.44	2.53	9	2	B.C. BROAD	C' HARPER	GARNER	0	1	5	.	.	3	Edged ball that lifted and left him to 3rd slip
2.55	4.18	62	3	D.I. GOWER *	C' LLOYD	SMALL	21	2	33	.	2	42	Edged off-drive low to 1st slip — bat 'left' him.
4.20	11.10	360	4	A.J. LAMB	C' DUJON	MARSHALL	110	8	290	.	13	259	6th Test. Edged drive.
4.23	5.33	70	5	M.W. GATTING	LBW	MARSHALL	29	4	88	.	4	49	Padded up to straight ball for second time in match (3 lbws = 21 lbws)
5.36	3.56	165	6	I.T. BOTHAM	LBW	GARNER	81	5	216	1	9	111	(1000 runs when 62) 50 off 40 balls. Pushed forward – misjudged line
3.58	4.43	25	7	P.R. DOWNTON	LBW	SMALL	4	6	230	.	.	20	Yorked on foot by late inswinger
4.45	5.41	56	8	G. MILLER	BOWLED	HARPER	9	7	273	.	1	33	Beaten by off-spin – off stump hit.
5.43	11.19	40	9	D.R. PRINGLE	LBW	GARNER	8	9	300	.	1	26	Played back – beaten by breakback. 12th LBW - TEST MATCH RECORD
11.13	(11.19)	6	10	N.A. FOSTER	NOT OUT		9			.	2	4	—
			11	R.G.D. WILLIS	DID NOT BAT								
				EXTRAS	b 4 lb 7 w 1 nb 6		18					1h 34m	600 balls (including 9 no balls)

* CAPTAIN † WICKET-KEEPER

TOTAL (98.3 OVERS, 443 MINUTES) 300-9 DECLARED at 11.19 am on fifth day.

13 OVERS 2 BALLS / HOUR
3.05 RUNS / OVER
50 RUNS / 100 BALLS

BOWLER	O	M	R	W	HRS	OVERS	RUNS
GARNER	30.3	3	91	3	1	13	21
MARSHALL	22	6	85	2	2	13	49
SMALL	12	2	40	3	3	13	53
BAPTISTE	26	8	48	0	4	12	59
HARPER	8	1	18	1	5	14	28
			18		6	14	23
	98.3	20	300	9	7	14	50

© BILL FRINDALL 1984

(SETTING WEST INDIES 342 TO WIN IN 270 MINUTES PLUS 20 OVERS)

	RUNS	MINS	OVERS	LAST 50 (in minutes)
TEA: 20-1	50	91	19.3	91
STUMPS: 114-4 (3rd DAY) (155 AHEAD)	100	162	35.3	71
LUNCH: 144-4 (185 AHEAD)	150	208	45.0	46
TEA: 226-5 (267 AHEAD)	200	277	59.5	69
STUMPS: 287-7 (328 AHEAD)	250	375	83.5	98
	300	440	98.0	65

[12 OVERS] [56 MIN.] FOWLER 6* (56 min) GROWER 13* (45 min)
LAMB 30* (100 min) BOTHAM 17 (24 min) 38 OVERS; 175 MIN
LAMB 44 (86), BOTHAM 21* (64) 43.5 OVERS; 205 MIN 115 MIN LOST. RSP 12.30-2.05
[75 OVERS] LAMB 72* (256 min) [331 MIN] DOWNTON 1* (13 min.)
[95 OVERS] LAMB 109* (351 min) [416 MIN] PRINGLE 6* (23 min)

WKT	PARTNERSHIP		RUNS	MINS
1st	Fowler	Broad	5	9
2nd	Fowler	Gower	28	62
3rd	Fowler	Lamb	3	1
4th	Lamb	Gatting	52	70
5th	Lamb	Botham	128	165
6th	Lamb	Downton	14	25
7th	Lamb	Miller	43	56
8th	Lamb	Pringle	17	32
9th	Pringle	Foster	10	6
10th			(300)	

WEST INDIES — 2ND INNINGS

SET TO SCORE 342 RUNS IN A MINIMUM OF 328 MINUTES

IN	OUT	MINS	No.	BATSMAN	HOW OUT	BOWLER	RUNS	WKT TOTAL	6s	4s	BALLS	NOTES ON DISMISSAL
11:32	(5:31)	300	1	C.G. GREENIDGE	NOT OUT		214		2	29	241	HS in TESTS
11:32	12:34	62	2	D.L. HAYNES	RUN OUT (LAMB)		17	1	57	.	2	29	Attempted run to backward square leg - sent back - slipped
12:36	(5:31)	236	3	H.A. GOMES	NOT OUT		92		.	13	140	
			4	I.V.A. RICHARDS								
			5	C.H. LLOYD*								
			6	P.J. DUJON†		Did not bat						
			7	M.D. MARSHALL								
			8	E.A.E. BAPTISTE								
			9	R.A. HARPER								
			10	J. GARNER								
			11	M.A. SMALL								
				EXTRAS	b 4 lb 4 w - nb 13		21		2 6 4 44			
				TOTAL	(66.1 OVERS, 300 MINUTES)		344 – 1				410 balls (including 13 no balls)	

*CAPTAIN †WICKET-KEEPER

© BILL FRINDALL 1984

13 OVERS / HOUR
5:12 RUNS / OVER
84 RUNS / 100 BALLS

WKT	PARTNERSHIP		RUNS	MINS
1st	Greenidge	Haynes	57	62
2nd	Greenidge	Gomes	287*	236
				344

BOWLER	O	M	R	W	nb	HRS	OVERS	RUNS		RUNS	MINS	OVERS	LAST 50 (in mins)
WILLIS	15	5	48	0	9	1	14	57		50	54	12.3	54
BOTHAM	20.1	2	117	0	.	2	13	53		100	112	25.0	58
PRINGLE	8	0	44	0	4	3	12	80		150	149	33.1	37
FOSTER	12	0	69	0	.	4	13	66		200	199	42.3	50
MILLER	11	0	45	0	.	5	14	84		250	231	49.4	32
			21							300	271	58.4	40
	66.1	7	344	0									

LUNCH: 82 – 1 [20 OVERS] GREENIDGE 54*
                 [90 MIN] GOMES 4* (24)

TEA: 214 – 1 [45 OVERS] GREENIDGE 125' (210)
             [210 MIN] GOMES 52* (146)

WEST INDIES WON BY NINE WICKETS
WITH 11.5 OVERS TO SPARE

MEN OF THE MATCH: I.T. BOTHAM and
(FIRST JOINT AWARD) C.G. GREENIDGE
Adjudicator: T.G. EVANS

TOTAL TIME LOST: 3 HOURS 25 MIN (NET)

Third Test: Headingley, July 12, 13, 14, 16.
West Indies won by eight wickets

For two days England held their own in the third Test, though hopes were never high that this would last. The potential of West Indies was too great. Whereas they had the experienced Michael Holding fit again, England had brought in Paul Terry for his first Test, besides recalling Paul Allott and Nick Cook.

On a cloudy first morning, the West Indies bowling was soon without Malcolm Marshall, who broke his left thumb in two places while fielding in the slips. But the other bowlers moved the ball awkwardly off the pitch and England were soon 87 for 4, a state from which Allan Lamb, with his second hundred in successive Tests, lifted them up to 237 for 6, supported by Botham and Downton. Rain and bad light then ended play 40 minutes early.

Lamb did not add to his 100 next day and the innings ended for 270, but there was a point on the second evening when West Indies' score stood at 206 for 7. Willis for once had been hit to all parts, but Allott was accurate enough on a pitch of uneven bounce and movement to cause mistakes and in 20 overs took 5 for 42. As at Lord's, Gomes provided the most obdurate opposition, and next day developed an eighth-wicket stand with the aggressive Holding who made 54 off 52 balls. They put on 82. The score was 290 for 9 and Gomes was 94 when Marshall, who had previously been said to be out for 10 days, re-entered the fray, batting one-handed for long enough to allow the patient Gomes to add a second hundred to the one made at Lord's.

If Marshall could bat, it was then realized, he could certainly bowl and, having covered the white plaster with a darker bandage to avoid distracting the batsman, he bowled 22 overs for 38 runs and three wickets. With all their main batting gone, England, though they had been only 32 behind on first innings, had been reduced to 135 for 6, a third-wicket stand of 91 between Fowler and Gower providing the only hope of recovery after a start of 13 for 2. Fowler had been out to a return catch which Marshall dexterously took in the right hand using the left hand in support in case the ball tried to escape.

Downton had once again played the fast bowling with placid lack of concern and would have provided an ideal partner for any of the other batsmen who had established himself. But none did. Gower was out to the off-spinner Harper, who turned the ball enough on an always rather unpredictable pitch to provide a menacing alternative to the fast bowling.

On the Monday morning, Marshall quickly took the last four wickets, though Downton was only out when driving despairingly with the last man in.

West Indies needed only 128 to win. It was a target only two runs short of the one that Australia failed to reach in the memorable Headingley Test of 1981, but the circumstances were different. Willis was no longer a danger, Greenidge and Haynes gave West Indies a brisk and confident start of 106, and by early on the fourth afternoon of the Third Test England had lost the rubber.

114 WEST INDIES IN ENGLAND 1984

ENGLAND 1ST INNINGS v. WEST INDIES (3RD TEST) at HEADINGLEY, LEEDS on 12,13,14,16 JULY, 1984. TOSS: ENGLAND

IN	OUT	MINS	No.	BATSMAN	HOW OUT	BOWLER	RUNS	WKT	TOTAL	6s	4s	BALLS	NOTES ON DISMISSAL
11·00	11·36	36	1	G. FOWLER	LBW	GARNER	10	1	13	·	2	25	Misjudged line – padded up to ball that 'straightened'.
11·00	2·08	168	2	B.C. BROAD	C' LLOYD	HARPER	32	4	87	·	4	117	Edged backfoot square drive to 1st slip.
11·38	12·12	34	3	V.P. TERRY	C' HARPER	HOLDING	8	2	43	·	1	25	Edged outswinger low to 3rd slip's right.
12·14	12·30	16	4	D.I. GOWER *	LBW	GARNER	2	3	53	·	·	13	Played no stroke to ball that came back and kicked pad.
12·32	11·05	228	5	A.J. LAMB	BOWLED	HARPER	100	7	237	·	15	186	Off-break kept low – missed backfoot cover-drive.
2·10	3·26	76	6	I.T. BOTHAM	C' DUJON	BAPTISTE	45	5	172	1	7	61	Legside catch – followed short ball – ball hit gloves.
3·28	5·10	83	7	P.R. DOWNTON †	C' LLOYD	HARPER	17	6	236	·	2	54	Edged off-drive to 1st slip.
5·12	12·19	82	8	D.R. PRINGLE	C' HAYNES	HOLDING	19	10	270	·	3	74	HOLDING'S 200th TEST WICKET. Mishooked skier to mid-wicket.
11·06	11·24	18	9	P.J.W. ALLOTT	BOWLED	HOLDING	3	8	244	·	·	16	Off stump out – beaten by pace.
11·26	11·50	24	10	N.G.B. COOK	BOWLED	HOLDING	1	9	254	·	·	22	Beaten by outswinger that clipped off stump.
11·51	(12·18)	28	11	R.G.D. WILLIS	NOT OUT		4			·	·	13	54th 'not out' – world Test record extended.
				EXTRAS	b 4 lb 7 w – nb 18		29				1 6 34	606 balls (including 22 no balls)

* CAPTAIN   † WICKET-KEEPER

TOTAL (97·2 OVERS; 394 MINUTES) 270 all out at 12·19 pm second day.

14 OVERS 5 BALLS/HOUR
2·77 RUNS/OVER
45 RUNS/100 BALLS

	RUNS	MINS	OVERS	LAST 50 (in mins)
	50	85	20	85
	100	172	41·3	87
	150	212	51·5	40
	200	269	65·5	57
	250	349	85·4	80

LUNCH: 68-3 [28 OVERS / 120 MIN.]
TEA: 180-5 [59 OVERS / 240 MIN.]
STUMPS: 237-6 [77 OVERS / 315 MIN.] (1st DAY) BLSP at 5·15pm (46 lost)

BROAD 26" (100') 1" (2¾')
LAMB 60" (148')
DOWNTON 2' (12')
LAMB 100' (223')
PRINGLE 1' (3')

WKT	PARTNERSHIP		RUNS	MINS
1st	Fowler	Broad	13	36
2nd	Broad	Terry	30	34
3rd	Broad	Gower	10	16
4th	Broad	Lamb	34	56
5th	Lamb	Botham	85	76
6th	Lamb	Downton	64	83
7th	Lamb	Pringle	1	8
8th	Pringle	Allott	7	18
9th	Pringle	Cook	10	24
10th	Pringle	Willis	16	28
			270	

BOWLER	O	M	R	W	nb	HRS	OVERS	RUNS
GARNER	30	11	73	2	14	1	14	28
MARSHALL	6	4	6	0	1	2	14	40
HOLDING	29·2	8	70	4	4	3	15	40
BAPTISTE	13	1	45	1	·	4	16	72
HARPER	19	6	47	3	·	5	14	44
				29		6	15	29
	97·2	30	270	10				

2nd NEW BALL taken at 11·43 am 2nd day
- ENGLAND 253-8 off 88 overs.

© BILL FRINDALL 1984

WEST INDIES IN ENGLAND 1984

WEST INDIES 1ST INNINGS   IN REPLY TO ENGLAND'S 270 ALL OUT

IN	OUT	MINS	No.	BATSMAN	HOW OUT	BOWLER	RUNS	WKT	TOTAL	6s	4s	BALLS	NOTES ON DISMISSAL
12:31	12:56	25	1	C.G. GREENIDGE	c BOTHAM	WILLIS	10	1	16	.	2	23	Edged low to second slip.
12:31	2:06	55	2	D.L. HAYNES	BOWLED	ALLOTT	18	2	43	.	2	35	Bowled through gate attempting an on drive.
12:58	(12:58)	314	3	H.A. GOMES	NOT OUT		104	.	.	.	14	197	(7th in TESTS).
2:08	2:27	19	4	I.V.A. RICHARDS	c PRINGLE	ALLOTT	15	3	78	.	2	12	Mistimed on-drive — head-high catch to mid-on.
2:29	4:18	88	5	C.H. LLOYD *	c GOWER	COOK	48	4	148	.	7	75	Silly point catch — ball hit glove via pad.
4:20	5:20	60	6	P.J. DUJON †	LBW	ALLOTT	26	5	201	.	4	52	Hit across line (on drive) of full length ball.
5:22	5:29	7	7	E.A.E. BAPTISTE	c BROAD	ALLOTT	0	6	206	.	.	4	Drove wide half-volley to wide mid-off (2-handed catch to left)
5:31	5:32	1	8	R.A. HARPER	c DOWNTON	ALLOTT	0	7	206	.	.	2	Played inside straight ball — faint edge.
5:34	11:59	72	9	M.A. HOLDING	c ALLOTT	WILLIS	59	8	288	5	3	55	Hooked bouncer to long leg, well-judged catch.
12:01	12:08	7	10	J. GARNER	RUN OUT [TERRY/WILLIS]		0	9	290	.	.	1	Hesitated over second run to long-on (Gomes stroke).
12:10	12:58	16	11	M.D. MARSHALL	c BOTHAM	ALLOTT	4	10	302	.	1	8	Batted one-handed (right). Edged to 2nd slip.
				EXTRAS	b - lb 3	w - nb 15	18						

*CAPTAIN †WICKET-KEEPER

TOTAL (73.5 OVERS, 341 MINUTES)   302 all out at 12:58 pm on third day (LUNCH TAKEN).

5* 35* 464 balls (including 21 balls)

13 OVERS 0 BALLS/HOUR
4·09 RUNS/OVER
65 RUNS/100 BALLS

BOWLER	O	M	R	W	nb	HRS	OVERS	RUNS
WILLIS	18	1	123	2	11	1	13	47
ALLOTT	26.5	7	61	6	-	2	12	67
BOTHAM	7	0	45	0	-	3	15	43
PRINGLE	13	3	26	0	10	4	14	49
COOK	9	1	29	1	-	5	12	56
	73.5	12	302	10	18			

© BILL FRINDALL 1984

RUNS	MINS	OVERS	LAST 50 (in mins)
50	64	13.3	64
100	107	22.3	43
150	175	39.1	68
200	227	51.5	52
250	283	63.1	56
300	333	72.0	50

LUNCH: 19-1 [7 OVERS / 31 MIN.]
TEA: 138-3 [33 OVERS / 150 MIN.]
STUMPS: 239-7 [60 OVERS / 269 MIN.] (2ND DAY)

HAYNES 6* (31*)
GOMES 3* (4*)
GOMES 42* (23*)
LLOYD 46* (72*)
GOMES 75* (242*)
HOLDING 28* (27*)

WKT	PARTNERSHIP			RUNS	MINS
1st	Greenidge	Haynes		16	25
2nd	Haynes	Gomes		27	27
3rd	Gomes	Richards		35	19
4th	Gomes	Lloyd		70	88
5th	Gomes	Dujon		53	60
6th	Gomes	Baptiste		5	7
7th	Gomes	Harper		0	1
8th	Gomes	Holding		82	72
9th	Gomes	Garner		2	7
10th	Gomes	Marshall		12	16
				302	

116 WEST INDIES IN ENGLAND 1984

ENGLAND 2ND INNINGS
32 RUNS BEHIND ON FIRST INNINGS

IN	OUT	MINS	No.	BATSMAN	HOW OUT	BOWLER	RUNS	WKT	TOTAL	6s	4s	BALLS	NOTES ON DISMISSAL
1.40	4.52	160	1	G. FOWLER	c' AND BOWLED	MARSHALL	50	4	106	·	9	128	Held hard, waist-high catch two-handed.
1.40	1.51	11	2	B.C. BROAD	c' BAPTISTE	MARSHALL	2	1	10	·	·	9	Fended sharply lifting ball to backward square leg.
1.54	2.03	9	3	V.P. TERRY	LBW	GARNER	1	2	13	·	·	8	Missed push across line of straight full-length ball.
2.05	4.43	126	4	D.I. GOWER *	c' DUJON	HARPER	43	3	104	·	8	100	Pushed forward - edged off-break to 'keeper.
4.45	4.58	13	5	A.J. LAMB	LBW	MARSHALL	3	5	107	·	·	6	Hit on back leg. Late on break-back - through 'gate'.
4.54	5.57	63	6	I.T. BOTHAM	c' DUJON	MARSHALL	14	6	135	·	2	50	Offside edge - 'walked'.
5.00	11.30	92	7	P.R. DOWNTON †	c' DUJON	GARNER	27	10	159	·	4	67	Edged off-drive high to 'keeper.
5.59	11.09	12	8	N.G.B. COOK	c' LLOYD	MARSHALL	0	7	138	·	·	13	Tried to withdraw bat from outswinger. 1st slip - diving to right.
11.10	11.12	2	9	D.R. PRINGLE	LBW	MARSHALL	2	8	140	·	·	3	Beaten by break-back. Shuffled across stumps.
11.13	11.19	6	10	P.J.W. ALLOTT	LBW	MARSHALL	4	9	146	·	·	4	Played back to full-length low break-back.
11.21	(11.30)	9	11	R.G.D. WILLIS	NOT OUT		5			·	1	4	55m 'not out' - extended his world Test record.
				EXTRAS	b - 1b 6	w - nb 2	8			0	25	392 balls (including 2 no balls)	

*CAPTAIN †WICKET-KEEPER

TOTAL (65 OVERS, 260 MINUTES) 159 ALL OUT at 11.30 am on 4th day.

	RUNS	MINS	OVERS	LAST 50 (in mins)
	50	81	19.0	81
	100	135	34.4	54
	150	252	63.0	117

HRS	OVERS	RUNS	w
1	14	34	7
2	16	57	-
3	16	18	1
4	14	28	-

BOWLER	O	M	R	W	nb
MARSHALL	26	9	53	7	1
GARNER	16	7	37	2	-
HOLDING	7	1	31	0	1
HARPER	16	8	30	1	-
			8		
	65	25	159	10	

© BILL FRINDALL 1984

TEA: 85-2 [27 OVERS / 109 MIN]   FOWLER 37* (105) / GOWER 37* (84)

STUMPS: 135-6 [58 OVERS / 230 MIN]   DOWNTON 14* (62) / COOK 0* (3)
3RD DAY   103 AHEAD

4TH DAY: ENGLAND LOST LAST FOUR WICKETS for 24 runs in 30 minutes off 7 overs - Marshall's best analysis in Tests (today 4-0-15-4) - with his doubly-fractured left thumb encased in plaster.

15 OVERS 0 BALLS/HOUR
2.45 RUNS/OVER
41 RUNS/100 BALLS

WKT	PARTNERSHIP		RUNS	MINS
1st	Fowler	Broad	10	11
2nd	Fowler	Terry	3	9
3rd	Fowler	Gower	91	126
4th	Fowler	Lamb	2	7
5th	Lamb	Botham	1	4
6th	Botham	Downton	28	57
7th	Downton	Cook	3	12
8th	Downton	Pringle	2	2
9th	Downton	Allott	6	6
10th	Downton	Willis	13	9

WEST INDIES IN ENGLAND 1984

WEST INDIES 2ⁿᵈ INNINGS

REQUIRING 128 TO WIN IN A MINIMUM OF 680 MINUTES

IN	OUT	MINS	No.	BATSMAN	HOW OUT	BOWLER	RUNS	WKT TOTAL	6s	4s	BALLS	NOTES ON DISMISSAL
11.41	2.33	131	1	C.G. GREENIDGE	c⁺ TERRY	COOK	49	2 108	·	7	96	Edged via pad to forward short-leg – simple catch
11.41	2.25	123	2	D.L. HAYNES	c⁺ FOWLER	COOK	43	1 106	·	3	85	Edged on drive to extra-cover
2.27	(2.48)	21	3	H.A. GOMES	NOT OUT		2		·	·	11	
2.35	(2.48)	13	4	I.V.A. RICHARDS	NOT OUT		22		·	4	18	Made winning hit
			5	C.H. LLOYD*								
			6	P.J. DUJON†								
			7	E.A.E. BAPTISTE								
			8	R.A. HARPER	} Did not bat							
			9	M.A. HOLDING								
			10	J. GARNER								
			11	M.D. MARSHALL								
				EXTRAS	b – lb 2	w – nb 13	15		0	4	210 balls (including 15 no balls)	
				TOTAL	(32.3 OVERS, 146 MINUTES)		131-2					

*CAPTAIN †WICKET-KEEPER

13 OVERS 2 BALLS/HOUR
4.03 RUNS/OVER
62 RUNS/100 BALLS

WKT	PARTNERSHIP		RUNS	MINS
1ˢᵗ	Greenidge	Haynes	106	123
2ⁿᵈ	Greenidge	Gomes	2	6
3ʳᵈ	Gomes	Richards	23*	13
			131	

© BILL FRINDALL 1984

BOWLER	O	M	R	W	nb	HRS	OVERS	RUNS	RUNS	MINS	OVERS	LAST 50 (in mins)
WILLIS	8	1	40	0	10	1	12	50	50	59	11.5	59
ALLOTT	7	2	24	0	·	2	15	52	100	119	26.4	60
COOK	9	2	27	2	·							
PRINGLE	8.3	2	25	0	5							
			15									
	32.3	7	131	2								

LUNCH: 74-0 [15 OVERS / 79 MINUTES] [GREENIDGE 35* / HAYNES 23*]

WEST INDIES WON BY 8 WICKETS at 2.48 pm on the fourth day and so retaining the SIR FRANK WORRELL TROPHY

MAN OF THE MATCH: H.A. GOMES
Adjudicator: A.R. LEWIS

TOTAL TIME LOST: 1 HOUR 42 MINUTES

Fourth Test: Old Trafford, July 26, 27, 28, 30, 31.
West Indies won by an innings and 64 runs

West Indies went four up with an innings victory which was seldom in doubt after they had recovered from a start of 70 for 4 on the first day. The brown bare pitch promised to take spin earlier than it did, but in England's second innings the young off-spinner Roger Harper was able to wheel away for hours with much the same effect as another West Indian off-spinner, Lance Gibbs, did in two Old Trafford Test matches in the 1960s.

There was little in the pitch to justify West Indies' early losses. Haynes mishooked, and though Allott bowled well to remove Gomes, Richards, and Lloyd, three famous victims, in 13 balls, England knew only too well from past experience the depth of the West Indian batting. There was still Greenidge, and he batted through the day for 128, while Dujon played a fine innings of 101 in their fifth-wicket stand of 197, which ended just before the close.

England's performance was even more lacking in distinction next day, when between stoppages for rain Greenidge reached his second double hundred of the series and the nightwatchman Winston Davis made his highest first-class score of 77 with an ease that paid no compliments to an attack lacking the injured Willis. Davis's stand with Greenidge added 170, and at the end of the second day West Indies were all out for 500.

Pocock, on his return to Test cricket after an eight-year break, had bowled well to take four wickets, but this seemed to confirm that the West Indies fast bowlers would on this occasion have a powerful aide in Harper.

England started promisingly, Fowler and Broad making 90 for the first wicket. But once they were separated the innings went into a decline, accelerated by a ball that bounced less than expected and broke Terry's left arm. The bounce now was far from consistent.

On the Monday morning, Lamb played extremely well to reach 98, at which point the ninth and, he presumed, last wicket fell. However, after a pause, Terry appeared, not being required to take strike as the wicket had fallen to the last ball of an over. It was unclear whether Terry had come in to enable Lamb to reach his third hundred of the series or to try to stay while Lamb made the 23 runs still needed to avoid the follow-on. Lamb too appeared unsure and he took two runs off the last ball of the next over. It was then clear that Terry, one-handed, had no defence against Garner, and he was bowled second ball.

The second innings followed a predictable course and, though there was heavy rain during Monday night and though Gower showed improved form, West Indies had won by lunch on the fifth day.

WEST INDIES IN ENGLAND 1984

WEST INDIES 1ST INNINGS v. ENGLAND (4TH TEST) at OLD TRAFFORD, MANCHESTER on 26, 27, 28, 30, 31 JULY, 1984.

TOSS: WEST INDIES

IN	OUT	MINS	No.	BATSMAN	HOW OUT	BOWLER	RUNS	WKT	TOTAL	6s	4s	BALLS	NOTES ON DISMISSAL
11.00	6.30	588	1	C.G.GREENIDGE	c† DOWNTON	POCOCK	223	8	470		30	425	(11th in TESTS. (6th to score two 200s in a rubber.) HS in TEST. Edged cut. Pocock's SPmr.
11.00	11.12	12	2	D.L.HAYNES	c COWANS	BOTHAM	2	1	11			9	Hooked long-hop high to long-leg. Running catch.
11.15	12.23	68	3	H.A.GOMES	c BOTHAM	ALLOTT	30	2	60		5	59	Edged full-length offside ball low to 2nd slip.
12.25	12.28	3	4	I.V.A.RICHARDS	c† COOK	ALLOTT	1	3	62			3	Flicked full-length ball to mid-wicket.
12.30	12.45	15	5	C.H.LLOYD *	c† DOWNTON	ALLOTT	1	4	70			10	Edged push at off-stump ball via pad to 'keeper' (first ball in TESTS)
12.47	5.54	247	6	P.J.DUJON †	c† DOWNTON	BOTHAM	101	5	267		12	228	Attempted hook at bouncer skied gently off splice (3rd in TESTS)
5.56	3.24	184	7	W.W.DAVIS	BOWLED	POCOCK	77	6	437	1	10	146	Nightwatchman. HS in F.C. matches. Pushed at ball; ball hit off stump.
3.26	3.35	9	8	E.A.E.BAPTISTE	BOWLED	POCOCK	6	7	443		1	11	Made room to cut — then attempted pull. Ball kept low.
3.37	(6.56)	60	9	R.A.HARPER	NOT OUT		39				5	53	HS in TESTS.
6.32	6.36	4	10	M.A.HOLDING	BOWLED	COOK	0	9	471			8	Bowled behind legs — missed sweep.
6.38	6.56	18	11	J.GARNER	c† TERRY	POCOCK	7	10	500		1	12	Edged off-break to forward short leg.
				EXTRAS		b 4 lb 6 w 2 nb 1	13				3⁶	63⁴	
				TOTAL		(160·3 OVERS, 614 MINUTES)	500					964 balls (including 1 no ball)

500 all out at 6.56pm on 2nd day.

15 OVERS 4 BALLS/HOUR
3·12 RUNS/OVER
52 RUNS/100 BALLS

* CAPTAIN † WICKET-KEEPER

BOWLER	O	M	R	W	nb/w		HRS	OVERS	RUNS
BOTHAM	29	5	100	2	½		1	13	45
COWANS	19	2	76	0	½		2	12	31
ALLOTT	28	9	76	3	-		3	16	60
COOK	39	6	114	1	-		4	17	61
POCOCK	45·3	14	121	4	-		5	17	47
	160·3	36	500	10			6	18	29
							7	13	47
							8	19	60
							9	17	57
							10	15	35

2nd NEW BALL taken at 5.44 pm on 1st day -
WEST INDIES 264-4 after 80 overs.

© BILL FRINDALL 1984

	RUNS	MINS	OVERS	LAST 50
50	75	16·2	75
100	146	32·2	71
150	189	43·5	43
200	248	60·3	59
250	316	80·0	68
300	409	103·4	93
350	450	115·0	41
400	499	131·0	49
450	568	149·0	69
500	613	160·2	45

LUNCH: 77-4 26 OVERS / 121 MIN.
TEA: 198-4 59 OVERS / 242 MIN.
STUMPS (1st DAY): 273-5 93 OVERS / 362 MIN.
LUNCH: 342-5 (45 MIN LOST (LIGHT)) 110 OVERS / 437 MIN.
TEA: 443-7 (2 MIN LOST (RAIN)) 145 OVERS / 555 MIN.

GREENIDGE 36 (21) GREENIDGE 90 (86) GREENIDGE 128 (143) GREENIDGE 151 (185) GREENIDGE 214 (355)
DUJON 5 (14) DUJON 76 (185) DAVIS 2 (6) DAVIS 47 (81) HARPER 0 (11)

WKT	PARTNERSHIP		RUNS	MINS
1st	Greenidge	Haynes	11	12
2nd	Greenidge	Gomes	49	68
3rd	Greenidge	Richards	2	3
4th	Greenidge	Lloyd	8	15
5th	Greenidge	Dujon	197	247
6th	Greenidge	Davis	170	184
7th	Greenidge	Baptiste	6	9
8th	Greenidge	Harper	27	34
9th	Harper	Holding	1	4
10th	Harper	Garner	29	18
			500	

ENGLAND 1ST INNINGS

REQUIRING 301 RUNS TO AVOID FOLLOWING ON

IN	OUT	MINS	No.	BATSMAN	HOW OUT	BOWLER	RUNS	WKT	TOTAL	6s	4s	BALLS	NOTES ON DISMISSAL
1.33	3.53	140	1	G. FOWLER	BOWLED	BAPTISTE	38	1	90		5	112	Played on - edged drive via left boot into stumps.
1.33	5.11	195	2	B.C. BROAD	C' HARPER	DAVIS	42	2	112		3	146	Steered sharply lifting ball to 3rd slip (via Greenidge at 4th slip)
3.55 1.58	4.56 2.03	43	3	V.P. TERRY	BOWLED	GARNER	7	(1)	105 280			33	Left forearm (ulna) fractured by short ball from Davis. Retired 7*. Bowled right-handed with left arm in sling under sweater.
4.58	5.17	19	4	D.I. GOWER *	C' DUJON	BAPTISTE	4	3	117			14	Ticked at offside ball. Firm-footed stroke. Low catch.
5.13	(2.03)	251	5	A.J. LAMB	NOT OUT		100				15	185	6th in TESTS - (3rd in 4 innings)
5.19	5.56	37	6	I.T. BOTHAM	C' GARNER	BAPTISTE	6	4	138			23	Sliced wide half-volley to gully - very high right-hand catch
5.58	6.17	19	7	P.R. DOWNTON	† C' HARPER	GARNER	0	5	147			9	Edged outside push - low to 3rd slips left - ball left him.
6.19	12.07	109	8	P.J.W. ALLOTT	C' GOMES	DAVIS	26	6	228		3	86	Miscued hook - gentle skier to backward square-leg.
12.09	12.44	35	9	N.G.B. COOK	BOWLED	HOLDING	13	7	257		3	29	Off stump - misjudged grope at ball angled in.
12.46	1.51	25	10	P.I. POCOCK	BOWLED	GARNER	0	8	278			14	Off stump.
1.53	1.55	2	11	N.G. COWANS	BOWLED	GARNER	0	9	278			4	Off stump.
				EXTRAS	b 5	lb 21	44					6 0 4 30	
				TOTAL	(105.2 OVERS, 448 MINUTES)	W - nb 18	280		all out at 2.03 pm on 4th day.			655 balls (including 23 no balls)	

*CAPTAIN †WICKET-KEEPER

14 OVERS   1 BALLS/HOUR
2·66 RUNS/OVER
43 RUNS/100 BALLS

	RUNS	MINS	OVERS	LAST 50 (in mins)
	50	82	20.1	82
	100	163	42.1	81
	150	271	63.1	108
	200	350	82.2	79
	250	402	95.0	52

BOWLER	O	M	R	W	Nb
GARNER	22.2	7	51	4	4
DAVIS	20	2	71	2	14
HARPER	23	10	33	0	2
HOLDING	21	2	50	1	
BAPTISTE	19	8	31	3	
			44		
	105.2	29	280	10	

HRS	OVERS	RUNS
1	13	40
2	18	41
3	15	24
4	10	33
5	15	24
6	14	50
7	14	53

2ND NEW BALL TAKEN AT 11.56am 4th day.
ENGLAND 212.5 after 85 overs.

© BILL FRINDALL 1984

TEA: 92-1 (41 OVERS) (73 OVERS) BROAD 36* (157')
157 MIN 305 MIN TERRY 0* (15')

STUMPS: 163-5 LAMB 27* (108')
(337 BEHIND) ALLOTT 10* (42')

LUNCH: 270-7 (101 OVERS) LAMB 90* (230')
(230 BEHIND) 427 MIN POCOCK 0* (16')

WEST INDIES ENFORCED FOLLOW ON
- ENGLAND 220 BEHIND

WKT	PARTNERSHIP		RUNS	MINS
1st	Fowler	Broad	90	140
2nd	Broad	Terry Gower	15* 7	38 13
3rd	Gower	Lamb	5	4
4th	Lamb	Botham	21	37
5th	Lamb	Downton	9	19
6th	Lamb	Allott	81	109
7th	Lamb	Cook	29	35
8th	Lamb	Pocock	21	25
9th	Lamb	Cowans	0	2
10th	Lamb	Terry	2	5
				280

WEST INDIES IN ENGLAND 1984 121

ENGLAND 2ND INNINGS FOLLOWING ON 220 RUNS BEHIND

IN	OUT	MINS	No.	BATSMAN	HOW OUT	BOWLER	RUNS	WKT	TOTAL	6s	4s	BALLS	NOTES ON DISMISSAL
2:14	2:15	1	1	G. FOWLER	BOWLED	HOLDING	0	1	0	.	.	2	Played late half-cock push at breakback.
2:14	3:24	70	2	B.C. BROAD	LBW	HARPER	21	2	39	.	2	53	Padded up to 'arm' ball.
2:17	4:57	140	3	P.R. DOWNTON	BOWLED	HARPER	24	3	77	.	3	115	Played on - edged drive via bad into stumps.
3:26	(12:11)	177	4	D.I. GOWER*	NOT OUT		57	.	.	.	8	153	His first 50 of the rubber.
4:59	5:27	28	5	A.J. LAMB	BOWLED	HARPER	9	4	99	.	1	27	Down wicket - missed on-drive - bowled via pad.
5:29	5:36	7	6	I.T. BOTHAM	C† HAYNES	HARPER	1	5	101	.	.	8	Edged off break via pad to forward short leg - 'walked'.
5:38	11:36	30	7	P.J.W. ALLOTT	BOWLED	GARNER	14	6	125	.	3	28	Off stump removed - failed to play forward.
11:38	11:45	7	8	N.G.B. COOK	C' DUJON	GARNER	0	7	127	.	.	1	Followed away seamer.
11:47	11:56	9	9	P.I. POCOCK	C' GARNER	HARPER	0	8	128	.	.	5	'PAIR' Drove to mid-off. HARPER'S BEST TEST ANALYSIS.
11:58	12:11	13	10	N.G. COWANS	BOWLED	HARPER	14	9	156	1	2	12	Missed vast swing to leg - ball rebounded off pads.
			11	V.P. TERRY	ABSENT HURT		-						Fractured left forearm.
				EXTRAS	b 9 lb 3 w 1 nb 3		16					16 19	404 balls (including 4 no balls)
				TOTAL	(66.4 OVERS, 249 MINUTES)		156						all out at 12:11 pm on the 5TH DAY.

* CAPTAIN † WICKET-KEEPER

16 OVERS 0 BALLS/HOUR
2:34 RUNS/OVER
39 RUNS/100 BALLS

WKT	PARTNERSHIP		RUNS	MINS
1st	Fowler	Broad	0	1
2nd	Broad	Downton	39	67
3rd	Downton	Gower	38	71
4th	Gower	Lamb	22	28
5th	Gower	Botham	2	7
6th	Gower	Allott	24	30
7th	Gower	Cook	2	7
8th	Gower	Pocock	1	9
9th	Gower	Cowans	28	13
			156	

BOWLER	O	M	R	W	HRS	OVERS	RUNS		RUNS	MINS	OVERS	LAST 50 (in mins)
HOLDING	11	2	21	1	-/1	1	15	29	50	86	22.4	86
GARNER	12	4	25	2	1/-	2	17	47	100	175	47.1	89
HARPER	28.4	12	57	6	3/-	3	16	25	150	248	66.2	73
DAVIS	3	1	6	0	-	4	16	33				
RICHARDS	1	0	2	0	-							
BAPTISTE	11	5	29	0	-							
			16									
	66.4	24	156	9								

TEA: 56-2 (164 BEHIND) | 23 OVERS | DOWNTON 17*(84)
                          | 87 MINUTES | GOWER 10*(15)

STUMPS: 120-5 | 56 OVERS | GOWER 43*(36)
(4TH DAY) (100 BEHIND) | 208 MIN. | ALLOTT 10*(24)

WEST INDIES WON BY AN INNINGS
AND 64 RUNS - the first touring
team to win the first 4 Tests of a
rubber in England.

MAN OF THE MATCH: C.G. GREENIDGE
Adjudicator: E.R. DEXTER

TOTAL TIME LOST: 3 HOURS 10 MIN (NET)

© BILL FRINDALL 1984

Fifth Test: The Oval, August 9, 10, 11, 13, 14.
West Indies won by 172 runs.

West Indies became the first side ever to beat England 5-0 in England, which was a tribute not only to their superiority but to the excellence of an English summer that allowed almost uninterrupted play. England were comfortably beaten in the end, but were not disgraced in a widely contrasting first innings.

On the first day, the ball swung and moved off the pitch. England's bowlers, especially Botham, Allott, and, in his first Test, Richard Ellison, exploited the conditions with skill and accuracy, and it needed a typically stout innings by Clive Lloyd, barely recovered from a virus, to steer West Indies up to 190.

It could be argued at this point that if the conditions were similar on the second day, as seemed likely, the West Indies bowlers might be less well suited to them than England's had been.

Whether the ball would still swing next day was never established. The pitch had more pace in it than most and the West Indian fast bowlers merely thumped the ball in short, taking wicket after wicket with balls that lifted near the batsman's head and which he touched as he took evasive action. Fowler had to retire after a blow on the forearm but returned to become top scorer. Even Pocock, the nightwatchman, who held out for 40 minutes but without scoring, was bounced out by Marshall, who bowled with fire and stamina to take 5 for 35. What had been an exhibition of cricketing skills by both batsmen and bowlers on the first day had become a demonstration of the game's least attractive side, though in the umpires' view within the requirements of Law 42 relating to fair play.

The third day was sunny, the pitch good, and there was never much doubt that West Indies would build substantially on their first innings lead of 28.

England's new young bowlers, Agnew and Ellison, did make a good start by removing Greenidge, Gomes, and Richards for 69. But Botham in the changed conditions was wayward, and West Indies made their usual recovery, this time with Haynes as the anchor man and Lloyd and Dujon in support. Haynes had made only 110 in his seven previous Test innings, but batted through the day to finish at 111 not out, the lead by then 312.

Another 62 runs were added on the fourth morning by Haynes and a vigorous lower order, after which England set about the task of making 375, a last innings figure not reached successfully in over 100 years by England batsmen against far weaker bowling sides than the West Indians of 1984.

A second-wicket stand of 60 between Broad and Tavare gave the score a respectable look early on, but five wickets were down that night and, after some hefty blows by Botham, the remaining five fell in an hour on the last morning.

The presentation ceremony in front of the pavilion was marred by an unruly crowd, who caused players of both sides to retreat and doubtless put an end to the staging of such ceremonies on the playing area in future.

WEST INDIES IN ENGLAND 1984

WEST INDIES 1ST INNINGS v. ENGLAND (5TH TEST) AT KENNINGTON OVAL, LONDON, ON 9,10,11,13,14 AUGUST, 1984. TOSS: WEST INDIES

IN	OUT	MINS	No.	BATSMAN	HOW OUT	BOWLER	RUNS	WKT	TOTAL	6s	4s	BALLS	NOTES ON DISMISSAL
11.00	12.17	77	1	C.G. GREENIDGE	LBW	BOTHAM	22	2	45	·	3	51	Pushed across line – ball angled in.
11.00	11.33	33	2	D.L. HAYNES	BOWLED	ALLOTT	10	1	19	·	1	22	Drove across full-length ball. Middle and off stumps hit.
11.35	12.57	82	3	H.A. GOMES	C BOTHAM	ELLISON	18	3	64	·	1	57	Edged drive to 2nd slip – high, two-handed catch.
12.19	1.41	42	4	I.V.A. RICHARDS	C ALLOTT	BOTHAM	8	4	64	·	·	25	Hooked off-stump bouncer high to fine long-leg – running catch.
12.59	1.53	14	5	P.J. DUJON †	C TAVARÉ	BOTHAM	3	5	67	·	·	10	BOTHAM'S 300TH TEST WICKET Gloved bouncer to 1st slip.
1.43	(5.25)	202	6	C.H. LLOYD *	NOT OUT		60			·	5	112	Became 6th highest scorer, passing G.S. Chappell, when 48. (TEST).
1.55	1.59	4	7	M.D. MARSHALL	C GOWER	ELLISON	0	6	70	·	·	4	Edged drive at outswinger high to 3rd slip (two-handed catch).
2.01	3.14	73	8	E.A.E. BAPTISTE	C FOWLER	ALLOTT	32	7	124	·	5	58	Drove which ball low to cover.
3.16	4.37	61	9	R.A. HARPER	BOWLED	BOTHAM	18	8	154	·	3	46	Drove across inswinging yorker.
4.39	4.40	1	10	M.A. HOLDING	LBW	BOTHAM	0	9	154	·	·	2	Drove across late inswinger. Botham 5 wkts for 23rd time in Tests.
4.42	5.25	43	11	J. GARNER	C DOWNTON	ALLOTT	6	10	190	·	·	34	Edged off-drive to 'keeper.
				EXTRAS			13			b 1 lb 4 w 7 nb 1			
				TOTAL			190			(70 OVERS, 325 MINUTES)			all out at 5.25pm on 1st day.

*CAPTAIN †WICKET-KEEPER

0 19 4 421 balls (including 1 no ball)

12 OVERS 5 BALLS/HOUR
2·71 RUNS/OVER
45 RUNS/100 BALLS

BOWLER	O	M	R	W	H/R	OVERS/H	RUNS
AGNEW	12	3	46	0	1/3	13	37
ALLOTT	17	7	25	3	-	2	13	27
BOTHAM	23	8	72	5	1/3	3	12	29
ELLISON	18	3	34	2	4/1	4	14	43
						5	13	38
	70	21	190	10				

	RUNS	MINS	OVERS	LAST 50 (in mins)
	50	94	20.0	94
	100	181	38.5	87
	150	267	58.1	86

LUNCH: 64-3 [26 OVERS, 120 MIN.] RICHARDS 8* (4†) DUJON 0* (·)

TEA: 136-7 [52 OVERS, 240 MIN] LLOYD 24* (1NT) HARPER 8* (2x)

WKT	PARTNERSHIP		RUNS	MINS
1st	Greenidge	Haynes	19	33
2nd	Greenidge	Gomes	26	42
3rd	Gomes	Richards	19	38
4th	Richards	Dujon	0	2
5th	Dujon	Lloyd	3	9
6th	Lloyd	Marshall	3	4
7th	Lloyd	Baptiste	54	73
8th	Lloyd	Harper	30	61
9th	Lloyd	Holding	0	1
10th	Lloyd	Garner	36	43
			190	

© BILL FRINDALL 1984

ENGLAND 1ST INNINGS
IN REPLY TO WEST INDIES 190 ALL OUT

IN	OUT	MINS	No.	BATSMAN	HOW OUT	BOWLER	RUNS	WKT	TOTAL	6s	4s	BALLS	NOTES ON DISMISSAL
2.25	11.35	92	1	G. FOWLER	c Richards	Baptiste	31	(1)	21/116	.	2	61	Rehired hurt when 12* - hit on right forearm by lifting ball from Marshall. Edged drive to 2nd slip - shirt sleeve will retain two-handed.
2.17	2.57	19	2	B.C. BROAD	Bowled	Garner	7	2	10	.	.	13	Beaten by superb ball - pitched leg, hit middle & off.
5.38	5.57	42	3	P.I. POCOCK	c Greenidge	Marshall	4	1	22	.	.	21	Unable to avoid fast bouncer - simple catch to 4th slip (box handle)
5.59	11.43	92	4	C.J. TAVARÉ	c Dujon	Holding	0	2	64	.	2	55	Followed, quicker, sharply lifting, leg side ball.
11.34	1.49	41	5	D.I. GOWER*	c Dujon	Holding	16	4	45	.	2	34	Failed to avoid bouncer that cut back - off gloves.
11.45	12.26	67	6	A.J. LAMB	LBW	Marshall	12	3	84	.	.	40	Beaten by fast ball that cut back and kept low.
12.28	2.19	22	7	I.T. BOTHAM	c Dujon	Marshall	14	5	83	.	1	20	Unable to avoid fast bouncer that glanced gloves.
1.52	2.14	75	8	P.R. DOWNTON†	c Lloyd	Garner	16	8	133	.	.	62	Failed to evade fast lifting ball - off gloves to 1st slip.
2.21	3.36	77	9	R.M. ELLISON	Not out		20			.	2	43	
2.59	(5.35)	29	10	P.J.W. ALLOTT	Bowled	Marshall	16	9	156	.	1	24	off stump - played back to full length ball - first after resumption.
3.38	5.27	6	11	J.P. AGNEW	Bowled	Marshall	5	10	162	.	.	10	Played on via pads.
5.29	5.35			EXTRAS	b 2 lb 4 w - nb 10		16			b 4 / 6 10			
				TOTAL	(61.5 overs, 292 minutes)		162		all out at 5.35pm on 2nd day.			383 balls (including 12 no balls)	

*CAPTAIN †WICKET-KEEPER

13 OVERS 1 BALLS/HOUR
2·62 RUNS/OVER
42 RUNS/100 BALLS

BOWLER	O	M	R	W	nb	HRS	OVERS	RUNS
GARNER	18	6	37	2	5	1	12	22
MARSHALL	17.5	5	35	5	5	2	13	28
HOLDING	13	2	55	2	2	3	11	34
BAPTISTE	12	4	19	1	.	4	14	43
HARPER	1	1	0	0	.			
			16					
	61.5	18	162	10				

	RUNS	MINS	OVERS	LAST 50 (in mins)
	50	119	25	119
	100	192	39.1	73
	150	272	57.3	80

STUMPS: 10-1 | 5 OVERS 22 MIN | FOWLER 4* (22') POCOCK 0* (1')
LUNCH: 57-3 [TAKEN AT 12·50pm - BAD LIGHT] | 27 OVERS 129 MIN | TAVARÉ 15* (75') LAMB 4* (21')
TEA: 133-8 | 54 OVERS 259 MIN | ELLISON 12* (43') ALLOTT 0* (4')

MARSHALL took five wickets in an innings for the seventh time in his last 10 Tests

WEST INDIES 28 RUNS AHEAD ON FIRST INNINGS

WKT	PARTNERSHIP		RUNS	MINS
1st	Fowler	Broad	10	19
2nd	Fowler / Tavaré	Pocock	11*	31 / 9
3rd	Tavaré	Gower	23	41
4th	Tavaré	Lamb	19	38
5th	Lamb	Botham	19	22
6th	Lamb	Fowler	1	2
7th	Fowler	Downton	32	36
8th	Downton	Ellison	17	37
9th	Ellison	Allott	23	29
10th	Ellison	Agnew	6	6
			162	

© BILL FRINDALL 1984

WEST INDIES IN ENGLAND 1984

WEST INDIES 2ND INNINGS
28 RUNS AHEAD ON FIRST INNINGS

IN	OUT	MINS	No.	BATSMAN	HOW OUT	BOWLER	RUNS	WKT	TOTAL	6s	4s	BALLS	NOTES ON DISMISSAL
5·46	11:35	51	1	C.G.GREENIDGE	c⁺ BOTHAM	AGNEW	34	1	51	·	4	39	Short ball, cut back sharply - attempted cut steered to 2nd slip
5·46	11:59	436	2	D.L.HAYNES	BOWLED	BOTHAM	125	9	329	·	17	269	(7th Test), (1st or tour). Played on - aimed off drive at inswinger.
11·37	11·42	5	3	H.A.GOMES	c⁺ TAVARÉ	ELLISON	1	2	52	·	·	6	Edged drive low to 1st slip - Ellison's first ball of the innings
11·45	11:58	13	4	I.V.A.RICHARDS	LBW	AGNEW	15	3	69	·	2	11	Played back and across sharp breakback.
12·00	2·28	108	5	C.H.LLOYD*	c⁺ DOWNTON	ELLISON	36	4	132	·	3	62	Edged cut - diving catch in front of 1st slip.
2·30	4·09	77	6	P.J.DUJON†	c⁺ LAMB	ELLISON	49	5	214	·	8	63	Edged drive at outswinger to 1st slip.
4·11	5·21	70	7	E.A.E.BAPTISTE	c⁺ DOWNTON	ALLOTT	5	6	237	·	·	47	Edged offside push to 'keeper.
5·23	5·50	27	8	M.D.MARSHALL	c⁺ LAMB	BOTHAM	12	7	264	·	2	14	Hooked bouncer straight to deep square-leg.
5·52	11·19	30	9	R.A.HARPER	c⁺ DOWNTON	ALLOTT	17	8	293	1	2	17	Played back - inside edge diving - low, 2-handed to left.
11·21	12·19	58	10	M.A.HOLDING	LBW	BOTHAM	30	10	346	1	3	36	Plumb - played back to yorker.
12·01	(12·19)	18	11	J.GARNER	NOT OUT		10			·	1	15	-
				EXTRAS	b - lb 12	w - nb -	12				2b 4²	579 balls (0 no balls)	

*CAPTAIN   †WICKET-KEEPER

TOTAL (96·3 OVERS, 456 MINUTES)   346 all out at 12:19 pm on 4th day.

BOWLER	O	M	R	W	nb
BOTHAM	22·3	2	103	3	·
ALLOTT	26	3	96	2	·
POCOCK	8	3	24	0	·
AGNEW	14	2	51	2	·
ELLISON	26	7	60	3	·
			12		
	96·3	14	346	10	

© BILL FRINDALL 1984

2ND NEW BALL taken at 11:27am on 4th day
- WEST INDIES 295-8 after 85 overs

HRS	OVERS	RUNS
1	12	52
2	13	38
3	13	42
4	14	59
5	12	34
6	12	31
7	13	53

RUNS	MINS	OVERS	LAST 50 (in mins)
50	49	10·5	49
100	137	28·1	88
150	199	41·0	62
200	248	53·3	49
250	352	74·1	104
300	408	86·0	56

STUMPS: 15-0 (2ND DAY) (45 AHEAD)
LUNCH: 98-3 (136 AHEAD)
TEA: 212-4 (240 AHEAD)
STUMPS: 284-7 (3RD DAY) (212 AHEAD)

4 OVERS 16 MINUTES	GREENIDGE 10* HAYNES 4*
28 OVERS 136 MINUTES	HAYNES 28* (36) LLOYD 19* (64)
55 OVERS 256 MINUTES	HAYNES 72* (246) DUJON 48* (76)
79 OVERS 377 MINUTES	HAYNES 111* (377) HARPER 14* (11*)

12 OVERS 4 BALLS/HOUR
3·59 RUNS/OVER
60 RUNS/100 BALLS

WKT	PARTNERSHIP		RUNS	MINS
1st	Greenidge	Haynes	51	51
2nd	Haynes	Gomes	1	5
3rd	Haynes	Richards	17	13
4th	Haynes	Lloyd	63	108
5th	Haynes	Dujon	82	77
6th	Haynes	Baptiste	23	70
7th	Haynes	Marshall	27	27
8th	Haynes	Harper	29	30
9th	Haynes	Holding	36	38
10th	Holding	Garner	17	18
			346	

ENGLAND 2ND INNINGS — REQUIRING 375 RUNS IN A MINIMUM OF 629 MINUTES

IN	OUT	MINS	No.	BATSMAN	HOW OUT	BOWLER	RUNS	WKT	TOTAL	6s	4s	BALLS	NOTES ON DISMISSAL
12.31	1.47	37	1	G. FOWLER	C' RICHARDS	MARSHALL	7	1	15	.	1	30	Edged fast ball, angled across, to 2nd slip
12.31	4.17	167	2	B.C. BROAD	C' GREENIDGE	HOLDING	39	2	75	.	.	104	Unable to avoid faster lifter off long run - off glove to gully
1.49	5.30	201	3	C.J. TAVARÉ	C' RICHARDS	GARNER	49	5	135	.	4	153	(HS v WI) Edged off drive to 2nd slip - fast two-handed catch.
4.19	4.39	20	4	D.I. GOWER*	LBW	HOLDING	7	3	88	.	1	12	Beaten by late inswing - quicker ball off longer run.
4.41	4.44	3	5	A.J. LAMB	C' HAYNES	HOLDING	1	4	90	.	.	2	Fended short ball to right of short leg - longer run.
4.46	11.25	100	6	I.T. BOTHAM	C' MARSHALL	GARNER	54	6	181	.	6	51	50 off 49 balls. Skied hook to deep fine-leg.
5.32	11.37	66	7	P.R. DOWNTON†	LBW	GARNER	10	7	186	.	1	46	Played back - beaten by breakback.
11.27	12.01	34	8	R.M. ELLISON	C' HOLDING	GARNER	13	10	202	.	.	24	Edged backfoot force at lifting ball to gully
11.39	11.52	13	9	P.J.W. ALLOTT	C' LLOYD	HOLDING	4	8	200	.	1	6	Edged off-side ball to 1st slip - not in line.
11.54	11.55	1	10	P.I. POCOCK	C AND BOWLED	HOLDING	0	9	200	.	.	2	'PAIR' - second in successive Tests. Reaction catch - jm. drive.
11.57	(12.01)	4	11	J.P. AGNEW	NOT OUT		2			.	.	2	
				EXTRAS	b -	1b 2	16			0	15	4	432 balls (inc. 14 no balls)

TOTAL (69.4 OVERS, 332 MINUTES) w 1 nb 13

202 all out at 12.01 pm.

*CAPTAIN †WICKET-KEEPER

© BILL FRINDALL 1984

BOWLER	O	M	R	W		HRS	OVERS	RUNS		RUNS	MINS	OVERS	LAST 50 (in mins)
MARSHALL	22	5	71	1	1/-	1	13	24		50	105	21.5	105
GARNER	18.4	3	51	4	7/-	2	11	32		100	205	44.2	100
HOLDING	13	2	43	5	5/1	3	16	27		150	265	56.3	60
BAPTISTE	8	3	11	0	0/-	4	11	51		200	321	68.0	56
HARPER	8	5	10	0	.	5	13	48					
	69.4	18	202	10			16	10					

LUNCH: 15 - 0 [7 OVERS / 31 MINUTES] FOWLER 7* BROAD 7*

TEA: 71 - 1 [34 OVERS / 152 MINUTES] BROAD 38*(6s) TAVARÉ 19*(4)

STUMPS: 151 - 5 [58 OVERS / 271 MINUTES] BOTHAM 32*(75) DOWNTON 2*(26)

WEST INDIES WON BY 172 RUNS

MAN OF THE MATCH: D.L. HAYNES

PLAYER OF THE SERIES: C.G. GREENIDGE
(Ad (Lucozade - both awards - R. ILLINGWORTH)

TOTAL TIME LOST: 1 HOUR 1 MINUTE

12 OVERS 3 BALLS/HOUR
2·90 RUNS/OVER
47 RUNS/100 BALLS

WKT	PARTNERSHIP		RUNS	MINS
1st	Fowler	Broad	15	37
2nd	Broad	Tavaré	60	128
3rd	Tavaré	Gower	13	20
4th	Tavaré	Lamb	2	3
5th	Tavaré	Botham	45	44
6th	Botham	Downton	46	54
7th	Downton	Ellison	5	10
8th	Ellison	Allott	14	13
9th	Ellison	Pocock	0	1
10th	Ellison	Agnew	2	4
			202	

Statistical Survey: England v West Indies 1984 – England

England – Batting/Fielding	M	I	NO	HS	R	Avge	100	50	6s	4s	Min	Balls	r/hb	Ct	St
A.J. Lamb	5	10	1	110	386	42.88	3	–	–	50	1150	846	46	3	–
I.T. Botham	5	10	0	81	347	34.70	–	3	3	43	779	538	64	5	–
G. Fowler	5	10	0	106	260	26.00	1	1	–	34	961	719	36	3	–
B.C. Broad	4	8	0	55	195	24.37	–	1	–	18	795	560	35	1	–
P.R. Downton	5	10	1	56	210	23.33	–	1	–	19	983	723	29	10	–
R.G.D. Willis	3	5	3	22	43	21.50	–	–	–	5	112	56	77	1	–
D.I. Gower	5	10	1	57*	171	19.00	–	1	–	23	562	443	39	3	–
D.R. Pringle	3	6	1	46*	81	16.20	–	–	–	10	257	211	38	3	–
P.J.W. Allott	3	6	0	26	67	11.16	–	–	–	9	205	164	41	2	–
G. Miller	2	4	0	22	42	10.50	–	–	–	6	122	92	46	2	–
V.P. Terry	2	3	0	8	16	5.33	–	–	–	2	86	66	24	2	–
N.G.B. Cook	3	6	0	13	25	4.16	–	–	–	4	110	92	27	1	–
P.I. Pocock	2	4	0	0	0	0.00	–	–	–	–	77	42	0	–	–
Also batted:															
J.P. Agnew	1	2	1	5	7	7.00	–	–	–	1	10	12	58	–	–
N.G. Cowans	1	2	0	14	14	7.00	–	–	1	2	15	16	88	1	–
R.M. Ellison	1	2	1	20*	33	33.00	–	–	–	3	111	67	49	–	–
N.A. Foster	1	2	1	9*	15	15.00	–	–	–	2	30	28	54	2	–
M.W. Gatting	1	2	0	29	30	15.00	–	–	–	4	78	56	54	2	–
T.A. Lloyd	1	1	1	10*	10	–	–	–	–	1	33	17	59	–	–
D.W. Randall	1	2	0	1	1	0.50	–	–	–	–	14	12	8	1	–
C.J. Tavaré	1	2	0	49	65	32.50	–	–	–	6	293	208	31	2	–
Totals	55	107	11	(110)	2018	21.02	4	7	4	241	6783	4968	41	42	–

England – Bowling	O	M	R	W	Avge	Best	5wI	10wM	b/w	r/hb	NB	wides
R.M. Ellison	44	10	94	5	18.80	3-60	–	–	53	36	–	1
P.J.W. Allott	104.5	26	282	14	20.14	6-61	1	–	45	45	–	–
I.T. Botham	163.2	30	667	19	35.10	8-103	2	–	52	68	–	7
D.R. Pringle	71.3	10	257	5	51.40	5-108	1	–	86	60	42	1
N.G.B. Cook	95	15	297	5	59.40	2-27	–	–	114	52	–	–
R.G.D. Willis	85	15	367	6	61.16	2-48	–	–	85	72	55	3
Also bowled:												
J.P. Agnew	264	4	97	2	48.50	2-51	–	–	78	62	1	–
N.G. Cowans	19	2	76	0	–	–	–	–	–	67	1	–
N.A. Foster	18	2	82	1	–	–	–	–	–	76	–	–
G. Miller	28	1	142	1	142.00	1-83	–	–	168	85	–	–
P.I. Pocock	53.3	17	145	4	36.25	4-121	–	–	80	45	–	–
Totals	708.1	132	2506	61	41.08	(8-103)	4	–	70	59	99	12

*not out r/hb = runs per 100 balls b/w = balls per wicket 5wI = 5 wickets in an innings 10wM = 10 wickets in a match

Statistical Survey: England v West Indies – West Indies

West Indies – Batting/Fielding

	M	I	NO	HS	R	Avge	100	50	6s	4s	Min	Balls	r/hb	Ct	St
C.G. Greenidge	5	8	1	223	572	81.71	2	–	2	78	1229	929	62	3	–
H.A. Gomes	5	8	3	143	400	80.00	2	1	–	51	1141	773	52	1	–
C.H. Lloyd	5	6	1	71	255	51.00	–	2	–	28	699	477	53	9	–
I.V.A. Richards	5	7	1	117	250	41.66	1	1	1	37	447	317	79	5	–
P.J.L. Dujon	5	6	0	101	210	35.00	1	–	–	27	473	412	51	16	–
E.A.E. Baptiste	5	6	1	87*	174	34.80	–	1	–	24	399	307	57	1	–
M.A. Holding	4	5	0	69	158	31.60	–	2	10	14	249	181	87	2	–
D.L. Haynes	5	8	0	125	235	29.37	1	–	–	28	787	485	48	3	–
R.A. Harper	5	6	1	39*	96	19.20	–	–	2	14	212	161	60	8	–
M.D. Marshall	4	5	0	29	47	9.40	–	–	1	7	130	70	67	2	–
J. Garner	5	6	1	10*	29	5.80	–	–	1	1	118	87	33	3	–
Also batted:															
W.W. Davis	1	1	0	77	77	77.00	–	1	1	10	184	146	53	–	–
M.A. Small	1	1	1	3*	3	–	–	–	–	–	5	3	100	–	–
Totals	55	73	10	(223)	2506	39.77	7	8	18	319	6073	4348	58	53	–

West Indies – Bowling

	O	M	R	W	Avge	Best	5wI	10wM	b/w	r/hb	NB	Wides
M.D. Marshall	167.4	50	437	24	18.20	7-53	3	–	42	43	33	6
J. Garner	217.5	60	540	29	18.62	5-55	1	–	45	41	45	–
R.A. Harper	128.4	47	276	13	21.23	6-57	1	–	59	36	7	–
M.A. Holding	122.2	24	343	15	22.86	5-43	1	–	49	47	15	2
E.A.E. Baptiste	125	39	265	8	33.12	3-31	–	–	94	35	15	1
Also bowled:												
W.W. Davis	23	3	77	2	38.50	2-71	–	–	69	56	14	–
I.V.A. Richards	1	0	2	0	–	–	–	–	–	33	–	–
M.A. Small	21	2	78	3	26.00	3-40	–	–	42	62	–	–
Totals	806.3	225	2018	94	21.46	(7-53)	6	–	51	42	129	9

*not out   r/hb = runs per 100 balls   b/w = balls per wicket   5wI = 5 wickets in an innings   10wM = 10 wickets in a match

David Gower's season epitomized. West Indies rejoice as he is out for three in the first innings at Lord's.

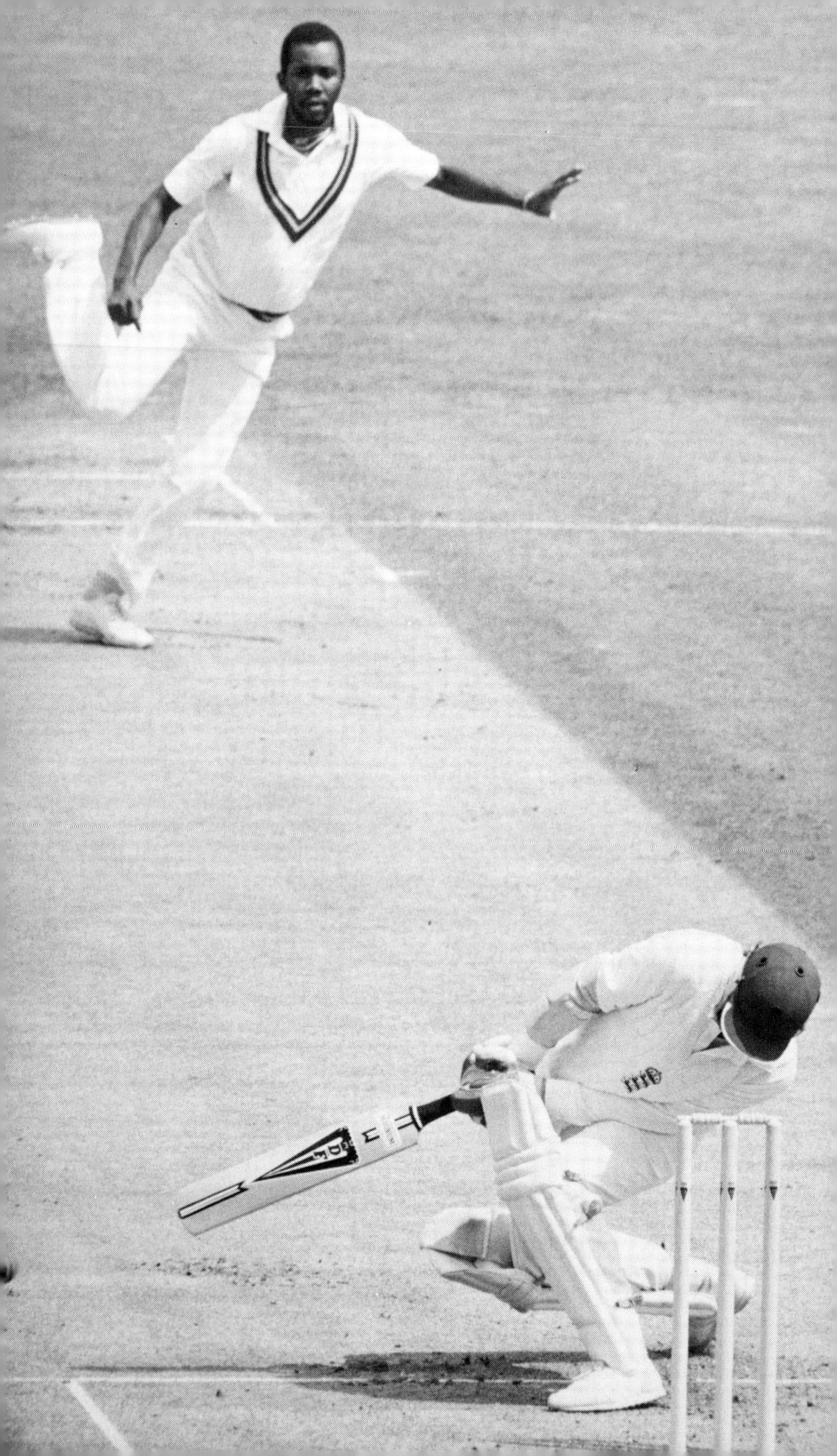

Left: Edgbaston, June 14. Andy Lloyd, misjudging a short ball from Malcolm Marshall, is hit on the side of the head. Impaired vision kept him out for the rest of the season.

Above: Headingley, third Test. Marshall, with his left thumb broken in two places, uses his right hand well enough to allow Larry Gomes to reach 100.

Right: Marshall, 7 for 53 in the second innings at Headingley, with one hand in plaster.

More Test action from the West Indies tour. Vivian Richards (above left), making 117 at Edgbaston, his first and, as it proved, best innings of the series. Gordon Greenidge (above right) drives Pringle for four during his brilliant innings of 214 not out on the last day of the Lord's Test. Graeme Fowler (below) makes sure that he is well under a steeply lifting ball from Joel Garner at Headingley.

The Oval. A rare moment of English jubilation. Jeffrey Dujon, trying not to play, is caught at slip and gives Ian Botham his 300th Test wicket.

Left: David Constant avoids a crowd invasion.

Right: Not what it looks. In a light-hearted moment, Allan Lamb is in fact congratulating Pat Pocock on his first run for England for eight years.

Below: An anxious moment for Janette Brittin, England's outstanding batsman in the women's series against New Zealand.

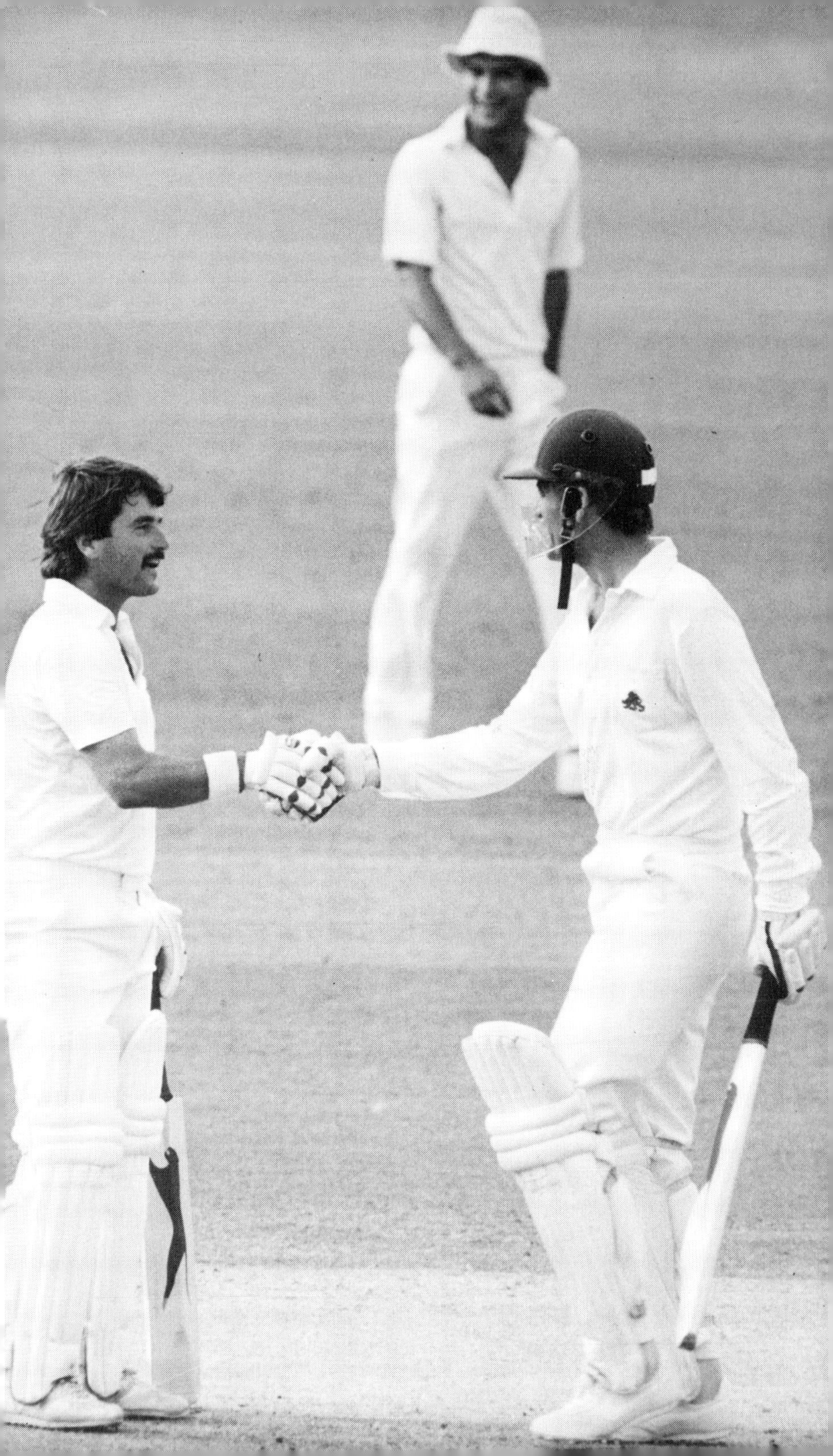

The *Daily Telegraph* Cricketers of the Year (see pages 17-18):
1 Mike Gatting (England)
2 Allan Border (Australia)
3 Peter Kirsten (S. Africa)
4 Malcolm Marshall (W. Indies)
5 Ian Smith (NZ)
6 Sunil Gavaskar (India)
7 Sarfraz Nawaz (Pakistan)
8 Ranjan Madugalle (Sri Lanka)

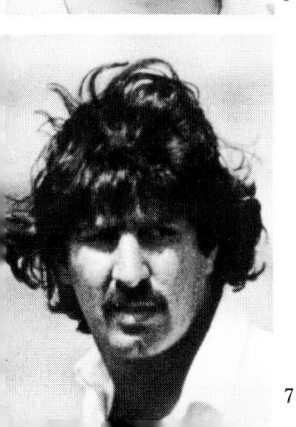

Right: Richard Hadlee, Britannic Assurance Player of the Season and the first player to do the double since 1967.

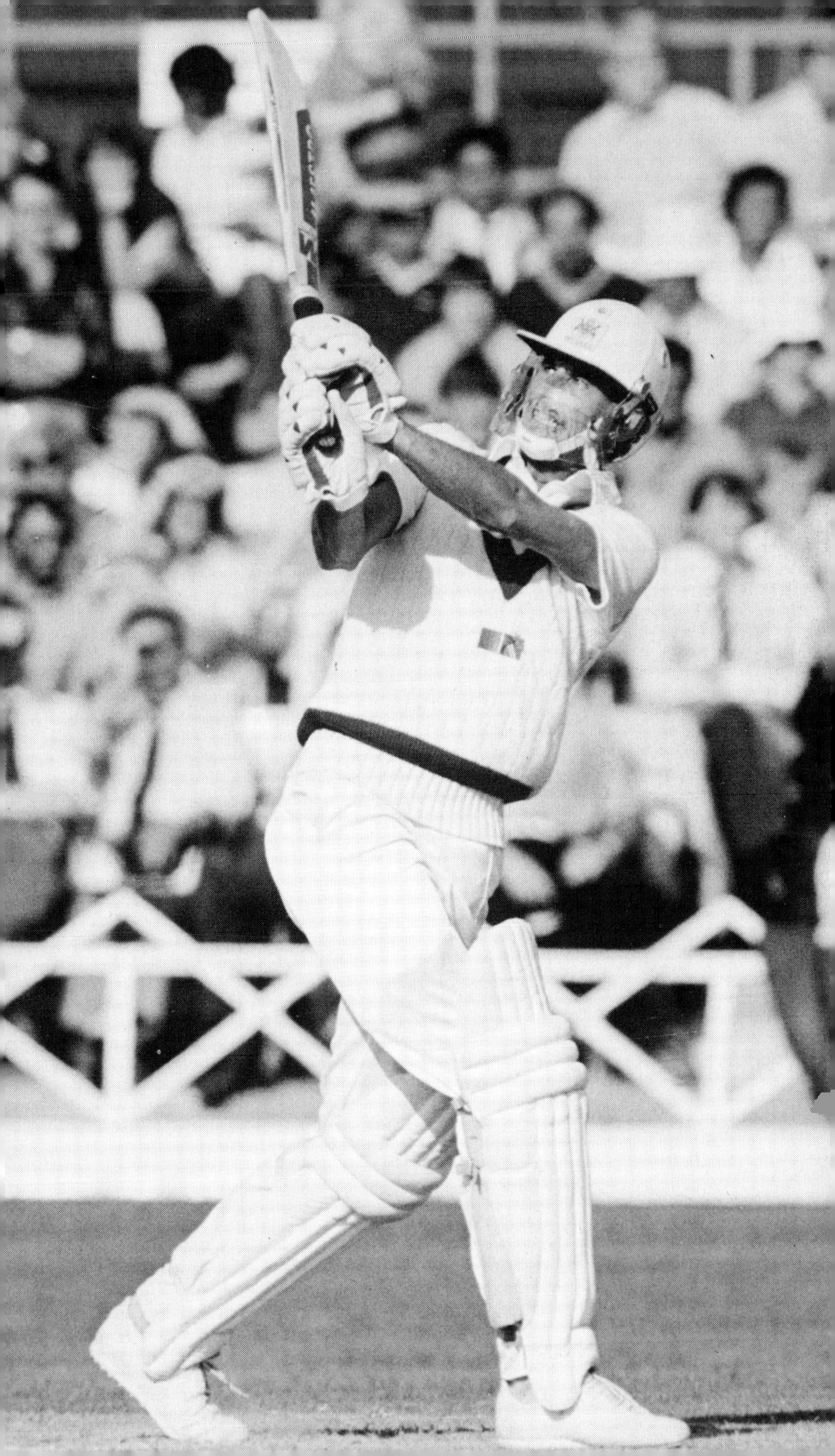

Essex, 1984 Britannic Assurance Champions and winners of the John Player Special League. Standing: D.E. East, C. Gladwin, A.W. Lilley, N.A. Foster, D.R. Pringle, K.R. Pont, B.R. Hardie, K.S. McEwan. Seated: D.L. Acfield, J.K. Lever, K.W.R. Fletcher (captain), G.A. Gooch, S. Turner.

Above: Man of the Match Clive Radley during the stand with Paul Downton that led Middlesex to their extraordinary victory in the NatWest final.

John Emburey after scoring the winning run in semi-darkness off the last ball of the thrilling NatWest final. Phil Edmonds still shows the strain of the last minutes.

England's new boys selected for the 1984-85 winter tour: Martyn Moxon (above), Bruce French (1), Richard Ellison (2), who had already made his Test debut against West Indies, Chris Cowdrey (3), and Tim Robinson (4).

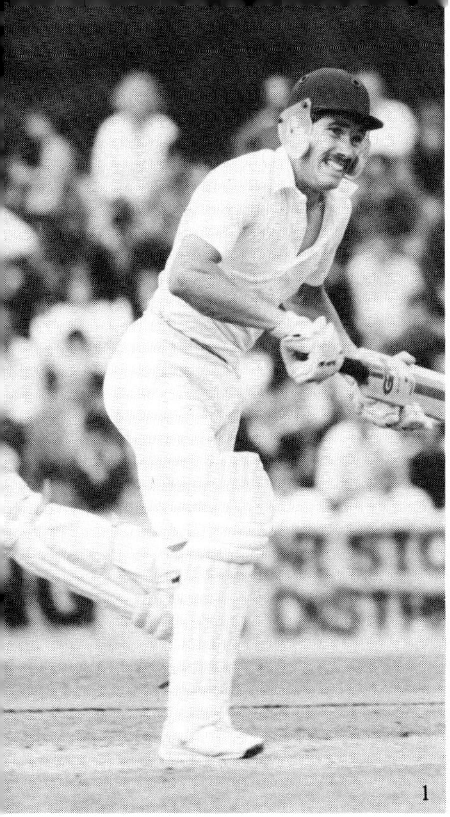

1

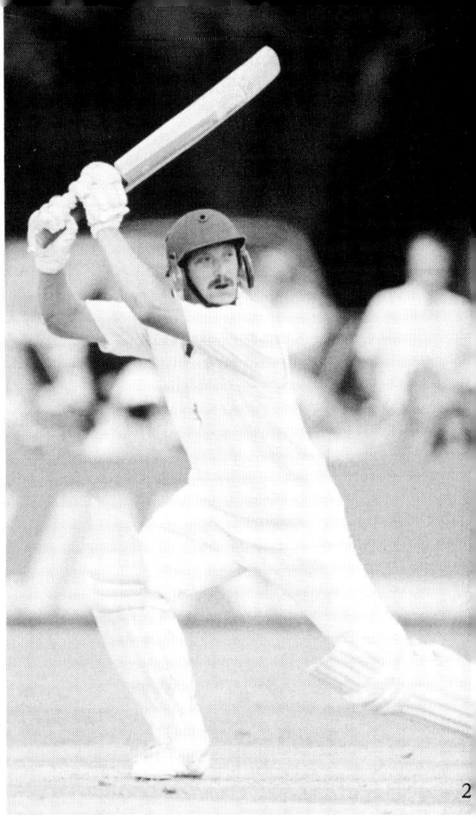

2

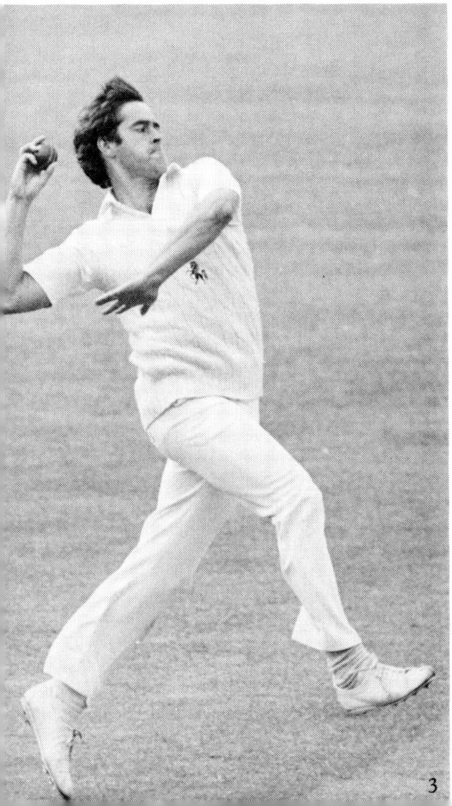

3

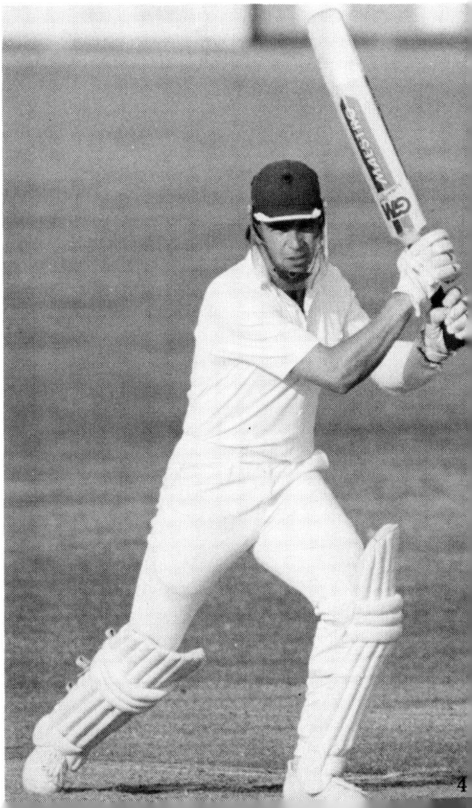

4

Left: Wettimuny's strokes off the back foot were one of the joys of his 190 for Sri Lanka at Lord's.

Below: The robust Duleep Mendis, the Sri Lankan captain, at Lord's, where he nearly made a hundred in each innings.

The unique follow-through of the Sri Lankan leg-spinner D.S. de Silva.

Winners of the *Daily Telegraph* 'Twin Hundreds' (see page 16): John Lever (left), still at 35 'the spearhead and mainstay of Essex'. Mike Gatting (right), who played many more valuable innings for Middlesex than his fastest hundred.

Statistical Highlights of the Tests

1st Test, Edgbaston. Andy Lloyd, from Oswestry, was only the second Shropshire-born cricketer to represent England and the first to do so in a home Test. The first was W. Newham, the Shrewsbury-born Sussex batsman, who made his only appearance in Test cricket against Australia at Sydney in 1887-88. P.N.F. Mansell, who played in 13 Tests for South Africa between 1951 and 1955, was also born in Shropshire, at St George's near Oakengates. West Indies compiled their highest total against England since 1976. Richards became the fourth batsman to score 5,000 runs for West Indies. His fifth Test hundred in England placed him second only to D.G. Bradman (11) in the list of Test hundreds scored by visiting batsmen. Baptiste and Holding shared a record West Indies ninth-wicket partnership of 150 against England. This was only the second time in 22 Tests that England had lost at Edgbaston, following Australia's victory in 1975.

2nd Test, Lord's. Lord's celebrated its centenary of Test cricket by staging its 76th official Test, to equal the record held by the Melbourne Cricket Ground. England employed their seventh different opening pair of batsmen within a sequence of eight Tests. Lloyd became the second batsman after G. St A. Sobers to score 7,000 runs for West Indies. Botham was the first bowler to take eight wickets in an innings against West Indies in a Test in England. Other notable career batting landmarks were reached by Botham and Greenidge (both 4,000 runs) and Gomes (2,000). Greenidge scored the first West Indies double century at Lord's. His unbroken stand of 287 with Gomes set a second-wicket record for either side in this series. West Indies lost a second-innings wicket for the first time in seven Tests. Their total of 344-1 was the fifth highest in a fourth innings to win a Test match. It was the first time since Headingley in 1948 that England had lost after declaring their second innings closed. The total of 12 lbw decisions by umpires Meyer (7) and Evans (5) equalled the Test record set in the New Zealand v West Indies Test at Dunedin in 1979-80.

3rd Test, Headingley. Holding became the fourth bowler after L.R. Gibbs, G.St A. Sobers, and A.M.E. Roberts to take 200 wickets in Tests for West Indies. Willis, playing in what proved to be his final Test, extended his world record of 'not out' innings to 55 and his record number of wickets by an England bowler to 325. On only one previous occasion – against Australia in 1921 – had England lost the first three matches of a series at home.

4th Test, Old Trafford. Old Trafford, also celebrating its centenary of Test cricket, enjoyed a first day uninterrupted by rain. This was in stark contrast to their very first day (10 July 1884), which was totally washed out. Pocock returned to England's team after missing 86 Tests – only H.L. Jackson (96 Tests) had had a longer wait for a recall. Greenidge became the first batsman to score a double century for West Indies at Old Trafford and the second after I.V.A. Richards (1976) to reach 200 twice for West Indies in the same series against any country. Lamb's hundred was his third in successive Tests. The last instance for England within the same rubber was achieved by K.F. Barrington against Pakistan in 1967.

5th Test, The Oval. Botham became the fifth bowler after F.S. Trueman, L.R. Gibbs, D.K. Lillie, and R.G.D. Willis to take 300 wickets in Test matches. Marshall claimed five wickets in an innings for the seventh time in his last 10 Tests. He ended the series with 24 wickets to bring his total for the last four series, played within only 18 months, to 99 wickets at a cost of 20.53 runs each. Pocock was dismissed for a pair for the second time in successive Tests; the only other such instance for England was inflicted upon R. Peel by Australia in 1894-95. West Indies equalled the world record of eight successive wins achieved by Australia against England in the 1920-21 and 1921 series. They also became the fifth side to win every match of a five-Test rubber. Only one previous West Indies side had managed this – F.M.M. Worrell's 1961-62 team beating India in the Caribbean. Only one of their last 38 Tests has ended in defeat. Their unbeaten run of 23 matches is the third-longest sequence in Test history.

TALES FROM FAR PAVILIONS
Compiled by Allen Synge and Leo Cooper

This unique collection of anecdotes, reportage and rare archive material explores cricket's frequently hilarious, sometimes disastrous and occasionally triumphant encounters with alien cultures. Here are eccentric and surprising tales of the Noble Sport played in the jungle, on the Trans-Siberian railway, on skates and in kilts.
An original and essential addition to every cricketer's bookshelf   £8.95

CRICKET CRISIS Bodyline and Other Lines
J.H. Fingleton
Introduction by Michael Parkinson

The long-awaited reprint of a classic of cricket literature *Cricket Crisis* is the definitive analysis of the 'Bodyline' controversy of 1932/3 by a member of the team that faced Larwood and Jardine and went on to become Australia's greatest cricket writer. Published with the original foreword by Neville Cardus.   £9.95

PAVILION
MICHAEL JOSEPH

West Indies Tour of Britain 1984

Results: Played 14; Won 8, Lost 0, Drawn 6

First-Class Averages

Batting and Fielding	M	I	NO	HS	R	Avge	100	50	Ct	St
C.G. Greenidge	11	16	3	223	1069	82.23	4	3	5	–
A.L. Logie	8	10	2	141	585	73.12	2	4	3	–
H.A. Gomes	12	17	5	143	841	70.08	4	3	2	–
C.H. Lloyd	9	9	2	72	364	52.00	–	3	12	–
I.V.A. Richards	12	15	1	170	625	44.64	2	3	12	–
P.J.L. Dujon	12	15	2	107	558	42.92	2	2	27	–
D.L. Haynes	12	17	1	125	632	39.50	1	5	9	–
T.R.O. Payne	7	8	3	44	191	38.20	–	–	4	1
W.W. Davis	4	4	1	77	112	37.33	–	1	1	–
R.B. Richardson	8	10	0	111	335	33.50	1	1	3	–
R.A. Harper	13	12	2	73	328	32.80	–	2	14	–
M.A. Holding	7	7	0	69	189	27.00	–	2	3	–
E.A.E. Baptiste	10	9	1	87*	196	24.50	–	1	1	–
M.D. Marshall	8	9	0	34	103	11.44	–	–	3	–
J. Garner	8	8	1	29	61	8.71	–	–	4	–
M.A. Small	5	3	2	3*	6	6.00	–	–	1	–
C.A. Walsh	8	5	2	2*	2	0.66	–	–	1	–

Bowling	O	M	R	W	Avge	Best	5wI	10wM
W.W. Davis	66	13	199	14	14.21	5-32	2	1
J. Garner	270.5	81	624	39	16.00	5-19	2	–
M.D. Marshall	260.4	75	646	40	16.15	7-53	4	–
R.A. Harper	302.1	106	632	37	17.08	6-57	3	–
M.A. Holding	178.5	42	486	21	23.14	5-43	1	–
M.A. Small	100	17	321	13	24.69	4-52	–	–
E.A.E. Baptiste	221.2	64	517	19	27.21	4-17	–	–
C.A. Walsh	156.1	32	557	14	39.78	3-33	–	–

Also bowled: H.A. Gomes 44-15-81-2; C.G. Greenidge 9-6-11-1; I.V.A. Richards 74-20-185-3.

*not out

Texaco Trophy

The first series of international limited-over matches to be sponsored by Texaco was doubly blessed – by three fine days amid a rainy period and by England's unexpected victory in the second match, which gave the third at Lord's the extra spice of a decider.

England, in fact, had made a promising start to the first match at Old Trafford, taking seven West Indian wickets for 103. But they had not shifted Vivian Richards, and his magnificent 189 not out, the highest ever in a one-day international and including 5 sixes and 21 fours, produced a score of 272. Baptiste played well in a stand of 55, but Garner was soon out, and at 166 for 9 England were within one wicket of being left a target probably within their scope. But despite losing wickets West Indies had scored at four runs an over and there were nearly 15 overs left. Holding played comfortably through them, making 12, while Richards hammered the England bowling mercilessly in an unbroken last-wicket stand of 106.

Only Lamb lasted long against the West Indies fast bowlers, and from a start of 8 for 2 England were always heading for a heavy defeat.

However, two days later at Trent Bridge they put West Indies in after a delayed start which reduced the match from 55 overs to 50. Again they made swift inroads into the West Indies batting. Miller, who had taken three wickets at Old Trafford, took the vital wicket of Richards, caught off the top edge while sweeping. From 75 for 5, there was only partial recovery this time, despite Lloyd's 52, and England needed only 180.

The long-held theory that good left-handers would more easily counter the massed West Indian fast bowlers than right-handers was fully borne out as Andy Lloyd, Fowler, and Gower moved steadily up to 103 before the second wicket fell. The ball still moved off the seam and the right-handers found the going harder, but they never looked like throwing away a winning advantage. Pringle's bowling and two catches had played a big part in the victory.

At Lord's, England brought in Randall for Gatting and West Indies the young off-spinner Harper for a batsman Richardson. This time before a capacity crowd, West Indies put England in on a pitch giving the fast bowlers some help early on, and, though the left-handers did well again to reach 91 for 1, there was a need for acceleration that their successors could not meet. The innings stumbled no further than 196. Botham briefly promised to produce what was needed, but was brilliantly caught by Harper who also ran out Lamb.

At tea, West Indies were 63 for 2, but any hope that Richards might fail and West Indies founder was swiftly killed afterwards. With Gomes playing very well in support, Richards played another superb innings, hitting 4 sixes and 10 fours and making 84 off 65 balls to bring West Indies racing home with eight overs to spare.

WEST INDIES IN ENGLAND 1984

England v West Indies 1st Texaco Trophy International
West Indies won by 104 runs
Played at Old Trafford, May 31
Toss: West Indies. Umpires: D.J. Constant and D.R. Shepherd
Man of the Match: I.V.A. Richards (Adjudicator: G. Pullar)

West Indies		Runs	Mins	Balls	6s	4s
C.G. Greenidge	c Bairstow b Botham	9	14	11	-	1
D.L. Haynes	run out (Botham)	1	6	5	-	-
R.B. Richardson	c and b Willis	6	37	24	-	-
I.V.A. Richards	not out	189	220	170	5	21
H.A. Gomes	b Miller	4	27	17	-	1
C.H. Lloyd*	c Pringle b Miller	8	29	21	-	1
P.J. Dujon†	c Gatting b Miller	0	2	1	-	-
M.D. Marshall	run out (Bairstow)	4	3	3	-	-
E.A.E. Baptiste	c Bairstow b Botham	26	51	49	-	2
J. Garner	c and b Foster	3	4	5	-	-
M.A. Holding	not out	12	60	27	-	2
Extras	(B 4, LB 2, W 1, NB 3)	10				
	(55 overs; 235 minutes)	**272-9**				

England		Runs	Mins	Balls	6s	4s
G. Fowler	c Lloyd b Garner	1	9	5	-	-
T.A. Lloyd	c Dujon b Holding	15	47	42	-	2
M.W. Gatting	lbw b Garner	0	3	5	-	-
D.I. Gower*	c Greenidge b Marshall	15	56	38	-	-
A.J. Lamb	c Richardson b Gomes	75	137	89	-	8
I.T. Botham	c Richardson b Baptiste	2	5	6	-	-
D.L. Bairstow†	c Garner b Richards	13	34	34	-	2
G. Miller	b Richards	7	17	24	-	-
D.R. Pringle	c Garner b Holding	6	14	21	-	-
N.A. Foster	b Garner	24	30	38	-	2
R.G.D. Willis	not out	1	2	2	-	-
Extras	(LB 6, NB 3)	9				
	(50 overs; 186 minutes)	**168**				

England	O	M	R	W
Willis	11	2	38	1
Botham	11	0	67	2
Foster	11	0	61	1
Miller	11	1	32	3
Pringle	11	0	64	0

West Indies	O	M	R	W
Garner	8	1	18	3
Holding	11	2	23	2
Baptiste	11	0	38	1
Marshall	6	1	20	1
Richards	11	1	45	2
Gomes	3	0	15	1

Fall of Wickets

Wkt	WI	E
1st	5	7
2nd	11	8
3rd	43	33
4th	63	48
5th	89	51
6th	98	80
7th	102	100
8th	161	115
9th	166	162
10th		168

*Captain †Wicket-keeper

England v West Indies 2nd Texaco Trophy International
England won by 3 wickets
Played at Trent Bridge, June 2
Toss: England. Umpires: H.D. Bird and D.O. Oslear
Man of the Match: D.R. Pringle (Adjudicator: A.R. Lewis)

West Indies		Runs	Mins	Balls	6s	4s
C.G. Greenidge	c Botham b Pringle	20	53	38	–	2
D.L. Haynes	lbw b Willis	4	32	23	–	–
R.B. Richardson	c Gower b Pringle	10	28	30	–	1
I.V.A. Richards	c Pringle b Miller	3	15	12	–	–
H.A. Gomes	b Pringle	15	44	39	–	–
C.H. Lloyd*	c Pringle b Miller	52	78	66	3	3
P.J. Dujon†	run out (Miller)	21	59	36	–	1
M.D. Marshall	run out (Bairstow)	20	30	22	–	1
E.A.E. Baptiste	lbw b Willis	19	28	16	–	1
M.A. Holding	b Botham	0	2	2	–	–
J. Garner	not out	6	13	11	–	–
Extras	(LB 7, NB 2)	9				
	(48.3 overs; 199 minutes)	**179**				

England		Runs	Mins	Balls	6s	4s
G. Fowler	b Baptiste	25	96	62	–	2
T.A. Lloyd	c Dujon b Baptiste	49	117	103	–	1
D.I. Gower*	lbw b Marshall	36	59	42	–	3
A.J. Lamb	b Gomes	11	24	24	–	–
I.T. Botham	c Gomes b Holding	15	45	23	–	1
M.W. Gatting	b Garner	6	15	14	–	–
D.L. Bairstow†	b Holding	9	22	16	–	–
G. Miller	not out	3	8	6	–	–
D.R. Pringle	not out	2	1	3	–	–
N.A. Foster	did not bat					
R.G.D. Willis	" "					
Extras	(B 4, LB 14, NB 6)	24				
	(47.5 overs; 201 minutes)	**180-7**				

England	O	M	R	W
Willis	9.3	0	26	2
Botham	9	1	33	1
Pringle	10	3	21	3
Miller	10	2	44	2
Foster	10	0	46	0

West Indies	O	M	R	W
Garner	9	1	22	1
Holding	8.5	1	29	2
Marshall	10	1	30	1
Baptiste	10	2	31	2
Richards	5	0	23	0
Gomes	5	0	21	1

Fall of Wickets

Wkt	WI	E
1st	24	75
2nd	38	103
3rd	39	131
4th	43	145
5th	75	157
6th	128	173
7th	148	177
8th	160	
9th	161	
10th	179	

*Captain †Wicket-keeper

WEST INDIES IN ENGLAND 1984

England v West Indies 3rd Texaco Trophy International
West Indies won by 8 wickets
Played at Lord's, June 4
Toss: West Indies. Umpires: D.G.L. Evans and B.J. Meyer
Man of the Match: R.A. Harper (Adjudicator: D.C.S. Compton)

England		Runs	Mins	Balls	6s	4s
G. Fowler	b Holding	34	79	72	–	1
T.A. Lloyd	b Harper	37	117	83	–	–
D.I. Gower*	b Marshall	29	85	57	–	–
A.J. Lamb	run out (Harper)	0	1	1	–	–
I.T. Botham	c Harper b Baptiste	22	28	27	1	1
D.W. Randall	c Dujon b Marshall	8	24	13	–	–
D.L. Bairstow†	b Marshall	8	26	22	–	–
G. Miller	b Holding	10	45	27	–	–
D.R. Pringle	lbw b Garner	8	31	22	–	–
N.A. Foster	not out	4	16	8	–	–
R.G.D. Willis	not out	6	11	9	–	–
Extras	(B 1, LB 17, W 4, NB 8)	30				
	(55 overs; 239 minutes)	**196-9**				

West Indies		Runs	Mins	Balls	6s	4s
C.G. Greenidge	c Bairstow b Pringle	32	95	81	–	3
D.L. Haynes	c Randall b Miller	18	74	51	–	2
H.A. Gomes	not out	56	113	90	–	4
I.V.A. Richards	not out	84	94	65	4	10
C.H. Lloyd*	did not bat					
P.J. Dujon†	,, ,,					
M.D. Marshall	,, ,,					
E.A.E. Baptiste	,, ,,					
R.A. Harper	,, ,,					
J. Garner	,, ,,					
M.A. Holding	,, ,,					
Extras	(B 1, W 1, NB 5)	7				
	(46.5 overs, 189 minutes)	**197-2**				

West Indies	O	M	R	W
Garner	11	4	17	1
Holding	11	0	33	2
Marshall	11	0	38	3
Baptiste	11	1	40	1
Harper	11	0	38	1

England	O	M	R	W
Willis	10.5	2	52	0
Botham	8	0	25	0
Miller	9	1	35	1
Pringle	8	0	38	1
Foster	11	1	40	0

Fall of Wickets

Wkt	E	WI
1st	60	50
2nd	91	63
3rd	91	
4th	128	
5th	144	
6th	151	
7th	167	
8th	177	
9th	182	

*Captain †Wicket-keeper

Sri Lanka in England

Sri Lanka's tour and their first Test match in England will be remembered as a great success, not for their victories – they did not win a match – but for the quality and spirit of their batting at Lord's when they had easily the better of a draw with England.

A month's preliminaries had established that the Sri Lankans had plenty of batting, which thrived in some lovely weather. They lost to only one county, Surrey, and that on a rough Oval pitch. But they arrived at Lord's for the Test having bowled out only one county side. Even that one, Kent, having succumbed to the fast-medium John and the leg-spinner D.S. de Silva, made over 400 after following on.

Thus Sri Lanka had earned a reputation for efficient batting and weak bowling. England stuck to the team that had played in the last Test against West Indies and which was entitled, most were agreed, to be retained for a more normal cricket match than the one-sided battering by West Indian fast bowlers had allowed.

Lord's produced a superb batting pitch. Gower won the toss and, putting a not unreasonable faith in the heavy atmosphere of an overcast late summer's day, chose to bowl first. But the ball did not swing. The talented Sri Lankan batsmen, notably Wettimuny and the young left-hander Ranatunga, were in their element and finished a shortened day 226 for 3, Wettimuny 116 not out.

The second day was affected even more by bad light and drizzle, but Sri Lanka reached 434 for 4. Wettimuny, a model of correctness mixing dazzling cover-drives with great competence off his legs, advanced to 187 not out, while the sturdy captain Duleep Mendis made 100 not out off 112 balls with spectacular strokes including three sixes off Botham's long-hops. Sri Lanka declared before lunch next day, having given a much appreciated display of refreshingly orthodox and positive batting. The defects of England's bowling were too well known to increase concern, especially on such a good pitch, but there were high hopes that their batsmen would now make a contribution of similar quality to Sri Lanka's.

During the rest of Saturday's play, England reached the nadir of their season, mustering only 139 for 2 in 4 hours 20 minutes off 61 overs from modest bowlers, some handicapped by injury. The kindest criticism would be that Broad (69 not out), Tavare (16 in over two hours), and even Gower were hopelessly out of form. It was in dismal contrast to Sri Lanka's batting.

There was only a little improvement on the fourth day, when England were bowled out for 370 despite Lamb's well made 107, his fourth Test hundred of the summer. It remained only for Sri Lanka to bat comfortably through the last day. Mendis, in two hours, all but reached his second 100 of the match, and the wicket-keeper, the left-handed Silva, one of the less obviously gifted of Sri Lanka's young batsmen, batted through the day for 102 not out, latterly with a runner. For good measure, he almost repeated the feat next day when, having cast off his cramp, he made 161 not out against Warwickshire.

SRI LANKA IN ENGLAND 1984

SRI LANKA 1st INNINGS v. ENGLAND (Only Test) at LORD'S, LONDON on 23, 24, 25, 26, 27, 28 AUGUST, 1984. TOSS: ENGLAND.

IN	OUT	MINS	No.	BATSMAN	HOW OUT	BOWLER	RUNS	WKT	TOTAL	6s	4s	BALLS	NOTES ON DISMISSAL
11.03	11.31	636	1	S. WETTIMUNY	c Downton	Allott	190	5	442	.	21	471	Record Sri Lanka score. Edged cover-drive off back foot. Highest score, 1st wicket
11.03	11.19	16	2	S.A.R. SILVA †	LBW	Botham	8	1	17	.	1	11	Drove across full length in-swinger (left-handed batsman)
11.21	11.56	35	3	R.S. MADUGALLE	Bowled	Ellison	5	2	43	.	1	24	Off stump - played outside in-swinger
11.58	3.07	152	4	R.L. DIAS	c Lamb	Pocock	32	3	144	.	3	104	Beaten by flight - low catch at mid-wicket
3.09	2.19	248	5	A. RANATUNGA	Bowled	Agnew	84	4	292	1*	8	183	† 2nd innings. Beaten by breakback - off bail removed
2.21	11.52	197	6	L.R.D. MENDIS*	c Fowler	Pocock	111	6	456	3	11	143	* By 4 Sri Lanka captain. HS in Tests. Drove to mid-wicket boundary
2.33	12.02	29	7	P.A. DE SILVA	c Downton	Agnew	16	7	464	.	3	27	Test debut. Edged leg glance to keeper. Well-judged catch
11.54	(2.28)	34	8	A.L.F. DE MEL	not out		20			.	3	25	
12.04	(2.28)	24	9	J.R. RATNAYEKE	not out		5			.	.	18	
			10	D.S. DE SILVA	} did not bat								
			11	V.B. JOHN									
				EXTRAS	b 2 lb 8 w 2 nb 8		20					5⁶ 51⁴	1006 balls (including 10 no balls)
				TOTAL	(166 OVERS, 692 MINUTES)		491-7 DECLARED						

*CAPTAIN †WICKET-KEEPER

© BILL FRINDALL 1984

BOWLER	O	M	R	W	nb	w	HRS	OVERS	RUNS
AGNEW	32	3	123	2	8	.	1	14	43
BOTHAM	29	6	114	1	-/1	2	2	14	38
ELLISON	28	6	70	1	.	.	3	14	42
POCOCK	41	17	75	2	.	.	4	17	50
ALLOTT	36	7	89	1	.	.	5	14	30
							6	15	43
			2D				7	15	25
	166	39	491	7			8	13	37
							9	14	62
							10	14	55
							11	15	31

2nd NEW BALL taken at 11.17am on 2nd day -
SRI LANKA 229-3 after 85 overs

	RUNS	MINS	OVERS	LAST 50 (in mins)
	50	79	18.3	79
	100	149	34.3	70
	150	215	52.0	66
	200	295	72.3	80
	250	365	89.5	70
	300	468	113.3	103
	350	520	125.0	52
	400	573	137.2	53
	450	652	157.1	79

LUNCH: 81-2 | 28 OVERS 121 MINUTES

TEA: 173-3 | 59 OVERS 240 MINUTES | WETTIMUNY 106 (166) / DIAS 7* (66)

STUMPS: 226-3 Bad light at 5.31pm - 29 min lost | 81 OVERS 330 MINUTES | WETTIMUNY 116 (188) / RANATUNGA 56 (121)

LUNCH: 271-3 Rain at 12.01pm (32 min lost) | 103 OVERS 419 MINUTES | WETTIMUNY 137* (464) / RANATUNGA 74 (211)

TEA: 370-4 | 130 OVERS 541 MINUTES | WETTIMUNY 173 (546) / MENDIS 52 (87)

STUMPS: 434-4 Rain 4.12-5.13 (26 min lost) | 144.5 OVERS 605 MINUTES | WETTIMUNY 187* (604) / MENDIS 100* (146)

14 OVERS 2 BALLS/HOUR
2.96 RUNS/OVER
49 RUNS/100 BALLS

WKT	PARTNERSHIP		RUNS	MINS
1st	Wettimuny	Silva	17	16
2nd	Wettimuny	Madugalle	26	35
3rd	Wettimuny	Dias	101	152
4th	Wettimuny	Ranatunga	148‡	248
5th	Wettimuny	Mendis	150	176
6th	Mendis	de Silva	14	19
7th	de Silva	De Mel	8	8
8th	De Mel	Ratnayeke	27*	24
			491	

‡ SRI LANKA 4th WICKET RECORD

138 SRI LANKA IN ENGLAND 1984

ENGLAND 1st INNINGS
IN REPLY TO SRI LANKA'S 491-7 DECLARED

IN	OUT	MINS	No.	BATSMAN	HOW OUT	BOWLER	RUNS	WKT	TOTAL	6s	4s	BALLS	NOTES ON DISMISSAL
12.40	2.10	50	1	G. FOWLER	c MADUGALLE	JOHN	25	1	49	.	4	41	Steered short ball to 2nd slip - two-handed, chest-high catch
12.40	12.21	339	2	B.C. BROAD	c SILVA	DE MEL	86	3	190	.	8	242	His in TESTS. Edged cut at short offside ball.
2.12	4.48	136	3	C.J. TAVARÉ	c RANATUNGA	DS DE SILVA	14	2	105	.	1	95	Mistimed pull-drive - mid-on catch.
4.50	1.46	194	4	D.I. GOWER *	c SILVA	DE MEL	55	4	210	.	5	151	Edged ball that 'left' him, up slope
12.24	5.50	267	5	A.J. LAMB	c DIAS	JOHN	107	9	369	1	10	195	(4th Test this season.) Pulled short ball to mid-wicket
1.48	1.54	6	6	I.T. BOTHAM	c SUB (V.n.HAGT)	JOHN	6	5	218	.	1	6	Pushed across line - edged to gully
1.56	4.09	114	7	R.M. ELLISON	c RATNAYEKE	DS DE SILVA	41	6	305	.	7	79	Mistimed pull - skier to extra-cover.
4.11	5.16	65	8	P.R. DOWNTON†	c DIAS	DE MEL	10	7	354	.	1	53	Mowed simple catch to mid-wicket.
5.18	5.19	1	9	P.J.W. ALLOTT	BOWLED	DE MEL	0	8	354	.	.	1	off stump out - 1st ball.
5.21	5.59	38	10	P.I. POCOCK	c SILVA	JOHN	2	10	370	.	.	21	First Test runs since 1976. Edged drive low to keeper's right
5.52	(5.59)	7	11	J.P. AGNEW	NOT OUT		1			.	.	8	
				EXTRAS	b5 lb7		23					1+37	892 balls (including 9 no balls)
				TOTAL	(147.1 OVERS, 618 MINUTES)	w5 nb6	370						all out at 5-59pm on fourth day

*CAPTAIN †WICKET-KEEPER

14 OVERS 2 BALLS/HOUR
2.51 RUNS/OVER
41 RUNS/100 BALLS

BOWLER	O	M	R	W	HRS	OVERS	RUNS	MINS	OVERS	LAST 50 (in mins)
DE MEL	37	10	110	4	3/1	1	13	53	50	53	12.2	53
JOHN	39.1	12	98	4	4/1	2	14	22	100	183	42.4	130
RATNAYEKE	22	5	50	0	-½	3	15	23	150	277	65.3	94
D.S. DE SILVA	45	16	85	2	-/1	4	13	32	200	364	87.1	87
RANATUNGA	1	1	0	0	.	5	16	28	250	424	100.1	60
MADUGALLE	3	0	4	0	.	6	13	39	300	500	118.4	76
			23			7	13	45	350	569	136.1	69
	147.1	44	370	10		8	14	38				
						9	17	39				
						10	13	42				

© BILL FRINDALL 1984

LUNCH: 32-0 [5 OVERS / 21 MINUTES] [FOWLER 15* / BROAD 17*]

TEA: 81-1 [32 OVERS / 141 MINUTES] [BROAD 36*(141) / TAVARÉ 12*(89)]

STUMPS: 139-2 [61 OVERS / 259 MINUTES] [BROAD 69*(229) / GOWER 16*(70)]

LUNCH: 210-3 [91 OVERS / 378 MINUTES] [GOWER 55*(185) / LAMB 10*(36)]

TEA: 300-5 [119 OVERS / 501 MINUTES] [LAMB 55*(159) / ELLISON 37*(107)]

SRI LANKA'S LEAD: 121 RUNS

WKT	PARTNERSHIP		RUNS	MINS
1st	Fowler	Broad	49	50
2nd	Broad	Tavaré	56	136
3rd	Broad	Gower	85	150
4th	Gower	Lamb	20	41
5th	Lamb	Botham	8	6
6th	Lamb	Ellison	87	114
7th	Lamb	Downton	49	65
8th	Lamb	Allott	0	1
9th	Lamb	Pocock	15	29
10th	Pocock	Agnew	1	7

370

SRI LANKA 2ND INNINGS (121 RUNS AHEAD ON FIRST INNINGS)

IN	OUT	MINS	No.	BATSMAN	HOW OUT	BOWLER	RUNS	WKT	TOTAL	6s	4s	BALLS	NOTES ON DISMISSAL
11·02	11·23	21	1	S. WETTIMUNY	c' Gower	Botham	13	1	19	·	2	21	Edged late outswinger to 3rd slip.
11·02	(5·20)	316	2	S.A.R. SILVA†	NOT OUT		102			·	12	255	HS in Tests. Runner from 83*. Maiden first-class hundred.
11·24	11·32	8	3	R.S. MADUGALLE	BOWLED	Botham	3	2	27	·	·	9	Beaten by break-back that clipped off stump.
11·34	2·06	112	4	R.L. DIAS	LBW	Botham	38	3	111	·	5	79	Beaten by break-back that kept low — played back.
2·09	2·15	6	5	A. RANATUNGA	LBW	Botham	0	4	115	·	·	6	Late on quicker ball that 'straightened'. Hit on back leg.
2·17	2·21	4	6	P.A. DE SILVA	c' Downton	Pocock	3	5	118	·	·	6	Edged 'arm' ball to 'keeper.
2·24	4·46	120	7	L.R.D. MENDIS*	c' Fowler	Botham	94	6	256	3	9	96	Edged pull — skier to extra-cover.
4·48	4·59	11	8	A.L.F. DE MEL	c' Ellison	Botham	14	7	276	·	3	8	Drove to deep mid-off.
5·02	(5·20)	18	9	J.R. RATNAYEKE	NOT OUT		7			·	1	15	
			10	D.S. DE SILVA	} Did not bat								
			11	V.B. JOHN									
				EXTRAS	b 5 lb 4 w - nb 11		20			3⁶	32⁴	495 balls (including 15 no balls)

TOTAL (80 OVERS, 316 MINUTES) 294-7 DECLARED at 5.20 pm on 5th day.

*CAPTAIN †WICKET-KEEPER

© BILL FRINDALL 1984

BOWLER	O	M	R	W	nb	HRS	OVERS	RUNS
AGNEW	11	3	54	0	15	1	11	48
ALLOTT	1	0	2	0	·	2	16	45
BOTHAM	27	6	90	6	·	3	17	42
POCOCK	29	10	78	1	·	4	14	45
ELLISON	7	0	36	0	·	5	16	98
LAMB	1	0	6	0	·			
TAVARÉ	3	3	0	0	·			
FOWLER	1	0	8	0	·			
	80	22	294	7	20			

2ND NEW BALL NOT TAKEN

RUNS	MINS	OVERS	LAST 50 (in mins)
50	60	11.3	60
100	124	28.4	64
150	213	51.2	89
200	252	61.4	39
250	280	68.4	28

LUNCH: 93-2 [27 OVERS] SILVA 39* (115)
(214 AHEAD) [119 MINUTES] DIAS 27* (81)

TEA: 180-5 [58 OVERS] SILVA 71* (229)
[239 MINUTES] MENDIS 37* (71)

MATCH DRAWN

MAN OF THE MATCH: S. WETTIMUNY
(Adjudicator: T.W. Graveney)

TOTAL TIME LOST: 1 HOUR 55 MIN (NET)

15 OVERS 1 BALLS/HOUR
3.68 RUNS/OVER
59 RUNS/100 BALLS

WKT	PARTNERSHIP		RUNS	MINS
1st	Wettimuny	Silva	19	21
2nd	Silva	Madugalle	8	8
3rd	Silva	Dias	84	112
4th	Silva	Ranatunga	4	6
5th	Silva	P.A. de Silva	3	4
6th	Silva	Mendis	138	120
7th	Silva	De Mel	20	11
8th	Silva	Ratnayeke	18*	18
			294	

Statistical Highlights of Lord's Test

Lord's, in its Test match centenary year, staged its 77th official Test to overtake the world record previously held by the Melbourne Cricket Ground. Gower (the only player to appear in all of England's 34 Tests since the 1981 Ashes series), Tavaré, Botham, and Allott were England's only survivors from the team that won the inaugural Test in Colombo in February 1982. Sri Lanka's total of 491-7 declared was the highest of their 12-match history. Wettimuny (190) recorded Sri Lanka's highest score in Test cricket, the highest innings by any visiting batsman playing his first Test innings in England, and the sixth-highest score against England at Lord's. Mendis, who made his highest score in Tests, became the first Sri Lankan captain to score a Test hundred while in office. Gower led the England team's applause from the dressing room balcony for Pocock's first run in Test cricket since 1976. Silva's hundred was his first in first-class cricket. This was England's 12th match without victory, equalling their longest sequence of non-success.

Sri Lanka Tour of England 1984

Results: Played 9; Won 0, Lost 1, Drawn 8

First-Class Averages

Batting and Fielding	M	I	NO	HS	R	Avge	100	50	Ct	St
S.A.R. Silva	7	12	3	161*	558	62.00	2	2	12	–
L.R.D. Mendis	7	10	2	111	442	55.25	1	3	1	–
S. Wettimuny	7	11	1	190	505	50.50	2	1	2	–
R.S. Madugalle	7	12	4	87*	336	42.00	–	3	3	–
A. Ranatunga	8	11	1	118	419	41.90	1	3	5	–
P.A. De Silva	7	8	0	75	236	29.50	–	3	3	–
D.M. Vonhagt	5	9	0	75	251	27.88	–	1	2	–
J.R. Ratnayeke	8	11	5	66	163	27.16	–	1	5	–
A.L.F. De Mel	6	7	1	37	117	19.50	–	–	3	–
R.L. Dias	9	12	0	38	224	18.66	–	–	5	–
D.S. De Silva	5	4	1	37*	55	18.33	–	–	2	–
D.S.B.P. Kuruppu	3	4	0	25	38	9.50	–	–	4	1

Also batted: S.D. Anurasiri (4 matches) 0*, 0, 5 (2 ct); R.G. de Alwis (2 matches) 74 (3 ct); V.B. John (5 matches) 4, 0, 0* (1 ct); A.D.A. Samaranayaka (5 matches) 5, 9* (3 ct); M.M. Yusuf (4 matches) 2*.

Bowling	O	M	R	W	Avge	Best	5wI	10wM
V.B. John	190.3	46	603	26	23.19	6-58	3	–
A.L.F. De Mel	153.2	31	470	19	24.73	4-110	–	–
A. Ranatunga	69	12	227	6	37.83	2-44	–	–
D.S. De Silva	216	62	532	13	40.92	5-39	1	–
J.R. Ratnayeke	227.2	43	730	16	45.62	4-93	–	–
A.D.A. Samaranayaka	133.2	24	499	9	55.44	4-142	–	–

Also bowled: S.D. Anurasiri 89.5-21-336-1; P.A. De Silva 4-0-19-0; R.L. Dias 6-3-18-1; R.S. Madugalle 31-6-75-2; L.R.D. Mendis 1-0-2-0; S. Wettimuny 5-1-7-1; M.M. Yusuf 74-10-282-1.

English season 1984

Britannic Assurance Championship

In its first season under the sponsorship of Britannic Assurance, the County Championship had probably the most spectacular finish of its long history. Four runs were needed off the last two balls for Nottinghamshire to beat Somerset at Taunton and finish champions ahead of Essex, who had won their own final match in two days at Old Trafford. Mike Bore, who had already hit 10 runs off the first three balls of the final over, drove again at the left-arm spinner Booth but this time was caught on the boundary. By a few feet the championship stayed with Essex, the holders.

Notts had been only 14th in 1983 when without Richard Hadlee, but this season had him back in outstanding form which earned him the first Britannic Assurance Player of the Year award. Not many choices will be easier than that of an all-rounder who averaged 50 with the bat and took over 100 wickets at 14 apiece.

Essex and Notts had disputed the lead throughout the second half of the season with Essex usually just ahead. On August 10, Notts seemed to have done their cause serious harm by losing to Derbyshire after making them follow on. However, they immediately hit back with an impressive win over Middlesex at Lord's, Hadlee's contribution to that being five wickets and an innings of 210 not out. Essex had just had a narrow victory over Middlesex.

Ten days later, Essex had a calamitous match against Kent who, helped by an inspired all-round performance by their acting-captain Christopher Cowdrey, beat them by 10 wickets in a day and a half.

Throughout the last few weeks, Notts had a match in hand over Essex. This fell in the penultimate round of matches and was against Sussex at Hove. Notts began it only one point behind Essex and were in a position to put the prize almost out of Essex's reach there and then. But a match in hand is no asset if the weather is bad, and what with obdurate Sussex batting and interruptions for bad light and drizzle, Notts gathered only five points out of the match.

Thus they started the last round of matches just four points ahead of Essex, who were clearly the more likely to achieve a definite result at Old Trafford, where bowlers had usually received some help in 1984, than Notts were at Taunton. Lancashire, moreover, were bottom but one in the table. In the event, Essex swamped them by 10 wickets.

Notts meanwhile had been interrupted by bad light at Taunton and only appeared with a chance of victory when Ian Botham made the ideal declaration – ideal because it gave his side a chance of victory by forcing Notts to take desperate chances on a pitch taking slow spin. He asked for 297 in a minimum of 52 overs, though this proved to be 60 overs as spin was used almost throughout.

In so close a finish it is hard to say dogmatically that the better side won the Championship. Both were deserving. At various times Notts provided England teams with Broad and Randall, Essex supplied Pringle and Foster. When they met at Chelmsford in May, Notts won handsomely, outbowling Essex on a pitch which ordinarily would have been considered a big help to the Essex fast-medium bowlers. Yet the championship is decided not on one match but over a season of 72 days' cricket, and Essex's ability to bowl sides out, Lever playing a bigger part than ever, and to make runs quickly through such as Gooch and McEwan, gave them a better chance of finishing matches than other sides enjoyed.

It was an added boost to the public interest in the Championship that a lovely summer allowed almost unprecedented continuity of play.

Until July, Leicestershire were in contention with Essex and Notts, but dropped away, even to the extent of giving Lancashire their only victory of the season in August. They rallied at the end in a close contest for third place with Middlesex, Kent, and Sussex, but could not quite catch Middlesex whose performance was one of the more remarkable of the season.

After winning their first match on May 1, Middlesex did not win another for 10 weeks, by which time they had dropped to 12th. With one exception, their batsmen were out of form. Their once formidable bowlers lacked penetration and they showed all the signs of a side needing an overhaul. They were revived by Mike Gatting in a period of five weeks in which he was out only twice for under 100 and made his runs at a pace that brought four wins in five matches. Gradually, the other batsmen, Barlow, Slack, Radley, and Butcher, began to find their form and Middlesex were within sight of the leaders when they were roundly defeated by both Essex and Notts in a week.

Gower's absences and loss of form were a handicap to Leicestershire. Kent moved up two places from 1983 and continued to look a side for the future, as perhaps did Sussex, who advanced from 11th to 6th. Somerset, without Richards and Garner but with a successful temporary import in the New Zealander Martin Crowe, did well to improve from 10th to 7th, though if that last match at Taunton, indeed the last stroke, had gone differently, they would have stayed 10th, such was the congestion in the middle of the table.

Hampshire's descent from 3rd to 15th was not unexpected in the absence of Greenidge and Marshall. Yorkshire's 14th place suggested that modest bowling rather than a week former administration was at the heart of their troubles. Gloucestershire at the bottom also suffered from a shortage of penetrative bowling, while the presence of the once powerful Lancashire in 16th place was a sad reminder that, whatever their successes at the limited-over game, they have not won the Championship outright since 1934.

Britannic Assurance County Championship 1984 – Final Table

	P	W	L	D	T	1st Innings Points Batting	1st Innings Points Bowling	Total Points
1 ESSEX (1)	24	13	3	8	–	64	83	355
2 Nottinghamshire (14)	24	12	3	9	–	68	81	341
3 Middlesex (2)	24	8	7	9	–	63	78	269
4 Leicestershire (4)	24	8	2	14	–	60	78	266
5 Kent (7)	24	8	3	11	2	45	65	254
6 Sussex (11)	24	7	6	10	1	54	79	249
7 Somerset (10)	24	6	7	11	–	60	78	234
8 Surrey (8)	24	6	6	12	–	62	72	230
9 Warwickshire (5)	24	6	7	11	–	71	60	227
10 Worcestershire (16)	24	5	5	14	–	66	74	220
11 Northamptonshire (6)	24	5	9	9	1	58	56	202
12 Derbyshire (9)	24	4	6	14	–	72	66	202
13 Glamorgan (15)	24	4	2	18	–	65	71	200
14 Yorkshire (17)	24	5	4	15	–	59	55	194
15 Hampshire (3)	24	3	13	8	–	58	62	168
16 Lancashire (12)	24	1	9	14	–	49	72	137
17 Gloucestershire (12)	24	1	10	13	–	56	61	133

1983 final positions are shown in brackets. The total for Sussex includes 12 points for winning a match reduced to one innings. Where sides are equal on points, the one with the most wins has priority.

Points

For a win: 16 points, plus any first innings points. For winning a match reduced to a single innings because it started with less than eight hours of playing time remaining: 12 points. First innings points (awarded during the first 100 overs of each first innings and retained whatever the result of the match):

Batting
150 to 199 runs 1
200 to 249 runs 2
250 to 299 runs 3
300 runs and over 4

Bowling
3 or 4 wickets 1
5 or 6 wickets 2
7 or 8 wickets 3
9 or 10 wickets 4

Final Positions 1890-1984

	D	E	Gm	Gs	H	K	La	Le	M	Nh	Nt	Sm	Sy	Sx	Wa	Wo	Y
1890	—	—	—	6	—	3	2	—	7	—	5	—	1	8	—	—	3
1891	—	—	—	9	—	5	2	—	3	—	4	5	1	7	—	—	8
1892	—	—	—	7	—	7	4	—	5	—	2	3	1	9	—	—	6
1893	—	—	—	9	—	4	2	—	3	—	6	8	5	7	—	—	1
1894	—	—	—	9	—	4	4	—	3	—	7	6	1	8	—	—	2
1895	5	9	—	4	10	14	2	12	6	—	12	8	1	11	6	—	3
1896	7	5	—	10	8	9	2	13	3	—	6	11	4	14	12	—	1
1897	14	3	—	5	9	12	1	13	8	—	10	11	2	6	7	—	4
1898	9	5	—	3	12	7	6	13	2	—	8	13	4	9	9	—	1
1899	15	6	—	9	10	8	4	13	2	—	10	13	1	5	7	12	3
1900	13	10	—	7	15	3	2	14	7	—	5	11	7	3	6	12	1
1901	15	10	—	14	7	7	3	12	2	—	9	12	6	4	5	11	1
1902	10	13	—	14	15	7	5	11	12	—	3	7	4	2	6	9	1
1903	12	8	—	13	14	8	4	14	1	—	5	10	11	2	7	6	3
1904	10	14	—	9	15	3	1	7	4	—	5	12	11	6	7	13	2
1905	14	12	—	8	16	6	2	5	11	13	10	15	4	3	7	8	1
1906	16	7	—	9	8	1	4	15	11	11	5	11	3	10	6	14	2
1907	16	7	—	10	12	8	6	11	5	15	1	14	4	13	9	2	2
1908	14	11	—	10	9	2	7	13	4	15	8	16	3	5	12	6	1

ENGLISH SEASON 1984/BRITANNIC ASSURANCE CHAMPIONSHIP 145

	D	E	Gm	Gs	H	K	La	Le	M	Nh	Nt	Sm	Sy	Sx	Wa	Wo	Y
1909	15	14	—	16	8	1	2	13	6	7	10	11	5	4	12	8	3
1910	15	11	—	12	6	1	4	10	3	9	5	16	2	7	14	13	8
1911	14	6	—	12	11	2	4	15	3	10	8	16	5	13	1	9	7
1912	12	15	—	11	6	3	4	13	5	2	8	14	7	10	9	16	1
1913	13	15	—	9	10	1	8	14	6	4	5	16	3	7	11	12	2
1914	12	8	—	16	5	3	11	13	2	9	10	15	1	6	7	14	4
1919	9	14	—	8	7	2	5	9	13	12	3	5	4	11	15	—	1
1920	16	9	—	8	11	5	2	13	1	14	7	10	3	6	12	15	4
1921	12	15	17	7	6	4	5	11	1	13	8	10	2	9	16	14	3
1922	11	8	16	13	6	4	5	14	7	15	2	10	3	9	12	17	1
1923	10	13	16	11	7	5	3	14	8	17	2	9	4	6	12	15	1
1924	17	15	13	6	12	5	4	11	2	16	6	8	3	10	9	14	1
1925	14	7	17	10	9	5	3	12	6	11	4	15	2	13	8	16	1
1926	11	9	8	15	7	3	1	13	6	16	4	14	5	10	12	17	2
1927	5	8	15	12	13	4	1	7	9	16	2	14	6	10	11	17	3
1928	10	16	15	5	12	2	1	9	8	13	3	14	6	7	11	17	4
1929	7	12	17	4	11	8	2	9	6	13	1	15	10	4	14	16	2
1930	9	6	11	2	13	5	1	12	16	17	4	13	8	7	15	10	3
1931	7	10	15	2	12	3	6	16	11	17	5	13	8	4	9	14	1
1932	10	14	15	13	8	3	6	12	10	16	4	7	5	2	9	17	1
1933	6	4	16	10	14	3	5	17	12	13	8	11	9	2	7	15	1
1934	3	8	13	7	14	5	1	12	10	17	9	15	11	2	4	16	5
1935	2	9	13	15	16	10	4	6	3	17	5	14	11	7	8	12	1
1936	1	9	16	4	10	8	11	15	2	17	5	7	6	14	13	12	3
1937	3	6	7	4	14	12	9	16	2	17	10	13	8	5	11	15	1
1938	5	6	16	10	14	9	4	15	2	17	12	7	3	8	13	11	1
1939	9	4	13	3	15	5	6	17	2	16	12	14	8	10	11	7	1
1946	15	8	6	5	10	6	3	11	2	16	13	4	11	17	14	8	1
1947	5	11	9	2	16	4	3	14	1	17	11	11	6	9	15	7	7
1948	6	13	1	8	9	15	5	11	3	17	14	12	2	16	7	10	4
1949	15	9	8	7	16	13	11	17	1	6	11	9	5	13	4	3	1
1950	5	17	11	7	12	9	1	16	14	10	15	7	1	13	4	6	3
1951	11	8	5	12	9	16	3	15	7	13	17	14	6	10	1	4	2
1952	4	10	7	9	12	15	3	6	5	8	16	17	1	13	10	14	2
1953	6	12	10	6	14	16	3	3	5	11	8	17	1	2	9	15	12
1954	3	15	4	13	14	11	10	16	7	7	5	17	1	9	6	11	2
1955	8	14	16	12	3	13	9	6	5	7	11	17	1	4	9	15	2
1956	12	11	13	3	6	16	2	17	5	4	8	15	1	9	14	9	7
1957	4	5	9	12	13	14	6	17	7	2	15	8	1	9	11	16	3
1958	5	6	15	14	2	8	7	12	10	4	17	3	1	13	16	9	11
1959	7	9	6	2	8	13	5	16	10	11	17	12	3	15	4	14	1
1960	5	6	11	8	12	10	2	17	3	9	16	14	7	4	15	13	1
1961	7	6	14	5	1	11	13	9	3	16	17	10	15	8	12	4	2
1962	7	9	14	4	10	11	16	17	13	8	15	6	5	12	3	2	1
1963	17	12	2	8	10	13	15	16	6	7	9	3	11	4	4	14	1
1964	12	10	11	17	12	7	14	16	6	3	15	8	4	9	2	1	5
1965	9	15	3	10	12	5	13	14	6	2	17	7	8	16	11	1	4
1966	9	16	14	15	11	4	12	8	12	5	17	3	7	10	6	2	1
1967	6	15	14	17	12	2	11	3	7	9	16	8	4	13	10	5	1
1968	8	14	3	16	5	2	6	9	10	13	4	12	15	17	11	7	1
1969	16	6	1	2	5	10	15	14	11	9	8	17	3	7	4	12	13
1970	7	12	2	17	10	1	3	15	16	14	11	13	5	9	7	6	4
1971	17	10	16	8	9	4	3	5	6	14	12	7	1	11	2	15	13
1972	17	5	13	3	9	2	15	6	8	4	14	11	12	16	1	7	10
1973	16	8	11	5	1	4	12	9	13	3	17	10	2	15	7	6	14
1974	17	12	16	14	2	10	8	4	6	3	15	5	7	13	9	1	11
1975	15	7	9	16	3	5	4	1	11	8	13	12	6	17	14	10	2
1976	15	6	17	3	12	14	16	4	1	2	13	7	9	10	5	11	8
1977	7	6	14	3	11	1	16	5	1	9	17	4	14	8	10	13	12
1978	14	2	13	10	8	1	12	6	3	17	7	5	16	9	11	15	4
1979	16	1	17	10	12	5	13	6	14	11	9	8	3	4	15	2	7
1980	9	8	13	7	17	16	15	9	1	12	3	5	2	4	14	11	6
1981	12	5	14	13	7	9	16	8	4	15	1	3	6	2	17	11	10
1982	11	7	16	15	3	13	12	2	1	9	4	6	5	8	17	14	10
1983	9	1	15	12	3	7	12	4	2	6	14	10	8	11	5	16	17
1984	12	1	13	17	15	5	16	4	3	11	2	7	8	6	9	10	14

Derbyshire

Derbyshire, who made such encouraging advances the previous summer, slipped back disappointingly in 1984, dropping two places to 11th in the Championship, finishing bottom of the John Player League, and making no impression in the other limited-over competitions.

With Michael Holding committed to the West Indies, Derbyshire's gamble in releasing experienced seamers Steve Oldham and Colin Tunnicliffe the previous September depended for success on two things – freedom from injuries to bowlers and the development of such as Paul Newman, Roger Finney, Bruce Roberts, and Devon Malcolm. In the event, Ole Mortensen, who had been expected to shoulder the heaviest burden, played only eight Championship matches because of a spinal lesion and, although Newman passed 50 wickets for the first time, only left-arm-seamer Finney was consistently fit and effective. Derbyshire supporters noted indeed that Finney, the most improved player on the staff, ended the campaign with more runs and wickets than England tourist Richard Ellison of Kent.

The spinners were more successful. Geoff Miller had his best-ever season with both bat and ball and, but for missing five Championship games through international duties and injury, may well have followed Richard Hadlee to the 'double'. Both Miller and left-arm-spinner Dallas Moir, who overcame a diffident start to claim 65 wickets, scored maiden first-class centuries, the former in his 11th season, and the disappointment of Derbyshire's collective under-achievement was to some extent mitigated by individual successes.

Kim Barnett's six first-class centuries and aggregate of 1,734 runs made it a career-best season for the young skipper and also, arguably, made him the unluckiest omission from England's touring party for India and Australia. Only Gatting and Robinson of eligible batsmen made more runs, and both were selected. There were, perhaps, times when Barnett's captaincy seemed a shade ambitious, considering his bowling resources, but Derbyshire will no doubt appreciate such a positive approach when Holding and Mortensen are in harness.

John Morris continued to reveal the richest promise, scoring three Championship hundreds and one in the John Player League, while the dependable Alan Hill compiled his best-ever aggregate. John Wright, the New Zealand opener, available only on an abbreviated contract, took only 19 games to pass 1,000 runs; Bill Fowler frequently gave the middle order some extra momentum; and with eight players scoring first-class centuries – a county record – Derbyshire recorded more batting bonus points than anyone else.

With Harry Elliott (1920-47), George Dawkes (1947-61), and Bob Taylor (1961-84), Derbyshire have a long and illustrious tradition of quality wicket-keeping. Taylor, the world-record-holder with 1,646 victims, retired at the end of the summer but will remain with the county, captaining the Second XI from the slips and taking part in their commercial activities. No decline in standards to prompt retirement was discernible, and there could be no harder act to follow for the patient Bernie Maher.

Britannic Assurance County Championship: 12th; Won 4, Lost 6, Drawn 14
All First-Class Matches: Won 4, Lost 7, Drawn 14
NatWest Bank Trophy: Lost to Leicestershire in 2nd round
Benson & Hedges Cup: Failed to qualify for Q-F (3rd in Group B)
John Player League: 17th; Won 4, Lost 11, No result 1

Championship Averages   *not out

Batting and Fielding	M	I	NO	HS	R	Avge	100	50	Ct	St
J.G. Wright	12	21	1	177	1201	60.05	2	9	10	–
K.J. Barnett	23	39	3	144	1703	47.30	6	9	20	–
J.E. Morris	14	26	1	135	896	35.84	3	3	4	–
I. Broome	2	4	3	26*	35	35.00	–	–	1	–
A. Hill	24	42	3	125	1345	34.48	1	11	13	–
G. Miller	19	28	4	130	817	34.04	1	4	25	–
W.P. Fowler	21	36	8	116	940	33.57	2	7	17	–
J.H. Hampshire	20	31	4	101*	790	29.25	1	4	20	–
D.G. Moir	19	26	6	107	534	26.70	1	2	18	–
B. Roberts	17	26	5	80	554	26.38	–	3	12	–
R.J. Finney	23	35	5	78	652	21.73	–	4	5	–
I.S. Anderson	14	23	1	79	454	20.63	–	1	14	–
R.W. Taylor	18	22	7	46	303	20.20	–	–	27	5
B.J.M. Maher	6	9	2	66	127	18.14	–	1	14	–
O.H. Mortensen	8	8	4	40*	63	15.75	–	–	4	–
P.G. Newman	15	19	1	40	223	12.38	–	–	3	–
D.E. Malcolm	6	6	1	23	37	7.40	–	–	3	–

Also batted: J.P. Taylor (3 matches) 11, 0 (2 ct).

Hundreds (17)

6 K.J. Barnett: 114 v Leics, Chesterfield; 144 v Middx, Derby; 104 v Worcs, Worcester; 120 v Somerset, Taunton; 102* v Leics, Leicester; 107* v Hants, Derby.
3 J.E. Morris: 116 v Yorks, Harrogate; 103 v Worcs, Worcester; 135 v Leics, Leicester.
2 W.P. Fowler: 116 v Glam, Derby; 101* v Hants, Derby.
  J.G. Wright: 141 v Yorks, Harrogate; 177 v Sussex, Derby.
1 J.H. Hampshire: 101* v Essex, Chesterfield.
  A. Hill: 125 v Warwicks, Chesterfield.
  G. Miller: 130 v Lancs, Manchester.
  D.G. Moir: 107 v Warwicks, Chesterfield.

Bowling	O	M	R	W	Avge	Best	5wI	10wM
G. Miller	850.3	250	2038	84	24.26	6-30	6	–
R.J. Finney	565.1	127	1704	60	28.40	5-55	2	–
O.H. Mortensen	212.3	55	570	18	31.66	3-37	–	–
P.G. Newman	474.2	85	1601	48	33.35	7-104	1	–
D.G. Moir	803.5	204	2342	64	36.59	6-60	3	1
D.E. Malcolm	132.2	21	555	13	42.69	3-78	–	–
B. Roberts	277	43	1044	22	47.45	4-77	–	–

Also bowled: I.S. Anderson 55-10-176-3; K.J. Barnett 43-6-162-0; I. Broome 19.1-6-82-2; W.P. Fowler 117.3-27-398-5; J.H. Hampshire 1-1-0-0; A. Hill 50-10-191-3; J.E. Morris 11-0-73-1; J.P. Taylor 49.2-6-188-2; R.W. Taylor 6.2-1-23-1; J.G. Wright 22-2-114-1.

Essex

The batting of Graham Gooch, in becoming the first player to score 2,000 runs, and the bowling of John Lever, who won the *Daily Telegraph* Swanton Trophy as the first to take 100 wickets, were undoubtedly the highlights of Essex's feat in becoming champions in successive years. But their triumph was also decidedly due to an outstanding team effort, with only 15 players fielded all season.

One such example came when the slow left-arm spinner Ray East was brought back from retirement for three matches, after a finger injury to off-spinner Acfield in mid-season. East was later recalled again for the vital last match of the season against Lancashire, at Old Trafford, which necessitated victory for the Championship. Essex astutely selected both spinners for this match, and East certainly proved his worth again, with 3 for 24 in Lancashire's second innings. Acfield played a valuable part all season, with 46 wickets at 29.74, and indeed, for that telling match at Old Trafford, the champions could proudly boast the strongest of all county attacks in Lever, Foster, Pringle, Gooch, and the two spinners.

Lever captured the best figures of his career with 8 for 37 against Gloucestershire at Bristol, and also enjoyed his most successful season with 116 wickets. Foster likewise had his best season, with 87 wickets, and Pringle took 59 wickets at 25.88 apiece. But the surprise success of the Essex bowling arrived in the medium-pace of Gooch (38 wickets). The value of Gooch with the ball often came on his entering the attack as an opposition partnership was growing to dangerous size. He would quickly break the stand and enable Essex to regain the initiative. Such a duty was duly performed by Gooch on that telling last day at Old Trafford.

Gooch had a prime season as opening batsman, with the highest score of his career, 227 against Derbyshire at Chesterfield, and then his aggregate of 2,559 runs, beating the 50-year-old record of 2,308 runs held by Jack O'Connor. On the rare occasions when Gooch failed, the classical bat of McEwan invariably flowed. Even if McEwan did not quite recapture his great form of the previous season (2,176 runs), he still scored 1,755 runs at an average of 46.18.

The only two uncapped players for Essex were the young local batsmen Gladwin, 22, from East Ham, and the 19-year-old Prichard, from Billericay. The success of both provided much encouragement for the future, and opener Gladwin, with 1,396 runs, was awarded his county cap in August. On gaining his place, Prichard batted in the middle order, but later in the season his discerning captain Fletcher changed places and promoted Prichard to first wicket down. The Prichard potential was confirmed with 888 runs (average 32.89), and his maiden hundred came – as did many an Essex joy and achievement – in that last match at Old Trafford.

Essex suffered only three defeats – admittedly, comprehensively, at the hands of the runners-up Nottinghamshire, at Chelmsford, in May and then twice by Kent – and they finished as peerless champions with victories in 9 of their last 14 matches. Another stimulating point in the

ENGLISH SEASON 1984/ESSEX

Essex glory was that, apart from McEwan (South Africa), Phillip (West Indies), and Hardie (Scotland), all their players were either born or raised in the county.

Britannic Assurance County Championship: 1st; Won 13, Lost 3, Drawn 8
All First-Class Matches: Won 13, Lost 4, Drawn 10
NatWest Bank Trophy: Lost to Surrey in 2nd round
Benson & Hedges Cup: Lost to Lancashire in quarter-final
John Player League: 1st; Won 12, Lost 3, Tied 1

Championship Averages   *not out

Batting and Fielding	M	I	NO	HS	R	Avge	100	50	Ct	St
G.A. Gooch	23	40	7	227	2281	69.12	7	11	22	–
K.S. McEwan	24	39	6	142*	1563	47.36	4	8	19	–
P.J. Prichard	19	27	2	100	876	35.04	1	6	10	–
B.R. Hardie	24	32	6	99	886	34.07	–	5	25	–
K.W.R. Fletcher	22	33	4	131	932	32.13	3	3	20	–
C. Gladwin	23	40	3	94	1141	30.83	–	9	13	–
S. Turner	10	10	5	59*	128	25.60	–	1	4	–
D.R. Pringle	15	23	4	63	388	20.42	–	2	10	–
N. Phillip	12	16	1	71	284	18.93	–	1	1	–
N.A. Foster	18	21	5	54*	255	15.93	–	1	6	–
D.E. East	24	32	1	81	480	15.48	–	3	73	1
J.K. Lever	22	20	7	30	134	10.30	–	–	9	–
D.L. Acfield	22	20	8	7*	36	3.00	–	–	10	–

Also batted: R.E. East (3 matches) 22, 8 (2 ct); K.R. Pont (2 matches) 28, 32, 1 (1 ct).
A.W. Lilley (1 match) did not bat.

Hundreds (15)

7 G.A. Gooch: 220 v Hants, Southampton; 108 v Notts, Chelmsford; 113* v Leics, Hinckley; 227 v Derbys, Chesterfield; 131 v Yorks, Leeds; 105* v Middx, Lord's; 160* v Surrey, Oval.
4 K.S. McEwan: 101 v Derbys, Ilford; 142* v Hants, Colchester; 104 v Surrey, Oval; 132 v Lancs, Manchester.
3 K.W.R. Fletcher: 131 v Northants, Chelmsford; 106 v Yorks, Leeds; 122 v Worcs, Chelmsford.
1 P.J. Prichard: 100 v Lancs, Manchester.

Bowling	O	M	R	W	Avge	Best	5wI	10wM
G.A. Gooch	288.1	68	756	36	21.00	4-54	–	–
N.A. Foster	571.1	120	1727	78	22.14	6-79	4	–
J.K. Lever	801	177	2389	106	22.53	8-37	8	3
D.R. Pringle	420.4	100	1253	55	22.78	7-53	2	–
N. Phillip	250.2	45	835	32	26.09	5-48	1	–
S. Turner	226	77	481	18	26.72	3-29	–	–
D.L. Acfield	520.4	149	1256	43	29.20	6-44	2	–

Also bowled: D.E. East 3-0-11-0; R.E. East 114.4-40-197-8; K.W.R. Fletcher 5-0-20-0; C. Gladwin 10-1-26-0; A.W. Lilley 5.2-2-11-0; P.J. Prichard 1-0-5-0.

Glamorgan

On the face of it, Glamorgan had another moderate season in 1984, for though they managed a modest advance in the County Championship, from 15th to 13th, they did not improve on their 1983 position of 10th in the John Player League, while they signally failed to make an impact in either the Benson & Hedges or NatWest competitions. Nonetheless, there were signs that the Welsh county has built a nucleus of players capable of bringing about substantial improvement. Clear evidence of this was their late and merited flurry of success in August. Captained by Rodney Ontong in the absence of Mike Selvey, whose worn knees have caused his early retirement, they had the rare pleasure of recording successive Championship victories, against Northants at Sophia Gardens and Warwickshire at Edgbaston, and at last looked a side capable of winning matches rather than one merely difficult to beat.

The reasons for their improvement are not hard to find. Alan Lewis Jones, who reached 1,000 runs in a season for the first time in 1983, scored the first century of a 10-year career against Gloucestershire early in the season, followed it with four more, and scored over 1,800 first-class runs. This vast improvement owed much to the player's hard work during the winter when, with the invaluable help of county coach Alan Jones, he sought pretty successfully to eliminate weaknesses against faster bowling. His opening partner, John Hopkins, again batted solidly and had a good season. Geoff Holmes and Hugh Morris, given extended runs in the first team, rewarded the selectors with solid improvement, which augurs well for the future.

The class and consistency of Younis Ahmed were evident to most, and Ontong, again reliability itself with the bat, made a personal best 204 not out while defying Middlesex throughout the last day at Swansea. Steele also proved a most valuable recruit. He batted grittily down the order, took plenty of wickets with his slow left-arm bowling, and fielded brilliantly close to the bat. The balance that his and Ontong's all-round skills gave to the side was impossible to exaggerate.

The county's dilemma with regard to which of their overseas players, Javed Miandad or Winston Davis, should play was, at least temporarily, solved. Javed remains a great player, but with their batting more stable than for some years Glamorgan were able to opt for the erratic but occasionally formidable fast bowling of Davis. Davis's figures do not reflect his impact on opposing batsmen. Though he was inconsistent and regrettably prone to no-ball, his presence undoubtedly assisted the improving Barwick and Gregory Thomas, who even on the placid Sophia Gardens strips had the pace to make good batsmen hurry.

Ontong, now fully committed to off-spin, continued to develop his skills, as his tally of wickets indicates. Derrick's seamers showed promise, and with some good young players making their mark in the second XI Glamorgan approach 1985 with quiet confidence.

ENGLISH SEASON 1984/GLAMORGAN

Britannic Assurance County Championship: 13th; Won 4, Lost 2, Drawn 18
All First-Class Matches: Won 6, Lost 3, Drawn 18
NatWest Bank Trophy: Lost to Nottinghamshire in 1st round
Benson & Hedges Cup: Failed to qualify for Q-F (4th in Group C)
John Player League: 9th; Won 6, Lost 8, No result 2

Championship Averages

*not out

Batting and Fielding	M	I	NO	HS	R	Avge	100	50	Ct	St
Javed Miandad	7	13	1	212*	800	66.66	2	3	2	–
J. Derrick	10	15	7	69*	351	43.87	–	3	7	–
Younis Ahmed	18	31	3	122	1100	39.28	1	8	11	–
A.L. Jones	24	45	2	132	1550	36.04	5	4	25	–
J.A. Hopkins	24	46	5	128*	1435	35.00	2	8	18	–
R.C. Ontong	22	40	6	204*	1182	34.76	1	6	14	–
H. Morris	12	20	4	114*	542	33.87	1	4	2	–
J.F. Steele	23	38	12	60*	796	30.61	–	1	31	–
G.C. Holmes	20	36	1	90	1006	28.74	–	6	11	–
S.P. Henderson	7	12	0	90	340	28.33	–	3	4	–
W.W. Davis	16	18	6	50	271	22.58	–	1	7	–
J.G. Thomas	18	25	5	36*	313	15.65	–	–	7	–
T. Davies	24	32	7	43	364	14.56	–	–	36	7
C.J.C. Rowe	5	10	1	19	95	10.55	–	–	2	–
M.W.W. Selvey	13	15	7	20	82	10.25	–	–	8	–
S.R. Barwick	17	16	7	25	77	8.55	–	–	6	–

Also batted: D.A. Francis (1 match) 20, 7 (1 ct); R.C. Green (1 match) 3* (1 ct). M.R. Price (2 matches) did not bat.

Hundreds (12)

5 **A.L. Jones:** 129 v Glos, Cardiff; 122 v Middx, Swansea; 114 v Essex, Southend; 100 v Somerset, Taunton; 132 v Hants Cardiff.
2 **J.A. Hopkins:** 116* v Glos, Cardiff; 128* v Surrey, Oval.
  Javed Miandad: 212* v Leics, Swansea; 171 v Hants, Cardiff.
1 **H. Morris:** 114* v Yorks, Cardiff.
  R.C. Ontong: 204* v Middx, Swansea.
  Younis Ahmed: 122 v Sussex, Hove.

Bowling	O	M	R	W	Avge	Best	5wI	10wM
J.F. Steele	632.3	164	1780	65	27.38	5-42	4	–
R.C. Ontong	728.4	186	1941	65	29.86	7-96	4	–
W.W. Davis	458.5	102	1443	48	30.06	5-57	2	–
S.R. Barwick	391.3	98	1090	34	32.05	7-55	1	–
J.G. Thomas	383.3	77	1441	41	35.14	5-56	2	1
M.W.W. Selvey	280.4	62	913	19	48.05	4-40	–	–

Also bowled: J. Derrick 133.5-31-441-8; R.C. Green 14.5-3-65-2; G.C. Holmes 70-8-253-3; J.A. Hopkins 2.2-0-18-0; Javed Miandad 31.2-2-146-4; A.L. Jones 10-0-86-1; H. Morris 9-1-45-1; M.R. Price 29-4-96-2; C.J.C. Rowe 83-10-306-8; Younis Ahmed 12-3-34-0.

Gloucestershire

A harrowing season for Gloucestershire, in which they were bottom of the County Championship, avoided an unwelcome double wooden spoon only through a couple of late John Player League wins, and made no impression in either the NatWest or Benson & Hedges competitions (indeed in the latter they suffered embarrassing defeat at the hands of the Combined Universities at Bristol), ended with a petition of members seeking the resignation of the captain, David Graveney, and of the Cricket Committee. While the reaction of members, who in the 1970s had become used to a degree of success in all competitions, is understandable, one cannot but feel sympathy for Graveney himself. Mike Procter's retirement half-way through 1981 left Gloucestershire with one of the weakest attacks in county cricket, which was subsequently made even less effective through the decline of John Childs.

Last season, the county's signing of Courtney Walsh, the promising young West Indian fast bowler, was pre-empted by his country's surprise selection of him for their tour of England. In addition, Zaheer Abbas, one of the most feared batsmen on the county circuit for the last decade, made nothing like his usual quota of runs. Weary from continuous county and Test cricket, he faded sadly from the scene in July.

Bowling, as ever, was Gloucestershire's problem. Graveney himself topped the averages, but his wickets cost close to 30 runs apiece. Shepherd, tireless as ever at 40, bowled 800 overs, but his wickets were slightly more expensive than Graveney's. And Sainsbury, though admirably steady, again lacked penetration. Lawrence was at times genuinely fast, but was also frequently erratic; nevertheless, there was an improvement in his overall performance which, if maintained, could make him a real asset.

The batsmen were naturally under great pressure to score runs so as to cushion their bowlers, and none reacted better than the former Yorkshire batsman Bill Athey. He hit four centuries, and with over 1,800 runs had easily his best season, while the solid Romaines, despite a lean August, also passed the 1,800 mark. Neither Stovold nor Bainbridge was consistent, but both did enough to demonstrate their quality, and Shepherd at times laid about him effectively.

Of the younger players, Wright made an excellent maiden hundred against Surrey at Cheltenham and finished only just short of 1,000 runs, and Cunningham, though only moderately successful in the Championship, headed the Sunday League averages and should develop. Russell, the wicket-keeper, suffered from illness and injury, and his batting did not progress as had been hoped, but he remains a cricketer with a big future.

Graveney, confirmed in his appointment as captain for 1985 by the Club's management committee but with the annual general meeting still to be negotiated, will surely wish to forget this season. With Walsh and the Zimbabwean all-rounder Curran fully available and with Lloyds recruited from Somerset, Gloucestershire will next year be better balanced and should show long overdue improvement.

ENGLISH SEASON 1984/GLOUCESTERSHIRE

Britannic Assurance County Championship: 17th; Won 1, Lost 10, Drawn 13
All First-Class Matches: Won 1, Lost 10, Drawn 15
NatWest Bank Trophy: Lost to Lancashire in 2nd round
Benson & Hedges Cup: Failed to qualify for Q-F (4th in Group D)
John Player League: 13th; Won 5, Lost 9, No result 2

Championship Averages

*not out

Batting and Fielding	M	I	NO	HS	R	Avge	100	50	Ct	St
C.W.J. Athey	24	48	4	114*	1737	39.47	4	11	24	-
P.W. Romaines	24	48	0	141	1665	34.68	4	8	10	-
A.W. Stovold	24	48	2	139*	1490	32.39	2	11	17	2
Zaheer Abbas	14	28	4	157*	738	30.75	1	4	2	-
P. Bainbridge	21	40	6	134*	1012	29.76	1	6	8	-
J.N. Shepherd	23	37	6	87	846	27.29	-	6	13	-
A.J. Wright	21	37	3	139	842	24.76	1	5	11	-
R.C. Russell	20	26	5	63	513	24.42	-	1	26	9
C.S. Dale	7	7	2	49	98	19.60	-	-	1	-
D.A. Graveney	24	38	12	33	425	16.34	-	-	17	-
S.H. Wootton	3	6	1	33	72	14.40	-	-	4	-
E.J. Cunningham	5	9	2	24	99	14.14	-	-	-	-
C.A. Walsh	6	10	1	30	96	10.66	-	-	-	-
G.E. Sainsbury	20	19	14	10*	40	8.00	-	-	8	-
D.V. Lawrence	18	24	4	17	130	6.50	-	-	2	-
J.H. Childs	5	5	2	4*	10	3.33	-	-	2	-

Also batted: A.J. Brassington (1 match) 22, 0* (1 ct); D.A. Burrows (1 match) 0;
P.G.P. Roebuck (1 match) 5, 20; C.R. Trembath (2 matches) 17*, 0*, 8.

Hundreds (13)

4 **C.W.J. Athey:** 114* v Yorks, Bradford; 108* v Worcs, Worcester; 113 v Lancs, Bristol; 106 v Middx, Bristol.
 P.W. Romaines: 141 v Glam, Cardiff; 103 v Derbys, Gloucester; 120 v Yorks, Bradford; 114 v Worcs, Worcester.
2 **A.W. Stovold:** 126 v Worcs, Gloucester; 139* v Leics, Bristol.
1 **P. Bainbridge:** 134* v Essex, Bristol.
 A.J. Wright: 139 v Surrey, Cheltenham.
 Zaheer Abbas: 157* v Kent, Bristol.

Bowling	O	M	R	W	Avge	Best	5wI	10wM
J.N. Shepherd	783.3	206	2152	72	29.88	5-30	2	-
D.A. Graveney	623.4	181	1525	49	31.12	6-73	2	-
G.E. Sainsbury	536.2	132	1515	47	32.23	5-19	2	-
C.A. Walsh	185.2	48	622	18	34.55	6-70	1	-
D.V. Lawrence	446.1	75	1515	40	37.87	5-58	3	-
J.H. Childs	250	64	661	14	47.21	3-72	-	-
P. Bainbridge	303.2	73	959	18	53.27	4-76	-	-

Also bowled: C.W.J. Athey 9-1-36-0; D.A. Burrows 15-0-76-0; E.J. Cunningham
21-3-70-0; C.S. Dale 112.4-16-452-4; P.W. Romaines 0.3-0-8-0; C.R. Trembath 46.5-
5-225-5; Zaheer Abbas 5.4-4-1-0.

Hampshire

Hampshire's fall to 15th place after finishing third in the two preceding seasons was not as remarkable as it might seem. The depression was consistent with a pattern, in that the county's bad years have tended to coincide with West Indies tours of England. They were bottom in 1980 and 12th in 1976. Batting as Greenidge did for the tourists, his absence was, of course, vital. But bowling being Hampshire's weaker suit by far, they missed Marshall even more.

Milton Small, whom they had signed up as a stand-in for Marshall, was also called up for the tour, and Hampshire had to delve even deeper into Barbados's resources for a substitute. The best they could get was Elvis Reifer, left arm, who proved enthusiastic and industrious. But having come directly from club cricket, he lacked the experience to spearhead a county attack in unfamiliar conditions. There came a time, in fact, when Hampshire found it more worthwhile to give the overseas player's spot to a batsman, Robin Smith, who will have completed his English qualification next season.

Hampshire's bowling problems were mitigated somewhat by the recruitment of left-arm spinner Rajesh Maru from Middlesex, and Cardigan Connor, a domiciled Anguillan, who was serving an engineering apprenticeship in Slough while playing for Bucks. With only 16 isolated appearances for Middlesex behind him, Maru proved green, but he provided the attack with much-needed variety and at least once stood out as a match-winner.

Connor's arrival, when Hampshire's season was already four matches old, strengthened them significantly. Virtues of a full length and a straight line brought Connor more wickets than any Hampshire bowler except the indefatigable Tremlett, who gallantly carried a heavy burden. A haul of six wickets by Connor on his maiden appearance brought Hampshire the first of only three wins they scored all season. But even less pleasant was the debit side of 13 defeats. During the last 20 years, only Sussex (1975) and Lancashire (1965) were beaten as often in a single summer.

There were some chinks, too, in Hampshire's batting, although, in a dry summer of abundant runs, six of their batsmen passed the 1,000 mark. A model of consistency, Paul Terry, scoring five hundreds and six half-centuries, was picked for England, a deserved honour which, unfortunately, brought a long-term injury in its wake. With his early form, Mark Nicholas also gave the selectors more than a gentle nudge. Jesty, starting off with a double century against Cambridge, played several big and attractive innings.

A glaring batting problem was their vulnerability at the top of the order, with Chris Smith starting the season disastrously and then Terry getting injured. The repercussions were minimized by David Turner coming back from semi-oblivion to make runs with commendable consistency.

Pocock, the captain, was sadly out of touch when he broke a finger and decided against coming back, thus precipitating a crisis. Jesty, as vice-captain, led the side for a while and was then quite suddenly replaced by Nicholas, a move that could only have proved unsettling to a struggling side and one which obviously broke Jesty's heart.

Britannic Assurance County Championship: 15th; Won 3, Lost 13, Drawn 8
All First-Class Matches: Won 4, Lost 13, Drawn 9
NatWest Bank Trophy: Lost to Kent in 2nd round
Benson & Hedges Cup: Failed to qualify for Q-F (3rd in Group D)
John Player League: 9th; Won 7, Lost 9

Championship Averages   *not out

Batting and Fielding	M	I	NO	HS	R	Avge	100	50	Ct	St
V.P. Terry	13	24	3	175*	1055	50.23	4	6	13	–
D.R. Turner	18	33	4	153	1219	42.03	3	6	6	–
T.E. Jesty	23	41	4	143*	1329	35.91	4	4	14	–
M.C.J. Nicholas	24	44	1	158	1453	33.79	4	5	13	–
J.J.E. Hardy	11	17	4	95	436	33.53	–	4	8	–
R.A. Smith	6	11	3	62	254	31.75	–	1	4	–
N.G. Cowley	24	36	3	80	1020	30.90	–	6	10	–
C.L. Smith	24	45	2	125	1112	25.86	3	3	13	–
E.L. Reifer	18	26	8	47	357	19.83	–	–	5	–
T.M. Tremlett	22	30	6	74	428	17.83	–	2	4	–
N.E.J. Pocock	12	17	1	55	277	17.31	–	1	13	–
R.J. Parks	24	33	9	53*	355	14.79	–	–	57	10
R.J. Maru	15	19	3	36	235	14.68	–	–	20	–
S.J.W. Andrew	7	6	4	6*	12	6.00	–	–	1	–
C.A. Connor	20	23	9	13*	65	4.64	–	–	7	–

Also batted: S.J. Malone (2 matches) 0, 4 (2 ct); T.C. Middleton (1 match) 10, 5.

Hundreds (18)

4 **T.E. Jesty:** 143* and 141 v Worcs, Worcester; 131 v Lancs, Portsmouth; 120 v Essex, Colchester.
  M.C.J. Nicholas: 47 v Essex, Southampton; 100 v Worcs, Worcester; 128 v Yorks, Basingstoke; 158 v Lancs, Portsmouth.
  V.P. Terry: 105* v Glos, Southampton; 175* v Glos, Bristol; 136 v Sussex, Bournemouth; 102 v Surrey, Oval.
3 **C.L. Smith:** 125 v Glos, Southampton; 110* v Warwicks, Southampton; 121 v Derbys, Derby.
  D.R. Turner: 153 v Warwicks, Birmingham; 117 v Middx, Lord's; 124 v Derbys, Derby.

Bowling	O	M	R	W	Avge	Best	5wI	10wM
T.M. Tremlett	634.5	188	1403	67	20.94	5-48	2	–
C.A. Connor	621.5	150	1893	60	31.55	7-37	1	–
N.G. Cowley	538	115	1667	52	32.05	4-33	–	–
R.J. Maru	468.4	100	1494	43	34.74	7-79	2	–
T.E. Jesty	199.1	44	603	17	35.47	3-15	–	–
E.L. Reifer	469.3	86	1604	38	42.21	4-52	–	–
S.J.W. Andrew	162.2	43	530	11	48.18	4-30	–	–

Also bowled: J.J.E. Hardy 1-0-3-0; S.J. Malone 37-6-145-1; M.C.J. Nicholas 129-23-438-7; N.E.J. Pocock 10-0-61-0; C.L. Smith 143-16-650-9; D.R. Turner 5-1-9-0.

Kent

Considering Kent's immediate pre-season loss of two valuable strike-bowlers – Graham Dilley to a complex vertebral injury and Eldine Baptiste to the West Indies tour party – they produced a commendable standard of performance in all aspects of cricket: narrowly beaten finalists in the NatWest trophy and fifth in the Championship. This was due, in part, to the hasty but inspired recruitment of Terry Alderman as a replacement fast bowler but also to the burgeoning maturity of four young players – batsmen Neil Taylor, Mark Benson, and Derek Aslett, and all-rounder Richard Ellison.

Taylor, always difficult to dislodge as an opener, improved his mental attitude and, with it, his fluency. Benson overcame a tiresome cartilage injury to delight spectators all over the country with his phlegmatically forceful strokes. Aslett played innings of classic proportions, and Ellison batted and bowled with such determination and consistency as to earn himself a place in the England team. Christopher Cowdrey's all-round contributions and his success as acting captain were invaluable, and when, at the end of the season, the committee decided that Tavaré's loss of form was attributable to the burden of captaincy, Cowdrey was his natural successor.

With this quality of youth, if not at the helm then certainly in the prow, Kent invariably had the resilience to withstand such loss of form or fitness as inevitably overtook some of the senior players. Not the least of these were Chris Tavaré and Bob Woolmer. Tavaré gradually began to recapture some of his authority with the bat. The unlucky Woolmer, however, though untroubled in style and spirit, was forced to concede in mid-season that a recurring back injury called for his retirement.

Meanwhile, though, Derek Underwood, another senior statesman, indicated in two momentous matches that, far from considering retirement, his illustrious career was still in its infancy. The renaissance began at Canterbury when, during the Championship match against Hampshire, rain seeped under the covers, and those who had never seen Underwood – or anyone else – bowl on a wet wicket were in for a salutary ninety minutes. The left-arm specialist exploited the conditions to such effect that in 11.2 overs he claimed 7 wickets for 21 runs as Hampshire skidded to defeat.

Improbably, Underwood's next personal triumph exceeded the first when, at Hastings late in June, he came in as nightwatchman and proceeded to score his maiden century in a career of 22 summers. Not only that; this match against Sussex ended in the Championship's first tie for 10 years. And, if this were not enough, at Northampton, within three weeks, Kent were involved in another tied result.

Such events kept Kent bubbling along with a cheerfulness not always evident in recent years. All of which must have aroused mixed feelings among some of the ambitious players watching from the second XI wings. Wicket-keeper Stuart Waterton and Steven Marsh cheerfully alternated when Alan Knott was indisposed, but both were aware that the old master was by no means a past master.

Similarly, with Kent's incumbent younger batsmen in such good form, the hopes of others were seldom raised. Kevin Jarvis, meanwhile, supported Alderman with his customary enthusiasm and no little success to emphasize the value of the honest and uncomplicated club-man.

Britannic Assurance County Championship: 5th; Won 8, Lost 3, Tied 2, Drawn 11
All First-Class Matches: Won 9, Lost 3, Tied 2, Drawn 12
NatWest Bank Trophy: Lost to Middlesex in final
Benson & Hedges Cup: Failed to qualify for Q-F (3rd in Group C)
John Player League: 9th; Won 6, Lost 8, No result 2

Championship Averages   *not out

Batting and Fielding	M	I	NO	HS	R	Avge	100	50	Ct	St
R.A. Woolmer	8	14	3	153	427	38.81	1	2	4	–
M.R. Benson	12	23	2	127	805	38.33	3	3	6	–
N.R. Taylor	19	36	5	139	1039	33.51	2	5	4	–
C.S. Cowdrey	19	33	3	125*	951	31.70	2	5	18	–
D.G. Aslett	24	42	2	152	1231	30.77	4	3	13	–
C.J. Tavaré	21	37	0	117	1017	27.48	1	5	20	–
C. Penn	11	14	2	115	304	25.33	1	1	7	–
L. Potter	12	22	1	117	494	23.52	1	2	6	–
D.L. Underwood	24	33	9	111	498	20.75	1	–	11	–
G.W. Johnson	23	36	4	84	662	20.68	–	2	23	–
R.M. Ellison	18	28	6	79*	438	19.90	–	1	7	–
S.N.V. Waterton	5	8	0	50	151	18.87	–	1	7	3
S. Marsh	5	7	1	48	106	17.66	–	–	11	–
T.M. Alderman	20	27	13	52*	220	15.71	–	1	29	–
A.P.E. Knott	14	22	2	43	295	14.75	–	–	29	1
S.G. Hinks	6	11	0	39	118	10.72	–	–	2	–
K.B.S. Jarvis	22	24	13	19	38	3.45	–	–	6	–

Also batted: K.D. Masters (1 match) 0, 0.

Hundreds (16)

4 **D.G. Aslett:** 140 v Glos, Bristol; 129* v Middx, Dartford; 109 v Worcs, Worcester; 152 v Somerset, Taunton.
3 **M.R. Benson:** 120 v Surrey, Canterbury; 115 v Notts, Folkestone; 127 v Middx, Lord's.
2 **C.S. Cowdrey:** 102 v Surrey, Canterbury; 125* v Essex, Colchester.
  N.R. Taylor: 108 v Lancs, Maidstone; 139 v Somerset, Taunton.
1 **C. Penn:** 115 v Lancs, Manchester.   **D.L. Underwood:** 111 v Sussex, Hastings.
  L. Potter: 117 v Glam, Canterbury.   **R.A. Woolmer:** 153 v Glos, Bristol.
  C.J. Tavaré: 117 v Leics, Canterbury.

Bowling	O	M	R	W	Avge	Best	5wI	10wM
D.L. Underwood	676.4	250	1511	77	19.62	8-87	2	1
R.M. Ellison	451.5	125	1111	53	20.96	5-27	1	–
T.M. Alderman	559.4	149	1725	76	22.69	5-25	6	–
K.B.S. Jarvis	543.5	118	1715	63	27.22	5-49	1	–
C.S. Cowdrey	232.1	45	721	22	32.77	3-64	–	–
G.W. Johnson	374.1	87	1056	29	36.41	5-38	2	–

Also bowled: D.G. Aslett 9.4-0-58-0; S.G. Hinks 7-2-26-1; K.D. Masters 22-5-85-2; C. Penn 139-21-440-7; L. Potter 19-4-77-2; C.J. Tavaré 2-0-18-0; N.R. Taylor 5-0-19-0; R.A. Woolmer 20-3-51-5.

Lancashire

A year in which Lancashire won the Benson & Hedges Cup and were always in a challenging position in the John Player League could be considered successful. More discerning followers were alarmed by the fact that Lancashire escaped from finishing bottom of the Championship table, for the first time in their history, by two points. Fourteen Championship matches were drawn, bearing out the words of a former England player, now retired, who commented after playing at Old Trafford in May: 'If Lancashire don't do something about this pitch, they will have a terrible time. You cannot play winning cricket on it.'

With Allott, like Fowler, required by England and Folley still learning his trade as a slow left-arm bowler, Lancashire were rarely strong enough to win matches on pitches faster than Old Trafford's. Jefferies, on his day, could look a match-winner, but seems to be an attacker of moods. Watkinson, with four half-centuries including a dashing 70 against Essex, made more progress with the bat than the ball. It is hard to visualize a Lancashire team without Simmons, but the day must come.

Speak, regarded as the coming fast bowler two years ago, again failed to break into the first team, and in an effort to reinforce the seam bowling the club signed Balfour Patterson, a 22-year-old Jamaican and protégé of Clive Lloyd, in July. Patterson has the height, strength, and speed to become a formidable fast bowler, but has very limited experience of the first-class game.

The batting took a blow when Frank Hayes retired on medical advice before the season began, and neither of the Blues, Varey and Kevin Hayes, promised, in early career, to fill the gap. Ormrod arrived to do a solid professional job as he, Abrahams, the talented O'Shaughnessy, and the coming champion Fairbrother all passed 1,000 runs.

Where Lancashire were consistently impressive was in one-day cricket, and their fielding in the Benson & Hedges Final at Lord's will be remembered for a long time. They were a popular team, a pleasure to mix with, their good humour and generosity spreading from the captain and his always genial deputy, Simmons.

Clive Lloyd will return next summer, although he is likely to be seen more often in one-day games than in the Championship. Surprising departures include Radford, for whom Lancashire fought so hard to have registered as English, and the leg-spinner Nasir Zaidi, whose spirit and improving skills will surely win him a palce somewhere.

A first match will be played at Lytham next summer, temporarily supplanting Blackpool. No doubt, the West Coast support will again be of a sufficient size to raise the question, once more, of moving more matches from Old Trafford.

ENGLISH SEASON 1984/LANCASHIRE

Britannic Assurance County Championship: 16th; Won 1, Lost 9, Drawn 14
All First-Class Matches: Won 2, Lost 9, Drawn 14
NatWest Bank Trophy: Lost to Middlesex in quarter-final
Benson & Hedges Cup: Winners
John Player League: 4th; Won 10, Lost 6

Championship Averages

*not out

Batting and Fielding	M	I	NO	HS	R	Avge	100	50	Ct	St
G. Fowler	10	17	0	226	661	38.88	2	2	2	–
S.J. O'Shaughnessy	20	37	4	159*	1150	34.84	3	3	11	–
J. Abrahams	22	38	6	201*	1093	34.15	2	4	18	–
J.A. Ormrod	22	39	3	139*	1149	31.91	1	6	10	–
N.H. Fairbrother	22	38	1	102	1163	31.43	1	10	19	–
M. Watkinson	16	29	6	77	668	29.04	–	4	7	–
S.M.N. Zaidi	5	5	2	36	80	26.66	–	–	2	–
J. Simmons	21	34	5	72*	748	25.79	–	6	14	–
C. Maynard	14	21	5	50*	402	25.12	–	1	25	4
S.T. Jefferies	17	27	3	55*	568	23.66	–	1	4	–
M.R. Chadwick	7	14	0	61	293	20.92	–	2	2	–
D.P. Hughes	18	31	1	113	601	20.03	1	1	11	–
D.W. Varey	8	14	1	61	235	18.07	–	1	3	–
P.J.W. Allott	14	17	3	30	209	14.92	–	–	5	–
N.V. Radford	4	5	1	36	53	13.25	–	–	–	–
I. Folley	17	28	9	22*	194	10.21	–	–	6	–
D.J. Makinson	4	5	2	9	18	6.00	–	–	–	–
L.L. McFarlane	11	15	7	15*	41	5.12	–	–	2	–
J. Stanworth	10	10	3	6	18	2.57	–	–	16	1

Also batted: K.A. Hayes (1 match) 2, 13; B.P. Patterson (1 match) 0, 10.

Hundreds (10)

3 S.J. O'Shaughnessy: 159* v Somerset, Bath; 103* v Hants, Portsmouth; 129 v Warwicks, Manchester.
2 J. Abrahams: 201* v Warwicks, Nuneaton; 100* v Leics, Leicester.
  G. Fowler: 107 v Yorks, Leeds; 226 v Kent, Maidstone.
1 N.H. Fairbrother: 102 v Derbys, Buxton.
  D.P. Hughes: 113 v Somerset, Bath.
  J.A. Ormrod: 139* v Hants, Portsmouth.

Bowling	O	M	R	W	Avge	Best	5wI	10wM
P.J.W. Allott	424.4	123	1014	59	17.18	7-72	5	–
J. Simmons	619.4	177	1644	63	26.09	7-176	7	1
I. Folley	369	91	1015	34	29.85	5-65	2	–
L.L. McFarlane	256.5	39	843	28	30.10	4-65	–	–
S.T. Jefferies	429.5	73	1361	39	34.89	6-67	2	–
N.V. Radford	106.4	17	390	10	39.00	5-95	1	–
S.J. O'Shaughnessy	187.3	33	684	17	40.23	3-76	–	–
M. Watkinson	349	71	1202	29	41.44	6-39	1	–

Also bowled: J. Abrahams 68-10-222-3; N.H. Fairbrother 4.1-1-20-1; G. Fowler 2.1-0-8-0; K.A. Hayes 4-0-25-0; D.P. Hughes 76-13-219-1; D.J. Makinson 93-17-313-7; C. Maynard 2-0-8-0; B.P. Patterson 21-3-51-0; S.M.N. Zaidi 59-9-253-1.

Leicestershire

Leicestershire, fourth in the Championship the previous year and second in 1982, maintained their place among the leaders with fourth place again, but could not sustain their title challenge. That they should do as well as they did, however, was something of an achievement, considering injuries to key players. Captain David Gower was limited by international duties and by a mysterious hand infection to only nine first-class matches for the county. And at least as debilitating to their ambitions was the loss of Les Taylor and George Ferris, who had been expected to share the new ball. Taylor, plagued by elbow problems which required surgery, took only eight wickets, while Ferris, who made such an impact the previous summer, was unable to bowl a single delivery in the Championship because of a hairline fracture of the knee-cap.

The response to extra responsibilities from Jon Agnew was startling, his 72 wickets fulfilling the potential that had been dormant in the three previous seasons, but his subsequent promotion to the England side further depleted Leicestershire's bowling resources.

The accelerated development of Agnew, Gordon Parsons, Tim Boon, and James Whitaker was widely regarded as proof of the mature and, to some people, surprisingly sensitive leadership of Peter Willey, captain for most of the season. The former Northants all-rounder also contributed much with bat and ball. He scored five first-class centuries and his flourishing start with his new County underwrote their potent form in the first half of the season. With Nick Cook undergoing a crisis of form and confidence, Willey's off-spin was an invaluable extra option and earned him 40 wickets.

Andy Roberts came out of retirement in Antigua to answer Leicestershire's SOS in mid-season, refreshing their title hopes with 33 wickets from only 264 overs. But Ian Carmichael, the Yorkshire-born Australian who arrived via a period on scholarship with Essex, took longer than expected to adjust.

If Agnew made the greatest advance, Boon was not far behind. The 22-year-old right-hander managed only 18 runs in 7 innings the previous season, but Gower's absences provided greater exposure and he responded impressively, scoring a maiden century against Gloucestershire and adding three more in compiling 1,177 runs.

Whitaker, another youngster of rich promise, impressed with his uncomplicated approach and the power and cleanness of his hitting, while Ian Butcher and the unflagging Chris Balderstone performed with their usual consistency to compensate for a decline in productivity from Paddy Clift and Nigel Briers. Caps were awarded to Butcher and Parsons, in the latter case the reward for a best-ever season which yielded 65 wickets and 815 runs, a good many made at a gallop.

Mike Garnham remained something of an enigma, keeping wicket efficiently and batting sturdily, but twice getting himself suspended by the county for breaches of discipline which apparently involved salty outbursts on the field.

ENGLISH SEASON 1984/LEICESTERSHIRE

Britannic Assurance County Championship: 4th; Won 8, Lost 2, Drawn 14
All First-Class Matches: Won 9, Lost 2, Drawn 15
NatWest Bank Trophy: Lost to Northamptonshire in quarter-final
Benson & Hedges Cup: Failed to qualify for Q-F (3rd in Group A)
John Player League: 13th; Won 4, Lost 8, No result 4

Championship Averages
*not out

Batting and Fielding	M	I	NO	HS	R	Avge	100	50	Ct	St
D.I. Gower	9	13	1	117*	660	55.00	2	4	4	–
T.J. Boon	20	35	5	144	1177	39.23	4	4	9	–
J.J. Whitaker	18	30	2	160	1077	38.46	2	6	20	–
J.C. Balderstone	19	35	2	181*	1155	35.00	2	5	14	–
P. Willey	24	42	2	167	1322	33.05	5	2	17	–
G.J. Parsons	24	36	9	63	815	30.18	–	6	8	–
I.P. Butcher	22	38	1	130	1086	29.35	3	3	16	–
R.A. Cobb	3	5	0	48	142	28.40	–	–	2	–
M.A. Garnham	17	27	5	84	599	27.22	–	5	43	2
M.D. Haysman	4	8	3	34	127	25.40	–	–	8	–
A.M.E. Roberts	8	12	4	89	188	23.50	–	1	2	–
P.B. Clift	18	27	7	58	429	21.45	–	1	6	–
N.E. Briers	20	33	3	47	500	16.66	–	–	8	–
N.G.B. Cook	18	23	8	44	230	15.33	–	–	16	–
J.P. Agnew	20	20	5	30	148	9.86	–	–	4	–
L.B. Taylor	6	5	1	16*	37	9.25	–	–	–	–
P. Whitticase	7	8	2	14	32	5.33	–	–	16	–
I.R. Carmichael	7	6	3	4*	6	2.00	–	–	3	–

Hundreds (18)

5 P. Willey: 102 v Derbys, Chesterfield; 104 v Northants, Leicester; 159* v Warwicks, Leicester; 156 v Hants, Southampton; 167 v Yorks, Leicester.
4 T.J. Boon: 103* v Warwicks, Leicester; 113 v Glam, Swansea; 144 v Glos, Leicester; 123* v Derbys, Leicester.
3 I.P. Butcher: 130 v Derbys, Chesterfield; 102 v Sussex, Leicester; 130 v Yorks, Sheffield.
2 J.C. Balderstone: 181* v Glos, Leicester; 143* v Derbys, Leicester.
  D.I. Gower: 103 v Worcs, Worcester; 117* v Warwicks, Birmingham.
  J.J. Whitaker: 160 v Somerset, Leicester; 117 v Derbys, Leicester.

Bowling	O	M	R	W	Avge	Best	5wI	10wM
N.E. Briers	99	20	243	12	20.25	3-48	–	–
A.M.E. Roberts	265	70	769	33	23.30	7-74	3	–
P.B. Clift	587.1	161	1488	59	25.22	8-26	2	1
J.P. Agnew	572.3	110	2077	72	28.84	5-44	4	1
P. Willey	512.1	152	1197	40	29.92	6-78	2	–
G.J. Parsons	616.1	129	2013	65	30.96	5-42	2	–
I.R. Carmichael	208	40	661	17	38.88	5-84	1	–
N.G.B. Cook	618.2	176	1616	39	41.43	4.45	–	–

Also bowled: J.C. Balderstone 12-1-66-0; I.P. Butcher 1-0-13-0; L.B. Taylor 123-36-338-8.

Middlesex

Middlesex, whose season began with disappointments and, perhaps, a whiff of discord, emerged at the end with a creditable record: NatWest winners, third in the County Championship, and fifth in the John Player League. All credit, then, to Mike Gatting who, in his second year of captaincy, recognized and tackled the early symptoms that threatened to lead a successful galleon into the doldrums.

The portents were painfully evident in the Benson & Hedges zonal match at Taunton where, with almost truculent resignation, the holders were eliminated from the competition. Gatting's problems were subsequently exacerbated by injuries and illness – not the least the indisposition of Clive Radley, with mumps. Even so, there was no clinical explanation for the side's inability to score substantial totals, as when at Lord's they failed to exceed 200 in either innings against Northants.

Reviewing that period, Gatting later remarked that morale was certainly low, and for a time, when there was no significant improvement, he began to doubt his ability as a captain. However, victories over Worcestershire at Uxbridge and over Yorkshire in two days at Lord's (Gatting 131 not out) were followed by another by 7 wickets in the return match against Northants – and Middlesex had zoomed from 12th to 5th in the Championship table.

That match at Northampton served to illustrate perfectly all aspects of Gatting's determination. He scored 146 in the first innings and 91 not out in the second to confirm that, if some batsmen were letting the side down, he was certainly not among them. At all events the worst was over and even the dread memory of a double defeat by Surrey, in June, began to recede at last.

Back to Lord's and the next fillip – a splendid 9-wicket victory over Hampshire and another personal success for Gatting; run out for 41 and undefeated with 128. There was also a century from Roland Butcher to endorse a general revival in the run-scoring department.

Meanwhile, Middlesex had moved into the quarter-finals of the NatWest with a hard-fought away win against Notts by 5 runs. On August 1, they reached the semi-finals by routing Lancashire by 171 runs and, here at Lord's, it was Graham Barlow's turn to come good with a magnificent 158. Of equal significance was Wayne Daniel's 5 wickets for 14 – a signal that Middlesex, at last, were firing on all cylinders. More importantly, perhaps, young players were taking their chances well – not least, in Paul Downton's Test absences, reserve wicket-keeper Colin Metson.

It was, then, a genial company who beat Hampshire by 7 wickets at Bournemouth, and none more so than Phil Edmonds who, on a Dean Park wicket of extraordinary turn and bounce, claimed a career-best 8 for 53. Too late seriously to challenge for the Championship or John Player titles, Middlesex nevertheless made an impact in the final reckoning by denying Essex victory over three enthralling days at Chelmsford.

Keith Fletcher and his men were not amused, but Gatting gave every impression that he was coasting towards the end of the season with an understandable degree of contentment. Certainly there was much to smile about at Lord's, where the revenue from increased attendances, together with competitive prize and place money, had comfortably exceeded those early-season expectations.

Britannic Assurance County Championship: 3rd; Won 8, Lost 7, Drawn 9
All First-Class Matches: Won 8, Lost 7, Drawn 11
NatWest Bank Trophy: Winners
Benson & Hedges Cup: Failed to qualify for Q-F (5th in Group C)
John Player League: 5th; Won 9, Lost 5, Tied 1, No result 1

Championship Averages   *not out

Batting and Fielding	M	I	NO	HS	R	Avge	100	50	Ct	St
M.W. Gatting	20	37	7	258	1998	66.60	7	8	18	-
R.O. Butcher	21	36	6	116	1251	41.70	2	10	16	-
W.N. Slack	23	43	7	122*	1420	39.44	3	6	20	-
C.T. Radley	23	37	7	128*	1065	35.50	2	7	21	-
P.R. Downton	12	18	6	88	351	29.25	-	2	23	6
G.D. Barlow	18	34	2	96	875	27.34	-	5	10	-
C.P. Metson	12	17	5	96	300	25.00	-	2	28	2
P.H. Edmonds	23	32	3	142	598	20.62	1	2	20	-
K.P. Tomlins	8	14	0	47	238	17.00	-	-	5	-
J.E. Emburey	24	34	2	57	539	16.84	-	3	16	-
N.F. Williams	16	20	2	44	272	15.11	-	-	5	-
S.P. Hughes	13	14	4	41*	144	14.40	-	-	5	-
N.G. Cowans	18	23	1	66	255	11.59	-	1	7	-
A.J.T. Miller	3	5	0	29	57	11.40	-	-	1	-
W.W. Daniel	21	24	14	16*	87	8.70	-	-	4	-

Also batted: K.R. Brown (1 match) 6 (1 ct); J.D. Carr (2 matches) 0, 0; C.R. Cook (2 matches) 47, 16, 43 (1 ct); R.G.P. Ellis (2 matches) 18, 33, 3; K.D. James (1 match) 2. A.R.C. Fraser (1 match) did not bat.

Hundreds (15)

7 **M.W. Gatting:** 258 v Somerset, Bath; 104 v Worcs, Uxbridge; 131* v Yorks, Lord's; 146 v Northants, Northampton; 128* v Hants, Lord's; 116 v Essex, Lord's; 100* v Kent, Lord's.
3 **W.N. Slack:** 100 v Worcs, Uxbridge; 106 v Leics, Leicester; 122* v Essex, Chelmsford.
2 **R.O. Butcher:** 104 v Kent, Dartford; 116 v Hants, Lord's.
  C.T. Radley: 128* v Glam, Lord's; 118* v Surrey, Lord's.
1 **P.H. Edmonds:** 142 v Glam, Swansea.

Bowling	O	M	R	W	Avge	Best	5wI	10wM
N.G. Cowans	419.1	71	1300	65	20.00	6-64	2	-
P.H. Edmonds	802.3	227	2031	77	26.37	8-53	2	1
W.W. Daniel	462	86	1463	54	27.09	4-53	-	-
J.E. Emburey	806.5	227	1884	67	28.11	5-94	1	-
S.P. Hughes	270.3	45	895	31	28.87	4-27	-	-
N.F. Williams	390.5	76	1384	32	43.25	4-55	-	-

Also bowled: J.D. Carr 30-5-73-4; A.R.C. Fraser 34-7-124-1; M.W. Gatting 84-20-197-7; K.D. James 10-3-22-2; W.N. Slack 24-2-73-0; K.P. Tomlins 5-1-9-0.

Northamptonshire

Northants had a frustrating season, with injuries continuously playing a depressing part and the team seldom at full strength. At the start Williams had flu and then a chipped finger, followed by the captain, Cook, who himself was the most consistent of the batsmen and topped the averages, absent for three weeks with a broken thumb. Then Boyd-Moss suffered a broken thumb and a recurrence of hepatitis, while the wicket-keeper Sharp missed two months with his broken thumb. Both the opening bowlers Mallender and Hanley were afflicted with knee injuries.

On top of these withdrawals, Northants were, of course, frequently without the services of England's top batsman, Lamb. In fact, it was not until the last match of the season, against Worcestershire, that Lamb scored a county hundred. Hitherto, his aggregate had been 583 runs (average 29.15).

Williams also failed to score a hundred before that last match, when his 169 brought him belatedly past the 1,000 mark. Indeed, it was a poor season for Williams as an all-rounder, with his 32 wickets of off-spin costing 42 runs apiece. Larkins and Steele were the only capped players available throughout and, in spite of one lean patch of 12 innings for 122 runs, Larkins was once again the leading batsman with 1,656 runs.

One decided mark of favour for Northants with their handicap of injuries was the advance of younger players in filling those vacant roles, notably the success in batting of Bailey and Wild and the wicket-keeping of Ripley. Bailey was selected for the first match of the season, against Warwickshire at Edgbaston, only because Williams had flu. But he certainly took his chance in style, with a maiden hundred, and all promise was handsomely fulfilled. This tall, attacking batsman hit three championship hundreds, played a magnificent innings of 95 against West Indies at Milton Keynes, and finished with an aggregate of 1,404 runs in his first full season.

Wild, 21, was a successful left-handed bat, with two hundreds. His maiden century came in the first ever tied match at Northampton, against Kent.

There was particular concern for the county when Sharp was injured, for he had been the regular wicket-keeper for the past dozen years or more. His place was taken by Ripley, a 17-year-old from Farsley, and by the end of the season the wicket-keeping of this young Yorkshireman had matured with encouraging results (28 catches, 12 stumpings), to say nothing of his development as a batsman. He played an excellent innings of 61 against Surrey.

The Northants bowling was the real weakness, and it was only in the last match that the team gained maximum points for both bowling and batting – and that match, against Worcestershire, was lost. On this front, at least, came the most significant news for the county in next season's signing of the West Indian off-spinner Roger Harper.

Northants, Somerset, and Sussex are the only counties never to have won the Championship, but Northants have certainly been a force to reckon with, as runners-up in 1957, 1965, and 1976. During that period they have been fortunate to have had the secretarial powers of Ken Turner in office. Turner, who started as assistant to Lieut-Colonel A. St. G. Coldwell in 1947, has now retired after 26 years as secretary of the club.

Britannic Assurance County Championship: 11th; Won 5, Lost 9, Tied 1, Drawn 9
All First-Class Matches: Won 5, Lost 9, Tied 1, Drawn 10
NatWest Bank Trophy: Lost to Middlesex in semi-final
Benson & Hedges Cup: Failed to qualify for Q-F (4th in Group A)
John Player League: 12th; Won 6, Lost 9, No result 1

Championship Averages   *not out

Batting and Fielding	M	I	NO	HS	R	Avge	100	50	Ct	St
G. Cook	21	41	4	102	1507	40.72	2	9	14	–
A.J. Lamb	11	21	3	133*	693	38.50	1	5	10	–
W. Larkins	24	47	3	183*	1601	36.38	3	7	11	–
R.J. Bailey	24	43	7	114	1291	35.86	3	7	13	–
R.G. Williams	18	34	4	169	1025	34.16	1	5	9	–
D.J. Wild	14	25	1	144	819	34.12	2	2	4	–
D.J. Capel	16	27	5	81	726	33.00	–	5	8	–
R.J. Boyd-Moss	17	32	2	105	905	30.16	1	6	11	–
M.J. Bamber	5	10	1	51	220	24.44	–	1	1	–
D.S. Steele	24	38	12	78*	623	23.96	–	3	28	–
D. Ripley	13	19	3	61	237	14.81	–	1	26	12
G. Sharp	11	12	0	28	168	14.00	–	–	15	2
N.A. Mallender	20	30	5	33*	261	10.44	–	–	7	–
R.W. Hanley	16	20	7	33*	131	10.07	–	–	2	–
A. Walker	13	15	4	19	64	5.81	–	–	4	–
B.J. Griffiths	17	20	9	12	48	4.36	–	–	4	–

Hundreds (13)

3 **R.J. Bailey:** 100* v Warwicks, Birmingham; 114 v Somerset, Northampton; 106* v Sussex, Northampton.
  W. Larkins: 151 v Lancs, Northampton; 108 v Somerset, Northampton; 183* v Sussex, Northampton.
2 **G. Cook:** 102 v Warwicks, Birmingham; 102 v Derbys, Northampton.
  D.J. Wild: 128 v Kent, Northampton; 144 v Lancs, Southport.
1 **R.J. Boyd-Moss:** 105 v Lancs, Southport.
  A.J. Lamb: 133* v Worcs, Worcester.
  R.G. Williams: 169 v Worcs, Worcester.

Bowling	O	M	R	W	Avge	Best	5wI	10wM
B.J. Griffiths	452	110	1279	42	30.45	5-52	2	–
N.A. Mallender	508	114	1533	47	32.61	4-45	–	–
R.W. Hanley	387.1	83	1148	34	33.76	6-21	3	–
D.S. Steele	715	225	2056	60	34.26	5-86	2	–
R.G. Williams	428.2	103	1275	31	41.12	4-22	–	–
A. Walker	308.5	52	1118	27	41.40	4-50	–	–
D.J. Capel	139	18	615	14	43.92	5-28	1	–

Also bowled: R.J. Bailey 21-6-45-1; M.J. Bamber 2.3-1-3-0; R.J. Boyd-Moss 55-12-268-1; G. Cook 15.1-1-99-0; W. Larkins 63-16-170-5; G. Sharp 1-1-0-0; D.J. Wild 81.4-15-299-9.

Nottinghamshire

Notts captain Clive Rice adheres to that school of thought in professional sport that believes that to come second is to come nowhere. Judged thus, the summer was one of unalloyed disappointment for his side, second in the Championship, second in the John Player League, and semi-finalists in the Benson & Hedges Cup. The kinder and more realistic view, surely, is that it was in fact a marvellous season for Notts and they could be consoled that their total of 341 points would have been enough to claim the Championship in any other season since the introduction of the present points system.

Only a well-equipped county could have stayed in contention with a quite exceptional Essex squad, and there can hardly have been a more palpitating climax than that which saw Notts fail to overtake them with one ball remaining in their final match at Taunton. There was, in the end, the small matter of three yards in it, the distance by which Mike Bore's powerful heave failed to reach the boundary for the four runs that would have defeated Somerset and relegated Essex to runners-up. Perhaps, in a more detailed examination, a defeat at Trent Bridge a month earlier was more significant, Derbyshire preying on some uncharacteristic timidity and tactical mistakes to win after following on 222 runs behind.

The foundation of Nottinghamshire's re-emergence in 1984 was the colossal performance of Richard Hadlee, the first player to achieve the 'double' of 100 wickets and 1,000 runs since Fred Titmus in 1967. Hadlee's 210 not out against Middlesex at Lord's in August was arguably the innings of the summer, enabling him to finish with a batting average of better than 51, and he topped the national bowling lists with 117 victims at a fraction over 14 apiece; a phenomenal all-round display that found a positive response right through the side.

Tim Robinson was one of only two batsmen eligible for England's winter tour to top 2,000 runs, and Chris Broad, though absent for five Tests, still managed more than 1,250 runs for the county. Robinson, Derek Randall, and Clive Rice each scored three Championship centuries. John Birch provided strength in depth by getting close to becoming the sixth player to reach 1,000 runs in first-class matches. And, though limited by such competition to only 14 innings, 19-year-old Paul Johnson scored consecutive hundreds against Kent and Lancashire.

While dropped catches elsewhere undermined Notts on occasion, wicket-keeper Bruce French had a splendid season, his 86 dismissals overtaking the county's previous record, set by Geoff Millman in 1961.

With Kevin Saxelby and Kevin Cooper claiming close to 100 wickets between them, the absence of Mike Hendrick for all but three games was not critical, and Notts were superbly served by their two off-spinners, Eddie Hemmings and Peter Such. Hemmings, who began the season slowly after surgery on a shoulder, claimed 94 wickets, and Such, his 20-year-old protégé, finished in the top dozen in the national bowling averages.

ENGLISH SEASON 1984/NOTTINGHAMSHIRE

Britannic Assurance County Championship: 2nd; Won 12, Lost 3, Drawn 9
All First-Class Matches: Won 14, Lost 3, Drawn 11
NatWest Bank Trophy: Lost to Middlesex in 2nd round
Benson & Hedges Cup: Lost to Lancashire in semi-final
John Player League: 2nd; Won 10, Lost 5, No result 1

Championship Averages

*not out

Batting and Fielding	M	I	NO	HS	R	Avge	100	50	Ct	St
P. Johnson	6	9	1	133	424	53.00	2	1	5	–
R.J. Hadlee	24	31	8	210*	1179	51.26	2	7	23	–
C.E.B. Rice	24	39	7	152*	1553	48.53	3	6	20	–
R.T. Robinson	24	43	5	171	1700	44.73	3	10	16	–
D.W. Randall	21	35	3	136	1427	44.59	3	11	23	–
B.C. Broad	16	29	4	94	1072	42.88	–	10	14	–
J.D. Birch	18	28	4	110*	641	26.70	1	1	18	–
B.N. French	23	29	5	98	627	26.12	–	3	66	7
B. Hassan	15	23	3	70	386	19.30	–	1	20	–
K. Saxelby	19	18	8	27	190	19.00	–	–	1	–
R.A. Pick	8	6	3	22*	43	14.33	–	–	3	–
E.E. Hemmings	22	23	6	35	239	14.05	–	–	7	–
M. Newell	3	5	1	18*	33	8.25	–	–	3	–
K.E. Cooper	22	18	5	19	106	8.15	–	–	9	–
P.M. Such	11	10	5	16	29	5.80	–	–	5	–

Also batted: M.K. Bore (3 matches) 1, 27 (1 ct); C.W. Scott (1 match) 15 (2 ct). J.A. Afford (1 match – 1 ct) and M. Hendrick (3 matches – 2 ct) did not bat.

Hundreds (14)

3 D.W. Randall: 136 v Yorks, Nottingham; 110* v Sussex, Nottingham; 113 v Warwicks, Nottingham.
  C.E.B. Rice: 129 v Warwicks, Birmingham; 152* v Kent, Folkestone; 103* v Northants, Nottingham.
  R.T. Robinson: 171 v Leics, Leicester; 169 v Yorks, Nottingham; 117 v Lancs, Nottingham.
2 R.J. Hadlee: 100* v Hants, Bournemouth; 210* v Middx, Lord's.
  P. Johnson: 133 v Kent, Folkestone; 104 v Lancs, Blackpool.
1 J.D. Birch: 110* v Glos, Nottingham.

Bowling	O	M	R	W	Avge	Best	5wI	10wM
R.J. Hadlee	772.2	245	1645	117	14.05	7-35	6	1
P.M. Such	265.3	82	640	28	22.85	5-52	1	–
E.E. Hemmings	754.5	216	2080	86	24.18	6-49	6	1
K.E. Cooper	578.2	200	1266	47	26.93	8-44	1	–
C.E.B. Rice	206	53	569	19	29.94	4-61	–	–
K. Saxelby	492.5	132	1516	47	32.25	5-43	1	–
M.K. Bore	131.2	28	389	12	32.41	5-30	1	–
R.A. Pick	142	24	495	11	45.00	4-52	–	–

Also bowled: J.A. Afford 34.3-14-104-4; J.D. Birch 3-0-20-0; B.C. Broad 31.2-6-131-2; B.N. French 1-0-22-0; M. Hendrick 72.1-33-86-8; P. Johnson 2-0-14-1; D.W. Randall 9.4-0-43-3.

Somerset

Somerset adjusted to the loss of Vivian Richards and Joel Garner to the West Indian tour and to the restriction of Ian Botham's appearances owing to Test Match duties more successfully than they may have feared. Though they had a poor John Player League season, they reached the quarter-finals of the Benson & Hedges and NatWest competitions and to their credit climbed three places to seventh in the County Championship.

A characteristic of recent Somerset sides has been teamwork, and this quality was still much in evidence. No one, however, would deny the impact made by the 21-year-old New Zealand Test player Martin Crowe. Undaunted by the almost impossible task of replacing Richards, he batted most consistently after a quiet start and played some dazzling innings. Crowe, though strong and tall, was rarely brutal in his treatment of the ball, preferring to rely on timing and purity of stroke. He played some memorable innings, none more so than his unbeaten 152 at Southampton or his match-winning 190 a week later against Leicestershire at Taunton. As if this was not enough, he fielded brilliantly close-up or away from the bat and bowled most usefully.

Close behind Crowe's efforts came those of Marks and Roebuck. The former struck a rich vein of runs in August and easily passed 1,000 runs with an average of over 50. He increased his haul of wickets, finishing only 15 short of the double, and also reduced their cost. Roebuck, more fluent on the off-side than hitherto, discovered the knack of making hundreds, and his aggregate and average increased accordingly.

Popplewell also made useful contributions with the bat, though his natural aggression did not always sit easily at No. 3. Rose, despite injury problems, played some fluent innings and will be available in 1985. But Denning, who broke an arm after making a splendid start, has decided to retire.

Lloyds, though prospering with the bat, found few opportunities as an off-spinner and has decided to join Gloucestershire. Of the younger batsmen, neither Wyatt nor Felton developed as had been hoped. Both players' batting averages declined from the previous season, but their rich promise will surely be fulfilled.

A feature of the bowling was the advance of Mark Davis, the young fast-medium left-armer. With his ability to swing the ball into the right-hander, he enjoyed some destructive spells and was the most successful bowler after Marks. Dredge was his reliable self, but while his stamina and relish for battle were unimpaired, he was not particularly penetrative. The medium-paced Palmer still has some awkwardnesses in his action, but he certainly has life and an aggressive approach, while Booth's slow left-arm bowling developed steadily.

Somerset can look back on a season of satisfactory performance and will feel, too, that their long-term future is soundly based.

ENGLISH SEASON 1984/SOMERSET

Britannic Assurance County Championship: 7th; Won 6, Lost 7, Drawn 11
All First-Class Matches: Won 7, Lost 8, Drawn 11
NatWest Bank Trophy: Lost to Kent in quarter-final
Benson & Hedges Cup: Lost to Warwickshire in quarter-final
John Player League: 13th; Won 5, Lost 9, No result 2

Championship Averages
*not out

Batting and Fielding	M	I	NO	HS	R	Avge	100	50	Ct	St
P.W. Denning	4	7	3	90	289	72.25	-	3	2	-
V.J. Marks	22	31	9	134	1197	54.40	3	6	15	-
M.D. Crowe	23	38	5	190	1769	53.60	5	11	26	-
J.W. Lloyds	18	27	10	113*	780	45.88	1	5	20	-
P.M. Roebuck	22	34	0	159	1535	45.14	6	4	3	-
N.F.M. Popplewell	20	33	2	133	1056	34.06	1	6	21	-
I.T. Botham	11	15	1	90	444	31.71	-	4	2	-
B.C. Rose	19	31	4	123	847	31.37	1	4	5	-
S.J. Turner	5	6	3	27*	75	25.00	-	-	12	3
M.R. Davis	17	13	5	60*	178	22.25	-	1	6	-
N.A. Felton	14	24	1	101	499	21.69	1	3	4	-
J.G. Wyatt	14	25	0	87	449	17.96	-	2	6	-
G.V. Palmer	16	20	2	73*	299	16.61	-	1	15	-
S.C. Booth	12	14	7	42	100	14.28	-	-	12	-
C.H. Dredge	19	23	6	25*	194	11.41	-	-	8	-
T. Gard	19	21	4	26	192	11.29	-	-	45	10
R.L. Ollis	6	12	1	22	112	10.18	-	-	8	-

Also batted: M.S. Turner (1 match) 0, 1. P.H.L. Wilson (2 matches - 1 ct) did not bat.

Hundreds (18)

6 P.M. Roebuck: 145 v Yorks, Taunton; 102 v Warwicks, Birmingham; 128 v Leics, Taunton; 159 v Northants, Northampton; 101 v Hants, Taunton; 125 v Kent, Taunton.
5 M.D. Crowe: 125 v Middx, Bath; 113 v Lancs, Bath; 152* v Warwicks, Birmingham; 190 v Leics, Taunton; 108 v Glos, Bristol.
3 V.J. Marks: 134 v Worcs, Weston-super-Mare; 116* v Derbys, Taunton; 108 v Worcs, Worcester.
1 N.A. Felton: 101 v Surrey, Weston-super-Mare.
J.W. Lloyds: 113* v Worcs, Weston-super-Mare.
N.F.M. Popplewell: 133 v Middx, Bath.
B.C. Rose: 123 v Glam, Cardiff.

Bowling	O	M	R	W	Avge	Best	5wI	10wM
I.T. Botham	230.2	51	691	33	20.93	5-57	1	-
M.R. Davis	464.2	101	1432	59	24.27	7-55	3	1
V.J. Marks	733.4	196	2063	78	26.44	8-141	5	1
C.H. Dredge	490.4	113	1414	49	28.85	4-48	-	-
S.C. Booth	408.4	117	1172	38	30.84	4-50	-	-
M.D. Crowe	399	88	1248	39	32.00	5-66	1	-
G.V. Palmer	320.3	56	1231	30	41.03	4-58	-	-
J.W. Lloyds	183.2	45	563	10	56.30	2-24	-	-

Also bowled: N.A. Felton 0.1-0-4-0; N.F.M. Popplewell 116.3-26-359-7; P.M. Roebuck 10.2-5-18-0; M.S. Turner 29.8.85-0; P.H.L. Wilson 36-9-114-4; J.G. Wyatt 3-1-4-1.

Surrey

Surrey ended the season as might have been expected of a side generally workmanlike but inconsistent in corporate or individual personality. They collected no place money in the Championship or the John Player League and only modest rewards as losing quarter-finalists in the Benson & Hedges and NatWest competitions.

It is difficult, then, to escape an impression created in the past three or four years that Surrey are in a perpetual state of transition, with no reliable core of excellence on which to fashion a team of outstanding challenge.

They began the season with a new captain in Geoffrey Howarth, but an old failing in the slovenly approach for which they were punished, immediately, by Notts' 255-run victory and, subsequently, by manager Mickey Stewart's extra-curricular practice sessions.

Things could only get better, and by mid-May the batsmen, at least, were making the most of their opportunities – not least Grahame Clinton who, having languished in the second XI since July 1983, made a match-winning 94 against Gloucestershire in the Benson & Hedges match at the Oval.

The trend continued in the ensuing Championship match at Chesterfield, where Surrey, though finally frustrated by rain, raised 306 and 246 for 5. Stewart's hope that this marked a step forward in enterprise was somewhat tarnished, however, in the next match, at Chelmsford. On this occasion, in Howarth's absence, Surrey were led by Alan Butcher, who infuriated Essex by batting throughout the only day's play permitted by the weather. Furthermore, they were soon to realize that successful sides cannot live on runs alone when, though they aggregated 522 against Glamorgan, the Welsh side replied with 521 in a drawn match.

It was symptomatic of Surrey's chameleon qualities that, within 10 heady days in June, they achieved a much-prized double over Middlesex – at Lord's by 64 runs and at the Oval by an innings and 154 runs. At last the individual and collective personality had broken through. Monte Lynch scored a century in each match, Andrew Needham claimed an aggregate of 9 for 130 at Lord's, and Sylvester Clarke took 4 for 28 in the second innings at The Oval – figures he was to repeat in the home match against Hampshire who, coincidentally, provided Lynch with his fourth century of the summer.

Regrettably, the improvement was not maintained and Surrey lost all hope of significant success in the first two weeks of August when, in Stewart's words, they played badly. Nevertheless, there was hope for the future in the growing maturity of the younger players, of whom Alec Stewart and Mark Feltham particularly impressed.

Next season Roger Knight, the former captain who has proved more consistent than most in this season, as in other years, is to return to his principal vocation, teaching. However, he may still be available, as needed, to play during the summer holidays. Unless Surrey can recover and sustain the vitality they produced only fleetingly this summer, he may well be in some demand.

ENGLISH SEASON 1984/SURREY 171

Britannic Assurance County Championship: 8th; Won 6, Lost 6, Drawn 12
All First-Class Matches: Won 7, Lost 6, Drawn 13
NatWest Bank Trophy: Lost to Warwickshire in quarter-final
Benson & Hedges Cup: Lost to Nottinghamshire in quarter-final
John Player League: 8th; Won 7, No result 2

Championship Averages   *not out

Batting and Fielding	M	I	NO	HS	R	Avge	100	50	Ct	St
G.S. Clinton	18	27	6	192	911	43.38	2	5	6	–
R.D.V. Knight	20	33	3	142	1244	41.46	3	8	18	–
M.A. Lynch	24	39	1	144	1511	39.76	4	8	30	–
A.R. Butcher	23	39	4	135*	1362	38.91	4	5	11	–
A.J. Stewart	13	18	3	73	524	34.93	–	4	20	–
C.J. Richards	24	36	8	109	852	30.42	2	4	42	6
D.B. Pauline	9	15	1	88	354	25.28	–	3	8	–
G.P. Howarth	20	34	2	113	748	23.37	2	3	17	–
A. Needham	17	27	1	70	576	22.15	–	3	8	–
M.A. Feltham	11	14	5	44	183	20.33	–	–	4	–
G. Monkhouse	17	23	7	100*	292	18.25	1	1	8	–
D.J. Thomas	19	26	5	48	362	17.23	–	–	9	–
S.T. Clarke	23	25	3	35	329	14.95	–	–	20	–
P.I. Pocock	17	16	6	29*	110	11.00	–	–	8	–
K.T. Medlycott	4	4	3	7*	9	9.00	–	–	–	–

Also batted: I.J. Curtis (1 match) 1*; I.R. Payne (1 match) 0, 17 (2 ct); N.S. Taylor (1 match) 6* (1 ct); P.A. Waterman (2 matches) 0, 0* (2 ct).

Hundreds (18)

4 A.R. Butcher: 117* and 114 v Glam, Oval; 135* v Sussex, Guildford; 118 v Yorks, Oval.
  M.A. Lynch: 144 v Leics, Oval; 112 v Middx, Lord's; 118 v Middx, Oval; 104 v Hants, Oval.
3 R.D.V. Knight: 142 v Glos, Cheltenham; 114 v Somerset, Oval; 109 v Essex, Oval.
2 G.S. Clinton: 113* v Derbys, Oval; 192 v Yorks, Oval.
  G.P. Howarth: 108* v Sussex, Hove; 113 v Northants, Northampton.
  C.J. Richards: 109 v Derbys, Chesterfield; 100* v Worcs, Oval.
1 G. Monkhouse: 100* v Kent, Oval.

Bowling	O	M	R	W	Avge	Best	5wI	10wM
S.T. Clarke	651.1	165	1687	78	21.62	6-62	2	–
P.I. Pocock	515.2	125	1323	56	23.62	7-74	3	1
G. Monkhouse	439.5	116	1205	45	26.77	4-41	–	–
D.J. Thomas	480.1	109	1557	56	27.80	6-36	2	1
R.D.V. Knight	345.4	97	921	27	34.11	4-7	–	–
M.A. Feltham	256.2	42	932	26	35.84	5-62	1	–
A. Needham	316.4	75	1023	28	36.53	5-82	1	–

Also bowled: A.R. Butcher 38-9-134-4; G.S. Clinton 5-0-30-0; I.J. Curtis 11.3-3-36-1; M.A. Lynch 22.3-3-89-4; K.T. Medlycott 69-20-149-5; I.R. Payne 17-5-58-1; C.J. Richards 4-0-20-0; N.S. Taylor 27-5-85-2; P.A. Waterman 32-2-139-4.

Sussex

After two disappointing seasons that followed their vintage year of 1981, Sussex were again in ascendancy, finishing sixth and separated from the last of the prize money positions by only 17 points. They were not a brilliant side, but certainly efficient under the astute captaincy by John Barclay.

Sussex's prospects in 1983 were destroyed by long-term injuries to many of their bowlers. They were not wholly spared in 1984 either. Imran Khan was out for the whole season and Pigott, also a victim of stress fractures, could play only twice. But Sussex readily came to terms with these handicaps, and one of the factors that lifted them above mediocrity was the presence of two all-rounders in Colin Wells and Ian Greig, who both distinguished themselves.

Even though Mendis, Parker, Green, and both the brothers Wells scored over a thousand runs, Sussex's greater strength was in their bowling, and that despite the fact that the highest number of wickets taken by any bowler was 78, by Le Roux. However, Greig, Colin Wells, Reeve, and Waller all claimed between 53 and 62, and thus Sussex bowled out their opponents in the achievement of all their seven wins, as also in their memorable tie against Kent at Hastings. Le Roux's haul was his biggest since 1981, when he bowled a fair deal faster and when he had the advantage of hunting alongside the fearsome Imran. Reeve showed that his performance in his maiden season was no flash in the pan, and, when required to bowl with the new ball, Adrian Jones proved a useful apprentice.

In the humidity of a warm summer, Greig and Wells swung the ball purposefully, and when conditions were right Waller did his bit with left-arm spin. Thus their bowlers brought Sussex maximum points in 15 matches and achieved a total of 79 bowling points, which was very close to those of the champions and runners-up. This tally, which also reflected the high quality of Sussex's fielding, was particularly noteworthy as their home pitches were beyond reproach. In the circumstances, however, they did themselves less than justice by accumulating no more than 54 batting points. On this count, only Kent and Lancashire lagged behind them.

While Barclay was ever willing to issue or accept a challenge, Sussex in their first innings did not always produce the flair and spirit of adventure associated with the county. With Gould coming in at seven, sometimes even at eight, Sussex did have the depth of batting to be able to afford greater enterprise. To an extent, they might have been inhibited by some uncertainty at the very top of the order. True, Mendis made two hundreds and a double-century, but passed 50 on only three other occasions, while top score by his opening partner, Green, was 81. Parker could not have forgotten the miserable previous season and was therefore circumspect. But he really came into his own in August. Having made only one hundred hitherto, he scored five more in the remainder of the season, including one each against Essex and Notts. This fine run put him in contention for a tour place. Colin Wells, too, pressed his claims.

Sacrificing a degree of authority, he scored five hundreds, including a double-century.

Britannic Assurance County Championship: 6th; Won 7, Lost 6, Tied 1, Drawn 10
All First-Class Matches: Won 7, Lost 6, Tied 1, Drawn 12
NatWest Bank Trophy: Lost to Somerset in 2nd round
Benson & Hedges Cup: Lost to Yorkshire in quarter-final
John Player League: 3rd; Won 9, Lost 4, No result 3

Championship Averages

*not out

Batting and Fielding	M	I	NO	HS	R	Avge	100	50	Ct	St
C.M. Wells	24	36	6	203	1299	43.30	5	3	4	–
P.W.G. Parker	24	38	3	140	1411	40.31	4	6	18	–
G.D. Mendis	21	34	2	209*	1056	33.00	3	3	9	–
A.P. Wells	24	37	6	127	991	31.96	2	6	10	–
A.M. Green	22	37	2	81	973	27.80	–	4	11	–
D.A. Reeve	19	22	4	119	486	27.00	1	3	12	–
A.N. Jones	8	7	4	35	73	24.33	–	–	3	–
I.J. Gould	22	26	4	84	507	23.04	–	2	59	6
J.R.T. Barclay	24	33	2	82	713	23.00	–	4	21	–
I.A. Greig	24	33	4	64*	657	22.65	–	1	17	–
G.S. le Roux	23	24	6	68*	321	17.83	–	2	4	–
C.E. Waller	21	21	14	16*	56	8.00	–	1	2	–

Also batted: D.J. Smith (2 matches) 2, 1 (4 ct); D.K. Standing (2 matches) 5*, 7 (1 ct); D.J. Wood (2 matches) 15, 12, 5. A.C.S. Pigott (2 matches) did not bat.

Hundreds (15)

5 C.M. Wells: 203 v Hants, Hove; 127* v Northants, Horsham; 138* v Glam, Hove; 132* v Warwicks, Eastbourne; 121 v Glos, Hove.
4 P.W.G. Parker: 114 v Essex, Eastbourne; 122 v Warwicks, Eastbourne; 140 v Glos, Hove; 101 v Notts, Hove.
3 G.D. Mendis: 116 v Worcs, Worcester; 107 v Northants, Horsham; 209* v Somerset, Hove.
2 A.P. Wells: 105* v Leics, Leicester; 127 v Northants, Northampton.
1 D.A. Reeve: 110 v Surrey, Guildford.

Bowling	O	M	R	W	Avge	Best	5wI	10wM
G.S. le Roux	586.2	146	1612	76	21.21	6-57	2	–
A.N. Jones	150.5	29	476	20	23.80	5-29	1	–
C.E. Waller	591.3	214	1297	51	25.43	6-75	1	–
C.M. Wells	448.2	131	1281	50	25.62	5-25	2	–
D.A. Reeve	516.3	150	1339	49	27.32	4-28	–	–
J.R.T. Barclay	373	95	952	34	28.00	4-32	–	–
I.A. Greig	582	126	1770	56	31.60	4.39	–	–

Also bowled: A.M. Green 6-0-16-0; P.W.G. Parker 11.1-2-40-2; A.C.S. Pigott 32-5-96-2.

Warwickshire

Warwickshire began the season with Bob Willis and Andy Lloyd in the England team for the Texaco Trophy international series and for the first Test Match at Edgbaston. Subsequently, Lloyd did not play again for the county because of an eye injury and Willis made only two more Championship appearances before a recurrence of a viral infection, which first manifested itself in Pakistan, prematurely closed his career for England and Warwickshire.

In view of the loss of both their captain and leading strike bowler, especially in one-day competitions, and their most dependable opening batsman, Warwickshire's season could only be described as a triumph over adversity. Apart from dropping four places in the County Championship, they improved on the previous year's performances in the other competitions: John Player League (up two positions), Benson & Hedges Cup (beaten finalists), NatWest Trophy (semi-finalists).

Gifford, the favourite among the present staff to succeed Willis as captain, led the side with a firm, competitive example for much of the season. Warwickshire did not lose on that score, but Willis's bowling might have turned the results of several games, notably the NatWest semi-final against Kent. Gifford took 65 wickets, a noticeable decline on the previous halcyon year, but other than Underwood, there was no more effective spin bowler on the pitches which consistently favoured batsmen.

Warwickshire occasionally prepared 'result' wickets by leaving plenty of grass on their traditionally docile square. That was appreciated most by Ferreira, the South African all-rounder who continued his yearly improvement with 79 wickets and 777 runs. In many other counties, he would bat higher and probably score in excess of 1,000 runs. Small and Old each delivered match-winning figures, notably Old's achievement in taking 11 wickets to beat Yorkshire, his former county. But, not for the first time in recent years, Warwickshire's attack lacked a cutting edge. Aside from Willis's illness, they were also without Hogg because of a knee injury.

One area where they were supreme was their batting. Kallicharran set a county record of nine first-class centuries and, like Amiss, he scored over 3,000 runs in all cricket. Humpage made 1,891 first-class runs, a county best by a wicket-keeper, and Dyer, who replaced the unfortunate Lloyd, and Paul Smith both reached 1,000 for the first time.

Amiss, at 41, enjoyed the most productive year of even his distinguished career. He will take a testimonial in 1985, needing nine hundreds for the coveted century of centuries and fewer than 1,000 runs to become only the 14th player to make 40,000 in first-class cricket. He is now as much part of the Birmingham scene as Crossroads and roadworks around 'Spaghetti Junction'. Unlike those fixtures, however, he seems to get better every year.

After five seasons under Willis's leadership – he took them to one John Player League title and two knock-out finals – Warwickshire will move forward into a new era next summer. Its success may depend on their ability to find new bowlers, though Morton, a left-arm spinner from Scotland, and Wall, a swing bowler from Cumberland, showed obvious promise in their limited appearances.

Britannic Assurance County Championship: 9th; Won 6, Lost 7, Drawn 11
All First-Class Matches: Won 7, Lost 7, Drawn 12
NatWest Bank Trophy: Lost to Kent in semi-final
Benson & Hedges Cup: Lost to Lancashire in final
John Player League: 7th; Won 7, Lost 6, No result 3

Championship Averages   *not out

Batting and Fielding	M	I	NO	HS	R	Avge	100	50	Ct	St
D.L. Amiss	24	47	10	122	2137	57.75	6	13	15	–
G.W. Humpage	24	44	7	205	1813	49.00	5	9	51	9
A.I. Kallicharran	24	47	5	200*	2012	47.90	8	6	16	–
T.A. Lloyd	5	10	0	110	397	39.70	1	3	2	–
R.I.H.B. Dyer	17	34	2	106*	1047	32.71	1	7	6	–
A.M. Ferreira	24	37	13	76*	766	31.91	–	4	11	–
P.A. Smith	22	40	4	89	1032	28.66	–	8	9	–
C.M. Old	17	20	4	70	383	23.93	–	2	8	–
C. Lethbridge	13	15	2	41	274	21.07	–	–	4	–
G.C. Small	23	29	7	41*	400	18.18	–	–	6	–
K.D. Smith	19	37	1	93	598	16.61	–	2	3	–
G.J. Lord	3	5	0	55	79	15.80	–	1	2	–
Asif Din	6	9	2	35*	99	14.14	–	–	2	–
N. Gifford	24	24	10	28*	146	10.42	–	–	8	–
S. Wall	6	9	4	19	47	9.40	–	–	1	–
W. Morton	7	8	2	13*	39	6.50	–	–	3	–

Also batted: D.A. Thorne (1 match) 49, 20* (1 ct); R.G.D. Willis (5 matches) 4*, 4*, 5 (2 ct).

Hundreds (21)

8 **A.I. Kallicharran:** 200* and 117* v Northants, Birmingham; 101 v Lancs, Nuneaton; 116 v Notts, Birmingham; 100 v Essex, Ilford; 155 v Leics, Leicester; 117 v Lancs, Manchester; 155 v Glam, Cardiff.
6 **D.L. Amiss:** 100* v Notts, Birmingham; 121 v Northants, Northampton; 101* v Worcs, Worcester; 118 v Lancs, Manchester; 115* v Glam, Cardiff; 122 v Leics, Birmingham.
5 **G.W. Humpage:** 100* v Worcs, Birmingham; 205 v Derbys, Chesterfield; 101 v Hants, Birmingham; 112 v Yorks, Leeds; 127 v Glam, Cardiff.
1 **R.I.H.B. Dyer:** 106* v Glam, Cardiff.
T.A. Lloyd: 110* Northants, Birmingham.

Bowling	O	M	R	W	Avge	Best	5wI	10wM
A.M. Ferreira	728	142	2110	75	28.13	6-70	1	–
G.C. Small	629.4	124	1997	70	28.52	5-41	2	–
C.M. Old	468	125	1248	43	29.02	6-46	3	1
N. Gifford	758.4	219	1823	58	31.43	6-83	2	–
C. Lethbridge	220.1	31	792	21	37.71	4-35	–	–
P.A. Smith	172.4	19	754	18	41.88	4-41	–	–
W. Morton	146.5	35	462	11	42.00	4-85	–	–

Also bowled: Asif Din 11.3-1-55-5; T.A. Lloyd 3-0-35-0; D.A. Thorne 3-1-9-0; S. Wall 116.4-22-462-8; R.G.D. Willis 128-27-380-9.

Worcestershire

At first glance, Worcestershire's record in 1984 had a mundane appearance; solid rather than exciting and certainly giving no cause for a champagne party. Yet the county were delighted. They did not budget for winning a trophy but expected progress, and that is exactly what their young team delivered.

By winning their last three home games – their first hat-trick sequence at New Road since 1975 – they moved up six places on the previous year's performances in the County Championship. They also improved by five places in the John Player League, where they finished with four consecutive wins, but missed out on the prize money despite being within two points of the runners-up. The Benson & Hedges Cup, where they were eliminated at the zonal stage, and the NatWest Trophy, in which they have still to beat a first-class county since the change of sponsors, probably came too early for them. They were a much better side in August than in June and July.

Neale, the hard-working captain of the last three seasons, is clearly a competitor who responds to the demands of leadership. He scored over 1,700 runs, beating his personal best total for the second year in succession. Without wishing to burden him with an unwanted tag, he must be the best batsman among those who *never* seem to be mentioned as England candidates.

Patel is one of those contenders, but to the disappointment of his many admirers he was not called on by the selectors, and his form seemed to decline with each rejection. While he completed his double – 1,000 runs and 50 wickets – he has achieved both targets with a better average in the past.

Curtis and Weston, the newly-formed opening pair, both scored more than 1,000 runs, Weston winning the last home match with a career-best 145 not out and Curtis averaging over 40 after a remarkable August, in which he scored his maiden Championship century and made 523 Championship runs. Smith, the left-hander imported from Surrey, was troubled early in the season by a groin injury and in the middle by a broken finger, but he overcame those problems and periods of sketchy form to reach 1,000 runs, including a century on his return to The Oval. Worcestershire's batting stretched almost endlessly down the order, d'Oliveira flitting between brilliance and disappointment at No. 6, Humphries scoring two centuries from No. 7, and Illingworth taking part in century stands from No. 8.

Kapil Dev, when he had recovered from a knee operation, fitted into the middle with a number of innings bordering on the extravagant. He played in only half of the Championship programme, but made 640 runs and took 35 wickets, suggesting that he could transform Worcestershire in a full campaign.

Illingworth, the young left-arm spinner who was particularly effective in the John Player League, Pridgeon and Inchmore, the long-standing pace partners, and Newport and Ellcock, of the younger school, all did well at times. But, as with so many counties, bowling is Worcestershire's weakness.

Britannic Assurance County Championship: 10th; Won 5, Lost 5, Drawn 14
All First-Class Matches: Won 6, Lost 5, Drawn 15
NatWest Bank Trophy: Lost to Northamptonshire in 2nd round
Benson & Hedges Cup: Failed to qualify for Q-F (4th in Group B)
John Player League: 5th; Won 9, Lost 5, No result 2

Championship Averages   *not out

Batting and Fielding	M	I	NO	HS	R	Avge	100	50	Ct	St
P.A. Neale	24	42	6	143	1692	47.00	2	11	9	-
Kapil Dev	12	19	4	95	640	42.66	-	6	10	-
D.M. Smith	17	31	5	189*	1093	42.03	2	6	11	-
T.S. Curtis	20	34	2	124	1194	37.31	2	7	11	-
P. Moores	4	4	2	45	61	30.50	-	-	7	4
P.J. Newport	9	10	4	40*	180	30.00	-	-	2	-
D.N. Patel	23	40	1	153	1151	29.51	1	7	11	-
D.J. Humphries	20	31	8	133*	643	27.95	2	2	31	6
M.J. Weston	22	39	2	145*	1028	27.78	1	7	14	-
R.M. Ellcock	9	8	3	45*	134	26.80	-	-	1	-
R.K. Illingworth	19	20	7	43*	346	26.61	-	-	9	-
D.B. D'Oliveira	21	33	3	74	781	26.03	-	5	16	-
J.D. Inchmore	21	24	8	34	295	18.43	-	-	9	-
D.A. Banks	5	8	0	43	127	15.87	-	-	3	-
M.S.A. McEvoy	8	12	0	46	161	13.41	-	-	10	-
A.P. Pridgeon	23	23	7	67	211	13.18	-	1	13	-
A.E. Warner	6	7	2	27	62	12.40	-	-	3	-

Also batted: G.A. Hick (1 match) 82* (1 ct).

Hundreds (10)

2 T.S. Curtis: 124 v Northants, Wellingborough; 105 v Surrey, Oval.
   D.J. Humphries: 100* v Glam, Swansea; 133* v Derbys, Worcester.
   P.A. Neale: 143 v Yorks, Scarborough; 105 v Somerset, Weston-super-Mare.
   D.M. Smith: 189* v Kent, Worcester; 100* v Surrey, Oval.
1 D.N. Patel: 153 v Glam, Swansea.
   M.J. Weston: 145* v Northants, Worcester.

Bowling	O	M	R	W	Avge	Best	5wI	10wM
M.J. Weston	123.4	29	315	14	22.50	4-44	-	-
Kapil Dev	296.3	75	819	35	23.40	5-30	2	-
R.M. Ellcock	221.2	32	714	29	24.62	4-34	-	-
A.P. Pridgeon	683.5	160	1855	65	28.53	5-50	2	-
J.D. Inchmore	455	101	1250	41	30.48	4-37	-	-
R.K. Illingworth	647	178	1693	52	32.55	5-32	2	-
P.J. Newport	193.4	34	670	18	37.22	5-51	1	-
D.N. Patel	712.3	201	1936	50	38.72	5-117	1	-
A.E. Warner	137	24	482	11	43.81	5-27	1	-

Also bowled: D.A. Banks 4-0-17-0; T.S. Curtis 0.3-0-8-0; D.B. D'Oliveira 93-18-291-8; G.A. Hick 6-0-27-0; P.A. Neale 1.3-0-11-0; D.M. Smith 6-0-22-1.

Yorkshire

Yorkshire were mentioned in the context of the Charge of the Light Brigade more than once in a sweltering dry summer. Whatever the odds, whatever the difficulties, there was rarely a lack of spirit; their élan carried them to early victories until lack of experience, insufficient technique, and injuries dragged them down.

All political considerations aside, Illingworth's departure was a grievous loss. For a season and a half, Yorkshire had become accustomed to his generalship and had come to rely on his tactical planning. Suddenly that was withdrawn and, with it, the confidence he had shown in Carrick and Dennis, two of the most successful bowlers of 1983.

Sidebottom was promoted to strike bowler, a position for which he does not have the physical resources. Stevenson, starting with an injury, lost form and confidence to such an extent that only injuries to a succession of young seam bowlers, Jarvis, Fletcher, and Shaw, allowed him to regain his place. The two young spinners, Swallow and Booth, made encouraging progress, but it came through the school of hard knocks. Illingworth, one felt, could have shown them many a short cut.

When Sidebottom had form and fitness and before Moxon cracked a rib, in July, Yorkshire could hold their own. Headingley was packed for a Benson & Hedges semi-final lost by 3 runs, but the season went downhill from there until, by the end of August, Yorkshire's cricket was embarrassing. Essex and Warwickshire won at Leeds by record margins to leave the impression that the very foundations of Lord Hawke's great edifice were crumbling.

Not all was gloom, however. Sharp and Moxon passed 1,000 runs for the first time, Robinson appeared out of the Bradford League to average 40 in his first summer (his father says his two younger brothers are far better players), while the captain, storming on through a half-dozen injuries, played his cricket as if the coaching manual had been written by General George S. Patton.

Boycott, naturally, was the leading batsman and, in his 43rd year, was rarely less than one of great talents. Lumb has retired to South Africa and, like Athey before him, will be missed. Love's summer was dogged by injury and illness, while Metcalfe, despite two dramatic innings in the John Player League, seemed to struggle in the first-class game.

There cannot be a great Yorkshire team again until two great bowlers are found in the Ridings, and all that can be seen, in the far distance, is no more than a promise. However, the Second XI Championship, where the overseas professional is a little less influential, was won by the county.

Britannic Assurance County Championship: 14th; Won 5, Lost 4, Drawn 15
All First-Class Matches: Won 5, Lost 4, Drawn 15
NatWest Bank Trophy: Lost to Shropshire in 1st round
Benson & Hedges Cup: Lost to Warwickshire in semi-final
John Player League: 13th; Won 6, Lost 10

Championship Averages

*not out

Batting and Fielding	M	I	NO	HS	R	Avge	100	50	Ct	St
G. Boycott	20	35	10	153*	1567	62.68	4	9	13	-
P.E. Robinson	15	24	5	92	756	39.78	-	6	7	-
K. Sharp	24	39	2	173	1445	39.05	3	8	17	-
D.L. Bairstow	22	26	5	94	787	37.47	-	7	39	7
M.D. Moxon	18	31	3	126*	1016	36.28	2	6	19	-
R.G. Lumb	10	17	2	165*	534	35.60	2	1	2	-
A. Sidebottom	19	22	6	54*	511	31.93	-	2	1	-
S. Oldham	8	6	3	22	85	28.33	-	-	2	-
J.D. Love	15	23	2	112	568	27.04	1	3	7	-
S.N. Hartley	13	21	4	104*	437	25.70	1	1	2	-
I.G. Swallow	11	9	3	34*	136	22.66	-	-	9	-
S.J. Dennis	9	9	4	53*	104	20.80	-	1	1	-
P. Carrick	22	28	5	47*	400	17.39	-	-	13	-
A.A. Metcalfe	9	13	0	60	216	16.61	-	2	5	-
P.W. Jarvis	12	14	4	37	157	15.70	-	-	2	-
G.B. Stevenson	14	16	1	27	180	12.00	-	-	5	-
C. Shaw	3	5	2	17	32	10.66	-	-	-	-
S.D. Fletcher	8	5	1	28*	35	8.75	-	-	-	-
P.A. Booth	10	13	3	26	78	7.80	-	-	2	-

Also batted: S.J. Rhodes (2 matches) 6*, 35 (3 ct).

Hundreds (13)

4 **G. Boycott:** 104* v Kent, Tunbridge Wells; 153* v Derbys, Harrogate; 126* v Glos, Bradford; 101* v Glam, Cardiff
3 **K. Sharp:** 104 v Derbys, Harrogate; 132 v Glam, Cardiff; 173 v Derbys, Chesterfield.
2 **R.G. Lumb:** 165* v Glos, Bradford; 144 v Glam, Cardiff.
   M.D. Moxon 110 v Kent, Tunbridge Wells; 126* v Worcs, Scarborough.
1 **S.N. Hartley:** 104* v Glos, Bradford.
   J.D. Love: 112 v Somerset, Middlesbrough.

Bowling	O	M	R	W	Avge	Best	5wI	10wM
A. Sidebottom	479.1	103	1265	63	20.07	6-41	3	-
S.D. Fletcher	162	35	471	14	33.64	4-24	-	-
P.W. Jarvis	304	53	1115	32	34.84	6-61	2	-
P. Carrick	665.5	219	1606	44	36.50	6-32	3	1
S.J. Dennis	277.2	48	953	25	38.12	5-124	1	-
S. Oldham	244.5	57	703	18	39.05	4-59	-	-
I.G. Swallow	229.1	62	620	15	41.33	4-52	-	-
P.A. Booth	347	124	749	17	44.05	3-22	-	-
G.B. Stevenson	262.3	44	892	19	46.94	4-35	-	-

Also bowled: D.L. Bairstow 11-1-39-0; G. Boycott 11-0-25-0; S.N. Hartley 93-13-359-6; R.G. Lumb 1-0-5-0; M.D. Moxon 98-19-327-4; P.E. Robinson 2-0-12-0; K. Sharp 71-18-229-7; C. Shaw 53.4-5-177-5.

University Cricket

Oxford and Cambridge might have received harsh treatment at the hands of the counties in first-class matches last season, but University cricket was, at least, given a most welcome elevation by the fine efforts of the Combined team in the Benson & Hedges Cup. They beat Gloucestershire, at Bristol, and in the previous match against Surrey had lost only by one wicket.

In those two Benson & Hedges matches, Oxford and Cambridge owed much to the batting talents of their two Middlesex players, Miller and Carr. When it came to the 140th University Match at Lord's, these two again played the leading parts in Oxford's triumph by five wickets. Miller scored 128 not out in Oxford's first innings of 206 for 1 declared (still 65 runs behind), and here his batting achievement brought back many happy memories at Lord's of the last left-handed Oxonian to score a hundred in the University Match – the great M.P. Donnelly (142) in 1946.

Cambridge batted disappointingly in the second innings when all out for 195 – the left-arm Thorne taking 5 for 39 at slow medium – and Oxford were left with 261 to win in 160 minutes and 20 overs. This appeared an easy enough target on a wicket sadly pitched so near the Tavern boundary. But Cambridge hopes rose when Garlick soon bowled Miller off his pads, and Oxford confidence was fading fast as their batsmen showed little interest in anything aggressive to tea (53-2).

However, immediately after the interval, Carr changed all tactics and Dark Blues' spirit with a stirring array of attacking strokes and much good footwork. Carr, who had scored hundreds against Somerset and Lancashire in The Parks, made 68 to set Oxford up for victory, with an admirable partner in the 1983 captain Toogood. In 43 minutes after tea these two added 102 runs, and Toogood, with handsome straight driving, went on to complete his hundred. Hayes, Oxford's captain, hit two sixes in an innings of 35 not out and saw his team comfortable winners with five overs to spare.

A consolation for Cambridge was the form of their last two team choices, Burnley and Breddy. The opening batsman Burnley, playing in only his third match, was top-scorer in both innings, on each occasion receiving valuable support from Breddy.

Cambridge had a better balanced attack than Oxford, and now have much encouragement for 1985 with the same pair of opening bowlers in Garlick and Grimes and their two spinners, Cotterell and Andrew, all in residence again. The Cambridge attack however did suffer from the unhappy experience of their captain Pollock being banned by tutors from playing any cricket until after exams. He did, in fact, play in one match because of team injuries but, otherwise, at Fenners the University was led by their 1980-81 captain I.G. Peck – a master at Bedford School.

Cambridge University v Oxford University
Oxford won by 5 wickets
Played at Lord's, July 4, 5, 6
Toss: Cambridge. Umpires: N.T. Plews and D.R. Shepherd

Cambridge
A.E. Lea	*b* Thorne	39	*lbw b* Thorne	10
I.D. Burnley	*c* Thorne *b* Carr	86	*b* Carr	70
M.N. Breddy	*c* Edbrooke *b* Carr	61	*c and b* Rawlinson	17
P.G.P. Roebuck	*c* Carr *b* Toogood	31	(6) *c* Franks *b* Thorne	6
C.R. Andrew	*c* Thorne *b* Carr	0	(4) *lbw b* Thorne	30
D.G. Price	*c* Miller *b* Carr	25	(5) *c and b* Lawrence	20
A.G. Davies†	*not out*	17	*c and b* Carr	8
A.J. Pollock*	*c* Carr *b* Lawrence	4	(9) *c* Carr *b* Hayes	9
T.A. Cotterell	*did not bat*		(8) *c* Franks *b* Thorne	14
A.D.H. Grimes	,, ,,		*lbw b* Thorne	0
P.L. Garlick	,, ,,		*not out*	4
Extras	(B 3, LB 5)	8	(B 1, LB 6)	7
	(7 wickets declared)	**271**		**195**

Oxford
A.J.T. Miller	*not out*	128	*b* Garlick	5
R.M. Edbrooke	*c* Davies *b* Garlick	20	*b* Andrew	15
G.J. Toogood	*not out*	52	*c* Price *b* Pollock	109
J.D. Carr	*did not bat*		*st* Davis *b* Andrew	68
D.A. Thorne	,, ,,		*run out*	3
K.A. Hayes*	,, ,,		*not out*	35
W.R. Bristowe	,, ,,		*not out*	15
J.G. Franks†	,, ,,			
M.R. Cullinan	,, ,,			
H.T. Rawlinson	,, ,,			
M.P. Lawrence	,, ,,			
Extras	(LB 5, NB 1)	6	(B 1, LB 8, W 2)	11
	(1 wicket declared)	**206**	(5 wickets)	**261**

Oxford	O	M	R	W	O	M	R	W
Thorne	23	8	60	1	26.1	12	39	5
Hayes	12	5	33	0	15	3	50	1
Carr	34	6	93	4	35	16	49	2
Rawlinson	6	3	14	0	5	1	21	1
Lawrence	31.2	10	62	1	17	7	25	1
Toogood	1	0	1	1	4	3	4	0

Cambridge	O	M	R	W	O	M	R	W
Garlick	12	0	46	1	9	2	17	1
Grimes	6	1	21	0	6	2	13	0
Pollock	10	2	32	0	11	2	60	1
Andrew	20.1	6	38	0	20	2	75	2
Cotterell	14	5	48	0	12	0	85	0
Lea	2	0	15	0				

Fall of Wickets

Wkt	CU 1st	OU 1st	CU 2nd	OU 2nd
1st	76	58	32	10
2nd	143		91	39
3rd	200		104	155
4th	204		146	158
5th	231		152	225
6th	258		167	
7th	271		167	
8th			191	
9th			191	
10th			195	

*Captain †Wicket-keeper

ENGLISH SEASON 1984/UNIVERSITY CRICKET

Cambridge University

Results: Played 10; Won 0, Lost 7, Drawn 3

First-Class Averages

Batting	M	I	NO	HS	R	Avge
I.D. Burnley†	3	6	0	86	232	38.66
A.G. Davies†	7	14	5	69	308	34.22
P.G.P. Roebuck†	5	10	2	62	261	32.62
C.R. Andrew†	9	18	1	101*	405	23.82
A.E. Lea†	9	18	0	119	395	21.94
D.G. Price†	7	11	0	49	239	21.72
S.G.P. Hewitt	3	5	4	14*	20	20.00
S.N. Siddiqi	6	12	0	52	219	18.25
M.N. Breddy†	10	20	1	61	339	17.84
T.A. Cotterell†	10	16	1	52	247	16.46
I.G. Peck	4	7	1	49*	97	16.16
A.K. Golding	8	13	0	44	189	14.53
A.J. Pollock†	6	9	0	32	97	10.77
A.D.H. Grimes†	7	11	2	13	58	6.44
GFH McDonnell	2	4	0	5	7	1.75
P.L. Garlick†	10	15	6	6*	13	1.44

Also batted: P.C. Richardson (1 match) 7; I.E.W. Sanders (1 match) 0, 9; N.P. Thomas (1 match) 0, 0; T.J. Travers (1 match) 5, 15.

Hundreds (2)

1 C.R. Andrew: 101* v Notts, Nottingham
A.E. Lea: 119 v Essex, Cambridge

Bowling	O	M	R	W	Avge	Best
Siddiqi	23	6	90	5	18.00	5-90
Pollock	161.2	32	620	14	44.28	4-104
Cotterell	293.4	43	1074	13	82.61	3-95
Garlick	253	31	1092	12	91.00	2-69
Andrew	158.3	25	568	6	94.66	3-77
Golding	185.1	17	822	6	137.00	2-100

Also bowled: Grimes 123-22-427-3; Lea 19-5-92-2; Richardson 21-0-122-1; Sanders 25-5-93-3.

Fielding

11 Davies (9ct, 2st); 4 Hewitt (3ct, 1st); 3 Cotterell, Pollock, Price; 2 Andrew, Breddy, Golding, Grimes, Lea, Peck, Roebuck; 1 Burnley, Garlick, Siddiqi, Thomas.

*not out †Blue 1984

Oxford University

Results: Played 8; Won 1, Lost 5, Drawn 2

First-Class Averages

Batting	M	I	NO	HS	R	Avge
J.D. Carr†	7	12	0	123	468	39.00
G.J. Toogood†	8	15	1	109	425	30.35
R.M. Edbrooke†	8	16	1	66	420	28.00
A.J.T. Miller†	5	10	1	128*	196	21.77
W.R. Bristowe†	5	8	3	30*	104	20.80
D.A. Thorne†	8	14	2	69*	237	19.75
J.G. Franks†	8	13	2	42*	170	15.45
K.A. Hayes†	8	14	1	37	194	14.92
M.R. Cullinan†	7	12	0	59	155	12.91
S.M. Hewitt	4	6	1	22	60	12.00
H.T. Rawlinson†	4	6	1	19*	35	7.00
M.P. Lawrence†	8	11	3	17*	49	6.12
J.R. Turnbull	5	9	3	6	12	2.00

Also batted: J.G. Brettell (1 match) 0*, 0; A.A.G. Mee (1 match) 2; M.D. Petchey (1 match) did not bat.

Hundreds (4)

2 J.D. Carr: 123 v Lancs, Oxford; 100 v Somerset, Oxford.
1 A.J.T. Miller: 128* v Cambridge University, Lord's
G.J. Toogood: 109 v Cambridge University, Lord's

Bowling	O	M	R	W	Avge	Best
Hayes	95	28	259	9	28.77	4-58
Thorne	200.1	41	556	15	37.06	5-39
Carr	313	89	812	18	45.11	5-57
Lawrence	291.1	59	869	13	66.84	3-79

Also bowled: Brettell 15-3-74-1; Cullinan 2-1-4-1; Hewitt 64.5-8-232-4; Miller 1-0-4-1; Petchey 34-7-82-4; Rawlinson 95.5-18-346-4; Toogood 54.5-9-199-3; Turnbull 91-16-354-3.

Fielding

9 Carr, Franks (8ct, 1st); 6 Thorne; 4 Edbrooke, Hayes, Lawrence; 3 Toogood, Cullinan (2ct, 1st); 2 Bristowe, Rawlinson, Turnbull; 1 Brettell, Mee, Miller.

*not out †Blue 1984

ENGLISH SEASON 1984/FIRST-CLASS AVERAGES

First-Class Averages

Batting (Qualifications: 8 innings, average 10.00)

(*not out)

	M	I	NO	HS	R	Avge	100	50
M.W. Gatting	24	43	10	258	2257	68.39	8	10
P.W. Denning	5	8	3	90	338	67.60	-	3
G.A. Gooch	26	45	7	227	2559	67.34	8	13
Javed Miandad	8	15	2	212*	832	64.00	2	3
G. Boycott	20	35	10	153*	1567	62.68	4	9
J.G. Wright	12	21	1	177	1201	60.05	2	9
D.L. Amiss	26	50	10	122	2239	55.97	6	14
M.D. Crowe	25	41	6	190	1870	53.42	6	11
V.J. Marks	24	34	10	134	1262	52.58	3	6
A.I. Kallicharran	26	50	6	200*	2301	52.29	9	7
R.J. Hadlee	24	31	8	210*	1179	51.26	2	7
R.T. Robinson	27	47	7	171	2032	50.80	5	11
P. Johnson	10	14	1	133	647	49.76	2	3
T.A. Lloyd	8	14	2	110	590	49.16	2	4
C.E.B. Rice	24	39	7	152*	1553	48.53	3	6
G.W. Humpage	26	47	8	205	1891	48.48	5	9
V.P. Terry	16	28	3	175*	1208	48.32	5	6
R.A. Smith	7	13	3	132	483	48.30	1	2
P.A. Neale	25	43	7	143	1706	47.38	2	11
P.M. Roebuck	24	37	1	159	1702	47.27	7	4
P.W.G. Parker	26	40	4	181	1692	47.00	6	6
K.S. McEwan	27	44	6	142*	1755	46.18	4	10
K.J. Barnett	24	41	3	144	1734	45.63	6	9
B.C. Broad	23	40	5	108*	1549	44.25	1	13
Younis Ahmed	21	35	4	158*	1369	44.16	2	9
J. Derrick	10	15	7	69*	351	43.87	-	3
D.L. Haynes	13	18	1	125	743	43.70	2	5
C.M. Wells	26	39	7	203	1389	43.40	5	4
G.S. Clinton	19	28	6	192	948	43.09	2	5
W.N. Slack	25	46	8	145	1631	42.92	4	6
Kapil Dev	12	19	4	95	640	42.66	-	6
T.S. Curtis	22	36	3	129	1405	42.57	3	8
D.M. Smith	17	31	5	189*	1093	42.03	2	6
D.R. Turner	20	37	4	153	1365	41.36	3	7
D.W. Randall	25	40	3	136	1528	41.29	3	12
T.E. Jesty	25	44	4	248	1625	40.62	5	4
J.W. Lloyds	20	30	10	113*	812	40.60	1	5
A.J. Lamb	18	34	4	133*	1209	40.30	5	5
R.O. Butcher	23	40	7	116	1326	40.18	2	10
P.E. Robinson	15	24	5	92	756	39.78	-	6
T.J. Boon	21	37	6	144	1233	39.77	4	4
G. Cook	22	43	4	102	1539	39.46	2	9
R.D.V. Knight	21	35	3	142	1254	39.18	3	8
K. Sharp	24	39	2	173	1445	39.05	3	8
R.A. Woolmer	8	14	3	153	427	38.81	1	2
M.A. Lynch	25	41	1	144	1546	38.65	4	8
M.D. Haysman	5	10	4	102*	230	38.33	1	-
A.R. Butcher	24	41	4	135*	1415	38.24	4	5
M.R. Benson	14	26	2	127	914	38.08	3	4
R.J. Bailey	25	45	8	114	1405	37.97	3	8
C.W.J. Athey	26	52	4	114*	1812	37.75	4	11

ENGLISH SEASON 1984/FIRST-CLASS AVERAGES

(*not out)	M	I	NO	HS	R	Avge	100	50
D.L. Bairstow	23	26	5	94	787	37.47	–	7
J.C. Balderstone	20	36	2	181*	1260	37.05	3	5
A.L. Jones	27	51	2	132	1811	36.95	5	7
J. Abrahams	23	39	6	201*	1216	36.84	3	4
J.J.E. Hardy	13	20	6	95	513	36.64	–	4
J.J. Whitaker	19	32	2	160	1097	36.56	2	6
W. Larkins	25	49	3	183*	1656	36.00	3	7
P. Willey	26	45	4	167	1472	35.90	6	2
D.I. Gower	18	30	2	117*	999	35.67	2	6
R.C. Ontong	25	45	8	204*	1320	35.67	1	7
M.D. Moxon	19	32	3	126*	1034	35.65	2	6
R.G. Lumb	10	17	2	165*	534	35.60	2	1
D.G. Aslett	26	45	3	221*	1491	35.50	5	3
P.W. Romaines	26	52	0	141	1844	35.46	4	10
J.E. Morris	15	28	1	135	948	35.11	3	3
R.I.H.B. Dyer	18	36	2	106*	1187	34.91	1	9
B.R. Hardie	27	38	7	99	1077	34.74	–	6
G. Fowler	17	29	0	226	1007	34.72	3	4
C.T. Radley	24	38	7	128*	1072	34.58	2	7
S.J. O'Shaughnessy	21	38	4	159*	1167	34.32	3	3
D.J. Capel	17	28	5	81	789	34.30	–	6
A.G. Davies	7	14	5	69	308	34.22	–	3
D.J. Wild	15	27	2	144	855	34.20	2	2
M.C.J. Nicholas	26	48	2	158	1559	33.89	4	6
H. Morris	12	20	4	114*	542	33.87	1	4
D.N. Patel	25	41	1	197	1348	33.70	2	7
G.D. Mendis	23	36	2	209*	1141	33.55	3	4
J.D. Carr	9	14	0	123	468	33.42	2	2
J.A. Hopkins	26	50	5	128*	1500	33.33	2	9
C. Gladwin	26	45	3	162	1396	33.23	1	9
K.W.R. Fletcher	25	37	5	131	1056	33.00	3	4
A. Hill	25	44	3	125	1352	32.97	1	11
I.P. Butcher	24	42	1	130	1349	32.90	5	3
P.J. Prichard	20	29	2	100	888	32.88	1	6
N.F.M. Popplewell	22	36	2	133	1116	32.82	1	7
R.A. Harper	14	12	2	73	328	32.80	–	2
A.P. Wells	25	39	7	127	1045	32.65	2	7
R.G. Williams	20	37	4	169	1072	32.48	1	5
J.A. Ormrod	23	40	3	139*	1199	32.40	1	7
P. Bainbridge	22	42	7	134*	1133	32.37	2	6
J.D. Birch	22	33	5	110*	905	32.32	1	5
N.R. Taylor	21	39	5	139	1098	32.29	2	5
G. Miller	22	34	5	130	933	32.17	1	5
A. Sidebottom	20	22	6	54*	511	31.93	–	2
I.T. Botham	17	26	1	90	797	31.88	–	7
A.W. Stovold	25	50	2	139*	1524	31.75	2	11
A.J. Stewart	15	21	3	73	570	31.66	–	4
N.H. Fairbrother	23	39	1	102	1201	31.60	1	10
W.P. Fowler	22	38	8	116	948	31.60	2	7
P.J. Newport	10	11	5	40*	187	31.16	–	–
Zaheer Abbas	14	28	4	157*	738	30.75	1	4
N.G. Cowley	26	38	4	80	1042	30.64	–	6
C.S. Cowdrey	22	37	3	125*	1039	30.55	2	5

ENGLISH SEASON 1984/FIRST-CLASS AVERAGES

(*not out)	M	I	NO	HS	R	Avge	100	50
S.P. Henderson	10	17	1	108	487	30.43	1	3
G.J. Toogood	8	15	1	109	425	30.35	1	2
C.J. Richards	25	38	8	109	908	30.26	2	4
R.J. Boyd-Moss	17	32	2	105	905	30.16	1	6
A.M. Ferreira	26	39	13	76*	777	29.88	-	4
G.C. Holmes	21	37	2	90	1039	29.68	-	6
B.C. Rose	20	33	4	123	856	29.51	1	4
G.J. Parsons	26	39	10	63	853	29.41	-	6
C.J. Tavaré	24	41	0	117	1198	29.21	2	5
M. Watkinson	17	29	6	77	668	29.04	-	4
M.A. Garnham	18	29	6	84	666	28.95	-	6
P.G.P. Roebuck	6	12	2	62	286	28.60	-	2
J.H. Hampshire	21	32	4	101*	792	28.28	1	4
J.F. Steele	25	41	12	60*	820	28.27	-	1
C.L. Smith	26	49	3	125	1298	28.21	4	3
P.A. Smith	23	41	4	89	1040	28.10	-	8
R.M. Edbrooke	8	16	1	66	420	28.00	-	2
D.J. Humphries	22	32	9	133*	644	28.00	2	2
M.J. Weston	24	41	3	145*	1061	27.92	1	7
S.H. Wootton	4	8	1	97	194	27.71	-	1
J.N. Shepherd	24	39	7	87	885	27.65	-	6
I.A. Greig	26	35	5	106*	813	27.10	1	2
J.D. Love	15	23	2	112	568	27.04	1	3
D.A. Reeve	21	22	4	119	486	27.00	1	3
A.J. Wright	22	39	3	139	971	26.97	1	6
B.N. French	26	32	6	98	697	26.80	-	3
R.M. Ellcock	9	8	3	45*	134	26.80	-	-
R.K. Illingworth	21	20	7	43*	346	26.61	-	-
G.D. Barlow	19	36	2	96	903	26.55	-	5
A.M. Green	24	40	2	81	1006	26.47	-	4
B. Roberts	17	26	5	80	554	26.38	-	3
J. Simmons	21	34	5	72*	748	25.79	-	6
P.R. Downton	21	33	9	88	618	25.75	-	3
S.N. Hartley	13	21	4	104*	437	25.70	1	1
D.B. D'Oliveira	23	34	3	74	796	25.67	-	5
S.T. Jefferies	18	28	3	65	633	25.32	-	2
C. Maynard	15	21	5	50*	402	25.12	-	1
C.P. Metson	12	17	5	96	300	25.00	-	2
R.M. Ellison	21	32	7	108	620	24.80	1	1
S. Turner	12	13	5	59*	197	24.62	-	2
D.S. Steele	25	39	13	78*	639	24.57	-	3
G.P. Howarth	22	37	3	113	833	24.50	2	4
D.B. Pauline	10	16	1	88	367	24.46	-	3
M.J. Bamber	5	10	1	51	220	24.44	-	1
R.C. Russell	21	27	6	63	513	24.42	-	1
C. Penn	12	15	2	115	317	24.38	1	1
D.G. Moir	20	28	6	107	534	24.27	1	2
L. Potter	14	25	1	117	574	23.91	1	2
C.R. Andrew	9	18	1	101*	405	23.82	1	1
J.G. Wyatt	16	28	0	103	666	23.78	1	3
J.R.T. Barclay	26	35	3	82	761	23.78	-	4
D.A. Thorne	9	16	3	69*	306	23.53	-	1
D.R. Pringle	21	35	7	96	658	23.50	-	4

ENGLISH SEASON 1984/FIRST-CLASS AVERAGES

(*not out)	M	I	NO	HS	R	Avge	100	50
A.M.E. Roberts	8	12	4	89	188	23.50	-	1
C. Lethbridge	15	17	3	46	324	23.14	-	-
C.M. Old	18	21	4	70	393	23.11	-	2
P.B. Clift	19	28	7	58	483	23.00	-	2
I.J. Gould	23	27	4	84	529	23.00	-	2
W.W. Davis	21	24	7	77	390	22.94	-	2
D.P. Hughes	19	32	1	113	706	22.77	2	1
I.G. Swallow	11	9	3	34*	136	22.66	-	-
M.R. Davis	19	14	6	60*	178	22.25	-	1
A. Needham	19	30	1	70	644	22.20	-	4
A.E. Lea	9	18	0	119	395	21.94	1	1
D.G. Price	7	11	0	49	239	21.72	-	-
N.A. Felton	14	24	1	101	499	21.69	1	3
B. Hassan	17	27	4	103*	499	21.69	1	1
S.N.V. Waterton	7	10	1	50	193	21.44	-	1
G.W. Johnson	25	39	5	84	726	21.35	-	3
K.P. Tomlins	10	18	1	103*	363	21.35	1	-
R.J. Finney	24	37	5	78	679	21.21	-	4
M.R. Chadwick	7	14	0	61	293	20.92	-	2
W.R. Bristowe	5	8	3	30*	104	20.80	-	-
S.J. Dennis	9	9	4	53*	104	20.80	-	1
D.L. Underwood	24	33	9	111	498	20.75	1	-
P.H. Edmonds	25	33	4	142	600	20.68	1	2
I.S. Anderson	14	23	1	79	454	20.63	-	1
M.A. Feltham	12	15	5	44	206	20.60	-	-
E.J. Cunningham	6	11	3	61*	162	20.25	-	1
R.W. Taylor	18	22	7	46	303	20.20	-	-
E.L. Reifer	20	26	8	47	357	19.83	-	-
N.E.J. Pocock	13	18	2	55	314	19.62	-	1
N. Phillip	13	17	2	71	293	19.53	-	1
R.A. Pick	12	10	5	27*	96	19.20	-	-
N.A. Foster	22	27	8	54*	356	18.73	-	1
R.G.D. Willis	8	8	5	22	56	18.66	-	-
D.J. Thomas	20	28	5	48	425	18.47	-	-
J.D. Inchmore	23	24	8	34	295	18.43	-	-
S.N. Siddiqi	6	12	0	52	219	18.25	-	1
T.M. Tremlett	23	31	7	74	438	18.25	-	2
G. Monkhouse	18	25	7	100*	328	18.22	1	1
G.C. Small	24	30	8	41*	400	18.18	-	-
N.E. Briers	22	37	3	73	616	18.11	-	1
D.W. Varey	8	14	1	61	235	18.07	-	1
A.J.T. Miller	8	15	1	128*	253	18.07	1	-
M.N. Breddy	10	20	1	61	339	17.84	-	1
G.S. le Roux	24	24	6	68*	321	17.83	-	2
K. Saxelby	20	19	8	27	196	17.81	-	-
R.J. Parks	25	34	9	89	444	17.76	-	2
K.D. Smith	21	40	1	93	692	17.74	-	3
J.E. Emburey	26	35	2	57	579	17.54	-	3
P. Carrick	22	28	5	47*	400	17.39	-	-
C.J.C. Rowe	6	11	2	60*	155	17.22	-	1
C. Dale	8	8	2	49	100	16.66	-	-
A.A. Metcalfe	9	13	0	60	216	16.61	-	2
G.V. Palmer	16	20	2	73*	299	16.61	-	1

ENGLISH SEASON 1984/FIRST-CLASS AVERAGES

(*not out)	M	I	NO	HS	R	Avge	100	50
T.A. Cotterell	10	16	1	52	247	16.46	-	1
B.J.M. Maher	7	11	2	66	146	16.22	-	1
D.A. Graveney	26	40	13	33	430	15.92	-	-
N.F. Williams	19	21	3	44	285	15.83	-	-
O.H. Mortensen	8	8	4	40*	63	15.75	-	-
T.M. Alderman	20	27	13	52*	220	15.71	-	1
P.W. Jarvis	12	14	4	37	157	15.70	-	-
D. Ripley	14	21	3	61	281	15.61	-	1
P.J.W. Allott	19	25	4	50*	326	15.52	-	1
J.G. Franks	8	13	2	42*	170	15.45	-	-
R.J. Maru	17	20	4	36	246	15.37	-	-
S.T. Clarke	23	25	3	35	329	14.95	-	-
J.G. Thomas	20	26	5	36*	314	14.95	-	-
A.P.E. Knott	14	22	2	43	295	14.75	-	-
D.A. Banks	6	9	0	43	132	14.66	-	-
E.E. Hemmings	24	24	7	35	248	14.58	-	-
D.E. East	27	37	2	81	510	14.57	-	3
A.K. Golding	8	13	0	44	189	14.53	-	-
M.S.A. McEvoy	10	13	0	46	188	14.46	-	-
S.P. Hughes	15	14	4	41*	144	14.40	-	-
S.C. Booth	12	14	7	42	100	14.28	-	-
T. Davies	27	35	7	43	398	14.21	-	-
P.G. Newman	16	21	2	40	269	14.15	-	-
Asif Din	6	9	2	35*	99	14.14	-	-
G. Sharp	11	12	0	28	168	14.00	-	-
K.A. Hayes	9	16	1	37	209	13.93	-	-
A.P. Pridgeon	24	23	7	67	211	13.18	-	1
M.R. Cullinan	7	12	0	59	155	12.91	-	2
N.G.B. Cook	24	30	9	44	256	12.19	-	-
J.K. Lever	24	22	7	37	182	12.13	-	-
G.B. Stevenson	14	16	1	27	180	12.00	-	-
C.H. Dredge	21	26	8	25*	214	11.88	-	-
S.G. Hinks	8	14	0	39	162	11.57	-	-
N.G. Cowans	21	25	1	66	269	11.20	-	1
M.W.W. Selvey	15	18	8	20	111	11.10	-	-
T. Gard	21	24	5	26	209	11.00	-	-
A.J. Pollock	6	9	0	32	97	10.77	-	-
S.R. Barwick	20	19	9	25	105	10.50	-	-
N.A. Mallender	20	30	5	33*	261	10.44	-	-
N. Gifford	25	24	10	28*	146	10.42	-	-
I. Folley	17	28	9	22*	194	10.21	-	-
R.L. Ollis	6	12	1	22	112	10.18	-	-

Bowling (Qualification: 10 wickets in 10 innings)

	O	M	R	W	Avge	Best	5wI
R.J. Hadlee	772.2	245	1645	117	14.05	7-35	6
R.A. Harper	314.1	109	676	37	18.27	6-57	3
P.J.W. Allott	604.5	171	1496	79	18.93	7-72	6
D.L. Underwood	676.4	250	1511	77	19.62	8-87	2
T.M. Tremlett	669.5	209	1444	71	20.33	5-48	2
A. Sidebottom	488.1	105	1292	63	20.50	6-41	3

Bowling (contd)	O	M	R	W	Avge	Best	5wI
G.S. le Roux	604.2	154	1647	78	21.11	6-57	2
S.T. Clarke	651.1	165	1687	78	21.62	6-62	2
N.G. Cowans	493.1	76	1593	73	21.82	6-64	2
J.K. Lever	874.5	195	2550	116	21.98	8-37	8
N.E. Briers	109	24	264	12	22.00	3-48	–
P.M. Such	386.5	122	937	42	22.30	5-34	2
G.A. Gooch	321.1	75	850	38	22.36	4-54	–
R.M. Ellison	535.5	142	1323	59	22.42	5-27	1
M.J. Weston	123.4	29	315	14	22.50	4-44	–
T.M. Alderman	559.4	149	1725	76	22.69	5-25	6
A.M.E. Roberts	265	70	769	33	23.30	7-74	3
Kapil Dev	296.3	75	819	35	23.40	5-30	2
E.E. Hemmings	797.5	234	2220	94	23.61	7-47	7
C.M. Wells	497.2	146	1396	59	23.66	5-25	2
M.R. Davis	500.4	108	1569	66	23.77	7-55	4
N.A. Foster	687.1	148	2098	87	24.11	6-79	4
R.M. Ellcock	221.2	32	714	29	24.62	4-34	–
K.B.S. Jarvis	570.5	128	1788	72	24.83	5-30	2
A.N. Jones	208.1	44	636	25	25.44	5-29	1
C.E. Waller	610.3	221	1349	53	25.45	6-75	1
G. Monkhouse	459.5	120	1273	50	25.46	4-41	–
P.B. Clift	620.1	165	1608	63	25.52	8-26	2
G. Miller	897.3	257	2236	87	25.70	6-30	6
P.I. Pocock	638.5	169	1621	63	25.73	7-74	3
D.A. Reeve	572.4	175	1420	55	25.81	5-22	1
V.J. Marks	808	226	2233	86	25.96	8-141	5
J. Simmons	619.4	177	1644	63	26.09	7-176	7
S.R. Barwick	477.4	128	1314	50	26.28	7-38	2
I.T. Botham	449.4	93	1562	59	26.47	8-103	4
K.E. Cooper	623.2	217	1364	51	26.74	8-44	1
N. Phillip	275.2	48	911	34	26.79	5-48	1
W.W. Daniel	462	86	1463	54	27.09	4-53	–
P.H. Edmonds	823.3	233	2096	77	27.22	8-53	2
J.F. Steele	673	175	1867	68	27.45	5-42	4
J.E. Emburey	865.3	255	1978	72	27.47	5-94	1
D.J. Thomas	505.4	114	1654	60	27.56	6-36	2
W.W. Davis	547.5	118	1725	62	27.82	5-32	4
D.R. Pringle	580.1	127	1784	64	27.87	7-53	3
A.M. Ferreira	772.1	156	2208	79	27.94	6-70	1
L.L. McFarlane	272.5	45	875	31	28.22	4-65	–
J.R.T. Barclay	417	117	1023	36	28.41	4-32	–
R.J. Finney	584	130	1770	62	28.54	5-55	2
G.C. Small	643.4	127	2027	71	28.54	5-41	2
J.P. Agnew	670.1	127	2413	84	28.72	8-47	5
C.H. Dredge	533	125	1534	53	28.94	4-48	–
C.M. Old	496	134	1306	45	29.02	6-46	3
R.C. Ontong	837.4	231	2155	74	29.12	7-96	4
S. Turner	285	95	617	21	29.38	3-29	–
D.A. Graveney	665.4	202	1588	54	29.40	6-73	3
N. Gifford	812.4	238	1919	65	29.52	6-83	2
A.P. Pridgeon	719.5	168	1949	66	29.53	5-50	2
C.J.C. Rowe	135	41	356	12	29.66	3-20	–
C.S. Cowdrey	271.1	57	832	28	29.71	3-28	–

ENGLISH SEASON 1984/FIRST-CLASS AVERAGES

Bowling (contd)	O	M	R	W	Avge	Best	5wI
D.L. Acfield	577.4	174	1368	46	29.73	6-44	2
I. Folley	369	91	1015	34	29.85	5-65	2
C.E.B. Rice	206	53	569	19	29.94	4-61	-
P. Willey	544.1	163	1291	43	30.02	6-78	2
S.P. Hughes	314.2	53	1051	35	30.02	4-27	-
M.D. Crowe	435	101	1353	44	30.75	5-66	1
S.C. Booth	408.4	117	1172	38	30.84	4-50	-
I.A. Greig	648	153	1913	62	30.85	4-39	-
J.N. Shepherd	800.3	208	2225	72	30.90	5-30	2
R.A. Pick	243.5	52	773	25	30.92	5-25	2
B.J. Griffiths	474	114	1332	43	30.97	5-52	2
J.D. Inchmore	497	110	1364	44	31.00	4-37	-
G.W. Johnson	462.2	117	1220	39	31.28	5-38	3
C.A. Connor	642.5	155	1949	62	31.43	7-37	1
M.A. Feltham	291.2	53	1012	32	31.62	5-62	1
O.H. Mortensen	212.3	55	570	18	31.66	3-37	-
N.G. Cowley	588.1	133	1779	56	31.76	4-33	-
R.W. Hanley	401.1	87	1182	37	31.94	6-21	3
G.J. Parsons	662.1	140	2164	67	32.29	5-42	2
S.T. Jefferies	451.2	86	1392	43	32.37	6-67	2
N.A. Mallender	508	114	1533	47	32.61	4-45	-
P.J. Newport	204.4	36	689	21	32.80	5-51	1
R.K. Illingworth	744	220	1872	57	32.84	5-32	2
C. Lethbridge	279.5	42	987	30	32.90	4-35	-
D.J. Wild	91.4	18	329	10	32.90	3-15	-
G.E. Sainsbury	566.2	141	1596	48	33.25	5-19	2
J.G. Thomas	435.2	95	1575	47	33.51	5-56	2
S.D. Fletcher	162	35	471	14	33.64	4-24	-
N.F. Williams	474.1	95	1653	49	33.73	4-19	-
D.N. Patel	770	219	2063	61	33.81	5-28	2
K. Saxelby	516.5	140	1592	47	33.87	5-43	1
D.B. D'Oliveira	113	24	341	10	34.10	2-50	-
R.D.V. Knight	349.4	99	925	27	34.25	4-7	-
P.G. Newman	505.2	89	1717	50	34.34	7-104	1
D.S. Steele	732	227	2100	61	34.42	5-86	2
P.W. Jarvis	304	53	1115	32	34.84	6-61	2
T.E. Jesty	220.1	50	668	19	35.15	3-15	-
R.J. Maru	549.4	129	1664	47	35.40	7-79	2
E.L. Reifer	524.5	100	1761	49	35.93	4-43	-
A. Needham	328.5	79	1047	29	36.10	5-82	1
P. Carrick	665.5	219	1606	44	36.50	6-32	3
C.A. Walsh	341.3	80	1179	32	36.84	6-70	1
L.B. Taylor	142	42	369	10	36.90	2-22	-
D.G. Moir	822.5	206	2419	65	37.21	6-60	3
D.V. Lawrence	455.1	80	1531	41	37.34	5-58	3
D.A. Thorne	203.1	42	565	15	37.66	5-39	1
S.J. Dennis	277.2	48	953	25	38.12	5-124	1
I. Carmichael	208	40	661	17	38.88	5-84	1
S. Oldham	244.5	57	703	18	39.05	4-59	-
W. Morton	189.5	46	549	14	39.21	4-85	-
S.J. O'Shaughnessy	214.3	39	753	19	39.63	3-76	-
M.W.W. Selvey	311.3	69	997	25	39.88	6-31	1
J.D. Carr	343	94	885	22	40.22	5-57	2

ENGLISH SEASON 1984/FIRST-CLASS AVERAGES

Bowling (contd)	O	M	R	W	Avge	Best	5wI
G.V. Palmer	320.3	56	1231	30	41.03	4-58	–
I.G. Swallow	229.1	62	620	15	41.33	4-52	–
A. Walker	308.5	52	1118	27	41.40	4-50	–
N.G.B. Cook	769.3	209	2053	49	41.89	4-45	–
P.A. Smith	194.4	23	839	20	41.95	4-41	–
D.E. Malcolm	156.2	24	674	16	42.12	3-78	–
R.G. Williams	442.2	104	1348	32	42.12	4-22	–
A.E. Warner	186	33	632	15	42.13	5-27	1
M. Watkinson	359	73	1229	29	42.37	6-39	1
D.J. Capel	155	20	679	16	42-43	5-28	1
P.A. Booth	347	124	749	17	44.05	3-22	–
A.J. Pollock	161.2	32	620	14	44.28	4-104	–
G.B. Stevenson	262.3	44	892	19	46.94	4-35	–
B. Roberts	277	43	1044	22	47.45	4-77	–
S.J.W. Andrew	162.2	43	530	11	48.18	4-30	–
J.H. Childs	296	83	736	15	49.06	3-72	–
J.W. Lloyds	240.2	69	697	14	49.78	3-62	–
R.G.D. Willis	213	42	747	15	49.80	2-19	–
P. Bainbridge	303.2	73	959	18	53.27	4-76	–
M.P. Lawrence	291.1	61	869	13	66.84	3-79	–
T.A. Cotterell	293.4	43	1074	13	82.61	3-95	–
P.L. Garlick	253	31	1092	12	91.00	2-69	–

The following bowlers took 10 wickets but bowled in fewer than 10 innings:

N.S. Taylor	80	20	254	10	25.40	3-38	–
R.E. East	152.4	48	324	11	29.45	3-24	–
M.K. Bore	151.2	40	413	13	31.76	5-30	1
N.V. Radford	106.4	17	390	10	39.00	5-95	1

Fielding Statistics (Qualification: 20 dismissals)

Wicket-keepers
- 87 B.N. French (76 ct, 11 st)
- 77 D.E. East (76 ct, 1 st)
- 71 R.J. Parks (61 ct, 10 st)
- 67 I.J. Gould (61 ct, 6 st)
- 66 G.W. Humpage (56 ct, 10 st)
- 58 T. Gard (48 ct, 10 st)
- 54 T. Davies (43 ct, 11 st)
- 52 C.J. Richards (46 ct, 6 st)
- 48 P.R. Downton (42 ct, 6 st)
- 48 M.A. Garnham (45 ct, 3 st)
- 46 D.L. Bairstow (39 ct, 7 st)
- 43 D.J. Humphries (36 ct, 7 st)
- 38 D. Ripley (26 ct, 12 st)
- 35 R.C. Russell (26 ct, 9 st)
- 33 C. Maynard (28 ct, 5 st)
- 32 R.W. Taylor (27 ct, 5 st)
- 30 A.P.E. Knott (29 ct, 1 st)
- 30 C.P. Metson (28 ct, 2 st)

Fieldsmen
- 33 J.F. Steele
- 32 M.A. Lynch
- 30 A.L. Jones
- 29 T.M. Alderman
- 29 D.S. Steele
- 28 M.D. Crowe
- 27 G.A. Gooch
- 27 B.R. Hardie
- 27 G. Miller
- 27 N.F.M. Popplewell
- 26 C.W.J. Athey
- 26 G.W. Johnson
- 26 D.W. Randall
- 26 A.J. Stewart (including 5 ct as wicket-keeper)
- 23 M.W. Gatting
- 23 R.J. Hadlee
- 23 P.W.G. Parker
- 23 W.N. Slack
- 23 C.J. Tavaré
- 22 J.R.T. Barclay
- 22 C.S. Cowdrey
- 22 B. Hassan
- 22 J.W. Lloyds
- 22 R.J. Maru
- 21 K.J. Barnett
- 21 K.W.R. Fletcher
- 21 C.T. Radley
- 20 J.D. Birch
- 20 S.T. Clarke
- 20 P.H. Edmonds
- 20 J.H. Hampshire
- 20 K.S. McEwan
- 20 C.E.B. Rice
- 20 J.J. Whitaker

Benson & Hedges Cup

The Benson & Hedges Cup competition was blessed in 1984 by some of the best weather in its history, which has been plagued by wet springs. It lacked only a more stirring climax than the final at Lord's proved to be. Lancashire, winners of the Cup for the first time, proved far too good for Warwickshire, giving an outstanding exhibition of youthfully athletic fielding which tended to accentuate the one-sidedness of the final.

There are certain mornings at Lord's when it is a decided disadvantage to bat first. But, though Warwickshire, having been put in, did lose early wickets, they had repaired the damage and just before lunch at 102 for 2, with Kallicharran and Amiss going well, were well enough placed to set Lancashire a stiff task. But Amiss was out, and after lunch the remaining seven wickets fell for 24 runs in 17.4 overs of paralysed batting against Jeffries, O'Shaughnessy, and finally Allott.

Lancashire lost three wickets for 70, but there was never any doubt that they would make the 140 needed, which they did with six wickets and more than seven overs to spare. Peter May, the adjudicator, then had to decide on the recipient of the Gold Award, which was not easy as the only individual performance of any moment had been Kallicharran's 70 for the badly beaten Warwickshire. The outstanding feature had been Lancashire's fielding and, as an appropriate mark of commendation, their captain, John Abrahams, received the award.

The ups and downs of limited-over cricket were illustrated 11 days later when, on the same ground in the NatWest Trophy, Lancashire were routed by Middlesex by no less than 171 runs.

One outcome of the relatively fine dry spring of 1984 was that in the zonal rounds Scotland, the Minor Counties, and the Combined Universities all made their highest scores in the competition. The Universities, predominantly Oxford this year, beat Gloucestershire, were said even by their opponents to be unlucky to lose to Surrey by one wicket, and for a time even had Essex working hard.

Middlesex, the holders, never promised to qualify, though Sussex, their only victims in a strong group which also included Somerset, did scrape through by beating Kent by one wicket. Lancashire, having lost to Derbyshire, qualified only on a better rate of taking wickets, while Warwickshire beat Yorkshire at Edgbaston by seven runs, a result almost identical with that of the semi-final between the two sides at Headingley five weeks later.

Lancashire beat the 1983 runners-up Essex at Chelmsford in one of the four quarter-finals, which were all won comfortably, and scored another handsome victory in the semi-final against Nottinghamshire at Trent Bridge. The other semi-final provided the best match of the competition. For much of it, Yorkshire, set on their way by Moxon and Sharp, seemed certain to make the 277 required on a good pitch and fast-scoring ground. But Bairstow's final assault was for once halted and amid great excitement and local mortification Warwickshire just held on by three runs.

Zonal Results

Group A	P	W	L	Pts
WARWICKSHIRE	4	4	0	8
YORKSHIRE	4	3	1	6
Leicestershire	4	2	2	4
Northamptonshire	4	1	3	2
Scotland	4	0	4	0

Group B	P	W	L	Pts
NOTTINGHAMSHIRE	4	3	1	6
LANCASHIRE	4	3	1	6
Derbyshire	4	3	1	6
Worcestershire	4	1	3	2
Minor Counties	4	0	4	0

Group C	P	W	L	Pts
SUSSEX	4	3	1	6
SOMERSET	4	3	1	6
Kent	4	2	2	4
Glamorgan	4	1	3	2
Middlesex	4	1	3	2

Group D	P	W	L	Pts
ESSEX	4	4	0	8
SURREY	4	2	2	4
Hampshire	4	2	2	4
Gloucestershire	4	1	3	2
Combined Univers.	4	1	3	2

Note: where two or more teams in a group have equal points, their positions are based on the faster rate of taking wickets in all zonal matches (total balls bowled divided by wickets taken).

Final Rounds

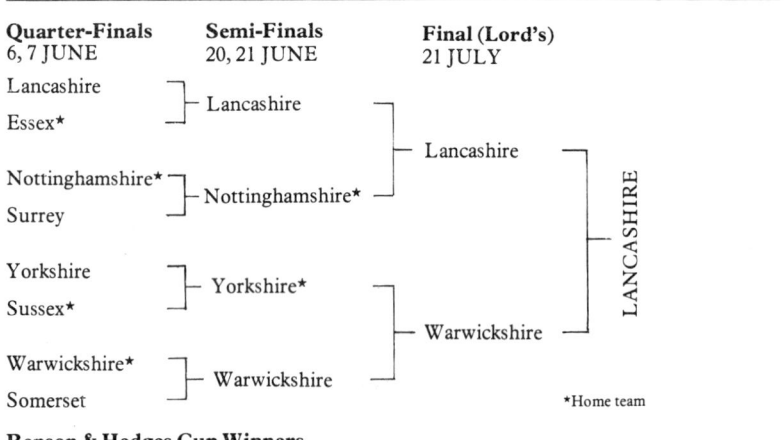

Quarter-Finals (6, 7 JUNE)
- Lancashire vs Essex*
- Nottinghamshire* vs Surrey
- Yorkshire vs Sussex*
- Warwickshire* vs Somerset

Semi-Finals (20, 21 JUNE)
- Lancashire
- Nottinghamshire*
- Yorkshire*
- Warwickshire

Final (Lord's) (21 JULY)
- Lancashire vs Warwickshire

Winner: LANCASHIRE

*Home team

Benson & Hedges Cup Winners

Year	Winner	Year	Winner	Year	Winner
1972	Leicestershire	1977	Gloucestershire	1982	Somerset
1973	Kent	1978	Kent	1983	Middlesex
1974	Surrey	1979	Essex	1984	Lancashire
1975	Leicestershire	1980	Northamptonshire		
1976	Kent	1981	Somerset		

Lancashire v Warwickshire 1984 Benson & Hedges Cup Final
Lancashire won by 6 wickets
Played at Lord's, July 21
Toss: Lancashire. Umpires: D.J. Constant and D.G.L. Evans
Gold Award: J. Abrahams (Adjudicator: P.B.H. May)

Warwickshire		Runs	Mins	Balls	6s	4s
R.I.H.B. Dyer	c Maynard b Watkinson	11	72	53	–	1
P.A. Smith	c Fairbrother b Allott	0	10	6	–	–
A.I. Kallicharran	c Abrahams b Jefferies	70	165	121	–	7
D.L. Amiss	c Maynard b Watkinson	20	54	46	–	1
G.W. Humpage†	c Maynard b Allott	8	17	21	–	–
A.M. Ferreira	c and b O'Shaughnessy	4	9	7	–	1
C.M. Old	b O'Shaughnessy	5	5	10	–	1
Asif Din	c Ormrod b Jefferies	3	16	13	–	–
G.C. Small	lbw b Jefferies	2	9	10	–	–
N. Gifford	not out	2	22	17	–	–
R.G.D. Willis*	c Jefferies b Allott	2	16	12	–	–
Extras	(LB 4, NB 8)	12				
	(50.4 overs; 207 minutes)	**139**				

Lancashire		Runs	Mins	Balls	6s	4s
G. Fowler	c Humpage b Willis	7	35	31	–	1
J.A. Ormrod	c Humpage b Ferreira	24	65	44	–	2
S.J. O'Shaughnessy	c Humpage b Ferreira	22	71	54	–	2
D.P. Hughes	not out	35	111	87	–	4
J. Abrahams*	c Humpage b Smith	0	8	3	–	–
N.H. Fairbrother	not out	36	57	49	–	6
S.T. Jefferies	did not bat					
J. Simmons	,, ,,					
C. Maynard†	,, ,,					
M. Watkinson	,, ,,					
P.I.W. Allott	,, ,,					
Extras	(LB 6, W 1, NB 9)	16				
	(42.4 overs; 177 minutes)	**140-4**				

Lancashire	O	M	R	W
Allott	8.4	0	15	3
Jefferies	11	2	28	3
Watkinson	9	0	23	2
O'Shaughnessy	11	1	43	2
Simmons	11	3	18	0

Warwickshire	O	M	R	W
Willis	9	0	19	1
Small	4	0	30	0
Ferreira	11	2	26	2
Old	10.4	3	23	0
Smith	6	0	20	1
Gifford	2	1	6	0

Fall of Wickets

Wkt	W	L
1st	1	23
2nd	48	43
3rd	102	70
4th	115	71
5th	121	
6th	127	
7th	132	
8th	133	
9th	134	
10th	139	

*Captain †Wicket-keeper

NatWest Bank Trophy

Middlesex, winners of the competition four years previously, under its former sponsorship, took the NatWest Trophy in 1984, beating Kent in a see-sawing final that had an appropriately tight finish.

It was a near echo of the 1981 final in which the issue rested on the very last ball. Dim lighting is often an element of theatrical tension, and at Lord's on this occasion, the eerie gloom of a September evening heightened the excitement. Low visibility was no less a handicap to Kent in the field than to Middlesex's batsmen.

The afore-mentioned cliff-hanger of 1981 ended with the rivals' totals level and Derbyshire prevailed by virtue of having conceded fewer wickets than Northamptonshire. Before the last ball was delivered in this instance, not only were the scores tied but the number of wickets lost was also identical. Had John Emburey not manoeuvred the ball from Ellison productively to mid-wicket, the yardstick would have been a comparison of respective totals at the 30-overs mark. Had it needed to be applied, Kent, 97-93, would have been the new champions.

Conditions were in favour of batting rather than bowling, and yet the highest score of the day was the crucial and award-winning 67 by Clive Radley, a buccaneering 58 by Chris Cowdrey being the only other exceeding 50. It delighted the connoisseur that the most effective bowling for both sides was supplied by a spinner, Emburey in Middlesex's case and Underwood for Kent. Emburey split Kent's formidable opening partnership and bowled his 12 overs for only 27 runs. Underwood stifled and dismissed Roland Butcher during a first spell of nine overs costing only 12 runs. And his firm check on the scoring compelled Gatting to chance his arm against Jarvis and hole out, a blow that put Kent in distinct ascendancy.

To deprive Middlesex of any credit for their revival would be unfair. Yet, if there was one factor that aided them, it was Tavaré's move in disengaging Underwood with a view to saving his three remaining overs to combat a future thrust. Control of the match was recovered for Middlesex by Radley, pugnacious and inventive, and Paul Downton, who contributed notably to the rise in momentum. Downton's dismissal, within six runs of Radley's, left Emburey and Edmonds needing 16 runs off 23 balls – not a daunting task except that by now, drivers on the Wellington Road had already felt the need of their headlights.

Enjoyment of a fine game and the dignity of a Lord's occasion were both enhanced by the suspension of the Tavern Bar. In the event, the grating, tuneless chanting that has become a feature of limited-overs cricket, was for once absent, or almost.

The big shock of the competition was dealt by Shropshire, eliminating Yorkshire in the first round. At the same stage, holders Somerset had a close call against Hertfordshire. In a season of many triumphs, Alvin Kallicharran set up a new record by scoring the first double-century in limited-overs cricket in England – against Oxfordshire, who had embarrassed his county, Warwickshire, in 1983.

ENGLISH SEASON 1984/NATWEST BANK TROPHY

Gillette Cup Winners

1963	Sussex	1969	Yorkshire	1975	Lancashire
1964	Sussex	1970	Lancashire	1976	Northamptonshire
1965	Yorkshire	1971	Lancashire	1977	Middlesex
1966	Warwickshire	1972	Lancashire	1978	Sussex
1967	Kent	1973	Gloucestershire	1979	Somerset
1968	Warwickshire	1974	Kent	1980	Middlesex

NatWest Bank Trophy Winners

1981 Derbyshire 1982 Surrey 1983 Somerset 1984 Middlesex

1984 Tournament

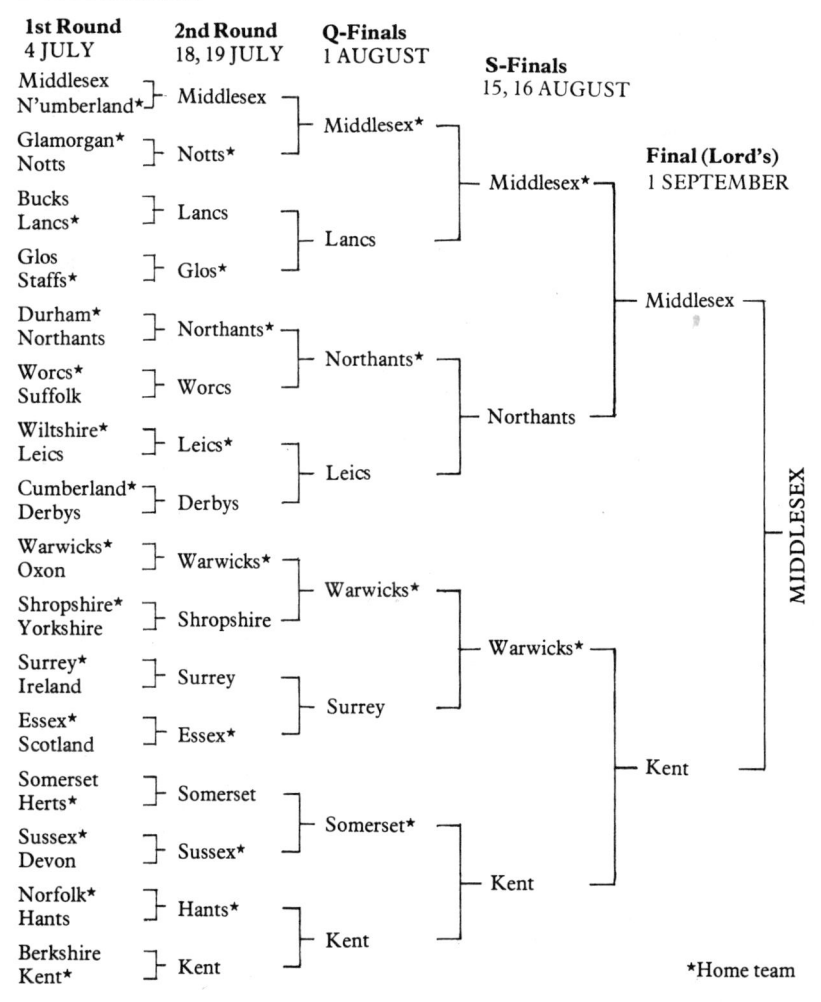

1st Round — 4 JULY
2nd Round — 18, 19 JULY
Q-Finals — 1 AUGUST
S-Finals — 15, 16 AUGUST
Final (Lord's) — 1 SEPTEMBER

Winner: MIDDLESEX

1st Round / 2nd Round / Q-Finals / S-Finals / Final:

- Middlesex / N'umberland* → Middlesex
- Glamorgan* / Notts → Notts*
  → Middlesex*
- Bucks / Lancs* → Lancs
- Glos / Staffs* → Glos*
  → Lancs
    → Middlesex*
- Durham* / Northants → Northants*
- Worcs* / Suffolk → Worcs
  → Northants*
- Wiltshire* / Leics → Leics*
- Cumberland* / Derbys → Derbys
  → Leics
    → Northants
      → Middlesex
- Warwicks* / Oxon → Warwicks*
- Shropshire* / Yorkshire → Shropshire
  → Warwicks*
- Surrey* / Ireland → Surrey
- Essex* / Scotland → Essex*
  → Surrey
    → Warwicks*
- Somerset / Herts* → Somerset
- Sussex* / Devon → Sussex*
  → Somerset*
- Norfolk* / Hants → Hants*
- Berkshire / Kent* → Kent
  → Kent
    → Kent
      → Kent

Final: MIDDLESEX

*Home team

Kent v Middlesex 1984 NatWest Bank Trophy Final
Middlesex won by 4 wickets
Played at Lord's, September 1
Toss: Kent. Umpires: H.D. Bird and B.J. Meyer
Man of the Match: C.T. Radley (Adjudicator: C.H. Lloyd)

Kent		Runs	Mins	Balls	6s	4s
M.R. Benson	*st* Downton *b* Emburey	37	122	89	–	2
N.R. Taylor	*b* Slack	49	129	90	–	4‡
C.J. Tavaré*	*c* Downton *b* Daniel	28	63	57	–	1
D.G. Aslett	*run out* (Butcher/Emburey)	11	31	33	–	1
C.S. Cowdrey	*c* Radley *b* Daniel	58	62	56	1	4
R.M. Ellison	*not out*	23	50	28	–	1
G.W. Johnson	*run out* (Gatting)	0	1	1	–	–
S.N.V. Waterton†	*not out*	4	11	10	–	–
D.L. Underwood	*did not bat*					
T.M. Alderman	” ”					
K.B.S. Jarvis	” ”					
Extras	(B 10, LB 8, W 3, NB 1)	22				
	(60 overs; 240 minutes)	**232-6**				

Middlesex		Runs	Mins	Balls	6s	4s
G.D. Barlow	*c* Waterton *b* Jarvis	25	42	43	–	2
W.N. Slack	*b* Ellison	20	76	54	–	1
M.W. Gatting*	*c* Tavaré *b* Jarvis	37	108	87	–	2
R.O. Butcher	*b* Underwood	15	26	21	–	1
C.T. Radley	*c* Tavaré *b* Ellison	67	108	82	–	2
P.R. Downton†	*c* Cowdrey *b* Jarvis	40	66	47	–	4
J.E. Emburey	*not out*	17	25	18	–	1
P.H. Edmonds	*not out*	5	19	10	–	–
S.P. Hughes	*did not bat*					
N.G. Cowans	” ”					
W.W. Daniel	” ”					
Extras	(LB 7, W 1, NB 2)	10				
	(60 overs; 240 minutes)	**236-6**				

Middlesex	O	M	R	W
Cowans	9	2	24	0
Daniel	12	1	41	2
Hughes	10	0	52	0
Edmonds	5	0	33	0
Slack	12	2	33	1
Emburey	12	1	27	1

Kent	O	M	R	W
Alderman	12	0	53	0
Jarvis	12	1	47	3
Ellison	12	2	53	2
Cowdrey	12	1	48	0
Underwood	12	2	25	1

Fall of Wickets

Wkt	K	M
1st	96	39
2nd	98	60
3rd	135	88
4th	163	124
5th	217	211
6th	217	217

*Captain †Wicket-keeper ‡Plus 1 five

John Player Special League

It is perhaps regrettable, though inevitable, that league championships are often determined before the competitive programme ends. Such was the case when Essex, though not engaged on the day, became John Player champions for the second time, on August 26, with two games in hand.

The anticlimax when their nearest challengers, Middlesex and Notts, were beaten by Sussex and Warwickshire respectively seemed particularly acute in view of the events of the preceding week when Essex were involved in one of the most remarkable matches of the season.

Essex, curiously prone to historic sequence, had been beaten by Sussex for the fifth consecutive year a fortnight earlier and now faced Hampshire, against whom they had not won a Sunday match since 1974. Accordingly, there was a strong sense of relief in the home camp when Graham Gooch hit a magnificent and undefeated 125 and Ken McEwan contributed 61 to a substantial 40-over total of 254 for 4. However, satisfaction turned to concern as Mark Nicholas and David Turner launched Hampshire's reply with a free-flowing opening partnership of 124.

When Turner and Robin Smith added 95 for the third wicket, there was considerable Essex anguish, until both were run out off successive balls – Turner for 114 and Smith for 51. Though Hampshire, at 239 for 4, were still looking odds-on winners, Fletcher's men bowled and fielded with such composure that four runs were still needed when Tim Tremlett faced the last ball from Derek Pringle. He hit it to Stuart Turner who lobbed it back, leaped in the air and Essex, as it transpired, became the John Player champions.

Significantly, success in that critical match owed much to the prolific batting of Gooch and McEwan, and the season's scoreboards endorse their value. When Essex first displaced Middlesex as leaders, on July 22, Gooch struck 99 and McEwan 52 not out against Kent. McEwan also topped the half century against Gloucestershire, Glamorgan, and Worcestershire; Gooch against Surrey, Warwicks, and Derbyshire. But, as in that palpitating match against Hampshire, Essex also were indebted to Keith Fletcher, whose meticulous captaincy – particularly in field-placing – was paramount.

If the victories of Warwickshire and Sussex, on August 26, were to prove conclusive, then Nottinghamshire's defeat at Trent Bridge must have been particularly galling for the home supporters – especially as Warwickshire were hugely indebted to an undefeated 107 from Dennis Amiss in reaching 231 for 5 off 40 overs. In the event, Notts made a sound but somewhat leisurely start and found themselves needing 70 off the last 10 overs. That they were beaten by a single run only hints at the frenetic finale.

At Hove, Middlesex suffered probably their most miserable Sunday of the season. Four points behind Essex, who would henceforth have a match in hand, it was essential they beat Sussex. Yet, though the home side mustered only a modest 194 for 4, Middlesex were hustled out in 30.4 overs for 120. Conversely, having now beaten both Essex and Middlesex, Sussex confirmed their right to challenge for an honourable third place in the final table.

As to Yorkshire, last year's champions, the purists among their supporters will doubtless cheerfully accept a decline to the anonymous regions of the league in exchange for a modest elevation from the bottom of the County Championship. Having achieved the top half of the table with a fourth consecutive win, on June 24, Yorkshire produced little thereafter to satisfy their limited-over fans.

Final Table	P	W	L	T	NR	Pts	6s	4w
1 ESSEX (6)	16	12	3	1	–	50	31	4
2 Nottinghamshire (15)	16	10	5	–	1	42	19	3
3 Sussex (4)	16	9	4	–	3	42	36	5
4 Lancashire (8)	16	10	6	–	–	40	39	2
5 Middlesex (8)	16	9	5	1	1	40	44	1
Worcestershire (11)	16	9	5	–	2	40	14	2
7 Warwickshire (15)	16	7	6	–	3	34	33	4
8 Surrey (11)	16	7	7	–	2	32	29	–
9 Glamorgan (10)	16	6	8	–	2	28	23	2
Hampshire (5)	16	7	9	–	–	28	37	2
Kent (3)	16	6	8	–	2	28	32	4
12 Northamptonshire (15)	16	6	9	–	1	26	28	2
13 Gloucestershire (14)	16	5	9	–	2	24	20	4
Leicestershire (11)	16	4	8	–	4	24	22	–
Somerset (2)	16	5	9	–	2	24	23	1
Yorkshire (1)	16	6	10	–	–	24	39	5
17 Derbyshire (6)	16	4	11	–	1	18	39	5

For the first four places only, the final positions for teams finishing with equal points are decided by the most wins.

1983 final positions are shown in brackets.

Winners

1969	Lancashire	1975	Hampshire	1981	Essex
1970	Lancashire	1976	Kent	1982	Sussex
1971	Worcestershire	1977	Leicestershire	1983	Yorkshire
1972	Kent	1978	Hampshire	1984	Essex
1973	Kent	1979	Somerset		
1974	Leicestershire	1980	Warwickshire		

1984 Awards and Distribution of Prize Money

£14,000 and League Trophy to champions – ESSEX

£7,000 to runners-up – Nottinghamshire

£3,500 to third-placing – Sussex

£2,000 to fourth-placing – Lancashire

£275 to winner of each match (shared in event of 'no results' and ties)

£400 to the batsman hitting most sixes in the season: M.W. Gatting (Middlesex) – 19

£400 to the bowler taking four or more wickets most times in the season: G.C. Small (Warwickshire) – 3

£250 to the batsman scoring the fastest 50 in a match televised on BBC2: R.J. Hadlee (Nottinghamshire) – 30 balls v Surrey at Trent Bridge, Nottingham, on September 2

Second XI Championship and Under-25s

Yorkshire, despite another season of struggle at the top level, won the First-Class County Second XI Championship in 1984, with an impressive 9 wins in 15 matches.

There were some fine individual performances during the season. Lancashire's David Varey hit the top score, 244 not out against Derbyshire, and shared in a massive seventh-wicket stand of 423 runs with Harry Pilling, whose 181 was a career best. Three bowlers took eight wickets in an innings, the best analysis being Peter Waterman's 8-15 for Surrey against Kent. The most remarkable bowling performance, however, was produced by Mike Bore, whose batting prowess was spotlighted at the end of the season when he came within a whisker of snatching the County Championship for Nottinghamshire. For the Second XI, he took 5 wickets in 6 balls against the hapless Derbyshire.

Second XI Championship 1984: Final Table

	P	W	L	D	Batting	Bowling	Total points	Avge
1 YORKSHIRE (2)	15	9	3	3	38	54	236	15.73
2 Surrey (3)	14	7	1	6	32	46	190	13.57
3 Worcestershire (8)	11	5	5	1	35	33	148	13.45
4 Warwickshire (7)	19	8	3	8	52	64	244	12.84
5 Middlesex (15)	14	5	3	6	46	42	168	12.00
6 Kent (4)	14	3	3	8	43	41	148*	10.57
7 Essex (11)	13	3	4	6	32	51	131	10.07
8 Lancashire (6)	18	3	4	11	53	65	166	9.22
9 Nottinghamshire (12)	16	4	2	10	32	50	146	9.12
10 Somerset (17)	11	2	2	7	28	32	92	8.36
11 Hampshire (13)	12	2	4	6	27	38	97	8.08
12 Northamptonshire (9)	14	3	3	8	27	38	113	8.07
13 Glamorgan (10)	17	3	6	8	49	39	136	8.00
14 Leicestershire (1)	12	2	5	5	24	36	92	7.66
15 Gloucestershire (16)	10	1	4	5	20	30	74†	7.40
16 Derbyshire (14)	12	1	5	6	27	43	86	7.16
17 Sussex (5)	12	1	5	6	26	34	76	6.33

1983 final positions are shown in brackets. *includes 16 points for batting second in two tied matches. †includes 8 points for batting second in a tied match

Surrey enjoyed a dramatic last-ball win over Middlesex in the final of the Warwick Under-25 Competition. Both sides, along with Nottinghamshire, had reached the semi-finals by dominating their zonal groups. Warwickshire won through by virtue of more away wins, after tying with Gloucestershire at the top of their group. In the semi-finals, Middlesex were taken to the last of their 40 overs before beating Warwicks by 2 wickets, while Surrey were convincing 36-run victors over Notts with 6 overs to spare.

In the final, Middlesex were well up with the pace before a middle-order collapse led to a tight finish. Feltham bowled Rose with the last ball to give Surrey a 1-run victory.

Surrey v Middlesex, Warwick Under-25 Final
Surrey won by 1 run
Played at The Oval, August 26 (40 overs)
Toss: Middlesex. Umpires: J. Birkenshaw and N.T. Plews

Surrey
D.B. Pauline*	b Sykes	23
N.J. Falkner	c Carr b Fraser	8
A.J. Stewartt	c Cook b De Freitas	58
D.M. Ward	c Brown b Sykes	10
N. Hicks	c Fraser b Rose	11
P. Marks	c Carr b De Freitas	29
M.A. Feltham	c Cook b De Freitas	12
K. Medlycott	b Fraser	6
C. Bullen	run out	5
N.S. Taylor	not out	4
P.A. Waterman	not out	1
Extras	(LB 3)	3
	(40 overs)	**170-9**

Middlesex
R.G.P. Ellis*	lbw b Bullen	46
A.J.T. Miller	lbw b Taylor	3
K. Brown†	lbw b Bullen	34
C.R. Cook	c Ward b Marks	41
J.D. Carr	run out	14
M. Blacket	c Pauline b Marks	0
K.D. James	run out	8
P. De Freitas	b Marks	0
G.D. Rose	b Feltham	13
J.F. Sykes	not out	0
A. Fraser	did not bat	
Extras	(B 2, LB 8)	10
	(40 overs)	**169-9**

Middlesex	O	M	R	W
James	8	1	25	0
Fraser	8	1	26	2
De Freitas	8	2	45	3
Sykes	8	0	40	2
Rose	8	0	31	1

Surrey	O	M	R	W
Waterman	7	0	34	0
Taylor	8	2	21	1
Marks	8	1	33	3
Medlycott	3	0	20	0
Feltham	8	3	28	1
Bullen	6	1	23	2

Fall of Wickets
Wkt	S	M
1st	20	20
2nd	34	84
3rd	58	95
4th	79	145
5th	120	147
6th	151	147
7th	155	148
8th	162	169
9th	166	169
10th		

*Captain †Wicket-keeper

Minor Counties Championship

Pride of place in 1984 must surely be given to Shropshire, the first 'giant killers' in the NatWest Trophy; an achievement in which they were so very nearly joined by Hertfordshire and Durham, the respective winners of the two 'domestic' Minor Counties competitions.

The English Estates Trophy – played earlier in the season than in its inaugural year – provided some fine cricket, and a gripping finale on a rain-affected Fenner's wicket. Hertfordshire dismissed Norfolk for a meagre 106, but had their captain, Collyer, to thank for rescuing them from an appalling start to their reply, in which they lost their first three batsmen for just one extra.

In the United Friendly Championship, Cheshire ran away with the Western Division with a string of impressive victories. The East was far more evenly contested; indeed, on the day when Cheshire clinched the Western leadership, it was still arithmetically possible for six of the Eastern teams to finish level on points at the top. Durham finally prevailed, thanks to successive victories in their last three matches. The final, sadly, proved an anticlimax, with Cheshire never recovering from a poor start.

Individual honours of the season went to two Pakistanis. Mudassar Nazar (Cheshire) won the Wilfred Rhodes Batting Trophy for the second year in succession, while the Frank Edwards Trophy for bowling was won by Parvez Mir (Norfolk), who, in taking over 50 wickets and scoring in excess of 500 runs, achieved the rare Minor Counties 'double'.

United Friendly Insurance County Championship: Final Tables

Eastern Division	P	W	L	U	B	NR	Pts	Western Division	P	W	L	U	B	NR	Pts
1 DURHAM*	9	4	2¹	2	1	–	50	1 CHESHIRE*	9	6	–	2	1	–	67
2 Staffs*	9	4	1	–	2	2	46	2 Bucks*	9	3	2	1	3	–	36
3 Norfolk*	9	3	3²	2	1	–	43	3 Shropshire*	9	2	2¹	2	2	1	33
4 Herts*	9	3	3	2	–	1	38	4 Somerset II	9	2	3¹	2	2	–	31
5 Suffolk*	9	2	3³	1	2	1	36	5 Devon*	9	2	1	1	4	1	29
6 Cumberland*	9	2	1	4	2	–	34	6 Berkshire*	9	1	–	5	3	–	28
7 Beds*	9	2	3²	–	4	–	30	7 Oxon*	9	1	3¹	4	1	–	26†
8 Lincs	9	2	3	–	2	2	26	8 Dorset	9	1	1¹	3	4	–	26
9 Cambs	9	1	3¹	4	1	–	26	9 Wiltshire	9	2	5¹	–	2	–	25
10 N'umberland	9	1	2¹	2	2	2	25	10 Cornwall	9	1	4	3	1	–	20

Points: 10 for win; U = up on 1st innings in match drawn (3pts), B = behind on 1st innings in match drawn (1pt); NR = no result (2pts); 1st innings lead in matches lost (L) 3 pts, the superior figure in the L column indicating the number of times 1st innings points were gained in matches lost.
*Qualified for 1985 NatWest Bank Trophy. †Oxfordshire take precedence over Dorset on batting average.

Leading UFI Averages

Batting	I	NO	HS	Runs	Avge	Bowling	O	M	R	W	Avge
Mudassar Nazar	8	2	121*	547	91.17	Parvez Mir	410.4	165	748	59	12.68
P. Bail	8	2	112*	454	75.67	D. Surridge	197.1	56	431	31	13.90
R.J. Lanchbury	14	3	143	754	68.55	D.R. Gilbert	193.3	37	587	40	14.68
G.D. Halliday	12	2	108*	628	62.80	M. Armanath	136	41	322	20	16.10
R.C. Shukla	13	7	98	338	56.33	J.A. Sutton	213.3	70	520	30	17.33
Agha Zahid	14	1	157*	722	55.54	S. Greensword	237.5	74	573	32	17.91

English Industrial Estates Knock-out Competition
Final: At Fenner's, Cambridge, July 15. HERTS beat NORFOLK by 3 wickets (55 overs). Norfolk 106 (41.1 overs; Handley 48; Johns 4-37); Herts 107-7 (49.1 overs; Collyer 68 not). Man of the Match: F.E. Collyer.

Cheshire v Durham, UFI Championship Play-off
Durham won by 6 wickets
Played at Worcester, September 8 (55 overs)
Toss: Durham. Umpires: D. Norton & D.S. Thompsett
Man of the Match: J.S. Wilkinson (adj. B.L. D'Oliveira)

Cheshire

Mudassar Nazar	*lbw b* Wilkinson	0
I. Tansley	*c* Mercer *b* Wilkinson	0
N.T. O'Brien	*lbw b* Lander	22
J.J. Hitchmough	*c* Mercer *b* Johnson	0
I.P. Davies	*b* Johnson	0
J.S. Hitchmough	*c and b* Lister	14
S.C. Yates	*b* Lister	6
J.A. Sutton*	*c* Atkinson *b* Lander	7
P.J. Hacker	*c and b* Lander	0
J.K. Pickup†	*lbw b* Johnson	3
A.J. Murphy	*not out*	0
Extras		6
	(35.2 overs)	**58**

Durham

J.W. Lister	*c and b* Mudassar	15
D.C. Jackson	*c* Mudassar *b* Murphy	15
S.R. Atkinson	*b* Mudassar	12
S. Greensword	*not out*	5
N.A. Riddell*	*c* J.S. Hitchmough *b* Murphy	0
G. Hurst	*not out*	6
R.A.D. Mercer†	*did not bat*	
B.R. Lander	,, ,,	
G. Johnson	,, ,,	
J.S. Wilkinson	,, ,,	
M. Roseberry	,, ,,	
Extras		8
	(16.5 overs)	**61-4**

Durham	O	M	R	W
Wilkinson	7	3	5	2
Johnson	8.2	4	13	3
Lander	11	4	14	3
Lister	9	2	20	2

Cheshire	O	M	R	W
Murphy	8.5	1	18	2
Hacker	2	0	13	0
J.S. Hitchmough	3	0	10	0
Mudassar Nazar	3	0	12	2

Fall of Wickets

Wkt	C	D
1st	0	18
2nd	5	46
3rd	9	51
4th	9	52
5th	39	
6th	45	
7th	48	
8th	54	
9th	56	
10th	58	

*Captain †Wicket-keeper

Village and Club Cricket

The traditional 'grassroots' weekend at Lord's, when clubs play the finals of their two championships – the William Younger Cup for senior sides, the Whitbread Trophy for villages – was advanced to accommodate the England-Sri Lanka Test. In superb weather, both underdogs came near to winning in close finishes.

William Younger Cup (45 overs). Lord's, August 18; Old Hill won toss.
Bishop's Stortford: 193-7 (C.S. Bannister 53, S.G. Plumb 45, R.H. Wacey 39, M.R. Gouldstone 24; C.N. Boyns 3-31); *Old Hill:* 196-5 (44.3 overs) (K.W. Wilkinson 76 not, C.N. Boyns 49; S.G. Plumb 2-33). *Old Hill won by 5 wickets.*

Plumb, Stortford's captain, and young Gouldstone opened with a brisk 63. Wacey and the massive Bannister hit out, Oliver, once of Warwickshire, taking much punishment as the score reached 193 for 7. Old Hill, of the Birmingham League, with former Worcestershire men Headley, Wilkinson, and Boyns, were held in check by Larlham, 9-5-15-0. Boyns made 49 before being beautifully caught by Bannister, and at 140-5 with five overs remaining Old Hill seemed doomed. Wilkinson, the captain, then took command and a towering six from the third ball of the final over brought victory. Surridge, Stortford's main bowler, was mismanaged, using only eight of his permitted nine overs. Old Hill, who had beaten former winners Shrewsbury and Scarborough, received £1,000, the runners-up £600. The competition is organized by the National Cricket Association.

Whitbread Village Championship Trophy (40 overs). Lord's, August 19; Marchwiel won toss.
Marchwiel: 159-7 (T. Roberts 55, D. Wallis 38, J. Bell 27; B. Loveridge 2-24, P. Mead 2-28); *Hursley Park:* 151-8 (A. Aymes 56, P. Wright 39; A. Morris 4-33). *Marchwiel won by 8 runs.*

The Clywd club, who had beaten another Hampshire village, Longparish, in the 1980 final, were clear favourites, but, apart from Roberts, a Welsh-speaking schoolmaster, and the Australian Wallis, scored below their form, totalling 159-7 in the 40 overs. For Hursley Park, Wright made three vital catches and then put on 97 with Aymes for the first wicket. But they needed 27 overs to do so and the required rate rose from four to nearly six runs an over. Hursley Park seemed unaware of the situation, and easy singles were not taken. Even the partisan crowd was strangely restrained and Hursley Park missed chances of glory and redeeming county pride. The President of MCC presented the trophy and £500 to Marchwiel and £250 to Hursley Park. *The Cricketer* has organized the competition since it began in 1972.

Schools Cricket

Exceptionally fine weather throughout the Summer Term had much to do with the glut of high scores, with several batsmen compiling remarkably large totals. Leading the field was Neil Lenham of Brighton, whose 1,534 runs was the most recorded for a school for at least 40 years. Michael Roseberry's 1,277 for Durham could have been even larger had he not missed several innings through other calls. There were comparatively few notable figures by bowlers, but two leg-spinners, S.D. Heath (King Edward's, Birmingham) and M.A. Atherton (Manchester GS), took 57 and 61 wickets, respectively, and P. Garratt's off-breaks accounted for 65 of Bedford Modern's opponents. J.D. Kudianavala scored 922 runs and took 70 wickets for Edinburgh Academy.

Although the firm wickets led to many draws, a few schools succeeded in winning most of their games. Foremost among these were Brighton, whose 15 victories set a new record for the school; Framlingham, who won 10 and drew 1 of their 11 school matches; and Shrewsbury, whose record of 13 wins, 6 draws, and 1 loss followed an equally good 1983 season.

The English Schools' Cricket Association (ESCA) enjoyed a record season. Over 600 inter-county games (not limited-over) were arranged in 1984. Support from the Lord's Taverners was increased, and their Cricketer Colts Trophy for Schools, contested by 1,586 schools over a two-year period, was won by Cheltenham College, who beat Arnold School, Blackpool, in the final at Edgbaston.

The ESCA Under-19s drew with the Public Schools, and representative matches against Scotland, Wales, and Ireland were also drawn. They beat a Zimbabwe Under-20 XI in a one-day match.

Millfield School won the Barclays Bank Cup (Under-17s), thanks to a match-winning innings by 15-year-old Harvey Trump in the final against Abbot Beyne School, Burton.

Of the annual Cricket Society awards, the Best Young Cricketer of the Year was Michael Roseberry of Durham. Harvey Trump won the Sir Jack Hobbs Award as the outstanding Under-15 cricketer.

The MCC Schools XI selected after the trials to play the NAYC was: M.A. Roseberry (Durham) capt, C.S. Mays (Lancing), M.A. Atherton (Manchester GS), D. Billington (Kirkbie Kendal), I. Bussey (Weston-super-Mare Tech), N. Cheeseright (Wetherby HS), D.G. Hills (Poole GS), T.J. O'Gorman (St George's, Weybridge), M.L. Roberts (Helston); T. Ward (Hextable, Kent), M. Robinson (Hull GS). Neil Lenham was not available for MCC because of commitments to Sussex.

Under-19 international caps were won by: M.A. Roseberry (Durham) capt, M.S. Atherton (Lancashire), P.A.C. Bail (Somerset), D.J. Billington (Cumbria), R.J. Blakey (Yorkshire), I.R. Bussey (Somerset), N.B. Cheeseright (Yorkshire), D.G. Hills (Dorset), C.S. Mays (Sussex), T.J. O'Gorman (Surrey), I. Redpath (Essex), M.L. Roberts (Cornwall), M.A. Robinson (Humberside), T.R. Ward (Kent), N.A. Willetts (Worcs).

Under-15 international caps were won by: H. Trump (Somerset) capt, T. Chadwick (Yorkshire), D. Graham (Gloucestershire), K. Krikken (Lancashire), J. Longley (Kent), P. Pollard (Nottinghamshire), M. Pooley (Cornwall), M. Proud (Yorkshire), A. Pugh (Devon), M. Ramprakash (Middlesex), G. Thorpe (Surrey), and J. Wood (Berkshire).

Women's Cricket

It makes a pleasant change to write about a successful England cricket team in the season of 1984. The England Women's team strode through the St George Assurance series against New Zealand undefeated. They won the St George Assurance Cup for the one-day internationals 3-0, with victories at Hastings, Leicester, and Bristol. The final game, at the Gloucestershire County Cricket Ground, received the Royal seal of approval. The guest of honour was HRH The Princess Anne, and she presented the cup to England's captain, Jan Southgate, who had top-scored in that game with a splendid 82.

The Test series resulted in three draws, so the St George Assurance Trophy was shared. In all the matches, batting reigned supreme and bowling lacked real penetration on the first-class wickets at Headingley, Worcester, and Canterbury.

Undoubtedly the highlight of the whole series was the amazingly consistent scoring of England's opener Janette Brittin, the 25-year-old Surrey physical education specialist. In her seven visits to the wicket, she notched up scores of 101, 88 not out, 144 not out, 96, 69, 63, and 35 (596 runs, average 119.20), using a bat earmarked for David Gower but passed on to her at the beginning of the season by the manufacturers.

After her third innings of 144 not out in the first Test at Headingley, Miss Brittin received the *Sunday Telegraph* Cricketer of the Week award – only the second woman to be so honoured. Another England player to emerge of high quality was Carole Hodges (Lancs & Cheshire). Promoted to open in the Canterbury Test, she scored a marvellous 158 not out. This season, Carole Hodges has played for Fylde CC men's third XI, which has considerably helped her power and ability.

Debbie Hockley, New Zealand's captain, was only 21 – the youngest international captain in the 50-year history of women's Test cricket. She made an instant impact in their opening match against Middlesex by fielding alarmingly close at short leg, wearing a helmet – the first time such millinery has been seen in women's cricket in this country.

Three representative sides made short 'overseas' tours during the summer. Junior England made an inaugural tour of Denmark, where interest in women's cricket is gaining pace. Young England visited Ireland. And a WCA side played in a triangular tournament in Holland with New Zealand.

The winter of 1984/85 finds England on a comprehensive tour of Australia, which includes five four-day Tests and three one-day Internationals. The two-month tour marks 50 years of Test cricket between the two countries. The England selectors curiously omitted from the touring team promising all-rounder Sarah Potter, who played for England in four out of six matches against the New Zealanders.

The England touring team chosen was: Jan Southgate (Sussex, capt), Jackie Court (Middx, vice-captain), Jan Aspinall (Yorks), Janette Brittin (Surrey), June Edney (Kent, wk), Carole Hodges (Lancs & Chesh), Megan Lear (Kent), Joan Lee (Yorks, wk), Gill McConway (E. Anglia),

Sue Metcalfe (Yorks), Jane Powell (Yorks), Avril Starling (Middx), Jill Stockdale (Yorks), Helen Stother (Middx), Chris Watmough (Surrey).

Test Series (St George Assurance Trophy)

First Test, played at Headingly, 6-8 July. MATCH DRAWN.
New Zealand 147-7 dec (A. McKenna 51, S. Rattray 33; J. Aspinall 3-26) and 194-8 (J. Dunning 71, S. Rattray 37; C. Hodges 2-25, J. Aspinall 2-33); England 256-5 dec (J. Brittin 144*, J. Southgate 35; L. Fraser 2-61, S. Brown 2-71).

Second Test, played at Worcester, 14, 16, 17 July. MATCH DRAWN.
New Zealand 225-6 dec (S. Rattray 57*, D. Hockley 47, N. Turner 45, A. McKenna 43; G. McConway 2-20) and 311-7 (N. Turner 57, E. Signal 55*; A. Starling 3-37); England 271-6 dec (J. Brittin 96, J. Edney 51*, J. Court 47; S. Gilchrist 3-42).

Third Test, played at Canterbury, 27-29 July. MATCH DRAWN.
England 214-7 dec (J. Brittin 63, J. Edney 49*; E. Signal 2-34, J. Dunning 2-35) and 297-5 dec (C. Hodges 158*, J. Southgate 59; S. Gilchrist 2-41); New Zealand 239-4 dec (D. Hockley 107*, A. McKenna 48) and 145-4 (D. Hockley 62, A. McKenna 33).

One-Day Internationals (St George Assurance Cup, 55 overs)

24 June at Hastings. ENGLAND won by 46 runs.
England 194-8 (55 overs; J. Brittin 101, C. Watmough 52; S. Brown 2-26, L. Fraser 2-23); New Zealand 148-7 (55 overs; D. Hockley 51; A. Starling 3-18, S. Potter 2-24).

30 June at Leicester. ENGLAND won by 6 wickets.
New Zealand 149-7 (53 overs; A. McKenna 37; J. Aspinall 2-29); England 151-4 (45.5 overs; J. Brittin 88*, C. Watmough 35; L. Fraser 3-27).

25 July at Bristol. ENGLAND won by 55 runs.
England 222-4 (54 overs; J. Southgate 82, J. Brittin 69); New Zealand 167-6 (54 overs; S. Rattray 60*, G. McConway 2-32).

Extras

Test Career Averages

The following individual career averages and records include all official Test matches played before 1 October, 1984. A dagger (†) indicates a left-handed batsman.

Key to bowling categories:

RF = right-arm fast
RFM = right-arm fast-medium
RMF = right-arm medium-fast
RM = right-arm medium
LF = left-arm fast
LFM = left-arm fast-medium
LM = left-arm medium
OB = right-arm slow off-breaks
LB = right-arm slow leg-breaks
LSA = left-arm slow leg-breaks

Australia

Batting/Fielding	M	I	NO	HS	R	Avge	100	50	Ct	St
T.M. Alderman	19	27	14	21*	79	6.07	-	-	16	-
A.R. Border†	61	107	20	162	4489	51.59	12	27	66	-
G.S. Chappell	87	151	19	247*	7110	53.86	24	31	122	-
T.G. Hogan	7	12	1	42*	205	18.63	-	-	2	-
R.M. Hogg	34	51	10	52	385	9.39	-	1	5	-
D.W. Hookes†	19	34	2	143*	1171	36.59	1	8	8	-
K.J. Hughes	66	116	6	213	4334	39.40	9	22	46	-
D.M. Jones	2	4	0	48	65	16.25	-	-	1	-
G.F. Lawson	23	37	7	57*	446	14.86	-	2	6	-
D.K. Lillee	70	90	24	73*	905	13.71	-	1	23	-
J.N. Maguire	3	5	1	15*	28	7.00	-	-	2	-
R.W. Marsh†	96	150	13	132	3633	26.51	3	16	343	12
G.R.J. Matthews†	3	4	1	75	111	37.00	-	1	-	-
W.B. Phillips†	10	17	1	159	620	38.75	2	2	17	-
C.G. Rackemann	4	3	0	12	16	5.33	-	-	1	-
G.M. Ritchie	8	16	1	106*	412	27.46	1	2	5	-
S.B. Smith	3	5	0	12	41	8.20	-	-	1	-
J.R. Thomson	49	69	16	49	641	12.09	-	-	19	-
K.C. Wessels†	12	20	1	179	815	42.89	3	1	12	-
G.M. Wood†	43	83	5	126	2642	33.87	7	12	32	-
R.D. Woolley	2	2	0	13	21	10.50	-	-	7	-
G.N. Yallop†	38	68	3	268	2753	42.35	8	9	22	-

Bowling	Type	Balls	R	W	Avge	Best	5wI	10wM
T.M. Alderman	RFM	4779	2258	70	32.25	6-135	4	-
A.R. Border	SLA	1462	539	15	35.93	3-20	-	-
G.S. Chappell	RM	5227	1913	47	40.70	5-61	1	-
T.G. Hogan	SLA	1436	706	15	47.06	5-66	1	-
R.M. Hogg	RF	6750	3025	112	27.00	6-74	6	2
D.W. Hookes	SLA	78	35	0	-	-	-	-
K.J. Hughes	LB	85	28	0	-	-	-	-
G.F. Lawson	RF	5132	2621	95	27.58	7-81	7	1
D.K. Lillee	RFM	18467	8493	355	23.92	7-83	23	7
J.N. Maguire	RMF	616	324	10	32.40	4-57	-	-
R.W. Marsh	OB	72	54	0	-	-	-	-
G.R.J. Matthews	OB	460	229	5	45.80	2-48	-	-
C.G. Rackemann	RFM	768	433	23	18.82	6-86	3	1
J.R. Thomson	RF	10199	5326	197	27.03	6-46	8	-
K.C. Wessels	OB	12	2	0	-	-	-	-
G.N. Yallop	LM	192	116	1	116.00	2-21	-	-

England

Batting/Fielding

	M	I	NO	HS	R	Avge	100	50	Ct	St
J.P. Agnew	2	3	2	5	8	8.00	-	-	-	-
P.J.W. Allott	9	13	2	52*	186	16.90	-	1	4	-
I.T. Botham	73	117	3	208	4159	36.48	13	18	84	-
B.C. Broad†	5	9	0	86	281	31.22	-	2	1	-
N.G.B. Cook	9	15	1	26	101	7.21	-	-	5	-
N.G. Cowans	13	23	5	36	143	7.94	-	-	7	-
G.R. Dilley†	18	28	8	56	330	16.50	-	2	5	-
P.R. Downton	10	18	2	56	279	17.43	-	1	21	-
P.H. Edmonds	23	28	6	64	430	19.54	-	2	23	-
R.M. Ellison†	2	3	1	41	74	37.00	-	-	1	-
N.A. Foster	6	8	2	18*	62	10.33	-	-	3	-
G. Fowler†	16	29	0	106	869	29.96	2	6	8	-
M.W. Gatting	30	52	4	81	1144	23.83	-	9	31	-
D.I. Gower†	65	113	10	200*	4486	43.55	9	23	42	-
A.J. Lamb	27	49	4	137*	1714	38.08	7	5	25	-
T.A. Lloyd†	1	1	1	10*	10	-	-	-	-	-
V.J. Marks	6	10	1	83	249	27.66	-	3	-	-
G. Miller	34	51	4	98*	1213	25.80	-	7	17	-
A.C.S. Pigott	1	2	1	8*	12	12.00	-	-	-	-
P.I. Pocock	20	32	2	33	167	5.56	-	-	13	-
D.R. Pringle	10	17	3	47*	247	17.64	-	-	3	-
D.W. Randall	47	79	5	175	2470	33.37	7	12	31	-
C.L. Smith	7	12	1	91	358	32.54	-	2	5	-
C.J. Tavaré	30	55	2	149	1753	33.07	2	12	20	-
R.W. Taylor	57	83	12	97	1156	16.28	-	3	167	7
V.P. Terry	2	3	0	8	16	5.33	-	-	2	-
R.G.D. Willis	90	128	55	28*	840	11.50	-	-	39	-

Bowling

	Type	Balls	R	W	Avge	Best	5wI	10wM
J.P. Agnew	RFM	414	274	4	68.50	2-51	-	-
P.J.W. Allott	RFM	1545	787	21	37.47	6-61	1	-
I.T. Botham	RFM	16881	8191	312	26.25	8-34	24	4
N.G.B. Cook	SLA	2990	1212	40	30.30	6-65	4	1
N.G. Cowans	RF	2163	1248	35	35.65	6-77	2	-
G.R. Dilley	RF	3130	1595	50	31.90	4-24	-	-
P.H. Edmonds	SLA	5220	1733	59	29.37	7-66	2	-
R.M. Ellison	RMF	474	200	6	33.33	3-60	-	-
N.A. Foster	RFM	1314	616	12	51.33	5-67	1	-
G. Fowler	RM	12	11	0	-	-	-	-
M.W. Gatting	RM	224	115	2	57.50	1-14	-	-
D.I. Gower	OB	12	2	1	2.00	1-1	-	-
A.J. Lamb	RM	12	6	0	-	-	-	-
V.J. Marks	OB	1082	484	11	44.00	3-78	-	-
G. Miller	OB	5149	1859	60	30.98	5-44	1	-
A.C.S. Pigott	RFM	102	75	2	37.50	2-75	-	-
P.I. Pocock	OB	5223	2321	54	42.98	6-79	3	-
D.R. Pringle	RMF	1520	752	16	47.00	5-108	1	-
D.W. Randall	RM	16	3	0	-	-	-	-
C.L. Smith	OB	102	39	3	13.00	2-31	-	-
C.J. Tavaré	RM	30	11	0	-	-	-	-
R.W. Taylor	RM	12	6	0	-	-	-	-
R.G.D. Willis	RF	17357	8190	325	25.20	8-43	16	-

West Indies

Batting/Fielding

	M	I	NO	HS	R	Avge	100	50	Ct	St
E.A.E. Baptiste	9	10	1	87*	224	24.88	-	1	2	-
W.W. Daniel	10	11	4	11	46	6.57	-	-	4	-
W.W. Davis	9	10	4	77	96	16.00	-	1	6	-
P.J.L. Dujon	24	30	2	130	1267	45.25	3	5	79	2
J. Garner	42	51	9	60	519	12.35	-	1	32	-
H.A. Gomes†	40	60	8	143	2232	42.92	7	9	12	-
C.G. Greenidge	57	96	11	223	4338	51.03	11	24	54	-
R.A. Harper	11	12	1	39*	152	13.81	-	-	16	-
D.L. Haynes	43	71	5	184	2643	40.04	7	13	24	-
M.A. Holding	49	64	10	69	763	14.12	-	5	15	-
C.H. Lloyd†	105	167	13	242*	7159	46.48	18	37	84	-
A.L. Logie	9	11	0	130	327	29.72	1	2	3	-
M.D. Marshall	31	38	2	92	536	14.88	-	2	12	-
I.V.A. Richards	68	101	5	291	5237	54.55	17	22	72	-
R.B. Richardson	6	7	1	154	353	58.83	2	-	5	-
A.M.E. Roberts	47	62	11	68	762	14.94	-	3	9	-
M.A. Small	2	1	1	3*	3	-	-	-	-	-

Bowling

	Type	Balls	R	W	Avge	Best	5wI	10wM
E.A.E. Baptiste	RFM	1224	486	15	32.40	3-31	-	-
W.W. Daniel	RF	1754	910	36	25.27	5-39	1	-
W.W. Davis	RF	1719	894	22	40.63	3-21	-	-
J. Garner	RFM	9886	3924	191	20.54	6-56	6	-
H.A. Gomes	RM	2017	793	11	72.09	2-20	-	-
C.G. Greenidge	RM	26	4	0	-	-	-	-
R.A. Harper	OB	1900	703	24	29.29	6-57	1	-
D.L. Haynes	RM	18	8	1	8.00	1-2	-	-
M.A. Holding	RF	10821	4947	209	23.66	8-92	12	2
C.H. Lloyd	RM	1716	622	10	62.20	2-13	-	-
A.L. Logie	RM/OB	1	4	0	-	-	-	-
M.D. Marshall	RF	6551	3117	133	23.43	7-53	8	-
I.V.A. Richards	RM/OB	2482	902	17	53.05	2-20	-	-
A.M.E. Roberts	RF	11135	5174	202	25.61	7-54	11	2
M.A. Small	RFM	270	153	4	38.25	3-40	-	-

New Zealand

Batting/Fielding	M	I	NO	HS	R	Avge	100	50	Ct	St
S.L. Boock	16	24	7	35	87	5.11	–	–	9	–
J.G. Bracewell	10	16	2	28	108	7.71	–	–	11	–
B.L. Cairns	37	58	7	64*	852	16.70	–	2	26	–
E.J. Chatfield	15	20	11	13*	80	8.88	–	–	2	–
J.V. Coney	30	51	9	174*	1567	37.30	1	11	37	–
J.J. Crowe	10	16	0	128	424	26.50	1	2	10	–
M.D. Crowe	13	21	1	100	429	21.45	1	–	12	–
B.A. Edgar†	27	48	3	161	1521	33.80	3	8	13	–
T.J. Franklin	1	2	0	7	9	4.50	–	–	–	–
E.J. Gray	2	4	0	17	38	9.50	–	–	–	–
R.J. Hadlee†	50	85	11	103	1820	24.59	1	9	28	–
G.P. Howarth	40	71	5	147	2270	34.39	6	10	27	–
W.K. Lees	21	37	4	152	778	23.57	1	1	52	7
J.F. Reid†	7	12	1	180	512	46.54	2	1	2	–
I.D.S. Smith	15	21	6	113*	416	27.73	1	–	45	1
M.C. Snedden†	10	12	2	32	147	14.70	–	–	2	–
J.G. Wright	31	54	2	141	1586	30.50	3	5	18	–

Bowling	Type	Balls	R	W	Avge	Best	5wI	10wM
S.L. Boock	SLA	3292	1103	37	29.81	5-28	1	–
J.G. Bracewell	OB	1827	810	25	32.40	5-75	1	–
B.L. Cairns	RMF	9096	3550	115	30.86	7-74	6	1
E.J. Chatfield	RFM	3509	1464	45	32.53	5-63	2	–
J.V. Coney	RM	1659	520	15	34.66	3-28	–	–
J.J. Crowe	RM	1	0	0	–	–	–	–
M.D. Crowe	RMF	471	225	3	75.00	2-35	–	–
B.A. Edgar	RM	18	3	0	–	–	–	–
E.J. Gray	SLA	288	128	4	32.00	3-73	–	–
R.J. Hadlee	RFM	12721	5626	235	23.94	7-23	18	4
G.P. Howarth	OB	560	254	3	84.66	1-13	–	–
W.K. Lees	RM	5	4	0	–	–	–	–
M.C. Snedden	RFM	1698	819	23	35.60	3-21	–	–
J.G. Wright	RM	6	2	0	–	–	–	–

India

Batting/Fielding	M	I	NO	HS	R	Avge	100	50	Ct	St
M. Amarnath	42	72	5	120	2660	39.70	7	16	34	-
R. Bhatt†	2	3	1	6	6	3.00	-	-	-	-
R.M.H. Binny	17	28	3	83*	605	24.20	-	4	7	-
D.R. Doshi†	33	38	10	20	129	4.60	-	-	10	-
A.D. Gaekwad	35	62	4	201	1776	30.62	2	8	13	-
S.M. Gavaskar	99	174	14	236*	8394	52.46	30	36	85	-
Kapil Dev	62	92	8	126*	2483	29.55	3	13	24	-
S.M.H. Kirmani	78	113	20	101*	2418	26.00	1	11	145	34
Kirti Azad	7	12	0	24	135	11.25	-	-	3	-
Madan Lal	37	59	16	74	1000	23.25	-	5	15	-
A. Malhotra	6	9	1	72*	199	24.87	-	1	2	-
Maninder Singh	12	14	4	15	54	5.40	-	-	3	-
Navjot Singh	2	3	0	20	39	13.00	-	-	1	-
S.M. Patil	25	41	4	174	1363	36.83	3	7	11	-
B.S. Sandhu	8	11	4	71	214	30.57	-	2	1	-
R.J. Shastri	27	41	6	128	1083	30.94	2	5	10	-
K. Srikkanth	6	9	0	65	147	16.33	-	1	2	-
D.B. Vengsarkar	69	113	10	159	3970	38.54	8	22	45	-
S. Venkataraghavan	57	76	12	64	748	11.68	-	2	44	-
N.S. Yadav	18	23	6	43	236	13.88	-	-	6	-
Yashpal Sharma	37	59	11	140	1606	33.45	2	9	16	-

Bowling	Type	Balls	R	W	Avge	Best	5wI	10wM
M. Amarnath	RM	3072	1525	27	56.48	4-63	-	-
R. Bhat	SLA	438	151	4	37.75	2-65	-	-
R.M.H. Binny	RM	1769	1021	24	42.54	3-18	-	-
D.R. Doshi	SLA	9322	3502	114	30.71	6-102	6	-
A.D. Gaekwad	OB	160	107	0	-	-	-	-
S.M. Gavaskar	RM	346	177	1	177.00	1-34	-	-
Kapil Dev	RFM	13341	6844	247	27.70	9-83	18	2
S.M.H. Kirmani	OB	18	13	1	13.00	1-9	-	-
Kirti Azad	OB	750	373	4	124.33	2-84	-	-
Madan Lal	RMF	5710	2704	67	40.35	5-23	4	-
A. Malhotra	RM	6	0	0	-	-	-	-
Maninder Singh	SLA	2328	970	15	64.66	4-85	-	-
Navjot Singh	RM	6	9	0	-	-	-	-
S.M. Patil	RM	645	240	9	26.66	2-28	-	-
B.S. Sandhu	RMF	1020	557	10	55.70	3-87	-	-
R.J. Shastri	SLA	6003	2368	62	38.19	5-75	2	-
K. Srikkanth	RM	36	10	0	-	-	-	-
D.B. Vengsarkar	RM	47	36	0	-	-	-	-
S. Venkataraghavan	OB	14877	5634	156	36.11	8-72	3	1
N.S. Yadav	OB	3804	1778	50	35.56	5-131	1	-
Yashpal Sharma	RM	30	17	1	17.00	1-6	-	-

Pakistan

Batting/Fielding	M	I	NO	HS	R	Avge	100	50	Ct	St
Abdul Qadir	27	34	4	50	454	15.13	–	1	7	–
Anil Dalpat	3	4	1	16*	38	12.66	–	–	5	2
Azim Hafeez†	10	12	3	24	69	7.66	–	–	1	–
Imran Khan	51	77	12	123	2023	31.12	2	7	16	–
Iqbal Qasim†	37	42	12	56	278	9.26	–	1	27	–
Javed Miandad	60	95	14	280*	4519	55.79	11	25	51	1
Mansoor Akhtar	13	22	3	111	484	25.47	1	2	7	–
Mohammad Nazir	14	18	10	29*	144	18.00	–	–	4	–
Mohsin Kamal	1	1	0	0	0	0.00	–	–	–	–
Mohsin Khan	33	54	5	200	2165	44.18	7	6	26	–
Mudassar Nazar	44	68	5	231	2542	40.34	6	11	31	–
Qasim Omar	9	16	1	113	484	32.26	1	2	5	–
Ramiz Raja	2	4	1	26	34	11.33	–	–	4	–
Rashid Khan	3	4	3	59	118	118.00	–	1	1	–
Salim Malik	16	22	2	116	775	38.75	3	4	19	–
Sarfraz Nawaz	55	72	13	90	1045	17.71	–	4	26	–
Shoaib Mohammad	3	5	1	80	108	27.00	–	1	–	–
Tahir Naqqash	14	17	5	57	299	24.91	–	1	2	–
Tauseef Ahmed	8	5	3	18	41	20.50	–	–	4	–
Wasim Bari	81	112	26	85	1366	15.88	–	6	201	27
Wasim Raja†	53	86	13	125	2678	36.68	4	16	19	–
Zaheer Abbas	69	112	10	274	4747	46.53	11	20	33	–

Bowling	Type	Balls	R	W	Avge	Best	5wI	10wM
Abdul Qadir	LB	7430	3380	96	35.20	7-142	7	2
Azim Hafeez	LFM	2097	1151	30	38.36	5-100	2	–
Imran Khan	RF	12551	5316	232	22.91	8-58	16	4
Iqbal Qasim	SLA	9444	3473	115	30.20	7-49	4	2
Javed Miandad	LB	1422	661	17	38.88	3-74	–	–
Mohammad Nazir	OB	3262	1123	34	33.02	7-99	3	–
Mohsin Kamal	RMF	192	125	2	62.50	1-59	–	–
Mohsin Khan	LB	86	30	0	–	–	–	–
Mudassar Nazar	RM	3054	1352	33	40.96	6-32	1	–
Qasim Omar	RM	6	0	0	–	–	–	–
Rashid Khan	RMF	546	263	6	43.83	3-129	–	–
Salim Malik	RM	36	20	2	10.00	1-3	–	–
Sarfraz Nawaz	RFM	13926	5798	177	32.75	9-86	4	1
Tahir Naqqash	RFM	2600	1317	31	42.48	5-40	2	–
Tauseef Ahmed	OB	1896	786	28	28.07	4-58	–	–
Wasim Bari	RM	8	2	0	–	–	–	–
Wasim Raja	LB	3729	1660	48	34.58	4-50	–	–
Zaheer Abbas	OB	284	93	1	93.00	1-14	–	–

Sri Lanka

Batting/Fielding

	M	I	NO	HS	R	Avge	100	50	Ct	St
A.M.J.G. Amerasinghe	2	4	1	34	54	18.00	–	–	3	–
R.G. de Alwis	5	10	0	28	102	10.20	–	–	9	1
A.L.F. De Mel	7	14	3	34	188	17.09	–	–	5	–
D.S. De Silva	12	22	3	61	406	21.36	–	2	5	–
P.A. De Silva	1	2	0	16	19	9.50	–	–	–	–
R.L. Dias	9	17	0	109	747	43.94	2	5	6	–
E.R.N.S. Fernando	5	10	0	46	112	11.20	–	–	–	–
V.B. John	6	10	5	27*	53	10.60	–	–	2	–
S.M.S. Kaluperuma	3	6	0	23	82	13.66	–	–	6	–
R.S. Madugalle	12	24	3	91*	681	32.42	–	4	7	–
L.R.D. Mendis	10	20	0	111	726	36.30	3	3	4	–
A. Ranatunga†	9	18	0	90	521	28.94	–	5	3	–
R.J. (Rumesh) Ratnayake	4	8	0	30	76	9.50	–	–	3	–
J.R. (Ravi) Ratnayeke†	8	16	4	29*	150	12.50	–	–	1	–
S.A.R. Silva†	2	4	1	102*	118	39.33	1	–	5	–
S. Wettimuny	11	22	1	190	819	39.00	2	4	4	–

Bowling

	Type	Balls	R	W	Avge	Best	5wI	10wM
A.M.J.G. Amerasinghe	SLA	300	150	3	50.00	2-73	–	–
A.L.F. De Mel	RFM	1515	1015	29	35.00	5-68	1	–
D.S. De Silva	LB	3031	1347	37	36.40	5-59	1	–
V.B. John	RMF	1281	614	28	21.92	5-60	2	–
S.M.S. Kaluperuma	OB	162	62	2	31.00	2-17	–	–
R.S. Madugalle	OB	24	4	0	–	–	–	–
A. Ranatunga	RM	432	173	5	34.60	2-17	–	–
R.J. (Rumesh) Ratnayake	RFM	678	405	8	50.62	4-81	–	–
J.R. (Ravi) Ratnayeke	RMF	1385	687	17	40.41	5-42	1	–
S. Wettimuny	RM	12	21	0	–	–	–	–

Back Numbers

The first two editions of the Daily Telegraph Cricket Year Book are still available, although in limited supply. Start to build up your collection now and watch it accumulate over the years.

Cricket Year Book 82/83 **Cricket Year Book 84**
£3.95 p/b £6.95 h/b   £4.95 p/b £6.95 h/b

Please indicate which book you require and send your order to
Dept. CYB, (Back Numbers) Daily Telegraph, 135 Fleet Street, London EC4
(please add 55p for postage and packing)

Guide to Newcomers

Register of New Players 1984

The following players made their first appearance in English first-class county cricket during the 1984 season. Three of them, I. Broome for Gloucestershire in 1980, P.J. Prichard for Essex in 1982, and J.J.E. Hardy for Hampshire in 1983, had appeared previously in limited-overs matches. Players indicated with a dagger (†) had already made their debuts in first-class cricket overseas, or, in the case of W. Morton, for Scotland.

Key to categories:

RH	Right-handed batsman		LFM	Left-arm fast-medium
LH	Left-handed batsman		LM	Left-arm medium
RF	Right-arm fast		OB	Right-arm slow off-breaks
RFM	Right-arm fast-medium		LB	Right-arm slow leg-breaks
RMF	Right-arm medium-fast		SLA	Left-arm slow leg-breaks
RM	Right-arm medium		WK	Wicket-keeper
LF	Left-arm fast			

Surname	Given Names	Birthdate	Place of Birth	Bat	Ball
Derbyshire					
Broome	Ian	6 May 60	Bradenstoke cum Clack, Wilts	RH	RFM
Malcolm	Devon Eugene	22 Feb 63	Kingston, Jamaica	RH	RF
Roberts†	Bruce	30 May 62	Lusaka, Northern Rhodesia	RH	RM
Taylor	Jonathan Paul	8 Aug 64	Ashby-de-la-Zouch, Leics	LH	LFM
Essex					
Prichard	Paul John	7 Jan 65	Billericay, Essex	RH	
Glamorgan					
Green	Russell Christopher	30 Jul 59	St Albans, Herts	RH	RMF
Price	Mark Richard	20 Apr 60	Liverpool, Lancashire	RH	SLA
Gloucestershire					
Burrows	Dean Andrew	20 Jun 66	Peterlee, Co Durham	RH	RMF
Dale	Christopher Stephen	15 Dec 61	Canterbury, Kent	RH	OB
Rolls	Lawson Macgregor	8 Mar 65	Bristol	RH	OB
Walsh†	Courtney Andrew	30 Oct 62	Kingston, Jamaica	RH	RFM
Hampshire					
Andrew	Stephen Jon Walter	27 Jan 66	London	RH	RM
Connor	Cardigan Adolphus	24 Mar 61	The Valley, Anguilla	RH	RMF
Hardy	Jonathan James Ean	2 Oct 60	Nakuru, Kenya	LH	
Middleton	Tony Charles	1 Feb 64	Winchester, Hampshire	RH	SLA
Reifer	Elvis Leroy	21 Mar 61	St Michael, Barbados	LH	LMF
Kent					
Cowdrey	Graham Robert	27 Jun 64	Farnborough, Kent	RH	RM
Lancashire					
Makinson	David John	12 Jan 61	Eccleston, Lancashire	RH	LMF
Patterson†	Belfour Patrick	15 Sep 61	Portland, Jamaica	RH	RFM
Leicestershire					
Carmichael†	Ian Robert	17 Dec 60	Hull, Yorkshire	LH	LFM
Haysman†	Michael Donald	22 Apr 61	Adelaide, Australia	RH	OB
Whitticase	Philip	15 Mar 65	Marston Green, Solihull	RH	WK
Middlesex					
Brown	Keith Robert	18 Mar 63	Edmonton, Middlesex	RH	WK
Fraser	Angus Robert Charles	8 Aug 65	Billinge, Lancashire	RH	RMF
Northamptonshire					
Hanley†	Rupert William	29 Jan 52	Pt Elizabeth, S. Africa	RH	RFM
Ripley	David	13 Sep 66	Leeds, Yorkshire	RH	WK

Register of New Players (contd)

Surname	Given Names	Birthdate	Place of Birth	Bat	Ball
Nottinghamshire					
Afford	John Andrew	12 May 64	Crowland, Lincolnshire	RH	SLA
Evans	Kevin Paul	10 Sep 63	Calverton, Notts	RH	RMF
Fraser-Darling	Callum David	30 Sep 63	Sheffield, Yorkshire	RH	RMF
Mee	Steven Robert	6 Apr 65	Nottingham	RH	RM
Newell	Michael	25 Feb 65	Blackburn, Lancashire	RH	LB
Somerset					
Turner	Murray Stewart	27 Jan 64	Shaftesbury, Dorset	RH	RMF
Turner	Simon Jonathan	28 Apr 60	Cuckfield, Sussex	LH	WK
Surrey					
Falkner	Nicholas James	30 Sep 62	Redhill, Surrey	RH	RM
Medlycott	Keith Thomas	12 May 65	Whitechapel, London E1	RH	SLA
Sussex					
Lenham	Neil John	17 Dec 65	Worthing, Sussex	RH	RMF
Wood	David John	10 Jan 65	Cuckfield, Sussex	LH	SLA
Warwickshire					
Morton†	William	21 Apr 61	Stirling, Scotland	LH	SLA
Wall	Stephen	10 Dec 59	Ulverston, Lancashire	RH	RMF
Worcestershire					
Hick†	Graeme Ashley	23 May 66	Salisbury, Rhodesia	RH	OB
Yorkshire					
Robinson	Phillip Edward	3 Aug 63	Keighley, Yorkshire	RH	LM
Shaw	Christopher	17 Feb 64	Hemsworth, Yorkshire	RH	RFM
Cambridge University					
Andrew	Christopher Robert	18 Feb 63	Richmond, Yorkshire	LH	OB
Breddy	Martin Nicholas	23 Sep 61	Torquay, Devon	RH	–
Burnley	Ian David	11 Mar 63	Darlington, Co. Durham	RH	–
Garlick	Paul Lawrence	2 Aug 64	Chiswick, London W4	RH	RMF
Grimes	Alexander David Hugh	8 Jan 65	Beirut, Lebanon	RH	RM
Lea	Antony Edward	29 Sep 62	Wolverhampton, Staffs	RH	LB
McDonnell	Guy Francis Henry	24 Jan 63	Lytham, Lancashire	LH	OB
Price	David Gregory	7 Feb 65	Luton, Bedfordshire	RH	OB
Richardson	Philip Charles	12 Jun 65	Paddington, London W2	RH	OB
Sanders	Ian Edward Wakefield	26 Feb 61	Edinburgh, Scotland	RH	RMF
Siddiqi	Shah Naweed	13 Sep 59	London	RH	RM
Thomas	Neill Peter	26 May 64	Tenterden, Kent	LH	SLA
Travers	Timothy James	28 Dec 62	Wimbledon, Surrey	RH	OB
Oxford University					
Brettell	James Gordon	19 Dec 62	Woking, Surrey	RH	SLA
Bristowe	William Robert	17 Nov 63	Woking, Surrey	RH	OB
Hewitt	Simon Mark	30 Jul 61	Radcliffe, Lancashire	RH	RMF
Mee	Adrian Alexander Graham	29 May 63	Johannesburg, S. Africa	RH	–

The following player made his first appearance in county cricket during 1964 but in limited-overs matches only. He has yet to make his debut in first-class cricket:

Surname	Given Names	Birthdate	Place of Birth	Bat	Ball
Surrey					
Ward	David Mark	10 Feb 61	Croydon, Surrey	RH	OB

Newcomers Record in English First-Class Cricket

Batting/Fielding		M	I	NO	HS	R	Avge	100	50	Ct	St
Derbyshire	I. Broome	2	4	3	26*	35	35.00	–	–	1	–
	D.E. Malcolm	7	8	1	23	40	5.71	–	–	4	–
	B. Roberts	17	26	5	80	554	26.38	–	3	12	–
	J.P. Taylor	3	2	0	11	11	5.50	–	–	2	–
Essex	P.J. Prichard	20	29	2	100	888	32.88	1	6	10	–
Glamorgan	R.C. Green	2	1	1	3*	3	–	–	–	1	–
	M.R. Price	3	2	0	7	8	4.00	–	–	–	–
Gloucestershire	D.A. Burrows	1	1	0	0	0	–	–	–	–	–
	C.S. Dale	8	8	2	49	100	16.66	–	–	1	–
	L.M. Rolls	1	–	–	–	–	–	–	–	–	–
	C.A. Walsh†	14	15	3	30	98	8.16	–	–	1	–
Hampshire	S.J.W. Andrew	7	6	4	6*	12	6.00	–	–	1	–
	C.A. Connor	21	23	9	13*	65	4.64	–	–	7	–
	J.J.E. Hardy	13	20	6	95	513	36.64	–	4	9	–
	T.C. Middleton	1	2	0	10	15	7.50	–	–	–	–
	E.L. Reifer	20	26	8	47	357	19.83	–	–	6	–
Kent	G.R. Cowdrey	1	1	0	7	7	7.00	–	–	1	–
Lancashire	D.J. Makinson	4	5	2	9	18	6.00	–	–	–	–
	B.P. Patterson	1	2	0	10	10	5.00	–	–	–	–
Leicestershire	I.R. Carmichael	7	6	3	4*	6	2.00	–	–	3	–
	M.D. Haysman	5	10	4	102*	230	38.33	1	–	9	–
	P. Whitticase	8	9	2	14	35	5.00	–	–	18	–
Middlesex	K.R. Brown	1	1	0	6	6	6.00	–	–	1	–
	A.R.C. Fraser	1	–	–	–	–	–	–	–	–	–
Northamptonshire	R.W. Hanley	17	21	7	33*	131	9.35	–	–	3	–
	D. Ripley	14	21	3	61	281	15.61	–	1	26	12
Nottinghamshire	J.A. Afford	3	–	–	–	–	–	–	–	1	–
	K.P. Evans	3	4	0	42	48	12.00	–	–	3	–
	C.D. Fraser-Darling	1	–	–	–	–	–	–	–	1	–
	S.R. Mee	1	–	–	–	–	–	–	–	–	–
	M. Newell	4	7	1	76	109	18.16	–	1	6	–
Somerset	M.S. Turner	1	2	0	1	1	0.50	–	–	–	–
	S.J. Turner	5	6	3	27*	75	25.00	–	–	12	3
Surrey	N.J. Falkner	1	1	1	101*	101	–	1	–	–	–
	K.T. Medlycott	6	6	5	117*	128	128.00	1	–	–	–
Sussex	N.J. Lenham	1	1	0	31	31	31.00	–	–	1	–
	D.J. Wood	2	3	0	15	32	10.66	–	–	–	–
Warwickshire	W. Morton	8	8	2	13*	39	6.50	–	–	3	–
	S. Wall	7	9	4	19	47	9.40	–	–	1	–
Worcestershire	G.A. Hick	1	1	1	82*	82	–	–	1	1	–
Yorkshire	P.E. Robinson	15	24	5	92	756	39.78	–	6	7	–
	C. Shaw	3	5	2	17	32	10.66	–	–	–	–
Cambridge U	C.R. Andrew	9	18	1	101*	405	23.82	1	1	2	–
	M.N. Breddy	10	20	1	61	339	17.84	–	1	2	–
	I.D. Burnley	3	6	0	86	232	38.66	–	2	1	–
	P.L. Garlick	10	15	6	6*	13	1.44	–	–	1	–
	A.D.H. Grimes	7	11	2	13	58	6.44	–	–	2	–
	A.E. Lea	9	18	0	119	395	21.94	1	1	2	–
	G.F.H. McDonnell	2	4	0	5	7	1.75	–	–	–	–
	D.G. Price	7	11	0	49	239	21.72	–	–	3	–
	P.C. Richardson	1	1	0	7	7	7.00	–	–	–	–
	I.E.W. Sanders	1	2	0	9	9	4.50	–	–	–	–
	S.N. Siddiqi	6	12	0	52	219	18.25	–	1	1	–
	N.P. Thomas	1	2	0	0	0	0.00	–	–	1	–
	T.J. Travers	1	2	0	15	20	10.00	–	–	–	–
Oxford U	J.G. Brettell	1	2	1	0*	0	0.00	–	–	1	–
	W.R. Bristowe	5	8	3	30*	104	20.80	–	–	2	–
	S.M. Hewitt	4	6	1	22	60	12.00	–	–	–	–
	A.A.G. Mee	1	1	0	22	2	2.00	–	–	1	–

*Not out †Includes 8 matches for the West Indies touring team

EXTRAS/GUIDE TO NEWCOMERS

Bowling		O	M	R	W	Avge	Best	5wI	10wM
Derbyshire	I. Broome	19.1	6	82	2	41.00	1-17	-	-
	D.E. Malcolm	156.2	24	674	16	42.12	3-78	-	-
	B. Roberts	277	43	1044	22	47.45	4-77	-	-
	J.P. Taylor	49.2	6	188	2	94.00	2-92	-	-
Essex	P.J. Prichard	1	0	5	0	-	-	-	-
Glamorgan	R.C. Green	31.5	9	92	2	46.00	2-65	-	-
	M.R. Price	31	4	109	2	54.50	1-43	-	-
Gloucestershire	D.A. Burrows	15	0	76	0	-	-	-	-
	C.S. Dale	125.1	22	467	7	66.71	3-10	-	-
	L.M. Rolls	15	1	49	0	-	-	-	-
	C.A. Walsh†	341.3	80	1179	32	36.84	6-70	1	-
Hampshire	S.J.W. Andrew	162.2	43	530	11	48.18	4-30	-	-
	C.A. Connor	642.5	155	1949	62	31.43	7-37	1	-
	J.J.E. Hardy	1	0	3	0	-	-	-	-
	E.L. Reifer	524.5	100	1761	49	35.93	4-43	-	-
Kent	G.R. Cowdrey	7	0	22	1	22.00	1-22	-	-
Lancashire	D.J. Makinson	93	17	313	7	44.71	2-49	-	-
	B.P. Patterson	21	3	51	0	-	-	-	-
Leicestershire	I.R. Carmichael	208	40	661	17	38.88	5-84	1	-
Middlesex	A.R.C. Fraser	34	7	124	1	124.00	1-68	-	-
Northamptonshire	R.W. Hanley	401.1	87	1182	37	31.94	6-21	3	-
Nottinghamshire	J.A. Afford	88.3	32	256	7	36.57	2-49	-	-
	K.P. Evans	48	8	173	2	86.50	2-31	-	-
	C.D. Fraser-Darling	29	9	55	3	18.33	2-14	-	-
	S.R. Mee	23	4	63	2	31.50	2-44	-	-
	M. Newell	4	0	14	0	-	-	-	-
Somerset	M.S. Turner	298	8	85	0	-	-	-	-
Surrey	K.T. Medlycott	98	34	186	7	26.57	2-15	-	-
Warwickshire	W. Morton	189.5	45	549	14	39.21	4-85	-	-
	S. Wall	140.4	28	545	9	60.55	2-65	-	-
Worcestershire	G.A. Hick	6	0	27	0	-	-	-	-
Yorkshire	P.E. Robinson	2	0	12	0	-	-	-	-
	C. Shaw	53.4	5	177	5	35.40	4-68	-	-
Cambridge U	C.R. Andrew	158.3	25	568	6	94.66	3-77	-	-
	P.L. Garlick	253	31	1092	12	91.00	2-69	-	-
	A.D.H. Grimes	123	22	427	3	142.33	1-24	-	-
	A.E. Lea	19	5	92	2	46.00	2-27	-	-
	P.C. Richardson	21	0	122	1	122.00	1-92	-	-
	I.E.W. Sanders	25	5	93	3	31.00	2-78	-	-
	S.N. Siddiqi	23	6	90	5	18.00	5-90	1	-
Oxford U	J.G. Brettell	15	3	74	1	74.00	1-74	-	-
	S.M. Hewitt	64.5	8	232	4	58.00	2-52	-	-

†Includes 8 matches for the West Indies touring team

The Cricketer International

Edited by Christopher Martin-Jenkins

Subscribe to The Cricketer — **GOOD WRITING**

Our team of writers, led by E. W. Swanton and Christopher Martin-Jenkins, with regular articles by Mike Brearley, Alan Gibson, Michael Melford, Peter Roebuck, Tony Pawson and many other leading names, covers cricket's major issues in depth and with style.

Subscribe to The Cricketer — **GOOD ACTION**

Adrian Murrell, *The Cricketer's* special photographer, was a recent winner of the Ilford Sports Photographer of the year and his vivid shots of Test and County cricket are colourful and compelling.

Subscribe to The Cricketer — **GOOD HUMOUR, FACTS AND VARIETY**

Robert Brooke and Bill Frindall find facts which no one else seems to spot. Neil Bennett, our brilliantly original cartoonist, makes you laugh and think! Plus news from clubs, schools, minor counties, women's cricket and a special Young Cricketer section.

Subscribe to The Cricketer — **GOOD IDEA!**

To open a 12 month subscription (12 issues) write to **The Cricketer Ltd., Dept. D.T., Beech Hanger, Ashurst, Tunbridge Wells, Kent, TN3 9ST.**
Inland, Ireland, Channel Islands, B.F.P.O. £12.45
All other countries: Surface mail £13.45
Airmail £21.70.

THE BIGGEST SELLER BECAUSE IT'S THE BEST

Obituary 1983-84

Deaths among famous cricketers over the period between the September of 1983 and 1984 were abnormally heavy, numbering 15 who had represented their countries, with varying distinction, as against 6 only in the previous 12 months. Most illustrious of all was *George Headley* (74), of Jamaica, the first of the great black West Indian batsmen, the measure of whose ascendancy it was in the 1930s that his Test average was apt to be twice that of the man who came next. When he made 106 and 107 against England at Lord's in 1939 there was only one other score higher than the 20s. He was a fascinating player and withal a modest one.

Sir Donald Bradman never saw a better wicket-keeper than *Don Tallon* (68) of Queensland, who was an integral part of the formidable post-war Australian teams. Likewise it could be said that among the left-arm opening bowlers of his type none perhaps should rank higher than *Bill Voce* (74) of Nottinghamshire, the other half of a formidable partnership with Harold Larwood.

Vijay Manjrekar (52), with his contemporary, Polly Umrigar, was the best of the early post-war Indian batsmen, a prolific player in Indian cricket and the scorer of 7 Test 100s, most of them when his side was up against it. The names of *Ian Cromb* (79), opening bowler, and *'Giff' Vivian* (70), left-handed all-rounder, take one back to New Zealand's early Test days and are a reminder of the happy spirit of those first teams. In at the start likewise was *Leslie Walcott* (90) of Barbados, the oldest West Indian Test cricketer at the time of his death. By contrast *Atholl McKinnon* (50), an affable South African and slow left-arm bowler, was still active as a coach, and was managing the 'rebel' West Indian team of 1983 when he died of a heart-attack. *A.W. Lampard* (98) of Victoria was the last survivor of the AIF team that toured England in 1919.

Back on the home front, we mourn 4 other Test cricketers, *Jack Ikin* (66) of Lancashire, *Johnny Arnold* (76) of Hampshire, *Maurice Tremlett* (61) of Somerset, and *Frank Lowson* (59) of Yorkshire. Ikin's qualities were such that he was chosen to take the first England Young Cricketers side to West Indies, having been assistant-manager to S.C. Griffith with MCC in Australia in 1965-66. Tremlett, an equally popular figure, became Somerset's first professional captain (1956-59).

Arnold, Hampshire's best bat of the 1930s, went on to serve as a first-class umpire, as also did *'Dusty' Rhodes* (67) of Derbyshire, whose leg-breaks brought him no fewer than 5 hat-tricks. *Harry Parks* (77) was a cheerful member of the family of Sussex Parkses. *Sir Denis Blundell* (77) of Waitaki was the leading bowler in the Cambridge sides of 1928 and 1929, and subsequently became Governor-General of New Zealand, his native country. *Patrick Dickinson* (64), going up from KCS, Wimbledon, was the first Cambridge freshman to score a hundred in the University Match since 1877, and was showing promise for Surrey when war came.

The Duke of Beaufort (83) was a considerable patron of cricket, with his own ground at Badminton and a past president of MCC and Gloucestershire. *Louis Duffus* (80) was the senior historian of South African cricket.

He reported more than 100 Tests between 1929 and 1970. Another overseas journalist, *Dick Whitington* (71) of South Australia, played for his state and also in the unofficial 'Victory Tests' in England in 1945. I conclude with two nonagenarians. *E.L. Kidd* (94) was the senior Cambridge and Middlesex cricketer. He led his university with much distinction in 1912 and achieved the rare double of a cricket Blue and a first-class degree. *Legh Winser* (99) kept wicket for Staffordshire, and on emigrating played for South Australia before World War I. He was a high-class golfer who holed the Barwon Heads course, in Victoria, in 76 strokes, 11 fewer than his age of 87!   E.W. Swanton

Career Details (b – born; d – died; F-c – first-class career)

ARNOLD, John; b Cowley, Oxon, 30 Nov 1907; d Southampton, Hants, 3 Apr 1984. Hampshire and England. F-c umpire 1961-1972. Soccer for Southampton, Fulham, and England. F-c (1929-50): 21,831 runs (32.82), 37 hundreds; 17 wkts (69.52).

BADCOCK, Frederick Theodore, MC; b North-West Frontier, India, 9 Aug 1898; d South Perth, Western Australia, 19 Sep 1982. Wellington, Otago, and New Zealand. F-c (1924-25 to 1945): 2383 runs (25.62), 4 hundreds; 221 wkts (23.57).

BARRETT, Peter; b Winchester, Hants, 3 Jun 1955; d Everton, Hants, 28 Oct 1983. Hampshire. F-c (1975-76): 138 runs (12.54).

BELL, Geoffrey Foxall, MC; b Stapenhill, Staffs, 16 Apr 1896; d Haslemere, Surrey, 17 January 1984. Oxford U (Blue 1919) and Derbyshire. F-c (1914-20): 336 runs (16.00).

BLUNDELL, Edward Denis (Sir Denis Blundell, GCMG, GCVO, KBE, OBE, QSO); b Wellington, NZ, 29 May 1907; d Townsville, Queensland, Australia, 24 Sep 1984. Cambridge U (Blue 1928-29), Wellington and New Zealand (2 unofficial Tests v MCC 1935-36). Governor-General of New Zealand 1972-77. President of NZ Cricket Council 1957-60.

BROWN, Lennox Sidney ('Len'); b Randfontein, South Africa, 24 Nov 1910; d Durban, South Africa, 1 Sep 1983. Transvaal, North-Eastern Transvaal, Rhodesia, and South Africa. Toured Australia and New Zealand 1931-32. Soccer for Huddersfield Town and Oldham Athletic. F-c (1930-31 to 1947-48): 778 runs (16.91); 147 wkts (24.77).

CROMB, Ian Burns; b Christchurch, New Zealand, 25 Jun 1905; d Christchurch 6 Mar 1984. Canterbury and New Zealand. F-c career (1929-30 to 1946-47): 3950 runs (29.04), 3 hundreds; 222 wkts (27.71).

DICKINSON, Patrick John; b Upper Barian, India, 28 Aug 1919; d London 28 May 1984. Cambridge U (Blue 1939), Surrey, Bombay, and Madras. F-c (1939 to 1952-53): 782 runs (20.58), 2 hundreds; 28 wkts (37.57).

GREENWOOD, Henry William ('Bill'); b East Preston, Sussex, 4 Sep 1909; d Horsham, Sussex, 16 Oct 1983. Sussex (1933-36) and Northamptonshire (1938-46). F-c (1933-46): 2590 runs (20.07), 1 hundred.

HEADLEY, George Alphonso; b Panama, 30 May 1909; d Kingston, Jamaica, 30 Nov 1983. Jamaica and West Indies. F-c (1927-28 to 1953-54): 9921 runs (69.86), 33 hundreds; 51 wkts (36.11).

HUNT, William Alfred ('Bill'); b Balmain, Sydney, Australia, 26 Aug 1908; d Sydney, 31 Dec 1983. NSW and Australia. F-c (1929-30 to 1931-32): 301 runs (14.33); 62 wkts (23.00).

IKIN, John Thomas ('Jack'); b Bignall End, Staffs, 7 March 1918; d Bignall End, 15 Sep 1984. Staffs, Lancashire, and England. F-c career (1938-64): 17,968 runs (36.81), 27 hundreds; 339 wkts (30.27).

KIDD, Eric Leslie; b London 18 Oct 1889; d Dunloaghaire, Co. Dublin, 2 July 1984. Cambridge U. (Blue 1910-11-12-13 – captain 1912) and Middlesex. F-c (1910-30): 5113 runs (24.94), 6 hundreds; 186 wkts (24.63); 129 ct.

LAMPARD, Albert Wallis ('Allie'); b Richmond, Melbourne, Australia, 3 Jul 1885; d North Balwyn, Victoria, 11 Jan 1984. Victoria. Toured England and South Africa (1919 AIF team) and New Zealand (1920-21 Australians). F-c (1908-09 to 1921-22): 2597 runs (30.91), 3 hundreds; 134 wkts (26.06).

LEWIS, Esmond Burman; b Shirley, Warwicks, 5 Jan 1918; d Dorridge, Warwicks. 19 Oct 1983. Warwickshire – made 9 dismissals on debut. F-c (1949-58): 553 runs (12.57); 94 ct, 26 st.

LOWSON, Frank Anderson; b Bradford, 1 Jul 1925; d Pool in Wharfedale Yorks, 8 Sep 1984. Yorkshire and England. F-c (1949-58): 15,321 runs (37.18), 31 hundreds; 191 ct.

McKINNON, Atholl Henry, b Port Elizabeth, South Africa, 20 Aug 1932; d Durban, 2 Dec 1983. Eastern Province, Transvaal, and South Africa. F-c (1952-53 to 1968-69): 1687 runs (15.06); 470 wkts (21.14).

MANJREKAR, Vijay Laxman; b Bombay, India, 26 Sep 1931; d Madras, 18 Oct 1983. Bombay, Bengal, Andhra, Uttar Pradesh, Rajasthan, Maharashtra, and India. F-c (1949-50 to 1972-73): 12,832 runs (49.92), 38 hundreds; 20 wkts (32.95).

MITCHELL, Frank Rollason; b Sydney, Australia, 30 Jun 1922; d Myton Hamlet, Warwicks, 4 Apr 1984. Warwickshire. Soccer for Birmingham City, Chelsea, and Watford. F-c (1946-48): 224 runs (8.30); 22 wkts (38.91).
PARKS, Henry William ('Harry'); b Haywards Heath, Sussex, 18 Jul 1906; d Taunton, Somerset, 7 May 1984. Sussex. F-c umpire. F-c (1926 to 1949-50): 21,725 runs (33.57), 42 hundreds; 13 wkts (54.30).
RHODES, Albert Ennion Groucott ('Dusty'); b Tintwhistle, Cheshire, 10 Oct 1916; d Barlow, Derbys, 18 Oct 1983. Derbyshire. Toured India with MCC 1951-52. F-c umpire 1959-79 (8 Tests 1963-73). F-c (1937-54): 7363 runs (18.98), 4 hundreds; 661 wkts (28.23).
TALLON, Donald; b Bundaberg, Queensland, Australia, 17 Feb 1916; d Brisbane, 7 Sep 1984. Queensland and Australia. F-c (1933-34 to 1953-54): 6034 runs (29.14), 9 hundreds; 303 ct, 129 st.
TREMLETT, Maurice Fletcher, b Stockport, Cheshire, 5 Jul 1923; d Southampton, Hants, 30 Jul 1984. Somerset and England. F-c (1947-60): 16,038 runs (25.37), 16 hundreds; 351 wkts (30.63); 257 ct.
VIVIAN, Henry Gifford ('Giff'); b Auckland, New Zealand, 4 Nov 1912; d Auckland, 12 Aug 1983. Auckland and New Zealand. F-c (1930-31 to 1938-39): 4443 runs (34.71), 6 hundreds; 223 wkts (27.62).
VOCE, William ('Bill'); b Annesley Woodhouse, Notts, 8 Aug 1909; d Nottingham 6 Jun 1984. Nottinghamshire and England. F-c (1927-52): 7583 runs (19.19), 4 hundreds; 1558 wkts (23.08); 280 ct.
WALCOTT, Leslie Arthur; b Barbados, 18 Jan 1894; d Barbados 28 Feb 1984. Barbados and West Indies. F-c (1924-25 to 1935-36): 555 runs (30.83); 16 wkts (29.50).
WARBURTON, Leslie, b Haslingden, Lancs, 1910, d Gloucester 11 Feb 1984. Lancashire. F-c (1929-38): 159 runs (39.75); 5 wkts (43.40).
WHITINGTON, Richard Smallpiece ('Dick'), LLB; b Unley Park, South Australia, 30 Jun 1912; d Sydney, 13 Mar 1984. South Australia and 'Victory Tests'. Writer. F-c (1932-33 to 1946-47): 2781 runs (32.33), 4 hundreds.
WILKINSON, Colonel William Alexander Carnac, DSO, MC and Bar, GM; b in Australia, 6 Dec 1892; d Storrington, Sussex, 19 Sep 1983. Oxford U. (Blue 1913), MCC, Gentlemen, the Army, and Free Foresters. MCC to Australasia 1922-23. F-c (1912-1939): 4332 runs (31.39), 9 hundreds.
WILLIAMS, Colonel Leoline; b Dursley, Glos, 15 May 1900; d St Austell, Cornwall, 29 Feb 1984. Sussex, Gloucestershire (1922), and the Army. F-c (1919-31): 1440 runs (22.86), 3 hundreds; 20 ct, 5 st.
WINSER, Cyril Legh, CMG, MVO; b Cheshire, 27 Nov 1884; d Barwon Heads, Victoria, Australia, 20 Dec 1983. Staffordshire (1906-09) and South Australia. F-c (1913-14 to 1920-21): 64 runs (8.00); 8 ct, 6 st.

Their Record in Tests

Batting/Fielding	M	I	NO	HS	R	Avge	100	50	Ct	St
J. Arnold (Eng)	1	2	0	34	34	17.00	-	-	-	-
F.T. Badcock (NZ)	7	9	2	64	137	19.57	-	2	1	-
L.S. Brown (SA)	2	3	0	8	17	5.66	-	-	-	-
I.B. Cromb (NZ)	5	8	2	51*	123	20.50	-	1	1	-
G.A. Headley (WI)	22	40	4	270*	2190	60.83	10	5	14	-
W.A. Hunt (Aus)†	1	1	0	0	0	0.00	-	-	1	-
J.T. Ikin (Eng)†	18	31	2	60	606	20.89	-	3	31	-
F.A. Lowson (Eng)	7	13	0	68	245	18.84	-	2	5	-
A.H. McKinnon (SA)	8	13	7	27	107	17.83	-	-	1	-
V.L. Manjrekar (Ind)	55	92	10	189*	3208	39.12	7	15	19	2
D. Tallon (Aus)	21	26	3	92	394	17.13	-	2	50	8
M.F. Tremlett (Eng)	3	5	2	18*	20	6.66	-	-	-	-
H.G. Vivian (NZ)†	7	10	0	100	421	42.10	1	5	4	-
W. Voce (Eng)	27	38	15	66	308	13.39	-	1	15	-
L.A. Walcott (WI)	1	2	1	24	40	40.00	-	-	-	-

†Left-handed batsman

Bowling	Type	Balls	R	W	Avge	Best	5wI	10wM
F.T. Badcock (NZ)	RM	1608	610	16	38.12	4-80	-	-
L.S. Brown (SA)	LB	318	189	3	63.00	1-30	-	-
I.B. Cromb (NZ)	RMF	960	442	8	55.25	3-113	-	-
G.A. Headley (WI)	LB	398	230	0	-	-	-	-
W.A. Hunt (Aus)	SLA	96	39	0	-	-	-	-
J.T. Ikin (Eng)	LB	572	354	3	118.00	1-38	-	-
A.H. McKinnon (SA)	SLA	2546	925	26	35.57	4-128	-	-
V.L. Manjrekar (Ind)	OB	204	44	1	44.00	1-16	-	-
M.F. Tremlett (Eng)	RFM	492	226	4	56.50	2-98	-	-
H.G. Vivian (NZ)	SLA	1311	633	17	37.23	4-58	-	-
W. Voce (Eng)	LF	6360	2733	98	27.88	7-70	3	2
L.A. Walcott (WI)	RM/OB	48	32	1	32.00	1-17	-	-

Looking forward

England on Tour 1984-85

England's Tour Party

	Age	Tests		Age	Tests
David Gower, captain (Leics)	27	65	Neil Foster (Essex)	22	6
Mike Gatting, vice-captain (Middx)	27	30	Graeme Fowler (Lancs)	27	16
			Bruce French (Notts)	25	0
Paul Allott (Lancs)	27	9	Allan Lamb (Northants)	30	27
Norman Cowans (Middx)	23	13	Vic Marks (Somerset)	29	6
Chris Cowdrey (Kent)	26	0	Martyn Moxon (Yorks)	24	0
Paul Downton (Middx)	27	10	Pat Pocock (Surrey)	37	20
Phil Edmonds (Middx)	33	25	Tim Robinson (Notts)	25	0
Richard Ellison (Kent)	24	2			

Tour Manager: Tony Brown (Somerset). Assistant Manager: Norman Gifford (Warwicks). Physiotherapist: Bernard Thomas.

Tour Itinerary

In India

October	31	*Arrive Delhi*
November	5, 6, 7	President's XI (Jaipur)
	9, 10, 11, 12	North Zone (Jammu)
	15	India (Chandigarh), one-day international
	17, 18, 19	Under-25s (Faridabad)
	22, 23, 24, 26, 27	INDIA (Delhi), First Test
	29, 30, Dec 1, 2	West Zone (Rajkot)
December	6, 7, 8, 10, 11	INDIA (Bombay), Second Test
	13	India (Pune), one-day international
	16	India (Bangalore), one-day international
	19, 20, 21, 22	East Zone (Gauhati)
	26, 27, 28, 30, 31	INDIA (Calcutta), Third Test
January	2	Bangladesh XI (Dhaka)
	5	India (Cuttack), one-day international
	7, 8, 9, 10	South Zone (Hyderabad)
	13, 14, 15, 17, 18	INDIA (Madras), Fourth Test
	21, 22, 23, 24	Central Zone (Indore)
	27	India (Nagpur), one-day international
	31, Feb 1, 2, 4, 5	INDIA (Kanpur), Fifth Test
February	7	Indian XI (Delhi), day/night charity match
	8	*Depart India for Australia*

In Australia (one-day international series)

February	17	Australia v England (Melbourne★)
	19	West Indies v New Zealand (Sydney★)
	20	Pakistan v India (Melbourne★)
	23	New Zealand v Sri Lanka (Melbourne★)
	24	Australia v Pakistan (Melbourne)
	26	England v India (Sydney★)
	27	West Indies v Sri Lanka (Melbourne★)
March	2	England v Pakistan (Melbourne★)
	3	Australia v India (Melbourne)
	5	Semi-Final (Sydney★)
	6	Semi-Final (Melbourne★)
	9	Plate Winners Final (Sydney)
	10	Final (Melbourne★)

★Day/night game; others are day games.

The 1985 Season

Few can have foreseen the West Indies' tour of 1984 as producing anything other than an England defeat, the severity of which would depend on how much interference there was from the weather. By contrast, there are enough uncertainties about the Ashes series of 1985 to raise hopes of far greater excitement. The cynic may say that it will be the meeting of two powers that have known better days, but it is not always the strongest sides that provide the most absorbing cricket.

Australia were brushed aside by West Indies in 1984 almost as easily as were England. They have to find replacements for Greg Chappell, Dennis Lillee, and Rodney Marsh, which will tax even their resilience and ability to produce good confident young players. The mere presence of new faces in the touring side should add to the interest, for the proliferation of Test cricket in recent years has taken away some of the mystery and unpredictability that used to accompany the four-yearly visit of formidable strangers in large green caps.

Some young Australians still gain experience of English conditions in the northern leagues. Terry Alderman augmented his in a season with Kent. But, unlike West Indies, who come here nowadays with such knowledge of English conditions through playing for counties (and such support from their expatriates) that it is practically a home match for them, Australia will have plenty to learn.

England are an almost equally unknown force. Anyone who six months before could name nine or ten of the side that takes the field for the first Test of 1985 against Australia would be worth a high-grade 'A' level. There is something to be said for starting from rock bottom, as England had to do after the completeness of their defeat by West Indies and their feeble effort against Sri Lanka, and it often takes only two bowlers to turn an ordinary side into a good one. Moreover, Test-class bowlers do tend to come more suddenly on the scene than batsmen.

There is the other intriguing question to be answered in 1985: how many of the banned players, by then available again, will be picked for England? Some of the team that went to South Africa in 1982 were nearing the end of their Test careers or past it. But others have almost increased their reputation *in absentia*. An opening batsman of Gooch's dominance, a slow bowler of Underwood's accuracy, an off-spinner of Emburey's reliability on good pitches, a fast-medium bowler who stays as fit and effective as Lever (and a left-arm one to boot) - all have become attractive propositions to the selectors as few alternatives of comparable ability have appeared.

It looks promising. The main snag, perhaps, is that we are due a wet summer.

Fixtures 1985

Duration of Matches (*including play on Sunday)

Cornhill Tests	5 days	Texaco Trophy	1 day
Britannic Assurance		NatWest Bank Trophy	1 day
Championship	3 days	Benson & Hedges Cup	1 day
Tourist matches	3 days or as stated	John Player Special League	1 day
University matches	3 days	Other matches	as stated

APRIL 20, SATURDAY
Cambridge	Cambridge Univ v Essex
Oxford	Oxford Univ v Somerset

APRIL 24, WEDNESDAY
Lord's	MCC v Essex (three days)
Cambridge	Cambridge Univ v Notts
Oxford	Oxford Univ v Glamorgan

APRIL 27, SATURDAY
Britannic Assurance Championship
Derby	Derbyshire v Northants
Chelmsford*	Essex v Warwickshire
Southampton*	Hampshire v Kent
Old Trafford*	Lancashire v Sussex
Leicester	Leics v Yorkshire
Lord's	Middlesex v Worcs
Taunton	Somerset v Notts
The Oval*	Surrey v Glamorgan

Other Match
Cambridge	Cambridge Univ v Glos

MAY 1, WEDNESDAY
Britannic Assurance Championship
Bristol	Glos v Lancashire
Canterbury	Kent v Surrey
Trent Bridge	Nottinghamshire v Essex
Taunton	Somerset v Glamorgan

Other Matches
Cambridge	Cambridge Univ v Middlesex
Oxford	Oxford Univ v Leics

MAY 4, SATURDAY
Benson & Hedges Cup
Chelmsford	Essex v Sussex
Cardiff	Glamorgan v Kent
Bristol	Gloucestershire v Notts
Old Trafford	Lancashire v Leics
The Oval	Surrey v Combined Univ
Worcester	Worcestershire v Warwicks
	Scotland v Derbyshire
Shrewsbury	Minor Counties v Somerset

Britannic Assurance Championship
Northampton	Northants v Hampshire
Headingley	Yorkshire v Middlesex

MAY 5, SUNDAY
John Player Special League
Chelmsford	Essex v Sussex
Cardiff	Glamorgan v Kent
Bristol	Gloucestershire v Notts
Old Trafford	Lancashire v Leics
Northampton	Northants v Hampshire
The Oval	Surrey v Warwickshire
Worcester	Worcestershire v Somerset
Bradford	Yorkshire v Middlesex

Tourist Match
Arundel	Lavinia, Duchess of Norfolk's XI v Australia (one day)

MAY 8, WEDNESDAY
Britannic Assurance Championship
Leicester	Leics v Derbyshire
Lord's	Middlesex v Kent
The Oval	Surrey v Lancashire
Edgbaston	Warwicks v Glamorgan
Worcester	Worcs v Gloucestershire

Tourist Match
Taunton	Somerset v Australia

Other Matches
Cambridge	Cambridge Univ v Sussex
Oxford	Oxford Univ v Hampshire

Benson & Hedges Cup
Swansea	Glamorgan v Minor Counties
Canterbury	Kent v Hampshire
Leicester	Leicestershire v Yorkshire
Northampton	Northants v Gloucestershire
Hove	Sussex v Surrey
Edgbaston	Warwickshire v Lancashire
	Combined Univ v Middlesex
	Scotland v Notts

Tourist Match
Worcester*	Worcestershire v Australia

MAY 12, SUNDAY
John Player Special League
Derby	Derbyshire v Northants
Canterbury	Kent v Hampshire
Leicester	Leicestershire v Yorkshire
Lord's	Middlesex v Gloucestershire
Taunton	Somerset v Glamorgan
Hove	Sussex v Surrey
Edgbaston	Warwickshire v Lancashire

LOOKING FORWARD/FIXTURES 1985

MAY 14, TUESDAY
Benson & Hedges Cup
Derby	Derbyshire v Northants
Bristol	Glos v Scotland
Southampton	Hampshire v Glamorgan
Old Trafford	Lancashire v Yorkshire
Leicester	Leicestershire v Worcs
Taunton	Somerset v Kent
The Oval	Surrey v Essex
Hove	Sussex v Middlesex

Tourist Match
Trent Bridge	Notts v Australia (one day)

MAY 16 THURSDAY
Benson & Hedges Cup
Southampton	Hampshire v Somerset
Canterbury	Kent v Minor Counties
Lord's	Middlesex v Essex
Northampton	Northants v Scotland
Trent Bridge	Nottinghamshire v Derbyshire
Worcester	Worcestershire v Lancashire
Headingley	Yorkshire v Warwickshire
	Combined Univ v Sussex

Tourist Match
The Oval	Surrey v Australia (one day)

MAY 18, SATURDAY
Benson & Hedges Cup
Chesterfield	Derbyshire v Glos
Chelmsford	Essex v Combined Univ
Lord's	Middlesex v Surrey
Trent Bridge	Notts v Northants
Taunton	Somerset v Glamorgan
Edgbaston	Warwicks v Leics
Bradford	Yorkshire v Worcs
Reading	Minor Cties v Hampshire

Tourist Match
Hove*	Sussex v Australia (four days)

MAY 19, SUNDAY
John Player Special League
Southampton	Hampshire v Surrey
Old Trafford	Lancashire v Glos
Lord's	Middlesex v Glamorgan
Trent Bridge	Notts v Leics
Scarborough	Yorkshire v Derbyshire

MAY 22, WEDNESDAY
Britannic Assurance Championship
Chesterfield	Derbyshire v Lancashire
Cardiff	Glamorgan v Middlesex
Leicester	Leicestershire v Notts
Northampton	Northamptonshire v Kent
Taunton	Somerset v Hampshire
Hove	Sussex v Gloucestershire
Edgbaston	Warwickshire v Surrey
Sheffield	Yorkshire v Essex

Tourist Match
Lord's	MCC v Australia

Other Match
Oxford	Oxford Univ v Worcestershire

MAY 25, SATURDAY
Britannic Assurance Championship
Bristol	Glos v Somerset
Southampton	Hampshire v Glamorgan
Old Trafford	Lancashire v Yorkshire
Leicester	Leicestershire v Northants
Lord's	Middlesex v Sussex
The Oval	Surrey v Essex
Worcester*	Worcs v Warwicks

Tourist Match
Derby*	Derbys v Australia (four days)

MAY 26, SUNDAY
John Player Special League
Bristol	Gloucestershire v Kent
Basingstoke	Hampshire v Glamorgan
Leicester	Leics v Northants
Lord's	Middlesex v Sussex
Trent Bridge	Notts v Somerset
The Oval	Surrey v Essex

MAY 29, WEDNESDAY
Brittanic Assurance Championship
Basingstoke	Hampshire v Derbyshire
Northampton	Northants v Warwicks
Trent Bridge	Notts v Leics
The Oval	Surrey v Middlesex
Hove	Sussex v Glamorgan
Headingley	Yorkshire v Somerset

Other Match
Oxford	Oxford University v Kent

MAY 30, THURSDAY
Texaco Trophy (1st 1-day intl)
Old Trafford	England v Australia

JUNE 1, SATURDAY
Texaco Trophy (2nd 1-day intl)
Edgbaston	England v Australia

Britannic Assurance Championship
Derby	Derbyshire v Glos
Chelmsford	Essex v Leics
Canterbury	Kent v Worcs
Taunton	Somerset v Warwicks
Horsham	Sussex v Surrey
Middlesbrough	Yorkshire v Hampshire

Other Match
Oxford	Oxford Univ v Lancashire

LOOKING FORWARD/FIXTURES 1985

JUNE 2, SUNDAY
John Player Special League
Derby	Derbyshire v Glos
Chelmsford	Essex v Leics
Canterbury	Kent v Worcs
Northampton	Northants v Lancashire
Taunton	Somerset v Warwicks
Horsham	Sussex v Notts
Middlesbrough	Yorkshire v Hampshire

JUNE 3, MONDAY
Texaco Trophy (3rd 1-day intl)
Lord's   England v Australia

JUNE 5, WEDNESDAY
Benson & Hedges Cup
Quarter-Finals

Tourist Match
Headingley   Yorkshire v Australia
(or Warwickshire or Lancashire)

JUNE 8, SATURDAY
Britannic Assurance Championship
Ilford	Essex v Lancashire
Abergavenny	Glamorgan v Worcs
Tunbridge Wells	Kent v Notts
Lord's	Middlesex v Derbyshire
Northampton	Northants v Sussex
Bath	Somerset v Glos
Edgbaston	Warwicks v Hampshire

Tourist Matches
Leicester*	Leics v Australia (four days)
Oxford	Oxford Univ v Zimbabwe

Other Match
Cambridge   Cambridge Univ v Surrey

JUNE 9, SUNDAY
John Player Special League
Ilford	Essex v Lancashire
Ebbw Vale	Glamorgan v Worcs
Lord's	Middlesex v Derbyshire
Bath	Somerset v Glos
Edgbaston	Warwicks v Hampshire
Sheffield	Yorkshire v Sussex

JUNE 12, WEDNESDAY
Britannic Assurance Championship
Derby	Derbyshire v Sussex
Ilford	Essex v Northants
Bournemouth	Hampshire v Middlesex
Tunbridge Wells	Kent v Gloucestershire
Leicester	Leics v Warwicks
Bath	Somerset v Lancashire
The Oval	Surrey v Notts

Other Matches
Cambridge	Cambridge Univ v Worcs
Oxford	Oxford Univ v Yorkshire

JUNE 13, THURSDAY
First Cornhill Test
Headingley   ENGLAND v AUSTRALIA

JUNE 15, SATURDAY
Britannic Assurance Championship
Swansea	Glamorgan v Essex
Old Trafford	Lancashire v Derbyshire
Lord's	Middlesex v Leics
Northampton	Northants v Glos
Trent Bridge	Notts v Kent
Hove	Sussex v Hampshire
Worcester	Worcs v Surrey

Tourist Match
Taunton   Somerset v Zimbabwe

Other Match
Oxford   Oxford Univ v Warwicks

JUNE 16, SUNDAY
John Player Special League
Swansea	Glamorgan v Essex
Old Trafford	Lancashire v Derbyshire
Lord's	Middlesex v Leics
Northampton	Northants v Glos
Trent Bridge	Notts v Kent
Bath	Somerset v Yorkshire
Hove	Sussex v Hampshire
Worcester	Worcs v Surrey

JUNE 19, WEDNESDAY
Benson & Hedges Cup
Semi-Finals

Tourist Match
1st-Class County (not in B & H) v Zimbabwe

Other Matches
Harrogate   Tilcon Trophy (three days)

JUNE 20, THURSDAY
Tourist Match
Cambridge   Combined Univ v Australia
(one day)

JUNE 22, SATURDAY
Britannic Assurance Championship
Bristol	Gloucestershire v Sussex
Old Trafford	Lancashire v Kent
Leicester	Leicestershire v Glamorgan
Northampton	Northants v Essex
Trent Bridge	Notts v Middlesex
The Oval	Surrey v Somerset
Harrogate*	Yorkshire v Worcestershire

Tourist Matches
Southampton*	Hampshire v Australia (four days)
Edgbaston	Warwicks v Zimbabwe

LOOKING FORWARD/FIXTURES 1985

JUNE 23, SUNDAY
John Player Special League
Bristol	Gloucestershire v Sussex
Old Trafford	Lancashire v Kent
Leicester	Leicestershire v Glamorgan
Luton	Northants v Essex
Trent Bridge	Notts v Middlesex
The Oval	Surrey v Somerset

JUNE 26, WEDNESDAY
Britannic Assurance Championship
Derby	Derbyshire v Notts
Chelmsford	Essex v Kent
Cardiff	Glamorgan v Somerset
Bristol	Glos v Hampshire
Old Trafford	Lancashire v Warwickshire
Northampton	Northamptonshire v Surrey
Worcester	Worcs v Middlesex
Bradford	Yorkshire v Leics

Tourist Match
Scotland v Zimbabwe

JUNE 27, THURSDAY
Second Cornhill Test
Lord's   ENGLAND v AUSTRALIA

JUNE 29, SATURDAY
Britannic Assurance Championship
Derby	Derby v Glamorgan
Southampton	Hampshire v Essex
Leicester	Leicestershire v Surrey
Trent Bridge*	Notts v Gloucestershire
Hastings	Sussex v Lancashire
Edgbaston	Warwickshire v Northants
Worcester	Worcs v Yorkshire

Tourist Match
Cleethorpes   Minor Counties v Zimbabwe

Other Match
Taunton   Somerset v Cambridge Univ

JUNE 30, SUNDAY
John Player Special League
Derby	Derbyshire v Glamorgan
Bournemouth	Hampshire v Essex
Canterbury	Kent v Middlesex
Leicester	Leicestershire v Surrey
Hastings	Sussex v Lancashire
Edgbaston	Warwicks v Northants
Worcester	Worcs v Yorkshire

JULY 3, WEDNESDAY
NatWest Bank Trophy (First Round)
	Bedfordshire v Glos
	Cheshire v Yorkshire
Derby	Derbyshire v Durham
Chelmsford	Essex v Oxfordshire
Southampton	Hampshire v Berkshire
Canterbury	Herts v Worcs
	Kent v Surrey
	Middlesex v Cumberland
	Norfolk v Leics
Trent Bridge	Notts v Staffs
	Scotland v Glamorgan
	Shropshire v Northants
Taunton	Somerset v Bucks
Bury St Edmunds	Suffolk v Lancashire
Hove	Sussex v Ireland
Edgbaston	Warwickshire v Devon

Other Match
Lord's   Oxford Univ v Cambridge Univ

JULY 6, SATURDAY
Britannic Assurance Championship
Swansea	Glamorgan v Notts
Gloucester	Glos v Yorkshire
Liverpool	Lancashire v Hampshire
Northampton	Northants v Middlesex
Taunton	Somerset v Leics
The Oval	Surrey v Kent
Hove	Sussex v Warwickshire
Worcester	Worcs v Derbyshire

JULY 6, SATURDAY
Tourist Match
Chelmsford*   Essex v Australia (four days)

JULY 7, SUNDAY
John Player Special League
Knypersley	Derbyshire v Worcs
Swansea	Glamorgan v Notts
Gloucester	Glos v Yorkshire
Liverpool	Lancashire v Hampshire
Tring	Northants v Middlesex
Taunton	Somerset v Leics
The Oval	Surrey v Kent
Hove	Sussex v Warwickshire

JULY 10, WEDNESDAY
Britannic Assurance Championship
Southend	Essex v Somerset
Swansea	Glamorgan v Leics
Gloucester	Glos v Worcestershire
Portsmouth	Hampshire v Sussex
Maidstone	Kent v Yorkshire
Lord's	Middlesex v Notts
Northampton	Northants v Derbyshire
Edgbaston	Warwickshire v Lancashire

Tourist Match
League Cricket Conference v Zimbabwe (two or three days)

230 LOOKING FORWARD/FIXTURES 1985

JULY 11, THURSDAY
Third Cornhill Test
Trent Bridge   ENGLAND v AUSTRALIA

JULY 13, SATURDAY
Britannic Assurance Championship
Chesterfield	Derbyshire v Leics
Southend	Essex v Gloucestershire
Portsmouth	Hampshire v Worcs
Maidstone	Kent v Northants
Old Trafford	Lancashire v Glamorgan
Lord's	Middlesex v Somerset
Nuneaton	Warwickshire v Notts
Sheffield	Yorkshire v Surrey

Tourist Match
Hove   Sussex v Zimbabwe (one day)

JULY 14, SUNDAY
John Player Special League
Southend	Essex v Gloucestershire
Portsmouth	Hampshire v Worcs
Maidstone	Kent v Northamptonshire
Old Trafford	Lancashire v Glamorgan
Lord's	Middlesex v Somerset
Edgbaston	Warwickshire v Notts
Hull or Bradford	Yorkshire v Surrey

Other Match
Arundel   Lavinia, Duchess of Norfolk's XI v Zimbabwe (one day)

JULY 17, WEDNESDAY
NatWest Bank Trophy (Second Round)
Beds or Glos v Shrops or Northants
Chesh or Yorks v Somerset or Bucks
Essex or Oxon v Middx or Cumberland
Hants or Berks v Norfolk or Leics
Kent or Surrey v Derbys or Durham
Notts or Staffs v Warwicks or Devon
Scotland or Glam v Sussex or Ireland
Suffolk or Lancs v Herts or Worcs

Tourist Match
Canterbury or
The Oval   Kent or Surrey v Zimbabwe

JULY 18, THURSDAY
Tourist Match
Jesmond   Minor Counties v Australia (one day)

JULY 20, SATURDAY
Benson & Hedges Cup
Lord's   Final

Tourist Match
Bristol*   Glamorgan v Australia
Glos v Zimbabwe (will start on July 21 if Glos are in B & H final)

JULY 21, SUNDAY
John Player Special League
Derby	Derbyshire v Somerset
Chelmsford	Essex v Kent
Leicester	Leics v Warwicks
Northampton	Northants v Sussex
Guildford	Surrey v Notts
Worcester	Worcs v Middlesex

JULY 24, WEDNESDAY
Britannic Assurance Championship
Chesterfield	Derbyshire v Yorkshire
Dartford	Kent v Essex
Southport	Lancashire v Surrey
Uxbridge	Middlesex v Northants
Trent Bridge	Notts v Sussex
Edgbaston	Warwicks v Somerset
Hereford	Worcs v Glamorgan

Tourist Matches
Bristol	Glos v Australia
Leicester	Leics v Zimbabwe

JULY 27, SATURDAY
Britannic Assurance Championship
Bristol	Glos v Glamorgan
Leicester	Leics v Kent
Uxbridge	Middlesex v Lancashire
TB or Worksop	Notts v Yorkshire
Taunton	Somerset v Essex
Guildford	Surrey v Hampshire
Eastbourne	Sussex v Worcs
Edgbaston	Warwicks v Derbyshire

JULY 27, SATURDAY
Tourist Match
Northampton*   Northants v Australia (four days)

JULY 28, SUNDAY
John Player Special League
Bristol	Glos v Glamorgan
Leicester	Leics v Kent
Lord's	Middlesex v Lancashire
Trent Bridge	Notts v Yorkshire
Taunton	Somerset v Essex
Eastbourne	Sussex v Worcs
Edgbaston	Warwicks v Derbyshire

JULY 31, WEDNESDAY
Britannic Assurance Championship
Leicester	Leics v Lancashire
Lord's	Middlesex v Glos
The Oval	Surrey v Warwickshire
Eastbourne	Sussex v Kent
Bradford	Yorkshire v Derbyshire

LOOKING FORWARD/FIXTURES 1985

AUGUST 1, THURSDAY
Fourth Cornhill Test
Old Trafford   ENGLAND v AUSTRALIA

AUGUST 3, SATURDAY
Britannic Assurance Championship
Derby   Derbyshire v Surrey
Chelmsford   Essex v Middlesex
Swansea   Glamorgan v Kent
Bournemouth   Hampshire v Somerset
Northampton   Northants v Notts
Edgbaston   Warwicks v Yorkshire
Worcester   Worcs v Lancashire

AUGUST 4, SUNDAY
John Player Special League
Derby   Derbyshire v Surrey
Chelmsford   Essex v Middlesex
Southampton   Hampshire v Somerset
Northampton   Northants v Notts
Edgbaston   Warwickshire v Yorkshire
Worcester   Worcs v Lancashire

AUGUST 7, WEDNESDAY
NatWest Bank Trophy
Quarter-Finals

AUGUST 8, THURSDAY
Tourist Match
                 Ireland v Australia (one day)

AUGUST 10, SATURDAY
Britannic Assurance Championship
Colchester   Essex v Derbyshire
Cardiff   Glamorgan v Warwicks
Cheltenham   Glos v Leics
Southampton   Hampshire v Surrey
Canterbury   Kent v Sussex
Trent Bridge   Notts v Worcs
Weston-s-Mare   Somerset v Northants
Headingley   Yorkshire v Lancashire

Tourist Match
Lord's*   Middlesex v Australia (four days)

AUGUST 11, SUNDAY
John Player Special League
Colchester   Essex v Derbyshire
Cardiff   Glamorgan v Warwicks
Cheltenham   Glos v Leics
Canterbury   Kent v Sussex
Trent Bridge   Notts v Worcs
Weston-s-Mare   Somerset v Northants
Headingley   Yorkshire v Lancashire

AUGUST 14, WEDNESDAY
Britannic Assurance Championship
Buxton   Derbyshire v Worcs
Colchester   Essex v Sussex
Cardiff   Glamorgan v Hampshire
Cheltenham   Glos v Notts
Canterbury   Kent v Warwickshire
Lytham   Lancashire v Northants
Weston-s-Mare   Somerset v Middlesex
The Oval   Surrey v Yorkshire

AUGUST 15, THURSDAY
Fifth Cornhill Test
Edgbaston   ENGLAND v AUSTRALIA

AUGUST 17, SATURDAY
Britannic Assurance Championship
Cheltenham   Glos v Warwicks
Old Trafford   Lancashire v Notts
Leicester   Leics v Hampshire
Lord's   Middlesex v Surrey
Wellingborough   Northants v Glamorgan
Hove   Sussex v Derbyshire
Worcester   Worcs v Essex
Scarborough   Yorkshire v Kent

AUGUST 18, SUNDAY
John Player Special League
Cheltenham   Glos v Warwickshire
Old Trafford   Lancashire v Notts
Leicester   Leics v Hampshire
Lord's   Middlesex v Surrey
Wellingborough   Northants v Glamorgan
Hove   Sussex v Derbyshire
Worcester   Worcs v Essex
Scarborough   Yorkshire v Kent

AUGUST 21, WEDNESDAY
NatWest Bank Trophy
Semi-Finals

AUGUST 24, SATURDAY
Britannic Assurance Championship
Chelmsford   Essex v Surrey
Swansea   Glamorgan v Yorkshire
Bournemouth   Hampshire v Glos
Old Trafford   Lancashire v Somerset
Northampton   Northants v Leics
Trent Bridge   Notts v Derbyshire
Hove   Sussex v Middlesex
Edgbaston   Warwickshire v Worcs

Tourist Match
Canterbury*   Kent v Australia (four days)

232 LOOKING FORWARD/FIXTURES 1985

AUGUST 25, SUNDAY
John Player Special League
Heanor	Derbyshire v Notts
Swansea	Glamorgan v Yorkshire
Bournemouth	Hampshire v Glos
Old Trafford	Lancashire v Somerset
The Oval	Surrey v Northants
Worcester	Worcs v Warwicks

AUGUST 28, WEDNESDAY
Britannic Assurance Championship
Derby	Derbyshire v Somerset
Bristol	Glos v Essex
Bournemouth	Hampshire v Leics
Trent Bridge	Notts v Glamorgan
Hove	Sussex v Yorkshire
Worcester	Worcs v Kent

Other Match
Lord's	MCC v Ireland (two days)

AUGUST 29, THURSDAY
Sixth Cornhill Test
The Oval	ENGLAND v AUSTRALIA

AUGUST 31, SATURDAY
Britannic Assurance Championship
Cardiff	Glamorgan v Glos
Folkestone	Kent v Derbyshire
Leicester	Leics v Worcs
Trent Bridge	Notts v Lancashire
Taunton	Somerset v Sussex
Edgbaston	Warwicks v Essex
Headingley	Yorkshire v Northants

SEPTEMBER 1, SUNDAY
John Player Special League
Cardiff	Glamorgan v Surrey
Southampton	Hampshire v Middlesex
Folkestone	Kent v Derbyshire
Leicester	Leics v Worcs
Taunton	Somerset v Sussex
Edgbaston	Warwicks v Essex
Headingley	Yorkshire v Northants

SEPTEMBER 4, WEDNESDAY
Britannic Assurance Championship
Bristol	Glos v Northants
Folkestone	Kent v Hampshire
Leicester	Leics v Middlesex
The Oval	Surrey v Sussex
Worcester	Worcs v Somerset

Other Match
Scarborough	Yorks v Derbys (ASDA Cricket Challenge, one day)

SEPTEMBER 5, THURSDAY
Scarborough	Lancs v Notts (ASDA, one day)

SEPTEMBER 6, FRIDAY
Scarborough	ASDA final (one day)

SEPTEMBER 7, SATURDAY
NatWest Bank Trophy
Lord's	Final

Britannic Assurance Championship
Hove	Sussex v Leics (Will be played on Sep 11 if either county in NatWest Final)

SEPTEMBER 8, SUNDAY
John Player Special League
Moreton-in-Marsh	Glos v Worcs
Southampton	Hampshire v Derbyshire
Canterbury	Kent v Warwickshire
Trent Bridge	Notts v Essex
The Oval	Surrey v Lancashire
Hove	Sussex v Leics

SEPTEMBER 11, WEDNESDAY
Britannic Assurance Championship
Chesterfield	Derbyshire v Warwicks
Southampton	Hampshire v Northants
Lord's	Middlesex v Essex
Taunton	Somerset v Worcs
Hove	Sussex v Leics (if not played on Sep 7)
Scarborough	Yorkshire v Notts

SEPTEMBER 14, SATURDAY
Britannic Assurance Championship
Chelmsford	Essex v Yorkshire
Cardiff	Glamorgan v Sussex
Canterbury	Kent v Somerset
Old Trafford	Lancashire v Leics
Trent Bridge	Notts v Hampshire
The Oval	Surrey v Glos
Edgbaston	Warwicks v Middlesex
Worcester	Worcs v Northants

SEPTEMBER 15, SUNDAY
John Player Special League
Chesterfield	Derbyshire v Leics
Chelmsford	Essex v Yorkshire
Cardiff	Glamorgan v Sussex
Canterbury	Kent v Somerset
Trent Bridge	Notts v Hampshire
The Oval	Surrey v Glos
Edgbaston	Warwicks v Middlesex
Worcester	Worcs v Northants

Fixtures are the copyright of the Test and County Cricket Board 1985